SUPER COMMUNITY BANKING

BANKING

A SUPERSTRATEGY FOR SURVIVING AND THRIVING IN THE YEAR 2000

ANAT BIRD

A BANKLINE PUBLICATION
PROBUS PUBLISHING COMPANY
Chicago, Illinois
Cambridge, England

A Bankline Publication

ISBN 1-55738-388-X

Printed in the United States of America

BB

2 3 4 5 6 7 8 9 0

To my parents who gave me a great start; To Guy who taught me what accomplishment is all about; and To all the Birds who make me fly, and most especially Big Bird. Thanks.

Special thanks to all the supercommunity bankers who taught me so much, shared their insights with me, and practiced supercommunity banking well before I gave it a name.

Thanks to Richard Israel for his contribution to the Centralization vs. Decentralization chapter; to Judy for typing this manuscript in such an organized and professional manner; to David DiCristofaro and David Harvey for their work on the supercommunity banks' performance data; and to Nikki for being the best at what she does.

And to Dick, who reads everything I write, and without whom this book would have remained a figment of my imagination.

CONTENTS

PREFACE

Supercommunity Banking— An American Innovation

Yankee ingenuity has permeated American business for hundreds of years. We are known for being first in many fields: the semiconductor, the car, the airplane, the light bulb, the telephone, the telegraph, the reaper, and the computer. And we also are known for our management acumen. Some people think that Yankee ingenuity is a thing of the past. This is not so!

We also have another unique invention which does not exist in other financial markets around the world: the supercommunity bank. Most of the developed countries and the G-7 have either one or two kinds of banks. More often, you will see a banking system that is highly concentrated among seven to ten banking giants. These megabanks not only provide financial services but also interface with major industrial concerns and are fully integrated into the country's economy. In some countries, such as Japan, this megasystem is complemented by hundreds of country banks that are analogous to our community banks. Those are little banks that serve remote geographical areas and do not offer the product sophistication nor the financial depth of their giant counterparts.

The United States has had a dual banking system, which resulted in the fragmentation of the depository institutions system since inception and by design. However, as the capital markets globalized, our system began to mirror, to some extent, other financial systems around the world. We are in the process of creating our own megabanks, evidenced by the creation of Chemical Banking Corporation, the Bank of America franchise,Key Corp and NationsBank. We also have over 10,000 community banking institutions serving local communities nationwide. In addition, however, a new kind of bank is evolving in our country that does not exist anywhere else around the world: the supercommunity bank. These are multi-bank holding companies, typically, that try to marry the best of both worlds. They are committed to the service levels and culture typically associated with community banks. Yet they also take advantage of their full asset base by achieving cost efficiencies that do not penalize service levels and offer scale-sensitive products that cannot be offered by small banks. In other words, the supercommunity banks try to get the competitive advantages of both large banks and small banks and create a winning formula.

This innovation appears to have worked very effectively in our financial system. Unlike European countries, the United States is comprised of fifty states with distinct geographic differences and economic environments. The supercommunity bank reflects this economic and cultural diversity. There are over 500 supercommunity banks in the country. As a segment, they outperform the rest of the industry in all measures of profitability by over 100 percent. Contrary to the megabank's conventional wisdom and design, supercommunity banks do not intend to be the lowest cost producer. They are prepared to make the investment necessary to offer unparalleled service levels to their customers. At the same time, those service levels create profitability dynamics and cross-selling ratios that result in superior performance.

Supercommunity banks are growing around the country and have been identified as the only growth segment in the depository institutions industry today.

Their growth is further evidence to market recognition of the unique opportunities associated with this strategic position. Many small banks recognize that although community banking is here to stay, not all community banks will survive. They seek to become supercommunity banks through mergers and acquisitions as a survival and prosperity strategy. Further, many larger banks that recognize they could not reach the economies of scale achieved by the megabanks opt as well for supercommunity banking. They recognize that their size is insufficient to enable them to become a low-cost producer in their market. The topography of the banking industry is therefore changing to a three-segment business. It is comprised of thousands of community banks, I believe, that will continue to survive, although not in full numbers. We are in the process of forming seven to ten megabanks that will become our low-cost producers and major global competitors. They, like the Japanese banks, can be of sufficient size and financial strength to compete in the global market, while coexisting with thousands of smaller, exclusively domestic banks. Finally, there are also hundreds of supercommunity banks bridging the gap between the megabanks and the small banks and doing so with superior profitability.

America, thanks to that still vibrant Yankee ingenuity, is leading the financial world with the creation of a new strategic position that has become a proven path to significant and sustained success for hundreds of companies. Their success not only provides fuel to their local economies, but also creates jobs and makes financial resources available to a broader spectrum of customers. Industry observers and investment analysts have recognized the potential embedded in this segment and, as a result, have placed significant premiums on their stock prices. Supercommunity banks' stocks outperform the industry not only as a consequence of their superior financial performance, but also in recognition of the additional potential for revenues and for capital appreciation they represent. They are further evidence to the underlying motto for success for many companies: Strategic focus works. Those banks that will recognize this and choose their path accordingly will have taken the first step to prosperity. Without that focus, success is unlikely to come.

CHAPTER ONE

Supercommunity Banking
Prescription for Success

Restructuring the
Banking Industry*

The banking industry is restructuring, and all but the megabanks are looking for a strategic position that will offer them a viable, long-term alternative for the future. Bank chief executives are struggling with fundamental issues that affect the very survival of their banks. Topics such as seeking effective cost-cutting measures, or building and capitalizing on core competencies through a realistic assessment of what the bank does well, are important, yet not at the core of future survival. These topics do not address the main issue at hand: how to win in an industry that is in the midst of restructuring and consolidation. What are the options available to bank CEOs as they plan for a future

in which the only clear fact is that fewer companies will be able to play?

The magnitude of change at hand is staggering. It is an accepted fact that the banking industry is experiencing an overwhelming overcapacity problem. The industry's woes are merely symptoms of this problem. Such symptoms, including loan losses resulting from commercial bankruptcies, have been increasing steadily throughout the years. There has been more than a seven-fold increase in failed bank assets from 1986 to 1991.

Product substitutes in the financial services industry have become widely available. It used to be that only banks made commercial loans. Today, everyone makes loans, from investment bankers and brokers to small consumer finance and mortgage companies. Similarly, the deposit

---

* Special thanks to BBB Research for their thoughts on the restructuring of the banking industry.

1

side is available to all and by all. The consumer can get a savings account or its equivalent from a thrift institution, commercial bank, mutual fund, brokerage company, investment bank, or from nonfinancial entities such as Alcoa, that will give uninsured certificates comparable to savings accounts. The increasing nonbank share of the financial services market is evidence to that effect.

- The gap between the most and least profitable banks is widening, yet another industry problem related to overcapacity. The lowest 5% of the industry has been earning less than a negative 1% return on assets annually since 1982 whereas the most profitable are at over 2% on assets.

- As a result of overcapacity, banks are unable to adequately price their services for the risk incurred. Loans to equally risky borrowers are priced well below the equivalent risk bond yields. In other words, bond issues for similarly risky borrowers are more expensive than the loans associated with the same borrowers. This is the result of intense price competition where banks are prepared to accept a lower rate in order to increase share. It may also be related to banks' lack of sophistication in risk measurement; however, market overcapacity seems to be the primary reason behind underpricing loans relative to the risk incurred.

- Banks are also hard-pressed these days to find profitable investments and quali-

FIGURE 1.1 Investors in U.S. Banking Industry Earning Consistently Shabby Returns for Placing Their Money at Risk

U.S. banking industry barely outperforming risk-free government securities . . .

. . . while unable to provide investors an adequate risk-adjusted rate of return

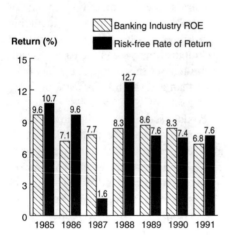

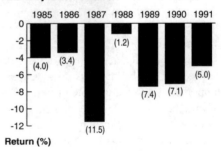

Sources: FDIC; *Economic Report of the President, 1991.*

ty assets. As a result, they are holding a greater portion of their assets in government securities than in commercial and industrial loans, which historically had been their bread and butter. The reason is partly due to regulatory constraints, harsh compliance regulations, and risk-based capital requirements. But a main component for a bank's reluctance to own commercial loans is the lack of availability. There are too many lenders and too few quality borrowers. As a result, the percentage of loans in the total asset portfolio of a bank's balance sheet has declined significantly.

- The poor returns earned by the U.S. banking industry (Figure 1.1) provide additional evidence to the fact that there are too many financial institutions chasing too little business. Banking's consistent failure to produce adequate risk-adjusted returns for investors is a classic indicator of overcapacity.

With so many banks competing for the same loans, borrowers have been able to play one lender against another for years. This, in part, precipitated banking's boom and bust loan cycle. Overcapacity, again, is one of the culprits behind the banking industry's pursuit of the next loan. Other causes, such as the "herd syndrome" in the business, where most loans flock onto the same coveted market segment, are also contributing elements to the industry's rush to book high-margin loans, which is responsible for banking's boom-and-bust cyclicity.

Examples of loan fads abound, as are listed below:

FIGURE 1.2 Demand for Financial Services Growing Across Past 25 Years

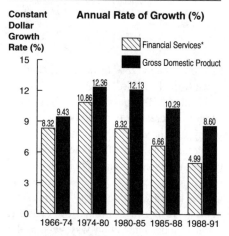

* Financial services includes U.S. commercial banks, foreign banks in the U.S., insurance companies, private pension funds, government employee retirement funds, finance companies, mutual funds, money market mutual funds, real estate investment trusts, security brokers and dealers, issuers of securitized credit obligations, savings institutions.

Sources: *Economic Report of the President, 1991;* Federal Reserve Board of Governors *Flow of Funds Accounts, Financial Assets & Liabilities Year-End, 1966-1989 & First Quarter 1992.*

Loan Type	Years
Real estate investment trusts	Mid 1970s
Agricultural allowance	Early 1980s
Oil and gas loans	Early to Mid 1980s
Less developed country debt	Mid 1980s
Highly leveraged transactions	Late 1980s
Acquisition, development and construction loans	Mid to late 1980s
Commercial real estate loans	Late 1980s, Early 1990s
Undocumented character loans	Mid 1990s?

It should be noted that the overcapacity in the banking industry is not the result of

FIGURE 1.3 Nonbank Financial Services Firms Growing over Four Times as Quickly as U.S. Banks

U.S. banking industry growth lagging far behind nonbank competitors . . .

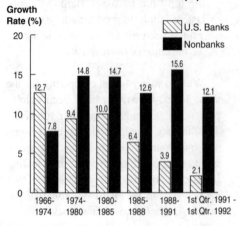

U.S. Banks vs. Nonbanks: Annual Rate of Growth of Financial Assets (%)

. . . causing bank market share to shrink dramatically

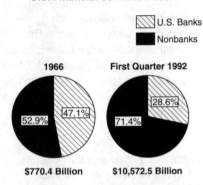

U.S. Financial Services Assets

Source: Federal Reserve Board of Governors. *Flow of Funds Accounts, Financial Assets & Liabilities Year-End, 1966-89 & First Quarter 1992.*

a declining demand for financial services. On the contrary, the entire financial services industry, including nonbanks, has been growing more quickly than the U.S. economy for each of the last twenty-five years, as shown in Figure 1.2.

There are many reasons why the expansion of the financial services industry did not result in a banking industry boom. Among the primary reasons are the ability of the nonbank competitors to absorb the majority of the growing demand, far outstripping the banking industry's growth. Nonbanks' rapid growth over the last twenty-five years (Figure 1.3), fueled by the introduction of near perfect and sometimes better than perfect substitutes for bank products and services, cut bank financial services market share almost in

half to a meager 28% of the entire market, down from 47.1% in 1966.

Nonbank financial companies have been more creative than the banks in marketing and product development. Lack of regulatory constraints facilitated their ability to quickly and efficiently develop innovative approaches to the marketplace as well as be fully responsive to the market's needs. Nonbank competition brought about product innovation way beyond the banking industry's capabilities and captured a significant share of the market. At the same time, today's bank and nonbank products are not as dissimilar as many believe. Many are essentially interchangeable, as demonstrated in Table 1.1. In other cases, while bank business lines are not perfect substitutes to competing nonbank

TABLE 1.1 Banks and Nonbanks Not as Dissimilar as Many Believe

Many bank and nonbank products are essentially interchangeable

Bank Products	Comparable Nonbank Products
Large Corporate Loans	Commercial Paper
Interest-Bearing Investment Accounts	Money Market Mutual Funds
Credit Cards	Credit Cards
Small Business Loans	Venture Capital Loans, Small Business Loans
Corporate Cash Management	Working Capital/Cash Management Accounts

. . . while entire bank business lines fighting nonbanks for market share

Bank Business Lines	Competing Nonbanks
Corporate Trust	Private Pension Funds and Life Insurance Companies
Leasing, Asset-Based Lending, Factoring	Commercial Finance Companies
Indirect Auto Lending	Captive Auto Finance Companies
Installment Lending	Consumer Finance Companies
Merger and Acquisition Advice Private Placements Municipal Bond Underwriting	Investment Banks

products, they are aimed at the same target market and designed to meet similar needs. For example, corporate trust services are designed to compete effectively with private pension funds and life insurance companies. Similarly, leasing, asset-based lending, and factoring are direct competitors to commercial finance companies. Indirect lending is banking's answer to captive auto finance companies, and installment lending is their response to consumer finance companies. Banks are also expanding into investment bankers' territory with the provision of merger and acquisition advice, private banking, private placements, municipal bond underwriting, municipal bond sales, money market desks, foreign exchange trading, mutual funds management, municipal bond dealings, and equity underwriting under Section 20. These innovative competitive products represent deregulation brought about by the marketplace, not by our regulators.

Domestic banks are losing share not only to creative nonbank banks, which are not bound by similar regulatory constraints, but also to increasingly aggressive

FIGURE 1.4 Foreign Competitors Capturing Larger Slice of U.S. Market

Foreign banks hold surprisingly large share of U.S. corporate loans . . .

. . . while steadily increasing control of U.S. banking industry assets

1991 Share of U.S. Commercial and Industrial Loan Market

Foreign Bank Financial Assets in the U.S. as Percentage of Entire Banking Industry

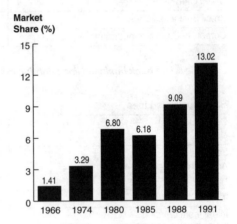

Sources: Federal Reserve Board of Governors. *Flow of Funds Accounts, Financial Assets & Liabilities Year-End, 1966-1989 & First Quarter 1992;* Robert McCauley and Roma Smith, "Foreign Bank Credit to U.S. Corporations: The Implications of Off-shore Loans," *Federal Reserve Bank of New York Quarterly Review* (Spring 1992): 54.

foreign bank competitors, who also enjoy a more favorable regulatory climate. Offshore banks now control nearly 50% of the U.S. market for commercial and industrial loans (Figure 1.4). They have increased their stake in the U.S. banking market from less than 2% in 1966 to over 13% of the industry assets today.

Surprisingly, declining market share and overcapacity did not erode the confidence of capital markets in banking's long-term prospects (Figure 1.5). This confidence is evident in the increasing rate at which investors are channeling new equity into the banking industry. After a lull in 1988, a steady growth in recent years indicates an affirmative vote of confidence on the banking industry's future.

At the same time, investors' confidence in the banking industry and its future prospects is benefiting only those banks that are superior performers and that earn steady and high profits. The industry's worst performers are starving for much needed capital, which may imply that we have not seen the end of the industry's shakeout and ongoing consolidation. Capital markets are imposing market discipline on the banking industry and eliminating the weak performers by withholding equity capital (Figure 1.6).

In the face of intensified competition, overcapacity problems, and regulatory constraints, many banks are hard-pressed to find their niche. Some ignore the problems and flawlessly execute a traditionalist

FIGURE 1.5 Capital Markets Cast Vote of Confidence on Banking's Prospects in Form of Increasing Equity

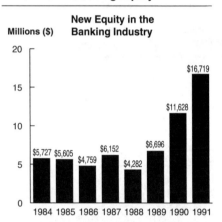

New Equity in the Banking Industry

Source: Federal Deposit Investment Corp. *Statistics on Banking* (1990).

FIGURE 1.6 ROE for Nation's Highest Earning Banks Well Above Investors' Required Rate of Return, in Completely Different Class than Nation's Poorest Performers

Average ROE for 10 Best, Worst Performers Out of 50 Largest U.S. Banks

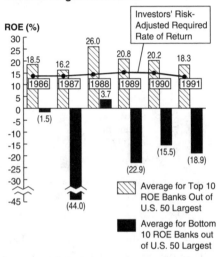

Sources: *Economic Report of the President,* 1991; *American Banker,* "Top Numbers," 1989, 1990, 1991, 1992.

banking strategy of slow growth, risk aversion, and conservatism. (Wachovia is a case in point.) Many, however, recognize that the only way to overcome overcapacity problems is by pursuing a clear strategic focus, differentiation, niche marketing, or low-cost production. As Michael Porter stated in *Competitive Strategy,* (New York: The Free Press, 1980), "The way to create a competitive advantage is by pursuing one of three classic competitive advantage strategies: differentiation, overall cost leadership, and focus. All require a full commitment to a strategic direction, and the ability to marshall resources to implement such a strategy in recognition of the company's core competencies, management, talent, and capital resources." (See Figure 1.7.)

The banking industry's intuitive response to Michael Porter's strategy is a three-way segmentation: low-cost producer, niche player, and supercommunity banks.

The Low-Cost Producer

In scale-sensitive businesses, such as mutual funds, custody services, or credit cards, large banks can establish a dominant position through size and low-cost services. They will continue to be successful and profitable through this defensible competitive position. Low-cost producers will outperform their competitors and prof-

FIGURE 1.7 Banks Employing Michael Porter's Three "Classic" Strategies To Gain Competitive Advantage

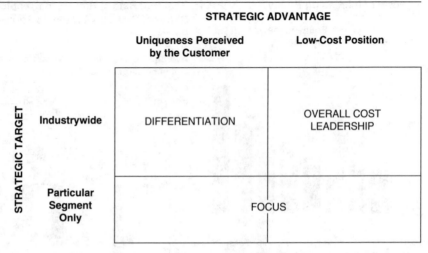

itably survive in those segments where cost is the primary factor in the buying decision. Services such as checking, savings, government securities purchasing, and other commodity-like products are examples of products where the low-cost producers can create cost-based competitive advantages in the long term. The government market, the money markets, Euro commercial paper, and foreign government securities all evidence this trend. Those institutions that concentrate on becoming the low-cost producers in these commodity businesses—often through superior technology and sheer volume—will become dominant scale players and eliminate the smaller players' market position. An example of such an institution is State Street Bank, the dominant custody service provider in the country. State Street made the necessary investments in technology to enter the business and continued to invest in cutting edge and customer supportive technology and product features. The result: market dominance, clear market identity, and intense profitability. In addition, and along the same lines, developing critical mass and dominating regional markets by rapidly growing in size, scope, and relative share creates economies of scale and size-related market power. Achieving such critical mass allows the bank to lower long-term production costs, rationalize pricing, and diversify the loan portfolio across economic regions, thereby reducing risk while achieving long-term earnings. Chemical Bank, Bank of America, and NationsBank are examples of such companies. Their profitability is a reflection of effective execution of this strategy and the fact that there is a powerful relationship between market share and returns.

Low-cost producers and critical mass players achieve profitability for reasons relating to market leadership, economies of scale, and economies of scope.

The market leadership is achieved through dominant market share relative to other geographic market and product line

---

. . . checking, savings, government securities purchasing . . . are examples of products where the low-cost producers can create cost-based competitive advantages in the long term.

---

competitors. The dominant share allows the banks to selectively cut prices to discipline discounters, set and enforce industry standards for product features and service performance, and have the depth to outspend rivals on research and development. An example of a bank that was successful in building dominant share through in-market acquisitions is Chemical Bank (Table 1.2).

Through acquisitions, Chemical Bank now operates 50% more branches than its closest competitors and does business with 50% of the small and middle-market companies in metropolitan New York. It is the lead bank with one out of every four companies in New York and is among the top

four players in interest and currency swaps, a classic scale-sensitive business.

Economies of scale are a powerful justification for greater size. The idea is that a large firm can produce the same goods or services less expensively than a smaller firm. This suggests that as a firm's operating size becomes larger, the cost of production of each unit decreases. This is because:

- Large firms produce more revenue and support more assets with the same expense base.
- Large firms are able to subdivide tasks, allowing employees to specialize.
- Large firms can use highly efficient specialized equipment that is often too expensive for small firms to use given their low-level output. (Source: David Kidwell and Richard Peterson, *Financial Institutions Markets and Money*, 3rd Ed., New York Dryden Press, 1987: 250–254).

This theory is not clearly evidenced in the banking industry. Studies conducted by Federal Reserve Banks do not support the hypothesis that economies of scale are a linear function in the banking industry. It appears that at some size, economies of scale diminish. That exact size level is a topic of much debate. Recent studies disagree on the size of banks of which economies of scale are exhausted. Nine different researchers estimated the asset size at which economies are exhausted to range between $300 million and $140 billion (Figure 1.8).

In-market direct competitor mergers offer the greatest opportunity for quietly

TABLE 1.2 Acquiring In-Market Competitors Banks' Best Means of Building Dominant Share

Case Example: Chemical Bank and Manufacturers Hanover Merger

Markets Served by Both Banks Prior to Merger	Post-Merger Market Position
Metropolitan NY Retail Banking	Chemical Bank Operates 50% More Branches Than Closest Competitor
Metropolitan NY Small Business, Middle Market	Chemical Does Business with 50% of Small, Middle-Market Companies, Is Lead Bank to One in Four
Large Corporate Finance	First in Primary Relationships with U.S. Corporations
	Largest Loan Syndicator
International Trading	Largest LDC Debt Trader
	Among Top Four Global Interest Rate, Currency Swap Arrangers
Fee-Based Operating Services	Leading U.S. Provider of Cash Management Services
	Largest U.S. Dollar Clearer

Source: Chemical Bank annual reports

capitalizing on scale economics, as evidenced by Donald Savages's study, shown in Figure 1.9. (Source: Donald Savage, "Mergers, Branch Closings and Cost Savings" Federal Reserve Working Paper, 1991): 5. However, it remains unclear whether they enhance franchise value as well as out-of-market and market augmentation mergers.

NationsBank is an excellent example of a bank seeking critical mass for all the right reasons. NationsBank is the result of the merger between the $66 billion NCNB and the $52 billion C&S/Sovran. That merger, which took place in July 1991, formed the largest Southern U.S. bank at the time and one which operated in nine out of the fourteen Southern states. The reasons for pursuing this critical mass strategy are consistent with the benefits described above:

- **Market Leadership.** "NationsBank is bigger than the three largest banks in the South combined and has more assets than all of the banks in Alabama, Arkansas, Mississippi and South Carolina collectively." *Bank Management Magazine*
- **Economies of Scale.** "NationsBank as a whole expects to produce revenues as large as the two predecessor banks with

FIGURE 1.8 Researchers Cannot Agree on The Right Size to Optimize Economies of Scale

Research studies completed to date disagree on size of bank at which economies of scale exhausted . . .

. . . but even researchers unable to find any efficiencies in greater scale acknowledge today's cost-conscious, megamerger environment makes current mergers unlike any before studied

Nine Different Research Estimates of Asset Size of Bank at Which Economies of Scale are Exhausted

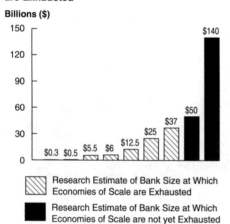

Billions ($)

Research Estimate of Bank Size at Which Economies of Scale are Exhausted

Research Estimate of Bank Size at Which Economies of Scale are not yet Exhausted

Excerpts from "Cost Savings Associated with Bank Mergers"

"This study estimates the magnitude of cost savings from bank mergers during the period 1982-1986. The results suggest that the non-interest expense ratio significantly increases after the merger.

The results in this study are subject to two important caveats:
1) the sample *does not include any mergers compar-able to the current megamergers,* and
2) the *acquiring banks' managers may not have intended to reduce costs.*"

Sources: Aruna Srinivasan and Larry D. Wall, "Cost Savings Associated with Bank Mergers," *Working Paper 92-2,* Federal Reserve Bank of Atlanta (February 1992): 25-26; Douglas Evanoff and Philip Israilevich, "Productive Efficiency in Banking," *Economic Perspectives,* Federal Reserve Bank of Chicago (July/August 1991): 24.

combined expenses that are $350 mil-lion lower than the two separate banks." *American Banker*

- **Economies of Scope.** "The economic and geographic diversity of our market should reduce the company's risk expo-sure to the individual state economies or specific business sector. Addi-tionally, product diversity helps protect the company from downturns in any one business segment."[1]

NationsBank achieved 31% of total cost savings by eliminating overlapping branch distribution systems. Within the first six months, it accomplished the following:

- Merged its two auto dealer finance groups into one group located in Greensboro, North Carolina.
- Consolidated credit card processing into one operation in Norfolk, Virginia.
- Merged marketing and administration

---

1. *NationsBank Annual Report,* 1991: 6. Arnold Danielson, "Southern Banking" "Life after Nation's Bank" *Bank Management,* September 1991: 14. Richard Layne, "Partner Shoot for Quick Fadings of $350 million a year." *American Banker,* July 23, 1991: 14.

FIGURE 1.9 In-Market, Direct Competitor Mergers Offer Greatest Opportunity for Capitalizing on Scale Economics

Redundancy in large bank competitors' branch systems . . .

Range of Branch Overlap Among 41 Largest U.S. Branch Banks

. . . implies large cost savings available from in-market acquisitions

Non-Interest Expense Overruns vs. Budget

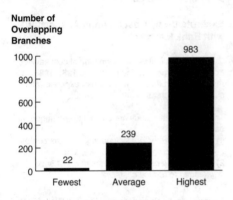

Sources: Donald Savage, "Mergers, Branch Closings, and Cost Savings" (Federal Reserve Working Paper, 1991): 5; *Analyzing Success and Failure in Banking Consolidation* (FMCG Capital Strategies, BAI, 1990): 42.

of support services and operations functions.

All resulted in significantly reduced costs. Overall, NationsBank strategy, much like other successful low-cost producers, paid off, as is evidenced in Figure 1.10.

Niche Player

It is not necessary to be all things to all people to achieve a sensible competitive position. For example, small banks in some communities are so well entrenched in their markets that the low-cost produc-

ers will not be able to displace them. The community bank niche will still be a viable strategic option, although not in as many markets as it is today. The personal service and business advice that the community banker gives will still be irreplaceable in many communities. Similarly, product-focused banks will survive through establishing an identity as providers of particular services. Examples include Northern Trust Company and U.S. Trust for trust services; Morgan Guarantee Trust Company for.both trust andexclusive, high-quality banking services; Bankers Trust New York Corp. for wholesale

FIGURE 1.10 Despite "Hit" to Earnings from Merger Activity, Scale Banking Strategy can be Extremely Profitable

Bank's ROE vs. U.S. Banking Industry Average ROE

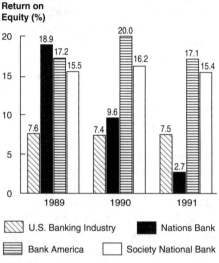

Return on Equity (%)

U.S. Banking Industry — Nations Bank
Bank America — Society National Bank

* This reflects $2 billion charge to earnings for credit-losses, merger expenses.

Source: FDIC call reports

investment and commercial banking services; State Street Bank & Trust Company for custody and securities handling services, and Marshal & Ilseley for operation support and data processing services. These banks are not the largest, nor are they perceived as providing full market coverage. Rather, each is clearly identified with a particular product or service family in which it has made the strategic decision to specialize. This commitment will continue to pay off as the industry identity of these banks helps them expand market share and command higher market premi-

ums for their stock. These banks are building franchise value through specialization.

The product specialization strategy has paid off for many companies. These companies have identified a core competency, a product or service that it provides as well as, or better than, anyone in the country in terms of quality, cost, service, delivery ability, and meeting customer needs. These companies recognized that sheer magnitude can be a barrier to entry in that particular product and were prepared to make the substantial incremental investment of capital, management talent, and other resources required to push that product line into a dominant position relative to other providers. The companies were also prepared to raise the capital needed to reach that size where magnitude and sophistication become a barrier to entry and attract the talent to become a superior service provider with significant economies of scale.

Bankers Trust exemplifies the "divest from weakness and invest in strength" concept. Bankers in general have traditionally been reluctant to implement divesti-

> *The personal service and business advice that the community banker gives will still be irreplaceable in many communities.*

tures. They found it hard to say no to those few customers who may have needed the unprofitable or marginal product or service that was draining management and capital resources. Bankers Trust had the foresight, vision, and intestinal fortitude to divest and reinvest its capital and management talent from non-core product offerings into designated areas of core excellence. Bankers Trust developed a sustainable advantage in a product expertise area that was dependent upon large-scale investments in technology and people in order to develop a tangible competitive advantage, achieve scale economies, and create a market identity and position. Bankers Trust initially divested itself of all its retail business, focusing exclusively on the commercial business. This in itself was considered drastic and was recognized as a leading move in the industry. Subsequently, the company found itself in a hemorrhaging condition when it came to its commercial loan portfolio. The bank elected to shrink its loan portfolio and expand its investment services and trading activities. As a result, the bank's loan portfolio has shrunk by 50% since this strategic shift was introduced in 1986, down to $14.5 billion from $28.6 billion. At the same time, return on equity exceeded 20% for each of the last five years, with the exception of two years where loan loss provisions left over from the previous strategy crippled results. (Figure 1.11).

U.S. Trust is another example of a company that made a strategic shift to achieve exceptional ROE through a focused, single-product strategy. The bank, which started as a large corporate international and middle-market lender, withdrew from commercial lending and refocused its resources on fiduciary and security services. High risks and poor performance compelled it to withdraw from international lending in 1979. During the early 1980s, continuing thin spreads forced U.S. Trust to withdraw from large corporate lending and to refocus on the middle market. The company had moderate success in middle-market lending, but pricing pressures persisted, and with it, poor performance. U.S. Trust realized that middle-market lending was not a long-term profitable niche to stay in. In 1987, the company made a major strategic shift. It exited commercial lending. The majority of its commercial loan portfolio was sold, and the remainder was carried as "liquidating commercial loans" on the balance sheet. U.S. Trust refocused all its resources on fee income businesses; specifically, asset management, mutual fund accounting, corporate trust, and other fiduciary and security services. Its profitability has not declined below 15% return on equity since 1987, and over 68% of its revenues in 1991 were derived from non-interest sources. (Figure 1.12).

Community banking is another example of niche playing. This is a profitable, sustainable strategy available to small companies with dominant market positions in small communities. A $50 million bank can have 70% market share in a 5,000-person community. Those community banks that offer the service levels, senior management accessibility, and plain vanilla product line required by their customers in small communities have been extremely successful.

It has been rumored that community banks are dinosaurs whose time has passed. The banking industry is quickly becoming the financial services industry, and with this transition come economies of

FIGURE 1.11 Bankers Trust Exemplifies "Divest from Weakness, Invest in Strength" Concept

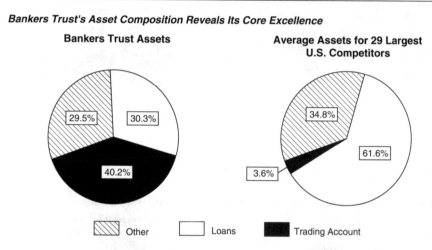

Bankers Trust's Asset Composition Reveals Its Core Excellence

Sources: Carol Loomis, "A Whole New Way to Run a Bank," *Fortune* (September 7, 1992): 74-85; Sheshunoff: *1000 Largest U.S. Banks* (1992); BBB Research.

scale, product diversification, and many other changes that the little community bank cannot accommodate. In the new banking industry, it is said, there is no room for the mom-and-pop operation. Figures are cited to support this assertion. For example, it costs the average small bank over $180 per year to process a credit card, while it costs Citibank under $60. Other lines of business, including mutual funds and installment loans, seem to be scale-sensitive as well. Moreover, the technological requirements to operate the business are becoming increasingly complex and expensive.

Some industry observers therefore assure that a small player cannot compete effectively in this environment. Bottom-line performance is essential, and the cuddly little community bank cannot produce

profitable results in a world where size and sophistication are critical to success. I beg to disagree.

The demise of the community bank was most eloquently predicted by McKinsey &

> *The banking industry is quickly becoming the financial services industry.*

Co. in 1985. That study suggested that there would be 100 banks in the United States by the year 1990. This prediction did not come true, and today we have 11,500 banks. In fact, de novo banking is stronger than ever. In New Jersey, there were more new charters granted in 1990

FIGURE 1.12 U.S. Trust Results Demonstrate the Effectiveness of Niche Player Strategy

Asset mix weighted toward securities, away from commercial & industrial loans . . .

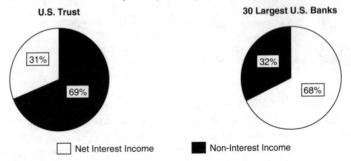

. . . results in a revenue stream composed primarily of non-interest income . . .

. . . which yields impressive returns on equity

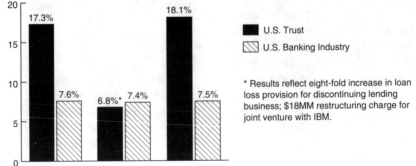

Source: FDIC.

than ever before. Similarly, in Pennsylvania, more new charter applications were approved that year than the combined total for the past 25 years. The strength of de novo banking is of particular significance since the requirements for granting new charters are tougher than ever, with greater minimum capital requirements, harsher scrutiny of the proposed management, and more strict criteria for demonstration of community need.

Why are these banks popping up now, when they are characterized as obsolete? Are these new bankers deluding themselves into believing they have something to offer that their big brothers cannot? New community banks are being created to meet a real need, one not met by the larger banks. Although they may not maximize cost efficiencies or offer a wide range of sophisticated services, community banks provide other benefits for which customers are prepared to pay. The assumption—implicit in the predictions of their demise—that cost is the overwhelming consideration for purchasing banking services has been proved unfounded by the resurgence of the community bank.

There are many reasons for the survival of the small bank. Historically, the U.S. banking system was designed to prevent concentration of financial power in too few hands. This is why the dual banking system was created, unit (not branch) banking established, and interstate banking prohibited, among other measures. This bias against the entrepreneurial spirit has not vanished, and it is exhibited in many industries. The respect for Yankee ingenuity, coupled with fear of monopolies and large conglomerates, is present all across

the country. This attitude, in turn, fuels the demand for the small bank, to ensure diversification of financial power.

Consolidation is creating a small group of very large banks, but it also breeds a new generation of small competitors. This phenomenon has occurred in many industries that experienced significant consolidation, but it is especially true for service businesses. In such industries, service is indeed a critical component of the product delivered, and it often suffers when consolidation takes place. Duplication of personnel facilities results in layoffs. As a consequence, many well-established, long-term relationships built up between a community bank and its customers are disrupted. Certain customers are not prepared to trade off the lower service levels for greater efficiency, lower cost of service, or broader product line. These customers seek the personal attention and advice they were accustomed to. The small institution can meet these needs.

Accounting and law firms are excellent examples of industries where the very large coexist with the very small. These two industries each meet the needs of different customer bases and offer different service levels. Both are viable in their own markets. A "Big Six" accounting firm is less likely to give a small business the same level of service it provides its largest prime clients.

The additional product diversification often accompanied by size is not especially relevant to the small business, whose needs are fairly limited in the first place. The same is true for banks.

Large banks are hard-pressed to be as community oriented as the small community banks. Although large banks may employ local people, their turnover is typically higher and their overall interest is lower than community banks. Conversely, for the local bank, their community is all there is. Consequently, the bank's interests, level of knowledge, and community relations reflect that single community focus. Community banks can be much more responsive to situations that require handling that is not by the book. The community bank is tied to its community. Its commitment to its community is unquestionable. The larger bank's business is much more defined by unemotional economics and numbers, which, in turn, may render certain communities less viable or attractive when their economies experience difficulties. The members of the community know that and often prefer to deal with the bank that is here to stay.

Although the community bank cannot possess the same technological capabilities as larger competitors, the rapid decline in the cost of technology makes it affordable even to smaller players. I found imaging technology in an $80 million bank. Similar examples abound. Hence, the small bank can still capitalize on certain technological features. For instance, vendors offer myriad features and services that the smaller bank can contract for, rather than own, thereby broadening its product offering and customer responsiveness.

Large and small banks successfully coexist all across the country. California is an example of a market where peaceful coexistence of large and small companies has been the norm for decades. They each meet a different set of needs of both differ-

ent and overlapping customers, and do so with great success.

In contrast to these arguments, there is a downside to community banks, which may indeed diminish their numbers during the 1990s. Simply stated, many are just not viable business entities. Size is a factor, particularly as the role of automation and technology in banking becomes more critical and the size of the community (and its bank) cannot support the necessary infrastructure. A community bank ties its fortunes to the economic condition of the community. The inevitable lack of diversification results in extreme vulnerability of the bank to local economic downturns, as was evidenced by both large and small banks that did not develop economic diversification in Texas and New England.

Smarter, larger banks ensure that, as they consolidate, their local unit is minimally altered. These branch offices are then in a position to offer a competitive alternative to the smaller, stand-alone community bank. Although this strategy may be more expensive than gutting the local, newly acquired bank, it also is more likely to provide continuity and to enhance customer retention.

Certain customers may outgrow their banks. Their needs become more sophisticated or geographically diversified, and the local bank can no longer meet them.

These and many other reasons explain my conviction that we will see a further reduction in the number of small community banks. Although the need for the community bank is strong in many areas, and although they provide a unique service package, not all community banks will be able to survive as consolidation continues and the economics of the business get even tougher. Those companies with clear strategic and market focus, and with relatively isolated markets, will continue to do well. Figure 1.13 demonstrates that the profitability of small banks outstrips the industry by far when they have a clear strategic focus and dominant position in their marketplace. Unfortunately, the number of communities where such strategic isolation is available and the undeniable aspect of economies of scale make this a declining niche available to fewer institutions in the future than today.

Supercommunity Banks

I believe that we will also see the emergence of a new institution—the supercommunity bank. Several of its kind are already in existence and doing very well.

FIGURE 1.13 ROA at the 100 Most Profitable Community Banks

Data are for banks with assets of $50 million to $1 billion

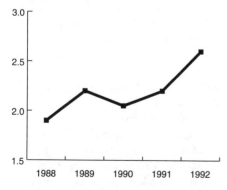

Sources: *American Banker,* Sheshundoff Information Services

A supercommunity bank is a bank that grows in order to achieve critical mass and economies of scale, yet consciously emphasizes its local presence and flavor, despite the additional costs incurred. Back office functions are consolidated, including accounting, purchasing, payroll, human resources, data processing, financial management, treasury, asset/liability management, and strategic planning. However, the benefits of these consolidations are not apparent to the customer. Local staffing remains stable, loan authority remains at the local level, and often even the local presidents are retained.

It is possible that these supercommunity banks are the answer to the profitability questions raised by today's scale considerations. Either way, the community bank in the form of the supercommunity bank is a longer-term survivor in the industry, and rumors of its extinction are premature.

The strategic alternatives reviewed above pertain primarily to large banks that can become larger still, and to small banks that can be all that they could be in a very finite market. What will become of the hundreds of those banking companies that do not fit into either strategy? Are they an extinct species? Absolutely not. They are the fastest growth segment of the U.S. banking industry and the most profitable by far. They are the supercommunity banks.

The supercommunity bank is emerging as one of the winners in the evolving financial services industry. This represents an important development for mid-sized banks seeking a viable strategic position and for small banks yearning to grow and combat strategic market isolation. The mid-sized banks, like much of the rest of the industry, have recognized that what has worked in the past is not likely to work in the future. Customers' preferences and needs are different. Expense structures are shifting toward technology. Competition has been reshaped, and product offerings are changing almost daily. Employees who were effective in the past are losing their effectiveness as the need to shift to a sales culture remains unmet by many. Sticking to one's knitting may be a good policy (when the knitting is still profitable), but it is not sufficient for future prosperity. The supercommunity strategy is an alternative for bankers who may feel caught in the middle—too small to be big and too big to be small.

Community banks generally know their limitations and their potential. Money-center banks, though struggling, have wide horizons for expansion in terms of geography, products, and size. What happens to the banks in between? On many levels, the medium-size bank cannot compete directly with money-center banks. Economies of scale work against the smaller banks' cost efficiencies and ability to pass on those savings to the customer through low prices for services. Similarly, achieving product sophistication to match the money-center banks is, in many cases, not feasible. It requires a broad customer base, a level of employee skill, and capitalization that are not available to medium-size banks. On the other hand, the small bank is well entrenched in its community and capable of meeting most of its customers' needs. The relationship between the community bank and its customer base is difficult to displace. Thus, it is no surprise that many mid-size banks are seeking a new strategic direction.

The supercommunity bank concept builds on the strength of the mid-size bank without trying to compete directly with either much smaller or much larger institutions in areas where they have a strong competitive advantage. What are the advantages of the supercommunity bank? On the one hand, the bank is not too big. It can still offer personal service to its customers. It is difficult to maintain that level of service in large banks. However, a supercommunity bank, regardless of size, can take steps to continue to capture the

> *The mid-sized banks, like much of the rest of the industry, have recognized that what has worked in the past is not likely to work in the future.*

community orientation, including the service levels and the senior management accessibility associated with it, even when asset size is $40 or $50 billion, as Bank One has proven. A constant effort to do so will capitalize on the community presence of the bank and permit it to compete effectively with the smaller banks. By the same token, it will put the company in a strong competitive position against the large banks that are incapable of maintaining the community orientation and the service levels associated with smaller institutions. The supercommunity bank will sacrifice certain cost efficiencies to ensure a strong community orientation. For example, installing an additional layer of management may not maximize cost efficiencies.

At the same time, regional presidents, local presidents, or high-level branch managers will help foster the community posture so essential to the success of the supercommunity bank. The purpose of the branches is not only to transact business at the local level with the requisite lending authorities, but also to get intensely involved in their own communities and essentially serve as individual community banks.

The supercommunity bank, then, maintains the community aspects of its operations through a measure of decentralization. The concept of decentralization may be unpopular in these days of cost-consciousness and economies of scale. However, the benefits in terms of strategic positioning that directly translate the bottom-line returns are significant and well worth the investment when properly managed. One does not mind investing a dollar to make four. The additional costs associated with the supercommunity bank strategy, although small, generate $2.00 in profits for every $1.00 in cost.

The supercommunity bank, as the name indicates, couples the strong community orientation of the smaller bank with the superior breadth of service of the large bank. It is not too big to be small and not too small to be big. Its aim is to outlocal the nationals and outnational the locals. The supercommunity bank takes advantage of its size to offer in-house services that the smaller bank is incapable of offering for many reasons. For example, most small banks cannot attract high-quality professionals in specialized services such as project finance and mortgage banking. Smaller banks do not have the customer base often required to offer services such

as corporate finance, money management derivatives, and other, more sophisticated transactions for the mid-size customer. On the other hand, large banks do not have the local presence needed to build a relationship with many middle-market companies and individual customers, and they sometimes do not have any interest in doing so. Small and mid-size companies do not bring to the table very large transactions, and money-center banks occasionally find that the cost-benefit relationships in dealing with such companies do not justify the effort.

The supercommunity bank can effectively serve certain segments of the market that may be shunned by the large banks and that cannot be well served by either large banks or small community banks. For example, although many mid-size corporations are strongly connected to their local community, some may need foreign exchange transactions, advice, and services, capitalization advice, risk management, or merger and acquisition assistance. These services can be effectively offered by the supercommunity bank, but not by the small community bank. It is conceivable that the supercommunity bank may even be able to do so more cost efficiently than larger competitors, since its overall cost base is typically lower than major money-center banks and the investment banks that are often the competitors for such transactions. Another segment that may be most effectively served by the supercommunity bank is the local affluent customer. The supercommunity bank can combine the local presence and hand-holding appreciated by the wealthy individual with the ability to transact and manage a more sophisticated package of services than the local bank can through a thriving top-notch trust department, which capitalizes on the total asset size of the supercommunity bank.

To some extent, the supercommunity bank marries the best of both worlds. It has the community bank attitude and delivery systems, but also provides a breadth of product line and sophistication of service that small banks lack, as well as economies of scale that are transparent to the customer and that cannot be accessed by small banks. Although they may not reach the diversity of product offerings available at the largest banks, supercommunity banks do provide a valuable combination of personal attention and service sophistication that appeals to a significant share of the middle-market customer base nationwide. The market vacuum in servicing these clients has been expanding as consolidation progresses. The supercommunity bank is the answer to the unmet need of this significant segment. As the large banks grow even larger, they tend to take advantage of the scale they are achieving. This, in turn, means a greater emphasis on commoditized services and low-cost production, which are diametrically opposed to the personalized, customized approach of the traditional community bank.

Another dimension of the growing number of large banks is the increasing sophistication of the product line. As the customer base grows, the economies of technology-intensive developmental products become more attractive. The result is a large, impersonal institution with an impressive array of products and services, many of which require an expensive technological infrastructure or highly skilled, highly paid personnel. A by-product of this transition is the large bank's decreasing ability to meet the needs of the service-oriented customer. Despite big banks' attempts to provide the personal touch through private banking departments, well-trained loan officers, and the like, most customers do not perceive that the level of service matches that of a smaller bank. This may be simply because it is uneconomical for a scale-sensitive business. The high rate of turnover, which rolled-up branch networks typically experience, has created further dislocation in the marketplace and irritated many customers.

While many customers are turned off by this continual change, they still seek some services that are too complex or too expensive for a small community bank to offer. Trust services, wire transfers, foreign exchange, and trade finance are among the services that few small banks offer but many customers need. The supercommunity bank delivers more products than most small community banks and more personalized service than low-cost producers do. It can offer profitable trust investment management and other services that require expertise, but vast size will not drive it to a configuration dictated by economies of scale. Banks that recognize the opportunity and position themselves to fill this niche are likely to be winners in the consolidation era. They must be prepared to sacrifice the optimal efficiencies created by a fully commoditized product line and service approach in order to maintain local presence and service levels at some slightly higher cost. Their customers are willing to pay the price for that additional attention, particularly when it is coupled with the products that meet their needs.

As industry experts expect megamergers to absorb the entire banking system into ten to fifteen giants, we still witness an industry fragmented into 10,000-plus institutions. Although plagued by overcapacity, consolidation will not go as far as some expect. I believe our industry will cluster into three strategic positions: megabanks, supercommunity banks, and community banks (within those segments, more refined strategic positions will exist as well). We may have half as many community banks in the future as we have today, but they will still exist. The industry seems to share my opinion. The recent Bank Administration Institute survey of hundreds of bankers on their views of the banking industry in the year 2000, called "Vision 2000," indicates wide agreement on the view of the multitiered industry with a single growth segment: the supercommunity bank.

Megamergers continue to create vacuums in customer service and displacement of customer relationships. The supercommunity bank is perfectly positioned to capture those relationships by offering the level of service that consumers crave without sacrificing the product breadth they seek. While the megamergers increase market share opportunities for supercommunity banks, they put pressures on them to increase size as a way of competing more effectively on the cost dimension. It is necessary for the full realization of the supercommunity opportunities to leverage both cost and product line. However,

growth for growth's sake may divert attention from the fundamental basic strength of the company, its culture, and its focus on service and the customer. Growth should be consistent with the strategic position and the "nonnegotiables" of the supercommunity bank:

- Community banking orientation
- Cost savings that are transparent to the customer
- Expansion of the product line

Supercommunity banks responded to overcapacity and the restructuring in the industry by moving closer to their customers. They focus on strengthening the personal ties with the customers. They are relationship oriented, not transaction oriented. They push authority down into the field and empower local decision makers close to the customers, while leveraging scale advantages to match large regional banks' and branch networks' lower production costs. The strategy achieves the often contradictory goals of getting closer to the customer while simultaneously slashing expenses by centralizing as many functions as possible. Banc One is a leader among supercommunity banks. As John B. McCoy said, "I very much abhor centralization. Our management structure is very decentralized with a president heading up the various affiliates. Each affiliate also has its own Board of Directors, its own business plan, and its own strategy for marketing and product pricing in its local territory. Consequently, each bank president is responsible for its performance."[2]

---

2   Natalie Baumer, "Banc One's Tactics for Excellence—An Interview with John D. McCoy," *Banker's Magazine* (Sept-Oct 1991): 9.

Supercommunity Banking—The Numbers Confirm the Strategy

Supercommunity banking is a strategic approach that uses customer-focused, community-oriented, people-intensive distribution coupled with customer-transparent cost savings in the back office. These elements are combined to deliver a cost-efficient and broad product line through locally rooted delivery channels. Typically, these organizations are structured as multibank holding companies, which delegate considerable autonomy to subsidiary banks. A central question has been how the supercommunity bank structure manifests itself in net interest margins, other income, expense, and credit risk. Some have argued that the strategy overstates the importance of local roots and personal service in both the pricing and credit quality equation and that it is an inherently expensive delivery strategy. The issue has become whether supercommunity banking is a fundamentally sound long-term strategy or a fad that will end in community bank roll-ups into large, centrally managed supermarkets.

in a recent analysis of a universe of over 1,500 American bank holding companies, I found impressive evidence that the supercommunity strategy is a winning and sustainable long-term approach to banking for the 1990s and beyond. Supercommunity bank holding companies were found to have substantially better net interest margins, roughly equal non-interest income and non-interest expense, and much lower levels of nonperforming loans and other real estate than their non-supercommunity bank peers.

The study compared the last fifteen quarters of performance data of a peer group of 270 supercommunity banks against 1,291 similarly sized non-supercommunity banks. The universe included all American bank holding companies except those held by larger bank holding companies or a limited number of institutions whose business has shifted away from core banking functions, such as J.P. Morgan or Bankers Trust Company. The findings indicated clear superior performance by the supercommunity banks.

Net Interest Margins

Supercommunity banks enjoy significantly wider net interest margins than those following alternative strategies. While non-supercommunity banks with assets over $5.0 billion had average net interest margins of 3.87%, their supercommunity bank peers generated a full 4.32% in average net interest margin. Similarly, non-supercommunity banks with assets under $5.0 billion had margins of 4.16% as contrasted with margins of 4.26% for their supercommunity bank peers. It appears that supercommunity banks price their loan products higher because of their market positions and highly personalized service levels. Similarly, supercommunity banks' interest expense levels are less than their non-supercommunity bank peers because of a superior mix of non-interest-bearing deposits and lower yields on interest-bearing deposits. The supercommunity customer does not change banks because loan products are priced somewhat less favorably than those available through branches of distantly owned and centrally managed non-supercommunity banks. It appears that fifty, or even 100, basis points will not lure the supercommunity bank customer away. (Figure 1.14).

Non-Interest Income

While non-supercommunity banks with assets greater than $5.0 billion generate non-interest income averaging 1.74% of assets, their supercommunity bank peers produce a roughly equal 1.74%. This figure confirms the strategic prescription that large supercommunity banks can move an equal amount of fee-generating products through subsidiary banks as the more integrated and centrally controlled non-supercommunity banks. We also found that for smaller supercommunity banks with assets less than $5.0 billion, non-interest income is also roughly equal to that of their non-supercommunity bank peers. Supercommunity banks under $5.0 billion generate non-interest income of 1.21% of assets in comparison to their non-supercommunity peers, which deliver 1.18%. Notwithstanding the fact that the two peer groups produce similar amounts of non-interest income, because the larger supercommunity banks are composed of smaller community banks, their ability to produce non-interest income equal to that of the large, integrated, non-supercommunity banks is a substantial improvement over their stand-alone capabilities. As affiliates of a supercommunity bank, smaller community banks are able to offer correspondent banking, investment management, mutual funds, and annuities that they would not otherwise ordinarily be capable of delivering (Figure 1.15).

Non-Interest Expense

Although supercommunity banks are often perceived to be managerially top heavy, and possess at least one layer of unnecessary middle management, $5+ billion supercommunity banks actually have roughly equal non-interest expense ratios to their non-supercommunity bank peers, and smaller supercommunity banks do substantially better than their peers. Supercommunity banks with assets in excess of $5.0 billion have ratios of non-interest expenses to assets of 3.6%, while their non-supercommunity bank peers have similar levels of 3.78% of assets. Similarly, those supercommunity banks with assets under $5.0 billion have non-interest expense to assets ratios of 3.52% compared their non-supercommunity bank peers, which have ratios of 3.56%. Apparently, supercommunity holding companies realize economies of scale through consolidation of back-office operations and maximization of cost efficiencies within product lines.

FIGURE 1.14 Net Interest Margin

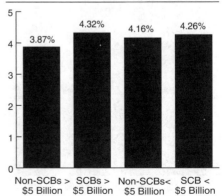

These efficiencies outweigh any higher costs that might otherwise be associated with the people-intensive, high-service, quality delivery strategy (Figure 1.16).

Asset Quality

Most significantly, asset quality at super-community banks far exceeds that of non-supercommunity bank peers. Nonperforming loans and other real estate as a percent of total loans was 5.00% for the non-supercommunity banks larger than $5.0 billion and 4.96% for the smaller non-supercommunity banks. These levels compare favorably with 3.18% and 3.02%, respectively, for the supercommunity bank institutions. Several possible explanations exist for the 2.00% variance. First, the more centralized non-supercommunity banks may be working off much greater lending limits and therefore have much greater concentrations of risk in their portfolios. Second, the more centralized non-supercommunity banks are more likely to

be involved in out-of-market lending, about which they have less knowledge. Third, the supercommunity banks are structured to maximize the benefit of local knowledge and contacts in the credit decision. Their local presidents and boards know the community thoroughly and make their lending decisions based on information often unavailable to non-local competitors. (Figure 1.17).

Return on Assets and Equity

As should be expected, because of the superior operating margins and credit quality at supercommunity banks, they have delivered much stronger returns over time. On both an average return on assets and return on equity basis, supercommunity banks have significantly outperformed their peers. Non-supercommunity banks delivered average returns on assets ranging from .41% to .45% of assets, as compared with returns of .79% and .76% for supercommunity banks. This performance was

FIGURE 1.15 Non-Interest Income to Assets

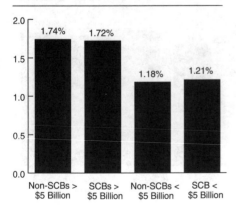

FIGURE 1.16 Non-Interest Expense to Assets

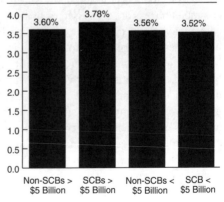

FIGURE 1.17 Nonperforming Loans & ORE to Total Loans & ORE

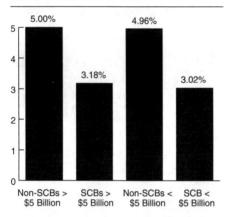

ance between non-supercommunity banks and supercommunity banks is less great in the case of return on equity, this is a reflection of the generally higher levels of equity capital found in the supercommunity bank. (Figures 1.18 and 1.19).

While supercommunity banking is sometimes criticized as being an unnecessarily expensive delivery mechanism adding little real value, our findings indicate that, over a period of time, the supercommunity strategy has offered significantly better operating margins and enhanced non-interest income opportunities all in the context of a relatively low-cost delivery structure. Furthermore, the strategy adds significant real value to the quality of credit decisions, which manifests itself in vastly higher-quality loan portfolios and favorable charge-off experiences.

mirrored in the return on equity numbers with non-supercommunity banks delivering returns ranging from 6.42% to 6.03% of equity compared with returns ranging from 11.83% to 10.19% of equity for the supercommunity banks. Although the variance

The question of whether supercommunity banking is a fundamentally sound long-term strategy or a passing fad appears

FIGURE 1.18 Return on Equity

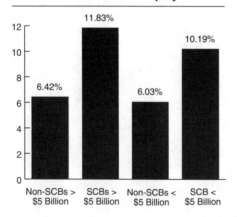

FIGURE 1.19 Return on Assets

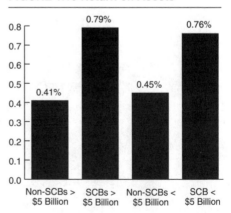

to be answered by the figures above. Further confirmation of their longevity is the vote of confidence they received from the capital markets. Supercommunity bank stocks command higher prices and are viewed as being less risky than their peers.

CHAPTER TWO

The Supercommunity Bank—
Outlocal the Nationals and
Outnational the Locals

Supercommunity Banking—
An Overview

What makes a bank a supercommunity bank? The definition is based on a three-pronged strategic approach:

1. Strong community orientation,
2. customer-transparent cost savings, and
3. a broad product line.

All combine to create a unique strategy that is defensible against both large and small banks, while building value in the franchise and generating strong profits (Figure 2.1). The attributes that define the supercommunity bank strategic position as they relate to the three major elements of the strategy are designed to capture the best of both worlds—the small and large banks (Figure 2.2).

First, let us consider the low-cost producers: Companies such as Citibank for retail services, State Street for global and domestic custody business, and Northern Trust for trust services are all trying to offer services at the lowest cost in their strategic niche. At the same time, boutique banks are growing. Companies with a clear market or product focus, such as US Trust in trust services, Morgan Guaranty in blue-chip banking, or Bankers Trust in investment banking are committed to achieving scale efficiencies and low-cost production in a specific product line. On the other hand, community banking is alive and well for small banks. Although there is overcapacity in that segment, it is a viable strategic alternative for many,

FIGURE 2.1 Supercommunity Banking—Prescription for Success

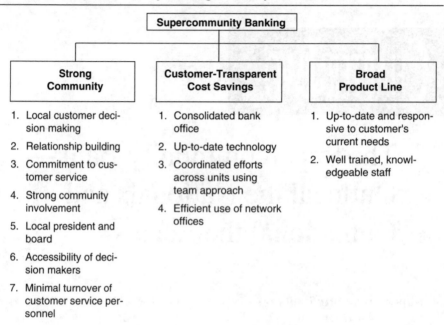

Strong Community	Customer-Transparent Cost Savings	Broad Product Line
1. Local customer decision making	1. Consolidated bank office	1. Up-to-date and responsive to customer's current needs
2. Relationship building	2. Up-to-date technology	2. Well trained, knowledgeable staff
3. Commitment to customer service	3. Coordinated efforts across units using team approach	
4. Strong community involvement	4. Efficient use of network offices	
5. Local president and board		
6. Accessibility of decision makers		
7. Minimal turnover of customer service personnel		

especially as consolidation creates customer relationship displacement. One interesting piece of evidence to the opportunities created by the megabank acquisition/slash-and-burn process are the start-ups, which are de novo banks that attempt to fill the vacuum created by the consolidation in the business.

As the industry resegments, every bank has to rethink its own strategic position and business focus. There is more than one viable strategic alternative available, as there is more than one way to turn a profit. Take an example from outside the banking business (Figure 2.3). McDonald's is a company that authored its strategy on a simple product line and simple delivery.

The product is standardized and fully commoditized. A Big Mac is a Big Mac whether you have it in Washington, D.C., Moscow, or Boise. No matter where you are in the world, McDonald's will deliver the same product, price, and environment. That predictability and consistency is not

FIGURE 2.2 Supercommunity Banking

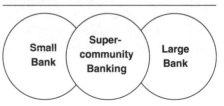

FIGURE 2.3 Bank Image Positioning

American Express	McDonald's
Superior Customer Service	Simple Product Line
Sophisticated Product Line	Simple Delivery

only an excellent way to achieve quality and cost efficiencies (variation is the nemesis of quality), but it is also a way to manage the customer's expectations. McDonald's builds its value around these features: product standardization, quality consistency, low-cost production, and speed and convenience of delivery.

The other side of the coin is that service becomes less important at McDonald's. Speed of delivery and consistency of product are key, but the person who serves you the Big Mac is immaterial to the transaction, and you do not develop a relationship with that person. Also, the product line

FIGURE 2.4 Bank Image Positioning: Implications

American Express	McDonald's
Service Critical	Service Less Important
Pricing Flexibility/ Value Pricing	Low Cost Production
Product Diversi- fication	Limited Line
Product Custom- ization	Standardization
Trained Sales Force	No Sales Force
Distribution Anchor: Sophistication	Distribution Anchor: Convenience

must be limited and fully standardized. Don't try to order your Big Mac without tomato; you can get the sandwich only one way—tomato included. That is one of the elements in the McDonald's formula for success. It facilitates low-cost production. McDonald's doesn't need a sales force either; it has the golden arches blanketing the United States and image advertising to build and support brand identification. To summarize, the company's strategic position anchor is low-cost production and product quality. Its distribution anchor is convenience (Figure 2.4).

American Express, on the other hand, is a company that offers superior customer service and a sophisticated, customized product line. Its strategy is diametrically opposed to McDonald's. Its product line is costly to manufacture and expensive to buy. With it comes tremendous product flexibility and diversification, as exemplified by the American Express platinum services. Platinum card customers are asked to fill out a profile of their personal and business preferences. Special programs are then tailored for the main lifestyle profiles identified among the customer base. Elements include sports (play tennis with Bjorn Borg or golf with Arnold Palmer), food (cook with Julia Child or Marcella Hazan), arts (meet Metropolitan Opera singers backstage), trips (an exclusive cruise down the Mississippi on the Delta Queen), and so on. American Express attempts to create a personalized approach to make each customer feel special and to have a product line that would meet the special needs of its various customers.

Product diversification and customization are accompanied with value pricing and price flexibility. The product is tiered, from the green card to the platinum card, and pricing is tiered accordingly, consistent with the customer's price sensitivity. A platinum cardholder is prepared to pay $400 a year for the amenities associated with the card, including status, service levels, cash availability, and the lifestyle product lines. A green cardholder is not prepared to pay for these services and, therefore, has a different product line available to him or her, which is much more narrow and less flexible. Either way, service is critical to the success of American Express. Consequently, its sales force is trained and capable of solving customers' problems without further transferring the customer to other points on the 800-number chain. That is an important feature to credit card customers who are used to being bounced from one phone extension to another until they, at last, reach the right person. Knowledgeable and empowered staff in customer service and sales is essential to the success of American Express. To summarize, the company's product line is complex and tiered to meet the needs of different segments. Product line sophistication is an important element to the strategy, and the distribution anchor is the effective sales and service focus.

Within this context of strategic repositioning between McDonald's low-cost production/low-service position and American Express's high-price/high-service position, the question bankers are asking is: "Is there room for community banks and supercommunity banks in the system?" It

appears that supercommunity banks are filling a void in the marketplace created by the megasize and depersonalization of the large banks and the super regionals. It is

---

Knowledgeable and empowered staff in customer service and sales is essential to the success of American Express.

---

responding to customers' preferences for local banks and for quality service as identified by the American Banker Consumer Surveys year in and year out. The evidence is that new bank charters continue to sprout despite the downcycle in the banking industry in the last couple of years. New banks are constantly being chartered around the country (Figure 2.5), flying in the face of overcapacity in the business. They gather investors behind them who are prepared to put their money on the per-

FIGURE 2.5 New Bank Charters Are at an All-Time High

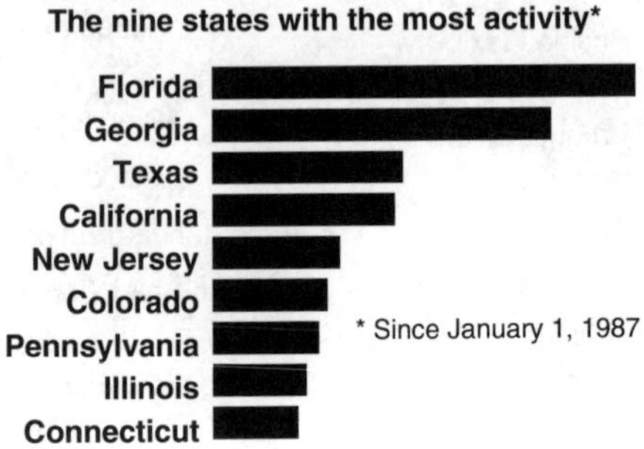

The nine states with the most activity*

State	
Florida	
Georgia	
Texas	
California	
New Jersey	
Colorado	
Pennsylvania	
Illinois	
Connecticut	

* Since January 1, 1987

Source: Federal Deposit Insurance Corp.

FIGURE 2.6 The Winning Formula

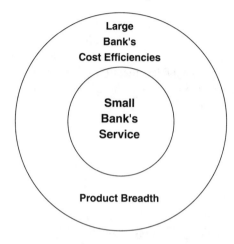

ception that, although there is overcapacity, there are market voids where customers are underserved. The same concept is the drive behind supercommunity banking, which takes it one step farther: "Outlocal the nationals and outnational the locals."

The supercommunity bank strategic position is committed to not being too big for personalized service, senior executive accessibility, and community identification, yet not being too small to achieve cost efficiencies and volume-sensitive businesses and to offer a sophisticated product line, meet a full range of the customer's needs; and to being able to attract the right kind of people to offer these services. Specialists are not easily attracted by small banks since it is not only money they're after but also type of clientele, size of transaction, and the passion of the game. These can be offered by supercommunity banks much more effectively than by small banks. The result—a winning formula (Figure 2.6).

Supercommunity banking does involve some key trade-offs (Figure 2.7). It involves several tension points that are not easily resolved and that represent a healthy conflict for the continuing prosperity of the organization. For example, cost-efficiencies imply fewer people, fewer branches, and so on. But community orientation, one of the nonnegotiables of the strategy, implies just the opposite. The tension between the two needs to be maintained and kept in check to make sure community orientation is not compromised, but not to the point of ignoring the cost implications of every decision in the course of offering superior community banking service.

Another balance that is difficult to attain is between centralization and decentralization. Centralization implies control, cost efficiencies, a sense of comfort, and standardization. At the same time, decentralization is another nonnegotiable of supercommunity banking because it keeps the decision maker close to the customer and enhances the community orientation of the company. One can continue to explore ways to centralize appropriately without affecting community orientation. At the same time, decentralization should not be totally yielded to as subsidiary presidents continue to exert pressure on the holding company to achieve more autonomy.

FIGURE 2.7 Supercommunity Bank: Key Trade-Offs

Cost Efficiencies — Community Orientation
Centralization — Decentralization
Product Diversity — Risk Containment

Another trade-off is between expansion of the product line and risk containment. Every new product introduction has a risk associated with it simply because it is new, but at the same time, product diversity is an essential strategic component of the program. As supercommunity banks continue to expand their product line, they should not go so far off a leverage point that they increase the risk beyond an acceptable risk-return trade point. Product expansion should build on strength and expertise (homegrown or imported), thereby limiting risk.

The tension between the holding company and the subsidiary is a healthy one and will continue throughout the process. It is to be expected; the presidents of the subsidiaries desire as much independence and autonomy as possible. They will resist standardization and centralization and attempt to continue to build their own infrastructure toward a self-contained environment that is natural, expected, and altogether not unhealthy for the sense of ownership the subsidiaries have over their business. By the same token, the holding company must continue to strive to centralize those areas that do not affect the community banking service levels to achieve benefits ranging from cost efficiencies to the controls that are so important in today's environment. It needs to do so while empowering the subsidiaries' presidents and other staff members to make the decisions within the parameters provided by the holding company, thereby freeing them from operational burdens to serve their customers the way they know best. Centralization is important also as a quality control measure because it implies

standardization and less variation. Supercommunity banks will continue to struggle with this trade-off and be frustrated by it on many occasions. This is a healthy frustration and should not bring one to abandon the strategic position or move too far in one direction or another to remove it.

The Role of Quality

Quality is integral to supercommunity banking. It is an elusive and fuzzy concept but can be quantified to a minute detail as will be described later on in this book. The market definition of quality (Figure 2.8) can range from general characteristics such as reliability, empathy, responsiveness, and assurance to friendliness, speed, accuracy, and personal service. The American Banker Consumer Survey indicates that customers give their primary financial institution high grades for specific aspects of the relationship, but have complaints about overall quality (Figure 2.9).

The importance of quality is twofold. The absence of quality creates a customer attrition, and the presence of quality creates customer retention. Therefore, no quality has a downside to it, while good quality has an upside to it. Quality counts,

FIGURE 2.8 Market Definition of Quality

Reliability	Friendliness (47%)
Empathy	Speed (40%)
Responsiveness	Accuracy (24%)
Assurance	Personal Service (13%)

Full product line, although important, is not at the top of the list.

FIGURE 2.9 Measuring Quality

Customers give their primary financial institutions high grades for specific aspects of relationships, but have qualms about overall quality

Mean scores on a scale of 1 (poor) to 5 (excellent). Percentages represent customers who gave poor or fair grades.

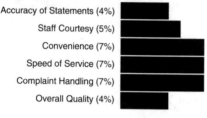

Accuracy of Statements (4%)
Staff Courtesy (5%)
Convenience (7%)
Speed of Service (7%)
Complaint Handling (7%)
Overall Quality (4%)

as Figure 2.10 indicates, to the most important customer segments in the business. Those that represent the greatest value, such as the highest income or the highest growth, will change a banking relationship because of quality problems. More than 50% of the 35- to 66-year-old population will switch banks if quality becomes a problem. Penalties for low quality are significant. At the same time, the benefits of quality service are significant as well. It results in strong customer loyalty, growth opportunities through cross-selling, reduced bank vulnerability to price wars as long-term customers become somewhat price-sensitive, and enhanced bank ability to command higher relative prices without affecting market share. Quality also implies retention, which, in turn, lowers marketing costs since cross-selling an existing customer or retaining an existing customer is seven times less expensive than acquiring a new one. Quality trans-

lates into market share, and market share translates into profitability.

Strong Community Orientation

A supercommunity bank is first and foremost a community bank. Being an effective local bank serving the community needs is the cornerstone of this strategy. In order to achieve this objective, the following characteristics are typically found among supercommunity banks.

Local Customer Decision-Making

The supercommunity bank does not centralize, by and large, the customer pricing decisions. The focus of each pricing decision is not the transaction itself, but the customer. The supercommunity bank, therefore, remains close to the customer and allows the authority and control of the pricing decisions to be left in the hands of the executives of each bank. Although coordination is important, sometimes even essential (for example, in the case of overlapping markets), the guiding philosophy is to leave the flexibility of the pricing structure, both deposits and loans, at the

FIGURE 2.10 Quality Counts: Bank Changes Because of Quality Problems

Group	Percentage
Total Population	42%
35-44 Years Old	56%
Income > $70,000	49%
Income < $20,000	34%

local level. This takes full advantage of the community banking element of the super-community bank position by allowing each bank's president and executive team to customize their pricing and transactions to individual customers and to their market conditions. Certain guidelines from the corporation may be imposed on each bank, particularly regarding liquidity levels, credit quality, asset quality, and fees. The purpose of these guidelines is to ensure that each bank acts consistently with the corporate objectives toward maximizing asset quality and increasing profitability. By the same token, decision-making autonomy at the individual bank level is essential to retaining the customer service edge, which is key to the success of the supercommunity bank and to maintaining the customer franchise.

Relationship Building

The supercommunity bank is geared toward building a relationship as opposed to being transaction oriented. It is interested in attracting and then retaining the customer. Strong customer retention is followed by increasing cross-selling activities and declining acquisition costs. The bank is not interested in maximizing the fees of one transaction. Rather, it is interested in a long-term approach to maximizing profits. Consequently, the management of each institution spends an extensive amount of time catering to customers and prospects, marketing at the local community level, and building the relationships. Flexibility in transaction structuring and pricing as well as quick turnaround time (which results from investing decision-making

authority at the local level) come into play when building the relationship.

Commitment to Customer Service

Service quality, a key element to achieving customer satisfaction and retention, is another major attribute to the supercommunity strategy. It is the small bank service level that the supercommunity bank is committed to offer, thus offsetting one of the important competitive advantages of small banks.

Strong Community Involvement

The individual members of the supercommunity bank maintain close involvement in their own community. The board, chief executive, and senior management team of each member bank get involved in a wide range of community-oriented activities. They strive to maintain civic leadership and participate actively in charity and other events that demonstrate their commitment to the local community. That commitment serves to defend their market position relative to both larger and smaller banks while leveraging resources already available to the bank in each community.

Local President and Board (with or without a local charter)

Local decision-making authority and strong ties to the community are critical to success. Hence, the presence of the local president and the support of a board of directors comprised of local community leaders are important components of the supercommunity bank identity. Although they represent a layer of overhead that otherwise can be eliminated, they also represent the bank's commitment to the community and to the service implications of that commitment. In turn, lower customer turnover and, often, lower price sensitivity represent the return on that investment. Local presence also facilitates growth of local market share through capitalizing on the president's and board members' local contacts.

Accessibility of Decision-Makers

One of the major competitive advantages of community banks is the accessibility of senior management and other decision makers to customers of all sizes. Small and large customers alike can speak with the department head and the president and get the decision-making and transactions flexibility resident only at the senior management level. The supercommunity bank ensures that those characteristics do not get lost in the process of creating a larger holding company.

Minimal Turnover of Customer Service Personnel

Much like the smaller community bank, the supercommunity banking organization strives to retain employees at the local level and maintain continuity of customer contact. Unlike the larger urban banks and the regional banks, which merge other institutions into their banks and follow the transaction by major turnover and maximizing cost efficiencies, the supercommunity bank is committed to keeping service continuity at each bank's level. Therefore,

mergers into a supercommunity bank are less painful to the smaller bank management, since most personnel are retained, particularly customer service personnel. Another benefit to this continuity is enhancing the bank's ability to fully understand its customers' needs and to design its product line and delivery systems to meet those needs.

Customer-Transparent Cost Savings

The supercommunity bank is committed to providing superior service levels, but not at all costs. Successful supercommunity banks seek ways to reduce costs without penalizing service levels, such that the customer is not aware of the cost-reduction measures under review by the bank. The holding company functions as a centralized production facility, whenever appropriate, to capitalize on the full asset size of the company, while the delivery system and line personnel often remain highly centralized and intact.

Cost Efficiencies

There are many opportunities available to the management of supercommunity banks to save money without penalizing service levels and sometimes with enhancing service levels. They range from further consolidation of functions, such as investment management, asset liability management, credit review, and policy functions, to achieving standardization of the product offering, which, in a sense, creates a shelf of uniform products that are available to all bank subsidiaries. Each bank subsidiary then selects the product array that is of interest to them. No single bank is obligated to market all products, but every bank is obligated to use a standardized product.

Standardization is one of the cornerstones of quality management as it implies minimal variation as illustrated in the McDonald's example. Product standardization is an aspect of quality since it creates predictability and a feeling of being at home. For example, at all Mcdonald's, the Big Macs will be the same; all the Ritz-Carlton Hotels have the same furniture and fixtures. Guests feel at home at both institutions. Similarly, if all bank branches throughout the system look the same, as Huntington Bancshares did throughout their 300-plus branch network, that creates not only cost efficiencies but a feeling of being at home for the customer, regardless of which branch the customer visits. The dual benefits of cost efficiencies and relationship enhancement are powerful.

Up-to-Date Technology

Technological investment is another scale-sensitive element to the strategy. Technological innovations carry a high fixed cost. The greater the volume of assets over which the cost is spread, the greater the efficiency. In addition, technology can be used to improve customer service levels, sales effectiveness, and so on. Platform systems and imaging are two prime examples of such applications.

The supercommunity bank does not aim to maximize the cost effectiveness of a large asset base. In other words, it does not attempt to minimize human resource costs and centralize all operations and decision-making activities to maximize savings. Rather, it strives to reach a balance between cost efficiencies and relationship management. This trade-off is typically achieved by centralizing functions that are transparent to the customer, ranging from accounting and investments to loan pro-

---

Businesses that require a major capital investment and, therefore, have a large fixed-cost component, lend themselves to cost efficiencies and a reduction of per item cost.

---

cessing and other data processing functions. Processing activities offer significant scale savings. At the same time, they are invisible to the customer. Hence, the consolidation of back-office processing functions provide an effective tool available to the supercommunity bank to take advantage of its size without sacrificing the community banking orientation.

The "nonnegotiable" goal should be cost efficiencies transparent to the customer. Cost efficiencies are essential to the competitive position of supercommunity banks. The most susceptible elements to cost efficiencies are volume-sensitive businesses, which are commoditized and not personalized. These range from check processing and proof-and-transit operations to mutual funds, investment management, trust services, custody (both global and domestic), credit card processing, data processing, and other technology-intensive services. Businesses that require a major capital investment, and therefore have a large fixed-cost component, lend themselves to cost efficiencies and a reduction of per item cost. In addition, businesslike investment management also lends itself to volume economies because it takes one person to manage $100,000 worth of equities, $100,000,000 worth of equities, or $1 billion worth of equities. The economies are obvious.

Centralization and standardization are effective tools for cost management at supercommunity banks so long as they do not diminish visible service levels. Reduced overhead is another cost-effective tool. Holding companies, like other bureaucracies, tend to multiply and grow. Keeping overhead under control is an important component of cost management at supercommunity banks. As the company grows (and growth, particularly through acquisition, is a typical feature of supercommunity banking), the holding company overhead should not grow in a linear function, thereby decreasing overhead relative to total assets.

The accelerating pace of technological change is continuing to make significant modifications in the mechanics and delivery of bank operations. In order to fully utilize the new technology and gain the most possible efficiencies to increase productivity, it is important to create a unified data processing and operations approach to the affiliate banking structure within the supercommunity banking strategy. First, a data processing conversion needs to be accomplished to convert existing affiliates and those to be acquired in the future to the same data processing systems. Second, economies of scale then can gradually be

developed as an increasing amount of the actual data processing work becomes centralized at the holding company level. Centralization and standardization are key to economies and savings realization as well as enhanced controls, quality, and other benefits.

Such programs as platform automation can be implemented to increase the productivity of line personnel in the branches. Platform automation also has the benefi-

---

As the company grows . . . the holding company overhead should not grow in a linear function, thereby decreasing overhead relative to total assets.

---

cial effect of standardizing the format of such processes as loan applications, new account openings, and customer information access. This standardization can have a significant human resource effect of allowing for the transfer of staff between affiliate banks without the tiresome and unproductive task of learning a new operations format. It will allow for the development of unified training manuals and programs for all affiliates and for easier comparison of operational details between affiliates to determine the relative efficiencies of each operation and facilitate learning across affiliates more successfully. Consistent with that approach, the multitude of unique products associated with a diverse system of affiliate banks must be reduced to retain those products of greatest benefits to the customer. One $1.5 billion supercommunity bank, for example, had over 1,000 deposit products. Another had over 170 variable-rate mortgage products. The result—customer confusion and an operations nightmare. Product simplification programs, such as the one described in Chapter 9 for Marquette's retail product line, can be used to determine which, if any, products might be merged into other products of greater value to the consumer.

In addition to creating cost-saving opportunities, technology can be used in conjunction with reengineering, a technique designed to reveal how to do things better and smarter and how to focus activities around the desired results rather than around the task performed in order to produce that result. Reengineering is particularly important in supercommunity banking because it treats all functions, including those that are geographically dispersed, as a single path to achieving the goal or the desired results. Supercommunity banking is a geographically dispersed system and, therefore, can reap special benefits from reengineering and technology, which make geographic distance invisible to the process and to the customers.

Units Using a Team Approach to Improve Cost Savings

Most supercommunity banks have a clear vision of their strategy and the desired market position. That vision is shared throughout the ranks. Employees and management alike understand the purpose of the bank, its philosophy, and its culture. This commonality goes a long way to increase staff productivity and to motivate employees at all levels to go the extra mile and be the best. Caring, responsive personnel are also conducive to creating a team approach whereby all resources are moving in the same direction. This, in turn, increases the effectiveness of resource utilization and promotes consistency across the individual banks.

Effective Use of Network Offices

Using the office network as a coordinated mechanism to generate low-cost deposits and efficiently distribute products is another aspect of the leverage element of the strategy. Increasing "production" of deposits, interest income, and fees per square foot and per employee is an important measure of that leverage. Mutual funds, annuities, and loans are among the arrows in the bank's quiver. Their goal is to become an effective distribution network for these and other products.

Broad Product Line

A supercommunity bank competes not only with the local community bank but also with large, money-center institutions. Having a broad product line is essential to effectively compete with the megabanks as well as to achieve customer relations and cross-selling. A broad product line is another cornerstone of the three-pronged supercommunity banking strategy. It is essential to offer a wide array of products and services that will meet the full range of customer's needs, so that customers will not outgrow the bank. Therefore, customer retention will be achieved, and the value of the franchise will be maximized.

The supercommunity bank does not leverage its franchise at the expense of the customer service level. Rather, it strives to maximize revenues through the franchise by combining effective relationship building with a broad, sophisticated product line. It is that combination that provides the winning formula by which the supercommunity bank can defend against the small bank's service, since smaller banks cannot offer the product breadth and sophistication, which can only be supported by a larger asset base. By the same token, that combination defends against the larger bank that can offer the product sophistication but loses the personal service and relationship management aspect.

The supercommunity bank boasts greater sophistication, which creates a competitive advantage vis-a-vis community bank competitors. The broader product line also produces fee-income growth opportunities.

The effectiveness of this element of the strategy hinges upon the bank's ability to offer training such that the staff is both knowledgeable of its various products and is sales oriented. The quality and salesmanship of the staff are essential to better leverage existing resources, including distribution channels and customer bases.

The supercommunity bank boasts greater sophistication, which creates a

competitive advantage vis-a-vis community bank competitors. The broader product line also produces fee-income growth opportunities. Some supercommunity banks use a broader product line to enhance their already strong margin business with a solid stream of fee income. The following are examples:

Bank	Fee-Income-Producing Service
M&I	Data Processing
Synovus	Service, Credit Card Processing
Bank Four	Credit Card Processing
Premier Bank	Mutual Funds and Annuities
Dime	Mutual Funds and Annuities
US Bancorp	Mortgage Banking

The broader product offering also permits the supercommunity bank to properly leverage existing customer base and distribution networks. The customer base is the franchise value of the company, and it is further enhanced as the relationship is built through the purchase of multiple products. Supercommunity banks truly believe in cross-selling. For them it is a way of life, not only a way to enhance current earnings by pushing more products through distribution networks. Cross-selling in a supercommunity bank is limited to creating long-term shareholder value by creating customer relationships, market share, and a predictable future income stream.

Examples of product expansion opportunities are varied. Supercommunity banks find their niche in many different ways, and individual banks should look for their own. The following list is a "mind tickler" for possible expansion. However, the acid test for product expansion is meeting customer needs (and building on a core competency whenever possible).

Consumer	Corporate
Mutual Funds	Derivatives
Annuities	Middle-market M&A
Insurance	Cash management
Investment management	Project finance
Personal	Corporate trust
Trust services	International banking
Travel services	Benefits management
Executive loans	Indirect auto lending
Customer finance	Data processing
Global investment	Credit card processing
Management	Correspondent banking

Some of the issues associated with product line expansion are discussed below.

Distribution

It is important to use the existing branch network as a distribution vehicle for additional products in order to create leverage. That, however, does not imply that current staffing is capable of offering new products. On many occasions, specialized personnel need to be trained or hired if present staff cannot gain the technical expertise or the sales attitude required to get the job done. It is also important to identify target segments within the customer base that are most likely to need the product introduced. Targeted marketing reduces the acquisition costs of new customers and enhances the value that the product brings to the prospect, since it is prescreened to ensure the product offered meets the target customers' needs.

Breadth of Product Expansion

How far should a supercommunity bank go in building a product line to fully meet customer needs? The answer depends on *what* the customer needs. Therefore, the first step in determining product expansion strategy is to identify the customer base's non-traditional product needs and to assess the customers' receptivity to the bank as a provider of these products and services. The American Banker Customer Survey and other surveys clearly indicate that customers are receptive to buying nontraditional financial services from their banks. They, in fact, prefer to be served by their banks/depository institutions since they trust them more than investment banks and brokerage firms.

It is important that products offered by supercommunity banks do not abuse that customer trust and ensure that the customer is not sold services that do not meet his or her needs. For example, a supercommunity bank that owns a discount brokerage or a full-service brokerage firm should not churn accounts like other brokerage firms do, but push for transactions only in those cases where the bank representative truly believes it is in the best interest of the customer. Supercommunity banks should be careful then not to squander the asset represented by the trust the customer puts in their bank.

It has also been indicated that customers like to be called by a bank representative about new products. They found this to be an information service as opposed to a pure sales call and appreciated the opportunity to learn more about aspects of the business they were unfamiliar with and new product offerings that might meet their needs. Therefore, bankers should be encouraged to call on the customers with such information and not perceive this to be a degrading experience or a pushy sales call. Instead, this is a valued information exchange, and the customer will determine whether it is in his or her best interest.

A secondary consideration in selecting product expansion opportunities is the competitive positioning of the bank. Not only should the product itself be attractive and potentially profitable to meet hurdle rates and retention criteria, but the competitive positioning itself should offer sufficient strength on which to build. In general, product expansion should build on strength and capitalize on leverage points available within the bank. Such leverage points can range from the customer base, to the distribution network, to technical knowledge. For example, cross-selling existing customers is less costly and enhances the relationship. Using the existing distribution network makes for better employees, more well-rounded staff, and greater profitability. Leveraging technical expertise is not only cost-efficient, but also makes for better career paths for one-track employees. For example, using trust services as a place to launch mutual fund management (if it meets the internal skills set requirements and the critical mass requirements) is a good way to leverage existing capability.

Another example is product innovation within one of the subsidiaries, which then is leveraged throughout the company. For example, at LaSalle Bank in Chicago, one of the smaller banks in the system developed expertise in municipal lease finance. They are now servicing the total system with that product capability, thereby leveraging the technical expertise developed in one of the subsidiaries. In a similar way within the same supercommunity bank,

another subsidiary developed expertise in construction finance. That bank now offers construction finance throughout the system.

Cannibalization

One product expansion issue that has more to do with perception than with reality is the issue of cannibalization. Many branch managers and traditional bank presidents perceive alternative investment products as direct competitors to the core deposits for which they received compensation for only so many years. As a result, explicitly or implicitly, they do not sell alternative investment products. They often do not realize that savings and investment funds are not direct substitutes and that customers, depending on their age and wealth, designate different buckets of funds to different uses, as depicted in Figure 2.11a-c. The purpose of product expansion on the liability side of the balance sheet is to capture funds that are currently outside the banking system and held in mutual funds and other investments. Although it is unlikely to expect no attrition, little attrition is a realistic objective.

Many supercommunity banks that have been very successful in the introduction of mutual funds find that cannibalization is a minor factor, in the range of under 20% of the total deposits within the first year. Integra, for example, gets 60% of the mutual fund growth from outside sources. Most of the funds captured are new funds. Within two years of product introduction, the new funds captured are reduced to about 25–40%, while the rest of the money represents rollovers. The common experience is, however, that while only

FIGURE 2.11a Investment Behavior
25-Year-Old Couple with Young Children

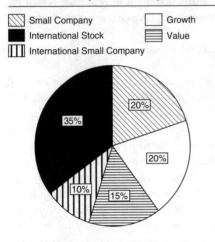

25% of the fund growth is "new" money, there is a reflow of money in time that brings back the deposits and effectively

broadens the customer relationship. Either way, although cannibalization cannot be ignored, it should be addressed and minimized so that it does not represent a real threat in the case of product expansion on the liability side. Supercommunity banks, however, should be aware of the sensitivity of the bank presidents to the introduction of such new liability-competing products, and attempt to allay the concerns of line people within the distribution network. One way to do so effectively is to compensate staff for total assets brought into the bank with different incentive compensation levels associated with different types of products depending on their profitability and growth potential for the bank. Either way, the message should be clear: new products need to be offered to fully meet the customer needs and capture the relationship.

FIGURE 2.11b Investment Behavior
48-Year-Old Couple Looking to Retirement

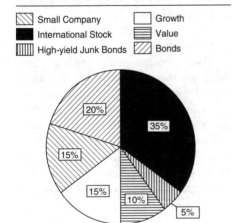

FIGURE 2.11c Investment Behavior
65-Year-Old Couple, Retired

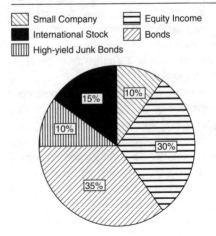

Costs

New product introduction can be very costly. Even if we assume that the supercommunity bank is a quick follower and, therefore, does not expend the funds and time necessary for research and development, the production itself could be expensive. Therefore, the make or buy decision needs to be made up front. In the mutual funds business, for example, the trade-off is clear. One needs certain minimal volume in order to make mutual funds successful, but the management fees associated with owning your own funds are 60 basis points, a significant annual income. When selling somebody else's funds, however, none of these expense and hurdle rates apply. Instead, you leverage your distribution network for 200-400 basis points (one-time fee) every time a fund is sold.

Choosing the correct risk-return trade-off is a key issue. Annual income is associated with product introduction/risk, while one-time fees, although less profitable, are also less risky. Training versus hiring is another trade-off associated with the cost of product expansion. Most supercommunity banks prefer to train their own people. However, in many cases, that is not an effective option since the technical expertise and attitudinal component of selling certain products, including mutual funds, may be quite different from the profile required to be a successful customer service representative. Training versus hiring should, therefore, be evaluated in a dispassionate manner to ensure successful product introduction. Some companies that have already integrated sales into their culture will be able to leverage existing staff for successful launch; others will not. One effective bridge technique is to use a third-party sales force initially to launch the product and to train internal staff in product sales. Once internal staff is integrated into the process, which usually occurs within one year to eighteen months, the internal staff sales force takes over and the third-party sales force gets terminated.

A product pro forma profit and loss statement is the acid test for product introduction. Short of the necessity to meet customer needs at a loss or to break even, profitability is the name of the game. Therefore, realistic financial statements need to be developed. Using peer information and experience is an effective way to project product performance. Vendor experience may not be as applicable since the vendors are typically dedicated full-time to the sales of that single product; whereas, supercommunity banks would often look at a product as a relationship filler or a retention vehicle in addition to the fee income opportunity.

The key success factor in product introduction and expansion is leverage. A supercommunity bank should leverage the existing cost base, including bricks and mortar, human resources, and the existing customer base, in order to make the whole greater than the sum of the parts. Sales capability and employee professionalism and expertise are also essential to a successful product.

Summary

The supercommunity bank attempts to combine the important characteristics of small community banks and large banks. It takes the community banking approach to the customer from the small bank and combines it with some measure of cost efficiencies that are created by economies of scale and the breadth of product offerings from the large banks. That combination is a winning strategy for the banking industry in the 1990s.

CHAPTER THREE

Successful
Supercommunity Banks

Successful supercommunity banks distinguish themselves by focusing on one key strength and building on it to maximize their franchise value. The following chapter contains illustrations of this point and how successful supercommunity banks have capitalized on a strength and used it to enhance their core earnings.

First Virginia Banks—Core Earnings and Indirect Auto Lending

First Virginia Banks exemplifies the supercommunity bank concept. The company is a $7 billion asset holding company operating across Maryland, Virginia, and Tennessee. It has twenty individual banks with 319 branches. Each bank has its own board of directors, president, and chief executive officer. In addition, there are fifty advisory board members. Directors are drawn from businesses in the local markets served and are invested in as a major corporate resource, including an annual retreat with spouses where they learn more about First Virginia and its role in their respective communities. The company has centralized its back-office operations and the technology for each of its banks. It also provides pricing guidelines and floors for loan products, but leaves the ultimate decision making at the local bank level. An excerpt from its 1991 annual report reads, "First Virginia has long prospered by operating what has now become popularly known as 'a supercommunity bank,' and we intend to continue to do so. This means we combine the best elements of local autonomy and focus. There are twenty separately chartered, fully owned banks, each

47

FIGURE 3.1

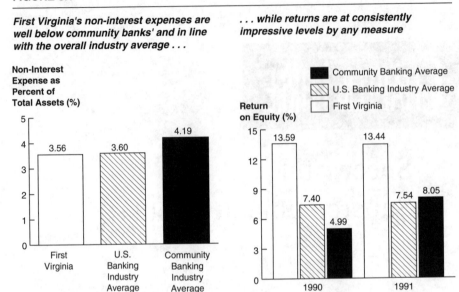

First Virginia's non-interest expenses are well below community banks' and in line with the overall industry average . . .

. . . while returns are at consistently impressive levels by any measure

Non-Interest
Expense as
Percent of
Total Assets (%)

- ■ Community Banking Average
- ▨ U.S. Banking Industry Average
- ☐ First Virginia

Return
on Equity (%)

Sources: American Banker, *Ranking the Banks*, 1992; FDIC; Sheshunoff Information Services; First Virginia.

with its own director concentrated primarily on local deposits, loan growth, and quality with the expertise and economies of having all staff functions provided by the holding company. The 'backroom' operation functions of the banks are carried out at full regional operation centers, and these centers, and the presidents of the member banks, report to regional executive officers who meet frequently with senior management of the holding company."

The secret to First Virginia's success, much like many of the superperformers among supercommunity banks, is a product focus beyond the margin business. Most superior supercommunity banks generate at least 1% ROA and 15% ROE off the core business. In addition, they develop a single product specialty, which is scale-

and expertise-driven, not relationship-driven, and which produces the extra 30 basis points on assets that create a supercommunity star.

First Virginia is a superior performer. What is interesting is that not only are the fundamentals excellent at First Virginia, but they have excelled in a business where few bankers have done well. They have been doing indirect auto lending since the early 1950s. The secret to the success is product expertise and discipline. For one thing, First Virginia has invested in relationship developments with the dealers. Says the company's CEO, Bob Zalokar, "We have trained our dealers well. We will not take junk and they know it. We are committed to competing effectively with the car manufacturers, captive finance

FIGURE 3.2 First Virginia Banks, Inc.

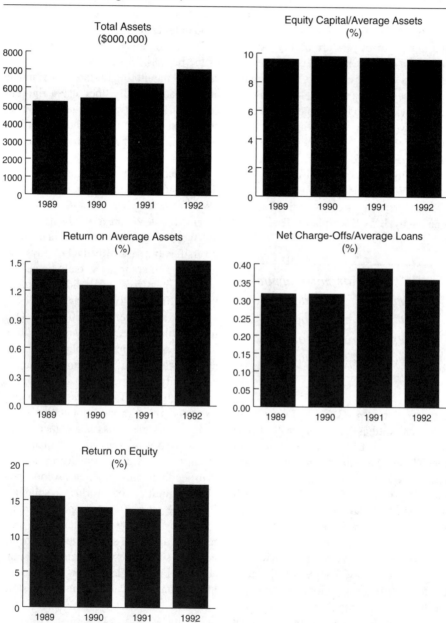

Source: FDIC Call Reports, 1989-1992.

companies, and with anyone else who will enter a market, but we will not sacrifice quality. Our dealers know what we buy, and our paper buyers are highly experienced. All of them have had at least seventeen years with our company, and the manager of the unit was a car dealer for several years in addition to being an effective auto paper buyer. He knows both sides of the business very well." Investment in the people, as well as the dealers, ensures that loan quality is not compromised.

First Virginia does business with over 100 dealers and finances individual car loans as well as floor plans. Their rates

---

This superior supercomunity bank performer demonstrates once again the effectiveness of strategic focus and a clear product orientation.

---

compete with GMAC, Ford Motor Credit, and even NationsBank. "We will always be in the market to meet their price and beat it," says Mr. Zalorar. In fact, the company is now opening an indirect car loan subsidiary in North Carolina. "If they can be up here, we can go down there," management says. When asked why the dealers continue to do business with First Virginia over the years, the answer is, "We're here to stay. The dealers like that. Even when times get tight, we will not touch indirect buying. We will curb other loans." Other lenders in the market do not offer the same commitment to their deal-

ers. First Virginia is a relationship lender, and they will be in the market through good times as well as bad times.

In addition to a thorough understanding of the business, a solid audit process and collateral monitoring for the floor planning are in place. Finally, they use a rigorous collection process where quality is never compromised. One rule of thumb: if a borrower misses the first payment, the car is gone.

Indirect lending is the icing on the cake for this supercommunity bank performer. "We know who we are and we are not ashamed of it. We are a small loan company. We like the retail business and find it diversifies our risk effectively," says Mr. Zalokar. The company's total charge-offs over the past five years did not exceed 0.33%, and the first quarter of 1993 appears even better at 0.14%. This includes the indirect car loan portfolio as well as a $78 million portfolio the company recently bought. This superior supercommunity bank performer demonstrates once again the effectiveness of strategic focus and a clear product orientation.

First Virginia Banks is a company that knows who it is. They are the supercommunity bank with a specialty in indirect auto lending. This strategic position provides the best of both worlds—a solid performance from the core operation augmented by the icing on the cake from indirect lending. Many supercommunity banks achieve superior results using the same strategy. First Virginia Banks can teach us all a lesson on how to implement this strategy well.

Figure 3.2 shows how First Virginia's strategy has paid off without sacrificing expense levels. The company's non-interest expense as a percent of total assets is below the industry average, while returns are consistently above average and impressive at any level, reaching 17% in 1992—two-and-a-half times the industry average of 7.54% for the year.

First Michigan Bank— Relationship Banking at its Best

Another example of an excellent supercommunity bank is First Michigan Bank Corp. Account officers of FMB conducted 8,000 visits last year to customers of the company's lead bank, many of whom are individuals and families. "We want to know their banking needs and talk about how things go, so we meet them at their kitchen tables—that's what it takes," says David M. Ondersma, Chairman, President, and Chief Executive Officer. Other FMB account officers set up shop at local factories in order to enroll workers in the bank's direct deposit payroll account program. "Teams of account officers show up at the beginning and the end of each shift, be it at 2 AM or 10 AM," says Ondersma. Other bank officers then go to work selling other products and services to the new customers, while yet another team of officers checks to make sure customers are satisfied with the services. First Michigan and other supercommunity banks are distancing themselves from the competitors by getting closer to their customers. While these banks may not all execute a letter of credit or a foreign currency swap with the dispatch of a Citicorp, they offer more than the traditional array of deposit and loan services of truly small-town banks. FMB,

for example, offers brokerage, trust, investment advisory services, life insurance, and mutual funds (owned by FMB) to the customers of its twelve affiliates. In a supercommunity bank, FMB "can do a lot of things associated with bigness" because of the ability to offer a full product mix. At the same time, they "can still retain the community banking aspect by keeping the local identity, our local directors dealing one-on-one and dealing with the local customer, the people, instead of just the facts and figures on the table before you," says Marvin A. Dreyer, owner of a tree farm and a director of First Michigan's Zeeland Bank.

Much of the higher expense is related to employees, an easy target for increasingly cost-conscious banks. The megamergers among banking giants announced in 1990 all share the goal of slashing operating costs by eliminating redundant jobs, and each of the combined banks will put thousands of workers on the street. Such drastic staff cuts would bleed a supercommunity bank. Providing one-on-one personal service, a hallmark of these institutions, requires many front-line employees, such as tellers and customer service representatives. Since each bank affiliate of a supercommunity organization operates autonomously, there are the additional costs of a president and a board of directors for each bank.

A bank's overhead ratio—operating expenses less non-interest income, divided by tax-equivalent net interest income costs, measures costs. The lower the ratio, the better. First Michigan's overhead ratio was 56.3% at year-end 1990. By comparison, the overhead ratio was 44.5% for Bank

America Corp., which with assets of $110.7 billion is more than 55 times larger than First Michigan.

Concedes First Michigan's Ondersma, "We're by no means the lowest-cost provider of banking services." Unable to compete on price, First Michigan has made service its sword in competition with other banks. Dedication, not just lip service, to quality, service, and the community must permeate the entire organization. If service falters, customers flock to other banks with lower prices. "When we buy a new affiliate, yes, we're buying the assets and the liabilities and all the financials that go with it, but also the people," says Merle J. Prins, Senior Vice President at FMC. "That's very, very important to us. The way they treat their customers, the way they take care of their customers, the way they interact in their community, being involved in their community, is very important." "As a matter of fact," says Prins, "the first question First Michigan's planners raise in considering a merger is, 'Do we think the chemistry is right that we can work together?'" Only after receiving a satisfactory answer to this query do they move on to the financials.

That's not to say FMB snubs the expense column. A former CPA, Ondersma points his cost eraser on backroom operations, the electronic and management systems brain center of First Michigan. "We've wrung out all the overhead we can from the banks in the backroom functions," explains Ondersma. "And while we pay a little more overhead in what we call the front room, the tellers . . . and in the boards and the presidents and so forth, we can make up for it by

having the back room as efficient and as consolidated and as up-to-date as we can get it."

Relationships with customers, Ondersma believes, are built by frontline employers. "That's where the expertise needs to be," he says, "and that's where we feel we need to spend our money." The result—superior performance. First Michigan even outperformed other supercommunity banks, posting a 14.7% ROE in 1990 compared to an average supercommunity bank ROE of 11.66%.

The two-tiered organization of supercommunity banks enables this kind of coveted financial performance without sacrificing customer service. Within First Michigan, for example, the top layer is First Michigan Bank Corp., the holding company. Its function is to provide all things common for affiliate banks to operate: auditing, human resources, loan processing and documentation, data processing, new products, strategic planning, accounting and tax preparation, and compliance. It's here where Ondersma extracts operation savings. Why here? This layer, while vital, is transparent to customers. They have no face-to-face contact with what goes on in this organizational tier. There's no expense to quality customer service if these tasks are consolidated to capture savings.

The second tier, FMC's network of eleven affiliate banks, is where the all-important customer contact occurs. Freed of having to provide back-office tasks and furnished with marketing and other services by the corporate parent, the affiliate banks focus on getting products and services to the customers. No scrimping here.

FIGURE 3.3 First Michigan Bank Corporation

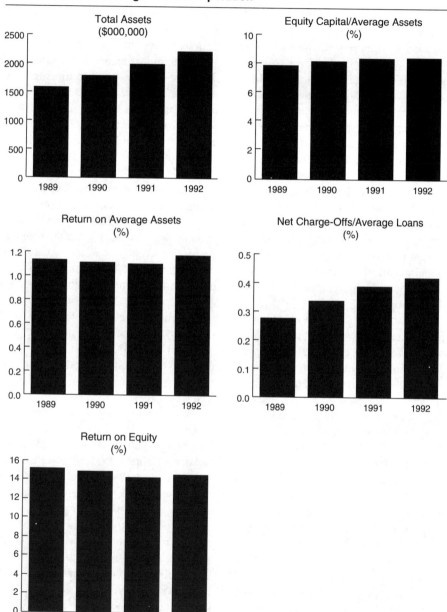

Source: FDIC Call Reports, 1989-1992.

Grass-roots banking is nurtured. Desert it and you court disaster. John F. Koetje saw it happen.

A dozen years ago, Koetje was a director of a community bank in Northern Michigan. The bank was acquired by an out-of-town bank holding company, which stripped it of its lending authority, centralizing the function at the parent company's home office several hundred miles away. The result: loan decisions were delayed, some creditworthy borrowers were denied credit. "The bank lost market share as a result," says Koetje, a construction company chairman who is now a director at First Michigan's Zeeland Bank. "The bank lost customers to other community banks. The community feeling was no longer there. There's not much community spirit in a situation like that."

At First Michigan, Ondersma and other senior executives of the corporate level do not interfere with decisions of the presidents of the affiliate banks. Each bank's president has latitude, for example, to set the interest rate paid on deposit accounts. But each bank president is accountable for generating a satisfactory return on assets. The target, set by the corporate parent, varies for each bank.

The president of the affiliates are free to decide how to hit the ROA targets. In the growing Grand Rapids market, Gerald R. Johnson Jr., President of the First Michigan affiliate, is dealing with a loan to deposit ratio of 80%. With money to lend, Johnson is expanding his loan staff and adding branches to reach more customers. On the other hand, Billie K. Fitz, President of FMC-Oceana Bank in Hart, has a small lending staff because loan demand in the bank's market is low. FMC-Oceana is a bond bank, generating earnings by trading government securities.

Joining all of the FMC affiliate banks to their communities are local boards of directors. Most of the directors are business people themselves who have an interest in assuring that the community remains vibrant in order for their personal businesses to succeed. Furthermore, directors use their knowledge of local community in their roles as bank directors. And they don't just exercise it to generate loans. For example, Robert J. Karpenga, a director of First Michigan's affiliate bank in Zeeland, is on the local Rotary Club committee that decides which private agencies get financial contributions from the organization. "I can take that committee knowledge and background to the Contribution Committee (on which he serves) at the bank and share the things I experience outside the bank," says Karpenga. "I could not do that if the decisions were made in another community by a parent bank company with centralized authority."

Directors of FMC's affiliate banks play an important role in assuring loan quality. For the first half of 1991, First Michigan had nonperforming loans of $14.2 million, or a tolerable 1.17% of total loans. That's far below the 3% ratio for what analysts consider a bank with serious loan problems. The directors' knowledge of the community and borrowers is key to keeping FMC's loan problems to a low level. "It's likely," explained Kenneth W. Elhart, a director of the Zeeland affiliate, "that through business contacts one of the directors will know the borrower or something about the borrower's business." Says

Elhart: "Besides looking at the numbers (as part of the loan) you're looking at a personality. You know what's in the company. You know what's happening with it. If the loan is going to be picked up by a correspondent bank, that decision is made at the correspondent bank, not the local level. And the decision is going to be made solely on the financial figures. Now they're important. But there's more to a company than that. You know where it's been, who's in it, how they're doing. You know it because you're involved in the community."

"That," he said, "is what community banking is about."

Marshall and Ilsley—A Supercommunity Bank with a Specialty Product: Data Processing

Marshall and Ilsley is an $8 billion supercommunity bank headquartered in Milwaukee. The company has performed at 1.35% or better on assets over the last ten years. The secret to M&I's success is excellent supercommunity banking operations enhanced by a data processing and transaction processing service. Marshall & Ilsley spent twenty years developing data processing excellence. Its subsidiary, M&I Data Services, Inc. began operation in 1964 as a bank department offering data processing services to downstream correspondents.

Many companies have started this way, but they did not invest in the core competency to create a stand-alone, separate business. M&I provided correspondent data processing services throughout the sixties and seventies as one small line of business among many within the bank. The deregulation of the industry in the early eighties caused many banks and thrifts to realize cost savings, simplify operations, and identify strategic core competencies. Outsourcing data and transaction processing became one of the most

FIGURE 3.4 Marshall & Ilsey Earning Hefty Returns on the Strength of M&I Data Services Revenues

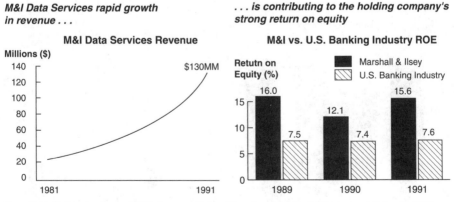

M&I Data Services rapid growth in revenue . . .

. . . is contributing to the holding company's strong return on equity

M&I Data Services Revenue

M&I vs. U.S. Banking Industry ROE

Sources: J. Christopher Svare, "M&I's Strategy: National Data Banking," *Bank Management* (February 1992): 16-19; *American Banker,* Top Numbers, 1991; FDIC.

FIGURE 3.5 Marshall & Ilsley Corporation

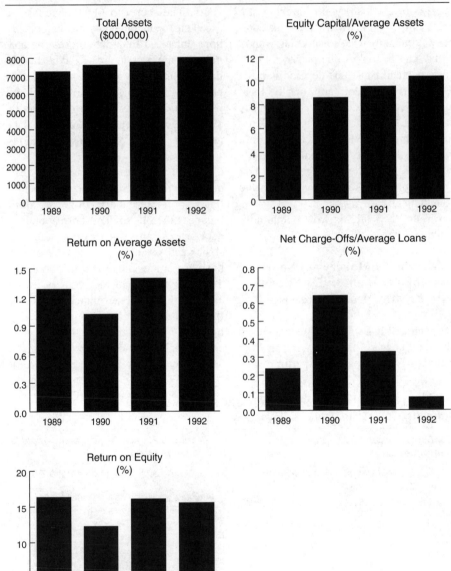

Source: FDIC Call Reports, 1989-1992.

promising options for members of the financial services industry that were looking for savings. M&I made, at that point, a strategic decision to capitalize on its twenty years of outsourcing experience. It started focusing even more capital investment on its data processing company and com-

---

The company's commitment to quality and service orientation, perfected through years of correspondent banking, gave it a competitive edge.

---

mitted to build it into a national transaction-processing powerhouse. The first out-of-state customer was signed in 1982. The company's commitment to quality and service orientation, perfected through years of correspondent banking, gave it a competitive edge. This, coupled with its competitive product line and strategic commitment to the business, made M&I one of the nation's premier data processing providers. M&I data services currently has 400 financial institutional customers in thirty-three states. The data company contributed 18% of the bottom line, or a total of $130 million in 1991 (Figure 3.4).

M&I, as a supercommunity bank, leveraged its data processing services in one more way. Correspondent banking became an important way to introduce the company to potential acquisition targets and resulted in a successful supercommunity core business expansion and intense profitability of the core margin business. The company yields 1.4% on assets and over

18% on equity and has done so, consistently outperforming the industry, for the past ten years. M&I is yet one more example of a company that executed the supercommunity bank strategy perfectly and supplemented it with a product specialization that made its performance jump from the very good to the superior category.

Marquette Banks—Quality Management as a Profitability Tool

Marquette Bank in Minneapolis was having difficulties in the late 1980s. Profitability wasn't what it should be, turnover was high, and overall performance was under question. Most companies would look for a quick carving of the cost base to achieve immediate results and appease the shareholders. Marquette, a supercommunity bank fully committed to supercommunity banking, did not take that route. Instead, management looked to quality as the answer to their profitability doldrums.

Executive Vice President and Chief Operating Officer Bert Colianni, together with the company's president, Tom Hurbst, and the chairman/owner, Carl Polahd (also owner of the Minnesota Twins) determined that a push to enhance quality in all facets of the business would yield greater income as well as cost savings. However, these cost savings will be sustainable (as opposed to a one-time hit) and increase efficiency and service levels at the same time. Senior management was committed to use the total quality management concept to enhance product and service levels while, at the same time, reducing the cost of producing them.

FIGURE 3.6 Marquette Banks

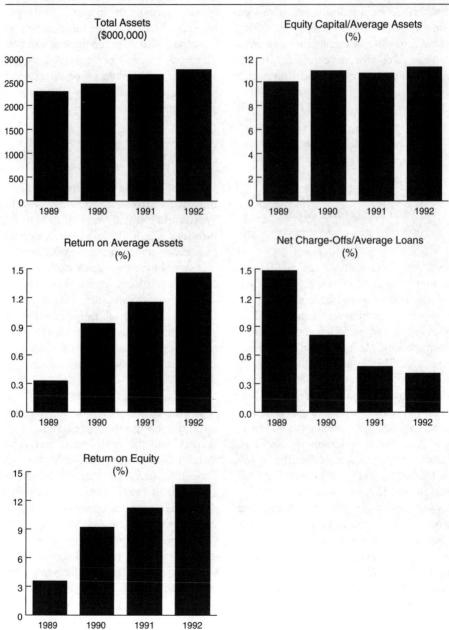

Source: FDIC Call Reports, 1989-1992.

The precondition to approving any new quality initiative was to satisfy two requirements: customer satisfaction improvement and profit enhancement. If both criteria were not satisfied, the initiative would not be approved. Accordingly, quantification of profit improvement and customer satisfaction became key to implementing quality management the Marquette way. As a result, profitability grew directly due to quality management initiatives by over $2 million a year, which amounted to 10% of the bank's total net income, and overall performance experienced a turnaround.

What were the key elements in Marquette's program that made it so effective?

1. Senior management was fully committed to the program and allocated the resources necessary to make it happen.
2. The cost of the program and the profits associated with it were carefully quantified and monitored.
3. All bank employees were directly exposed to the quality concept and what it means to them in the context of their day-to-day job.
4. A person was designated to take charge of quality and its implementation—someone's job depended on the initiative's success.

In addition, lessons on how not to do things were learned:

1. Unrealistic expectations were set at the project's onset. A quality integration process takes at least eighteen months to be truly incorporated into daily management.

2. Quality needs to be integrated into the bank's culture; it's a way of life, not a fad.
3. Senior management must be on board from the very start.
4. Executive compensation needs to be revised to reward not only profitability but also customer satisfaction.
5. Do not start the process until planning is completed and the bank is ready to involve the employees and clearly define management's expectations from them.

The company committed significant resources to its quality program. In the first six months of 1992, quantitative benefits associated directly with quality improvement exceeded the investment in the program fivefold. Profits increased 30%, and return on assets reached 1%.

Marquette and other financial institutions have come to realize that, although quality initiatives require significant investment, the benefits reaped far outweigh the costs within twelve months of program commencement. In addition to these quantitative benefits, quality programs enhance morale, esprit de corps, and overall service levels in banks where they are a true part of the corporate culture (as opposed to a lip-service program). Quality pays, and Marquette's bottom line is one piece of hard evidence to show for it.

Keystone—Building a Supercommunity Bank Through a Merger of Equals

In 1986, Keystone Bancorp was created through the sequential mergers of three

FIGURE 3.7 Keystone Bancorp, Inc.

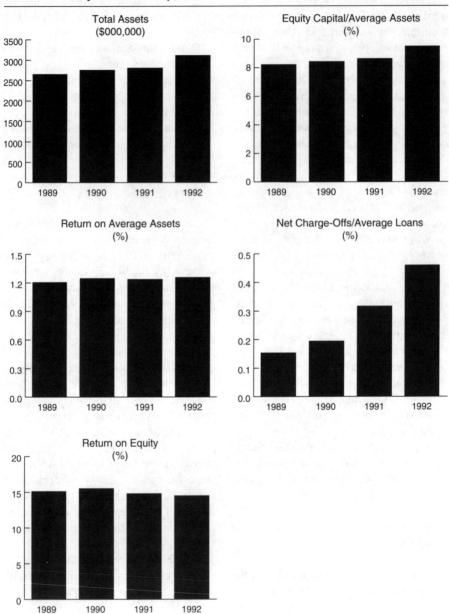

Source: FDIC Call Reports, 1989-1992.

equal companies. As the $3 billion new supercommunity bank was formed, management struggled with the building of a new corporate culture and style. Initially, the company elected not to initiate a drastic departure from the past. The three banks continued to run their business the way they used to, and even at the board level, constant comparisons among the banks were commonplace. Board members and managers alike were saying "our bank's way of doing things is the right one." The holding company management was reluctant to propose "the Keystone way" of banking. Instead, a coordinating position was created for all key management areas.

Keystone's management quickly found that although they successfully avoided conflict among the three entities, the lines of demarcation among the banks, albeit invisible, were very present. The coordinators, on the other hand, had full responsibility and no authority to execute their decisions. In short, a departure from the old ways was necessary to create a vibrant and effective company.

Once management had reached this conclusion, a lean and mean holding company was put together, where three executive vice presidents had responsibilities for the three major activities of the corporation: the banks; finance and operations; and administration, acquisitions, and human resources. Management invested time and resources in developing a clear mission and vision statements that described what kind of company Keystone was committed to being. It highlighted the important role each of the banks must play

in the overall success of the company, while acknowledging the need for some measure of standardization and common practices across the system.

Carl Campbell, the CEO, led the way with the definition of some "nonnegotiables," corporate-wide values that had to be implemented and kept at the forefront of all levels of management's thinking. The first was asset quality. An obsession with customer service soon followed. Further, Carl presented the supercommunity banking concept and strategic position to all of the officers of Keystone in a state of the company address and established reinforcing programs to provide constant reminders to all employees of the importance of service at all levels. Finally, a quality improvement program was initiated to "get things right the first time."

These initiatives created a new company out of the three banks that comprised Keystone. Consistent values, policies, and credit culture permeate the organization without regard to bank boundaries. Notwithstanding that, each bank has its own approach to its unique marketplace, and local decision making for credit and other decisions is closely guarded as a cornerstone of the supercommunity banking concept. Keystone is a lesson in the importance of creating a new culture and identity to a supercommunity bank that is the result of a merger of equals. Opting for one of the founding bank's cultures is not an effective alternative as it alienates the other equal banks who are part of the merger. At the same time, avoiding breaking down past barriers and letting each bank continue its past path is also a suboptimizing alternative, as it does not permit true supercommunity banking throughout the system and maintains unnecessary barriers and inefficiencies across the system.

A supercommunity bank depends on a clear culture and identity. A well-defined mission, vision, and corporate values statement that truly reflects the new company's desired identity and future path is critical to the success of any company, but especially so for supercommunity banks. Keystone is an example of a company that recognized this principle early on in its life and addressed it. Its current high performance and success are, in part, due to this recognition.

Branch Bank & Trust—Board Members Management

Hundreds of advisory board members—a nightmare of a clever marketing program? It works for BB&T!

Branch Bank & Trust is a $7 billion bank in North Carolina. The bank has been very successful throughout the years in defending and expanding its turf under the shadow of Wachovia and NationsBank and in the face of fierce competition from other supercommunity banks and small community banks in the state. As BB&T grew, it continued to reevaluate its competitive position. Once it reached several billion dollars in assets, management and John Allison, the CEO, decided to "break the bank down" into smaller, more local entities. These "banks," which did not have their own charters, official presidents, or legal boards, were to be BB&T's answer to the North Carolina banking giants and small banks alike. BB&T became a super-

community bank without incurring the charter, reporting, and board costs associated with stand-alone banks. At the same time, through proper decentralization and empowerment, the bank successfully created a perception and a reality of a network of local "banks" run by local decision makers and dedicated to the economic success of the communities they served.

As John Allison and Kelly King, the president of the lead bank, evaluated their strategy, they recognized the need for local representation at the community units level. However, they could not establish legal boards, which are a critical business development tool for small community banks, since there were no discreet charters permitting the establishment of such boards. Instead, Allison decided to build an extensive network of advisory boards to fill the business development role and provide an anchor into the community just like legal boards do. However, the advisory boards would be designed not to have the legal liabilities and responsibilities associated with full board membership.

The theory sounded nice, but implementation was challenging. The key to any successful board staffing is the perception that service on the board is of value and that the board itself is a prestigious body. How do you avoid the perception that an advisory board is merely a paper tiger, a business development ploy without any true impact on the bank's direction and operations? That was the challenge in front of BB&T's management. They met that challenge head-on, and through careful selection of the seed board members, created an aura of status and prestige around

FIGURE 3.8 Branch Bank & Trust Financial Corporation

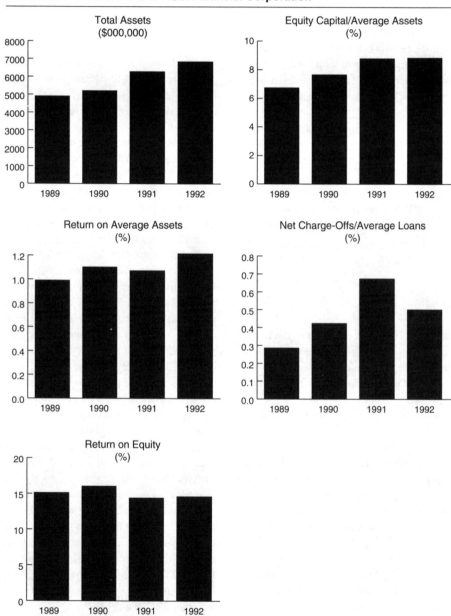

Source: FDIC Call Reports, 1989-1992.

its advisory boards. This, combined with some measure of compensation (although not nearly as high as legal board members' compensation), allowed the company to make membership in its advisory boards a coveted position. The best and the brightest of each community were selected and joined the boards.

Today, board membership in BB&T's network is a status position. The advisory boards work well, effectively fulfilling the

---

While many other Louisiana banks suffered through the recession and some even perished, Argent Bank continued to prosper.

---

range of functions expected of them. They help in business development and in community representation, as well as in opening new territories for the bank through supporting loan production offices (which typically precede branches in BB&T's case).

BB&T's success demonstrates the value that advisory boards can bring if carefully and effectively managed. The bank's expectations from its board members are clear, and monthly board meetings are anything but administrative or perfunctory gatherings. Both business development and marketing activities as well as matters pertaining to the community are discussed. In conclusion, advisory board members need not be a headache; they can be a cost-effective, irreplaceable community development tool.

First Interstate Bank of Southern Louisiana (Argent Bank)— Employee Retention

Donald L. Peltier is a visionary. Chairman of First Interstate of Southern Louisiana, to become Argent Bank, he wanted everything done exactly right. He realized that only quality of service and total commitment by the full complement of bank employees could bring the performance and results he was looking for. Together with Randy Howard, president of the bank, he built a successful supercommunity bank in Southern Louisiana. The company has weathered the ten-year recession in their marketplace without one year of losses.

While many other Louisiana banks suffered through the recession and some even perished, Argent Bank continued to prosper, and this year is showing record earnings of 1.35% on assets, with 9% capital and a 15.7% return on equity. How do they do it? They invest in their people. First they pay their people well. "We compare ourselves to the best run banks in the country and pay our people accordingly," says Howard. Bank management identified a cluster group for salary administration figures. These are highly successful banks, not necessarily in Argent's marketplace. The bank's compensation and other financial benefits are on a par with this elite group. "You have to pay well to attract the best" says Peltier. For example, retirement age has been lowered to 62 as an option, but the financial benefits have been reduced by only $40 a month relative to retirement at the age of 65.

Bank management is very attentive to employees and realizes that they are the

FIGURE 3.9 First Interstate Bank of Southern Louisiana

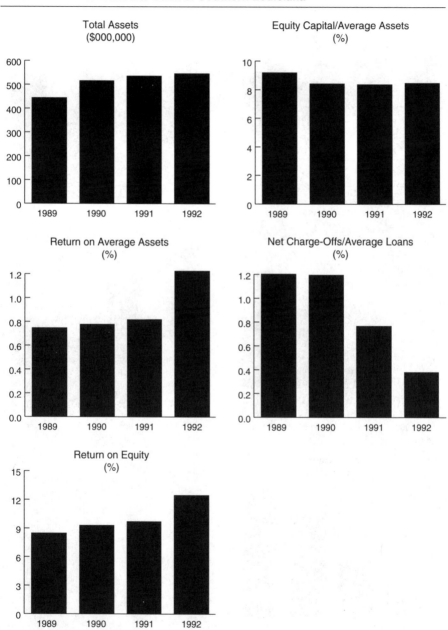

Source: FDIC Call Reports, 1989-1992.

FIGURE 3.10 Collective Federal

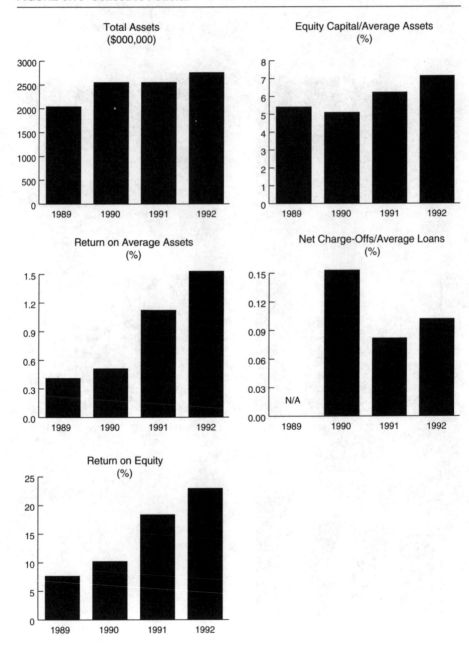

Source: FDIC Call Reports, 1989-1992.

prime resource of the company. They invest time, not only money. In the integration process of a recent acquisition, Randy Howard had breakfast with every single employee of the newly acquired company, which has turned into a bimonthly company gathering with fifteen to twenty people from all levels of the company every other

---

It has been demonstrated that the longer employee retention is, the longer your customers stay.

---

month. That means that Mr. Howard meets every single employee of the company within eighteen months. His accessibility to staff is unique in the business and, as many of his employees indicate, there is no fear factor in dealing with Bank President Randy Howard.

The results: a highly profitable company with an extremely low employee turnover. Over 30% of the staff have been with the company ten years or more. For supercommunity banks, this is of particular importance. The relationship orientation is a cornerstone to supercommunity banking. It has been demonstrated that the longer employee retention is, the longer your customers stay. Further, customer retention then gets translated into greater profitability. The reason is because as customers stay with the company longer, they expand their services and product involvement while increasing their price elasticity. In other words, they will not switch banks for a 50 basis point yield on

a CD or for 100 basis points on the price of a loan. First Interstate of Southern Louisiana has discovered that. Donald Peltier had the vision years ago to create a solid foundation of employee retention. The company has been reaping the benefits ever since.

Collective Federal—Cost Efficiencies

How can a supercommunity bank have an efficiency ratio of 43%? Ask Tom Hamilton of Collective Federal. This $4 billion thrift has converted itself to a supercommunity bank in recognition of the need to expand from its mortgage lending core into a full community banking service company. While undergoing this expansion, the company did not forget its cost-conscious roots. As Hamilton says, "We came from a small town, so we had to be cost-conscious." The company has been extremely cost-conscious from its inception. Corporate offices are a nondescript building in Egg Harbor, New Jersey. In its tradition of cost-consciousness, Collective built their own infrastructure, data center, check clearing, and servicing capacity. This is consistent with the company's belief that homebred infrastructure will yield better service and improve costs performance. Although counter-intuitive, this seems to work for Collective.

The company has grown through an interesting branching strategy. As it contemplates moving into new territories, it does not put the brick and mortar up first. Instead, a new branch will typically be initiated in a small rental space, often in a strip mall or a small shopping center. The branch manager and staff will announce the opening in the local high school basketball or football game on Sunday, with a celebration of hot dogs and balloons. Only when the branch achieves a critical mass of deposits will its location be traded up. In other words, the branch is expected to cover its own costs before it moves to a permanent location. This permits inexpensive and efficient branch-site testing. Also, break-even is achieved very quickly. This is quite different from the typical banking strategy, which involves fancy buildings and a break-even point of eighteen months or longer.

Collective augments its strong efficiency ratio with a low cost of funds. The company is pursuing transaction accounts actively and is in the process of changing its deposit mix to lower its already low cost of funds. A company in transition, they are looking for the younger customers, but refuse to attract them by being a high payer on deposits. "We were concerned that, given the no-frills nature of the branches, customers will expect us to compensate by offering higher rates to attract customers," says Tom Hamilton, Collective's CEO. However, true to their culture, Collective lowered rates to test the market's reaction. Like many others, they found that when they did so, it did not cause customer erosion. When asked what the secret was of this effective transaction, Hamilton said, "The timing was right; the industry was undergoing a bad publicity spell, and at that time high rates were associated with a perception of high risk. We were always perceived to be very prudent, and therefore we generated deposits despite the lower rates."

Collective knows its challenges in the future. It is a thrift in transition to a supercommunity bank. The company perceives its competitors to be commercial banks, not thrifts. Given Collective's strategic focus and sense of direction, its expansion is cautious but rapid. Its profitability is achieved through extremely low operating costs coupled with a wide-product offering ranging from the traditional mortgage to annuities and mutual funds as well as telephone discount brokerage services. "We sell to our customers' needs," says Hamilton. "Our biggest hurdle was to switch our branch people from deposit gatherers to a sales tool of both liabilities and assets. . . . Our underlying strength is that we are good to our customers. Many people say it, but we truly mean it." And an efficiency ratio of 43% certainly helps.

Community First— Acquisition Planning

Don Mengedoth knows where he's been and, more importantly, knows where he is going. He is the chief executive of Community First, a $1.2 billion North Dakota company. Community First is a unique supercommunity bank. It was created in 1986 when a group of investors bought several banks that were spun off First Bank Systems in North Dakota. The company conducted an initial public offering and used the capital to launch a unique and successful acquisition program. Mengedoth says, "We took acquisition planning seriously and spent a lot of time figuring out what we wanted to acquire and how." The plan was very specific. He and his people found out there were 3,000

FIGURE 3.11 Community First Bankshares

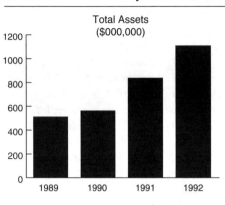

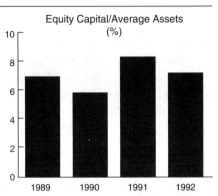

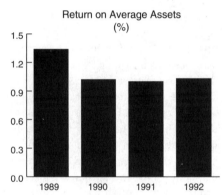

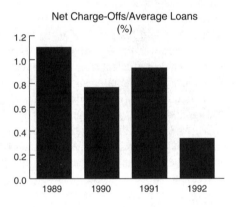

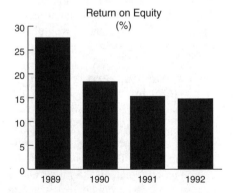

Source: FDIC Call Reports, 1989-1992.

community banks in the ten-state area around North Dakota. "We targeted the healthy and solid small community bank as our ideal acquisition candidate. We were not looking for RTC deals or for turnaround situations. We were looking for companies who had good market share in very small towns and who were solid performers." The results were incredible. Community First doubled its size in the last four years, with continuous improvement in ROE, which is now at 22%.

Community First went after the forgotten market—the small banks that everyone says cannot be acquired efficiently. But Mengedoth and his people figured out a way to acquire the $20 to $50 million banks in a cost-efficient manner. Although they make three to four acquisitions a year, their acquisition team consists only of Mengedoth and Chief Financial Officer Mark Anderson. The acquisition team that goes through due diligence is composed of internal people who understand the different components of the business and who are in charge of those components at Community First. The asset quality team at Community First is first to go out to an acquisition candidate and quickly determine the quality of the loan portfolio. Based on their assessment, the rest of the team goes out to look at the retail franchise and back-office operations and to develop an integration plan.

Mengedoth plays up being a supercommunity bank as a solution to small community banks' management who want to create liquidity in their stock, but not necessarily throw in the towel and retire. "As a supercommunity bank, we retain the integrity of our subsidiaries and maintain

management and board alike," he says. As a result, he is approached by half a dozen companies a month that wish to be acquired in a friendly transaction.

Another unique twist that Community First uses is minority interest. Mengedoth wants to make sure that the local people who make the company successful in the first place will not necessarily leave upon being acquired by Community First. Allowing them minority interest ensures continued interest and commitment to the bank as it becomes a subsidiary of the larger holding company.

In short, Community First has developed a well-oiled machine to acquire small community banks in their marketplace. They have identified up front clear acquisition criteria that get measured every time a candidate comes in the door or the company itself chooses to target a potential candidate. There is a lot of give and take during the acquisition process, and the transaction itself is friendly and structured so that both parties are satisfied. This is a tall order to accomplish for any bank, but especially for a $1 billion company. Don Mengedoth, indeed, had a vision, and he made it come true through a well-planned acquisition program.

Synovus—Supercommunity Banking with Product Specialization

Synovus is a successful supercommunity bank with a twist. First, it is committed to supercommunity banking. As their annual report states, "The concept of separate, local boards of directors for each affiliate is an essential facet of our decentralized

FIGURE 3.12 Synovus Nonperforming Assets as Percent of Total Assets

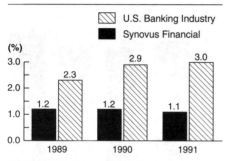

Sources: FDIC; Synovus Annual Report, 1991.

Synovus's nonperforming loan ratio is evidence to the success of this concept (Figure 3.12). It is three times lower than the industry average. The board members of Synovus and other supercommunity banks are rooted in the community and have a personal stake in the bank's success. They are much more active in referring friends, contacts, and other business development prospects to the bank than other non-supercommunity bank board members. "The Boards of Directors serve us in a number of ways. They help with credit decisions. They provide us with market knowledge, but most especially they serve as a business development network. These people are proud to be on the board of directors, and they really get into the role. They want us to do well and aren't shy about referring business our way," says one of the holding company's executives.

approach. Each board is made up of influential members of the community who provide valuable knowledge that leads to sound productive business decisions. No one is better equipped to make decisions about loans and maintain the relationship so important to successful community banking."

In addition to the core business of supercommunity banking, Synovus has a

FIGURE 3.13 Out-Invest Competitors and Rocket to Prominence

Total System's revenue is growing by leaps and bounds . . .

TSYS's Total Revenues

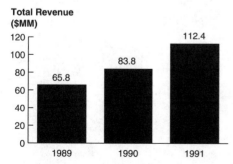

. . . contributing to the holding company's strong return on equity

TSYS vs. U.S. Banking Industry ROE

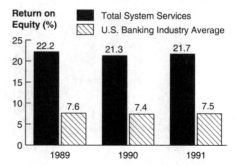

Sources: FDIC; Synovus Annual Report, 1991.

FIGURE 3.14 Synovus Financial Corporation

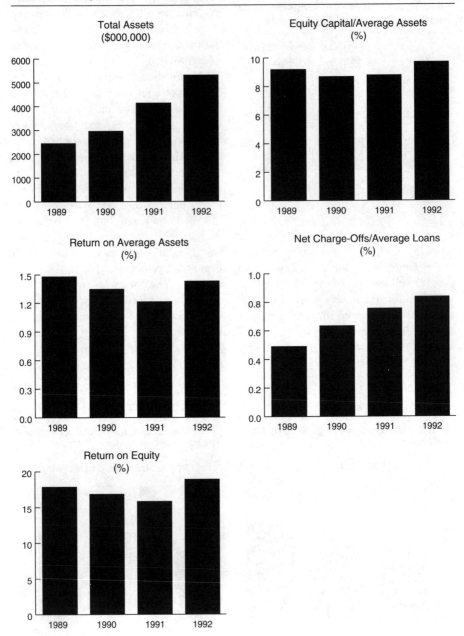

Source: FDIC call reports, 1989-1992.

specialty product. Total System Services, Inc. (TSYS) is a subsidiary of Synovus that provides bank card and private label credit card processing services for card issuers. In 1959, Columbus Bank & Trust, the lead bank in the formation of Synovus Financial, introduced a charge card to its customers. Seven years later, the company installed a computer system to handle its card processing. It continued to upgrade the hardware, software, and service levels such that by 1972 the company had a unique on-line accounting and processing system, which it named The Total System. Two years later, they commenced marketing the program to other financial institutions. TSYS did so well that revenue growth was remarkable. At the same time, it was tough to assess how well the company was doing. It was growing quickly, but as a bank subsidiary, costs were difficult to separate from the overall cost structure of the company, and revenues were commingled with other elements of the business. As a result, the requisite technology investments in equipment upgrades were more difficult to justify.

In 1983, management made the strategic decision to spin the credit card processing group off into a separate subsidiary. That subsidiary grew up to $112.4 million worth of revenues in 1991 with an impressive return on equity of 21.7% (Figure 3.13). This represents a growth of 7.5 times from $15 million in 1983. Today, TSYS accounts for 31% of the total holding company net income and is the second largest operation of its kind in the world, with 110 customers in thirty-four states.

Spinning off the company as an independent entity allowed for strategic focus and dedication to the business. TSYS is now out-investing, out-training, and out-innovating other card processors. For example, the company is opening a $24 million center for processing operations, which is the only facility designed for and solely dedicated to credit card processing. The company's size provides it with some scale advantages as well. It is the largest first-class mailer in the Southeastern United States, which allows it to negotiate on-site mail pickup from Atlanta, bypassing the smaller local post office that would be overwhelmed by the volume of mail generated by TSYS. Another example of the unique services TSYS provides and that reflect its dedication to the business is its joint venture with IBM to develop a computer science curriculum at a local college. TSYS will sponsor top graduates' education costs in return for service upon graduation.

Synovus has successfully kept a thriving supercommunity bank with a specialty service provider. The core earnings out of the supercommunity bank are augmented and enhanced by TSYS, a specialty product provider.

Summit Bancorp—Using Supercommunity Banking to Turn a Company Around

Two years of consolidation have allowed Summit Trust Company, a New Jersey-based bank holding company with $3.8 billion in assets, to recreate itself in the image of what Robert Cox, Summit's president, calls a supercommunity bank. "We decided to end up with three banks rather than one so we could pursue the concept of

FIGURE 3.15 Summit Bancorp

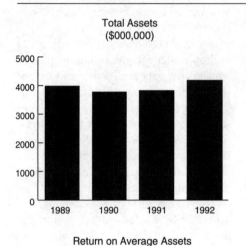

Total Assets
($000,000)

Equity Capital/Average Assets
(%)

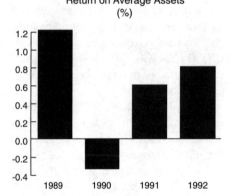

Return on Average Assets
(%)

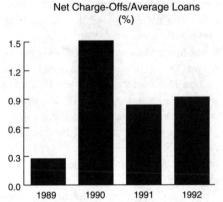

Net Charge-Offs/Average Loans
(%)

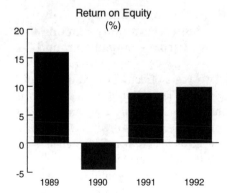

Return on Equity
(%)

Source: FDIC Call Reports, 1989-1992.

a supercommunity bank," Cox said. Summit's community banking approach, which places a premium on service over low costs, has gained a niche with the upscale retail customer and small- to mid-sized businesses. "Our claim to fame is service. This is our strength, and it has put us in a strong position," Cox said.

Summit, last fall, completed a two-year consolidation of eight banks into three in order to achieve efficiencies from centralized back-office operations and trust business, while at the same time aiming each of the three banks at different regional markets emphasizing community-oriented banking relationships. Lead bank Summit Trust Bank, which absorbed Chatham Trust, Maplewood Bank & Trust, and The Trust Co. of Princeton last fall, services north and north-central New Jersey. The south-central region is covered by Somerset Trust, which merged with Town & Country Trust in 1990, while Ocean National Bank, the result of the combination of Bay State Trust and Ocean National, handles the southern market.

Summit's organizational structure is a balance of centralized and decentralized approaches. Summit is about to shift each bank's operations and data processing department into a single central office, and all three banks are being put on a single software system, Systematic Software. "Somerset still uses Mellon Data Center to outsource its data processing, but we'll be taking that over soon," Cox said.

The cash management operations were folded into Summit Trust two years ago. The trust department is the third largest in the state, with almost $3 billion in assets under management. "Our investment department has a good performance record. The trust department's client base is growing; it has become an important source of income for us." Summit recently started selling insurance annuities from its branches and is making plans to offer mutual funds. "It's part of our strategy to grow the fee side of the business," Cox noted.

Otherwise, the individual banks have a fair amount of autonomy in operating their businesses. Cox, who is also the president of Summit Trust Bank, calls himself a fairly hands-off manager. "I spend more time on holding company matters and overall strategy these days. We give the other banks' directors a lot of leeway," he noted. Cox emphasizes attention to customers, pointing to regularly scheduled lunches and breakfast meetings between top executives and bank customers.

With an emphasis on returning to banking fundamentals, the holding company reported a year-end profit of $21 million after a $12 million loss in 1990 and expects to improve earnings this year.

Since taking a major provision at the end of 1990, Summit has worked to rectify its distressed loan portfolio. Non-performing loans (NPLs) stand at 4.2% of its $2.5 billion of total loans, down from 4.9% in 1990. "We're used to 1%, but I think our problem loans peaked out a couple of quarters ago," he said.

Summit's loan portfolio is heavily weighted toward real estate, the chief culprit of its delinquent loans. Over half of the banks' NPLs are in real estate. Cox credits a strong workout department with steering Summit toward a stable portfolio. "Workouts take time, but we're nearing the outer end of the problem," he said.

One quarter of the loan portfolio consists of commercial loans, and consumer loans account for about 16%. Residential loans represent the bulk of the institution's $1.48 billion real estate loan portfolio, with commercial loans at 37% and construction lending making up less than 1%. Cox expects to maintain Summit's commitment to being a major residential lender. "It's a good loan to have in the portfolio," he said. Summit Trust holds no leveraged buyout loans. "As a matter of policy we don't participate in national credits and don't get involved in the syndication market," he said. "We are returning to the fundamentals, things the industry did not pay attention to in the 1980s. We're looking for personal guarantees and collateral before we extend a loan."

Banc One—A Leading Example of Supercommunity Banking

Supercommunity banking is not a size-bound strategy. It is a strategic position, a philosophy, an attitude toward banking. As a result, we have supercommunity banks as little as $350 million and as big as Banc One, the granddaddy of all supercommunity banks. We can learn many lessons from the success of this $65 billion giant who managed to put on the small community bank face to its local customers, yet marshall the resources across the system toward superior performance. How does Banc One—the quintessential supercommunity bank—do it?

The company produces higher earnings per share every year with growing cash dividends. It has robust profitability ratios over the last fifteen years with a return on assets over 1% (1.66% in 1991) and return on equity averaging over 15%. Banc One avoids economic and industry concentration while developing an extensive branch system for gathering deposits and generating loans.

Banc One was founded by John H. McCoy in 1934. The founder and his son, John G. McCoy, saw the predecessor bank, City National Bank of Columbus, greatly expand during the 1950s and 1960s. They formed a holding company in 1968 and, later that year, made the first acquisition, The Farmer Savings Imprest Company in Mansfield, Ohio. Since then, the company has grown through acquisitions to become the largest supercommunity bank in the United States. John McCoy says, "The biggest reason we spend so much time on acquisitions is to increase earnings for our shareholders. . . . What we've done is to establish a philosophy: finding well-run banks, paying a fair non-dilutive price for them, and then using our systems to improve their performance. Because our buys are non-dilutive, those gains are funneled directly into improved earnings for our shareholders." Between 1984 and 1990, Banc One acquired fifty-four banks in five states.

Banc One does a variety of things to boost performance of its affiliates. For instance, they share expertise in such areas as electronic banking and specialized lending instruments. In addition, they centralize as many back-office operations as possible. The company also uses technology to gain a competitive edge. For example, they were able to use state-of-the-art software to improve the cash management system and achieve a leading credit card position.

Currently, they are working on branch software to increase the branch capacity to deal with many new checking accounts. Technology also helped Banc One to provide rapid feedback through their fabled management information system so that the company knows where it stands with various products, markets, and banks.

Banc One is a true supercommunity bank in its commitment to decentralization of decision making and community orientation. "I very much abhor centralization," says McCoy. "I feel much more comfortable having a decentralized organization with a president heading up the various affiliates. Each affiliate also has its own board of directors, its own business plan, and its own strategy for marketing and product pricing in its local territory. Consequently, each bank president is directly responsible for its performance. Although there is a great deal of local autonomy, the system is designed to motivate managers to perform. If the unit is underperforming in a given area, we analyze the problem and suggest solutions. A lot of constructive pressure is involved to motivate managers to focus on opportunities to improve performance. We have some forty performance ratios that we compare each bank against, and we encourage each bank to do the best it can. Of course, managers don't want their units to be the lowest performer in any category. As a result, we are able to 'turbocharge' the earnings of our affiliates." We are generally able to improve the bank's earnings by roughly 40% after an acquisition.

This is a formidable result because Banc One does not achieve the earnings improvement through a slash-and-burn

strategy. What the company attempts is to run a collaborative effort. "I don't care how small or big a bank is. We have never bought a bank that we haven't learned something from. For example, American

---

Banc One is a true supercommunity bank in its commitment to decentralization of decision making and community orientation.

Fletcher [now Banc One of Indiana] is a strong mortgage banker. On the other hand, Banc One has never been a great mortgage banker. So after the affiliation we sold Fletcher our mortgage company in Columbus, and they now do all the mortgage banking for the entire corporation out of Indianapolis," said McCoy.

Banc One also recognizes the power of the local boards. "I think it's important to have a local board of directors to tell us what's happening. I don't know what's taking place in Indianapolis or Milwaukee or Bloomington, but the local presidents and board do." Banc One also achieves other benefits from its supercommunity bank strategy. For one, the company now has a well-diversified loan portfolio and the loan size is much smaller, which makes the risk much smaller. Banc One, as a whole, has a legal lending limit of $300 million. The company set limits of no more than 10% of each of their bank's capital. On average, each bank has a lend limit below $10 million. If they exceed that, the loan must be approved at the state or corporate level. Loan review further supports loan quality. Banc One has tightened its loan review procedures and adheres to very strong and stringent credit principles. The individual loan committee, however, is only as good as the people who sit on it. Banc One, as a company, does not try to impose a directive on its affiliates of 'this is the way to operate,' so they are able to avoid making the big mistakes, such as committing to LDC loans, highly leveraged transactions, or commercial real estate. Each bank reflects its own marketplace and its own expertise, and the company as a whole does not have corporate-wide asset initiatives, which brought so many other strong banks to their knees."

Banc One's acquisition philosophy is also interesting. They do not go for unfriendly takeovers. Banc One management always looks for people who are willing to talk about being acquired and who have qualified management to run the organization. The company does not have ambitions to become a national bank per se. "If we wanted to be represented in every state, that would probably mean between 3,000 to 5,000 branches. We're a long way from there," says McCoy.

Banc One clearly knows the kind of company it wants to be. When asked about the secret of his success, John McCoy said, "I think our key achievement is that we are focused. . . . There has been an acknowledgement that we can't be all things to all people. We are not trying to be the tenth largest investment banking firm in the United States. We are not trying to be an overseas international banking company. Banc One's franchise has been built over the last thirty years with a focus on retail

and middle-market banking. We are retail bankers, mostly in small towns, and are always in-market lenders. We like to think of ourselves as the McDonald's of retail banking, selling the same thing everywhere: small and middle-market business loans, home mortgages, auto loans, trust services, credit cards, and the like. When it comes to risk, our managers think like small-town bankers. They are generally risk-averse, have no really large loans, and like broad economic diversity. What we are looking for are successful banks with good quality management in markets that offer opportunities for retail banking." This is an articulation of the supercommunity bank philosophy. Banc One, much like $300 and $500 million supercommunity banks, targets the small business, the middle market, and retail banking. This is the bread and butter of supercommunity banks, and it can feed $70 billion banks as successfully as $300 million banks.

There are other unique things about Banc One that make it a very successful supercommunity bank. The company pays a lot of attention to its culture. "We try to create a culture around here where you are not penalized for making a mistake. We don't expect everybody to be perfect. Some of our best people have had the biggest screwups," said McCoy. Further, where many banks are reluctant to invest in a new technology, Banc One commits 3% of its net income to research and development, an industry high. "The cornerstone of Banc One's success is operations, R&D, and marketing. It is a very well-run institution that has been able to spot trends before other banks have." The commitment to technology, autonomy, account-

FIGURE 3.16 Banc One Corporation

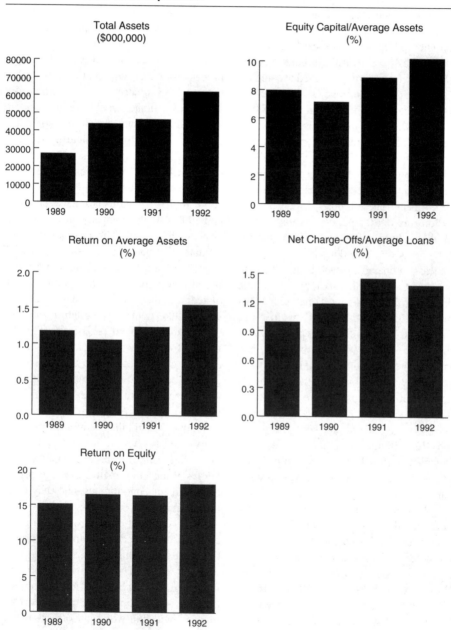

Source: FDIC Call Reports, 1989-1992.

ability, and service has provided the foundation for Banc One's stellar performance in such areas as consumer and middle-market banking and bank card operations (which has over 10 million bank affinity group and third-party processed accounts).

Another secret to Banc One's success is its management information control system, or MICS. It allows the company to decentralize with great comfort since irregularities, problems, and surprises will be spotted quickly. The system is literally a series of reports generated each month by all affiliates. These reports, which can run as long as eighty pages, display actual results on both the monthly and a year-to-date basis compared with budgets and forecasts prepared by each bank. The data is keyed to the affiliates knowing what the drivers of their businesses are. "Our focus on detail causes the user to want more information," McCoy explains. The reports include forecasts each month, and they also forecast the remainder of the year. One of the things that management attempts to do is to compare how we are doing versus what we said a month ago. As the year goes along, something that may be a budget variance may become less meaningful. The system also provides affiliates and management a way to compare the activities of like operations.

"We can take all our banks and we can compare them with one another to see where our margins are the strongest, where our productivity is the best, where our total return on assets is the best," says John Westman, Chief Financial Officer. "It creates a strong sense of internal competition. If one of our banks was seeking to improve its operations, it might be better

off to compare itself with the best banks in our system than with any other bank we could find. Peer comparison is the key to the uncommon partnership."

Despite its benefit, MICS is not an easy process to love. Banc One asks for a lot more analysis, scrutiny, and dedication than many affiliates would ever have given any financial system. Also, the competition it fosters, although healthy from a shareholder standpoint, is unhealthy to many a CEO's ulcers. Banc One has used MICS to manage its dramatic growth. (The company has tripled its size between 1986 and 1990.) As the company grew, the system mushroomed. The number of new affiliates that had to be migrated to MICS encouraged a hard look at the more user-friendly system, which incorporated a lot of features that are found in spreadsheet systems like Lotus. The system is capable of providing almost real-time status to what a forecast would look like as each affiliate goes along. When affiliates budget, the beauty of the system is that they will be able to use it for earnings modeling, so if they want to change a lot of assumptions about their volume or productivity, they are able to do that in a fairly user-friendly environment. The system allows Banc One to find discrete profit improvement opportunities, and they continue to pursue those very intensely.

Banc One collects an extraordinary amount of detailed and current information on each affiliate bank's internal and external performance. For example, the bank regularly publishes "league tables" on over forty ratios of operating performances, with the worst performers listed first. This encourages collaboration to improve the weakest affiliates rather than competition to be the best. The bank also continuously engages in workflow reeengineering and process simplification. The 100 most successful projects, known as the best of the best, are documented and circulated among affiliates. Banc One responds to local markets with the flexibility and friendly attitude of the traditional community bank. In addtion, they identify best practices of business processes and community banking around the system, and transfer those best practices across affiliate banks. They also empower the affiliate president and his people to get the job done. Banc One's capabilities are especially easy to transfer to new acquisitions. All the company needs to do is install its corporate MICS and intensively train the acquired bank's senior officers, a process that is often accomplished in a few months. Banc One has therefore made acquisition almost a separate line of business.

Similarly, Banc One is planning to improve its customer service to become more competitive with other money centers as well as supercommunity banks. "If you took a survey of the top 100 banks and rated them on service, the average score would be five out of ten. If we can score eight or nine, we consider ourselves apart from the others and get more market share. In order to do so, Banc One struggles with the issue of centralization versus decentralization much like every other supercommunity bank. One of the reasons we've been successful is because we are decentralized, which gives all affiliates the option of offering every Banc One product but doesn't obligate them to do so. We're

seeing that we need to bring more standardization to what we're doing and how our back rooms operate. Then we can offer the high standards of service to our customers," says McCoy. This push for standardization maintains the dynamics of the uncommon partnership.

"We have had something very special in this company in that we've had numerous, relatively autonomous, free-standing affiliates. To take advantage of technology, both from the cost and services standpoint, may sometimes involve surrendering some autonomy," says Westman. "The challenge is to keep the spirit of decentralization and keep some entrepreneurial spirit alive and well at the local level while trying to take advantage of what can be centralized and made more efficient and more productive."

To summarize, Banc One has successfully implemented supercommunity banking at its best. It has the distinctive ability to understand and respond to the needs of entire communities. To do community banking effectively, a bank has to have deep roots in the local community, but, traditionally, local banks have not been able to muster the professional expertise, state-of-the-art products, and highly competitive cost structures of large national banks like Citicorp. Banc One and other supercommunity banks compete by offering the customer the best of both these worlds. Striking the balance depends on two factors. One is the local autonomy. The center of the organizational role in the Banc One business system is played not by frontline employees but by the presidents of the sixty-plus affiliate banks in the Banc One network. Affiliate presidents have exceptional power within their own regions. They select products, establish prices and marketing strategies, make credit decisions, and set internal management policies. They can even overrule the activities of Banc One's centralized direct marketing businesses. But while Banc One's affiliate system is highly decentralized, its success also depends on an elaborate and highly centralized process of continuous organizational learning. Affiliate presidents have the authority to mold bank products and services to local conditions, but they are also expected to learn from this practice throughout the Banc One system and adapt it to their own operation.

Banc One is an excellent example of how a supercommunity bank can stay close to its communities even if it grows to be a megabank. Norwest, Barnett, First Empire, and others are walking in Banc One's shoes. The secret to their success is the clarity of the strategic focus, the rigorous financial information system, and a well-reasoned acquisition program.

CHAPTER FOUR

Community Banking

C ommunity banking is an approach to the customer. It is not necessarily a function of size, although it has been traditionally associated with small banks. In the broadest sense, a community bank is the one that derives most of its funding from the community it serves (as opposed to purchased funds) and invests these funds into those same communities. Given this definition, some large banks, such as Old Kent or Marshall & Ilsley, fall within the community bank category. It is the attributes of the community banking approach to the customer that differentiates community banks from other depository institutions. These attributes, which are key to the success of community banking, define the first prong of the supercommunity bank strategy.

Quality Service—A "Nonnegotiable" for Community Banking

Community banking is a way of life. It's an attitude that is the anchor to the supercommunity banking concept. Without it, the competitive advantage inherent in the strategic position is eliminated. Defining community banking is difficult. To some extent it is described in the definition of supercommunity banking. It is a behavioral and attitudinal concept; it's almost a matter of feeling and atmosphere. When you enter a first-class hotel, you know you're in a high-quality establishment within the first sixty seconds. Although the setting may be spectacular, it is the people who bring that setting to life: their smile, attentiveness, responsiveness, flexibility, and in general their ability to make you feel special.

Banks have the same opportunity when a customer enters the branch. Unlike by-mail operations, which cannot create the atmosphere and the sense of service and attentiveness through a written or phone communication, a bank has the opportunity to create an image in the customer's mind of an attitude toward service and a sense of customer importance. As the customer enters the branch, the bank needs to realize the opportunity to build relationships and retain customers as well as extend that opportunity into other communication modes, including telephone and mail.

A community banking institution must be committed to quality service and to capitalizing on the opportunity to satisfy the customer every time he or she enters the branch.

Quality service is a strategic concept:

- Customer dissatisfaction equals apathy.
- Customer apathy equals price/value attrition.
- Customer disservice equals attrition.
- Customer satisfaction equals relationships.
- Customer relationships equal retention.

In other words, satisfied customers empathize with the institution and reduce the importance of price in the purchasing decision. They perceive the empathy offered by the employee as a thing of value and attach that value to the price they have to pay for that sense of well-being. This is the first paradigm of quality service. Dissatisfied customers leave. More-than-satis-

> *Unlike by-mail operations, which cannot create the atmosphere and the sense of service and attentiveness through a written or phone communication, a bank has the opportunity to create an image in the customer's mind of an attitude toward service and a sense of customer importance.*

fied customers stay. Those customers who stay develop relationships. Relationships create retention. Retention creates profitability.

The second paradigm of quality service as the strategic concept involves the relationship between quality and market share:

- Customer-driven service equals customer satisfaction.
- Customer satisfaction equals customer relationships.
- Customer relationships equal customer retention.
- Customer retention equals market share.

We all know that market share is a powerful profitability enhancement tool. In service businesses it is especially important to exceed customer expectations. By so doing, a customer relationship is built, which in turn retains the customer. The longer a customer stays with you, the greater the market share you are going to get. That is why community banking is all

> *Empowerment is an integral part of the program. Relationships will be built by allowing the people who touch the customer the most to give the customer the service level he or she expects and to exceed that expectation. Empowering your staff to make decisions up to fifty dollars, for example, will result in greater customer satisfaction without breaking the bank.*

about relationships, and that is why relationships get translated into enhanced franchise value.

The third paradigm of quality service is that its absence is costly. Low quality results in customer defection, and is the root cause of 65% of account closings.

The secret to success of community banking is the commitment for relationship building. This is a tough proposition in this day of the microwave mentality. Customers do not have time to be served the

same way they used to be. Their expectations are higher than in the past. Some look for one-stop shopping and for the ability to obtain a broader range of core services at their bank. Many other competitors go after banks' customers using highly sophisticated segmentation techniques and marketing programs. In this day of commoditization, how does a community banking institution individualize its customers to achieve the relationship? In the past when the sea was calm, all ships proved masterful in floating. If the sea is no longer calm, a relationship focus is essential to staying afloat as a community bank. The old concepts for achieving a relationship are also not as valid today.

Using just-in-time technology and the sales-driven push approach in achieving customer satisfaction are no longer sufficient. Instead of a push approach to sales we need to create a pull demand through adopting values throughout the company that are customer driven. Instead of one-stop shopping, we want to create one-stop service that will exceed customer expectations and create a sense of individualization in this day of anonymity.

Empowerment is an integral part of the program. Relationships will be built by allowing the people who touch the customer the most to give the customer the service level he or she expects and to exceed that expectation. Empowering your staff to make decisions up to fifty dollars, for example, will result in greater customer satisfaction without breaking the bank. If you investigate every decision after it has been made, you will find that in many

cases you would have made the same decision as your staff did. Also, the overall
cost to the bank would be de minimus,
while the goodwill and relationship orientation benefits would be significant.

Service and guarantees are also an
important new tool to achieve service level
objectives. Both internal and external customer service staff should guarantee service within a certain quality range and a
certain time parameter. (See Chapter 9 for
specific parameter examples.) Benchmarking is key to achieving and exceeding
customer expectations by setting specific,
service-related benchmarks that will allow
the supercommunity bank to outservice its
competitors. The result: exceeding customer expectations and achieving the relationship.

Customer relationship requirements
vary. Many supercommunity banks believe
they know what the customer wants but do
not ask. By serving the customer and being
proactive in seeking input from the customer on what matters and what does not,
banks will be able to channel their
resources to get the most "bang" for the
buck, as well as achieve the service levels
that fully meet and exceed customer expectations. The following are typical components of the relationship requirements:

- *Accessibility.* The convenience expectations from the past are insufficient.
  Senior management accessibility is
  what the customer is looking for, and it
  is one of the cornerstones of the community banking approach. Being available to your customer when they need

you at any level of bank management is
a major differentiation factor and a
competitive advantage relative to most
larger banking companies. Good
responsiveness—the willingness and
the ability to make a quick decision that
may be specific to the customer needs,
as opposed to a commoditized approach—fills a vacuum created by fully

---

*Many supercommunity banks
believe they know what the
customer wants but do not ask.
By serving the customer and
being proactive in seeking input
from the customer on what matters and what does not, banks
will be able to channel their
resources to get the most
"bang" for the buck, as well as
achieve the service levels that
fully meet and exceed customer
expectations.*

---

commoditized companies. Responsiveness does not imply turnaround
time; it implies flexibility in the decision process and the interest in meeting
customers' needs. It does not imply
bending the credit quality rules; it simply implies an attitudinal change.
- *Professional/technical knowledge.*
  Customers expect competence. Bank
  personnel should know what they are

talking about. As the supercommunity bank plans product expansion into new asset and liability services, the people delivering those services and the sales force must be knowledgeable.

- *Promptness.* Promptness refers to turn-around time. The customer is entitled to know what the decision is regarding her mortgage, home equity loan, working capital line, or other decisions that are in the banker's hand. Again, that is where supercommunity banking can excel and offer the community banking service to the customer. By pushing down the decision to the bank sub-sidiary (within the guidelines of the holding company), any individual bank within the system has the capability to respond quickly to the customer and offer the service promptly. Rolled-up branch systems do not have that ability

---

Don't make a promise if you can't keep it. Customers under-stand that sometimes their requests are beyond the bank's ability to meet.

---

in many cases, nor do money-center banks. Community banks that know how to offer community service to the customer use promptness as a defensive tool. It is an integral part of supercom-munity banking.

- *Kept promises.* A community banking organization delivers on its promises. Don't make a promise if you can't keep it. Customers understand that some-times their requests are beyond the

---

Tell the customer what's going on with his account and with the company. A community bank has an interest in the customer's financial well-being beyond getting the loan repaid. A caring institution, the community bank keeps the customer informed of his financial condition, as wellas the bank's.

---

bank's ability to meet. What they do not understand is when a banker says he or she will take care of it and then forgets or ignores the request.

- *Personalization.* Community banking is relationship oriented, not transaction oriented. Supercommunity banks do not have numbers, they have customers. Unlike megacompanies, community banks have individual customers, and they treat them accordingly. In many cases, this goes way beyond knowing the name of the customer. It means treating the customer as a person. That is why keeping employees for a long time creates relationships, because long-term employees recognize long-term customers and know them beyond the name and into their personal preferences. Individualization of service is key to relationship building; it is the first floor of building the relationship.

- *Keeping informed.* Tell the customer what's going on with his account and with the company. A community bank has an interest in the customer's financial well-being beyond getting the loan repaid. A caring institution, the community bank keeps the customer informed of his financial condition, as well as the bank's. If changes occur, the community banker plans and initiates an information exchange with the customer to better meet the customer's needs. For example, an astute community banker will recognize that the customer does not keep all his funds at the bank, and

---

A customer who had a problem and whose problem was resolved satisfactorily is a more "linked-to-the-bank" customer than the one who did not have the problem in the first place.

---

when mutual funds and annuities are available through the holding company she will offer those services when the customer's financial profile warrants it as a way to meet and exceed the cus-

tomer needs, regardless of whether there is a sales initiative or not.

- *Do it right the first time.* Customers do not like mistakes. Management does not like mistakes. Doing it right the first

---

Creating a team of people who care about the customer and about the company is essential to service quality and to the community banking approach to the customer.

---

time is not only the most efficient way of doing things, it is also the most satisfying way of doing things.

- *Recovery.* Although doing it right the first time is an achievable objective, it cannot be lived up to at all times. When mistakes occur, the community banker owns up to them. "It is not how you fumble, it is how you recover" is the underlying principle here. A customer who had a problem and whose problem was resolved satisfactorily is a more "linked-to-the-bank" customer than the one who did not have the problem in the first place.
- *Follow-up.* A true community banker is not only a preemptor, he follows up as well to make sure the customer is indeed satisfied and to see whether anything else needs to be done. The follow-up creates another opportunity for contact, and every contact with the customer creates an opportunity to exceed

customer expectations. Every customer contact is a moment of truth and the community banker's chance to build a positive, ongoing relationship on human terms.

- *No surprises.* Community banking implies stability, continuity, and care. Therefore, if things change—for example service charges are to be imposed or interest rates are to be raised—customers should be told in advance to avoid surprises. By keeping the customers informed and by helping them anticipate change, they can deal with change better while realizing that their banker cares.

Community banking is about customer relationships. How do you measure the results of your efforts? Are you doing well in customer relationships or not? Surveying the customer base is one of the better ways of finding out. Elements to be followed up include how accurate the information provided was, how pleased or satisfied the customer was, and whether the banker was able to fulfill the customer's request.

Community bankers should recognize that roadblocks do exist. Sometimes the system simply cannot perform what the customer wants. Sometimes the support groups within the holding company do not offer the service the customer is looking for, which creates tension between the subsidiary and the bank holding company. Occasionally, the vendor cannot perform up to expectations; for example, when quality service agreements need to be incorporated into the vendor's contract and, if not met, the vendor needs to be replaced. Marketing strategies can also get in the way when the bank is pushing one product and then another. This week it is home equity loans, and next week it's auto loans. By pushing the product we do not meet customer needs, but our own. The product is being pushed for its profitability, its application to asset liability management, and other reasons that have little to do with customer needs. Although such marketing strategies are a long-time tradition for the industry, they do not maximize the relationship orientation.

Empowerment and pushing the decision down is an integral concept to super-community banking and to community banking. Creating a team of people who care about the customer and about the company is essential to quality service and to the community banking approach. With that concept comes empowerment. Part of employee ownership is the recognition that the buck stops with the employee himself or herself, i.e., the employee is responsible and has some say in how things are done. The most important concept is doing the right thing for the customer at the right time. Making mistakes is okay as long as they are reported and addressed. Breaking the fear barrier for reporting mistakes is a tough thing to do. People are reluctant to own up to errors and are fearful of the ramifications, but customer-oriented community banking teams can learn to surface mistakes and correct them.

The result is the "circle of quality" (Figure 4.1). A proud and an empowered

FIGURE 4.1 Correlation of CSR Retention to Customer Retention

employee is a happy employee. A happy employee stays with the bank. A longer-term employee implies lower cost since there are no recruitment costs, search costs, or training costs for a new employee, and so on. That, in turn, brings about higher service quality since the employee is thoroughly familiar with the way things are done at the bank and is less likely to make mistakes. Higher service quality brings about increased value, which makes for a happy and satisfied customer. A delighted customer leads to customer retention. Customer retention makes employees proud and happy, and the circle continues.

Supercommunity banking has to face the cost/service dilemma every day. If you are going to retain a high pricing structure, then you must achieve superior customer service or you will fail to meet the price/value expectations of today's more discerning customer (Figure 4.2). The way to achieve superior customer service is through the community banking attitude to the customer and through "customer listening." Identify who customers are and learn their preferences so that service delivery, distribution, and quality will be in the context of the customer's needs.

The way to achieve customer-centered service is by developing a culture of delivering perfect service every day. Setting high daily service quality expectations and standards as the goal and supporting that goal with a highly motivational work environment, and with the necessary technology and other resources, upgrades the whole company, even if the goal of perfection is not met each day. Sharing the vision of perfect service every day and the common

FIGURE 4.2 Service Quality Loop

"That which gets measured and rewarded gets done"

goal of preeminent customer service with each bank employee is the way to get superior service.

An organizational change of attitude needs to accompany the customer-centered service orientation. As Figure 4.3 demonstrates, quality-oriented companies are changing our pyramid. The customers are at the top, and management is at the bottom. From a customer relationship standpoint, the most important person is the teller or the customer service representative (CSR), with whom customers connect 95% of the time they contact the bank. Making sure the CSR buys into the concept of managing customer perceptions and exceeding their expectations is the way to achieve the quality service consistent with community banking and relationship orientation. If your CSRs and tellers do not feel a sense of ownership over the community banking approach to the customer, you will not achieve the retention and relationship orientation you are looking for.

Measurement of Quality as a Relationship Strategy

"In God we trust, all others bring data."
—Deming

Total quality management is different in the manufacturing industry than in the service industry as Figure 4.5 depicts. In the service industry the customer does not own an object, he or she owns a memory. The experience cannot be sold or passed on to a third party. It is also subjective. The goal of service, unlike a product, is to be unique. Each customer and each contact is special and different. Service happens and vanishes; it cannot be stockpiled or stored except in the customer's memory. The customer is an integral part of the pro-

FIGURE 4.3 Customer Service Excellence Pyramid

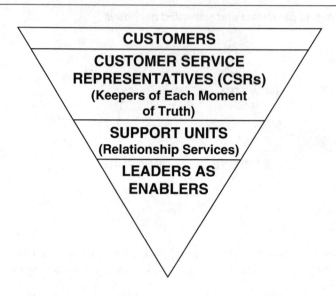

duction team and becomes a part of creating the service. The customer conducts quality control by comparing the expectations to what actually happened, unlike the manufacturing environment where quality

---

What gets measured and rewarded gets done.

---

control is simple. You know what the product specifications are and you see if the product meets those specifications. Since expectations are subjective, this makes quality an elusive concept to reach.

That is why the quality service that we are all seeking has to be customer-driven and achieved in the context of customers' expectations. As a result, if service does not meet the customers' expectations, the only means of recourse is to apologize, whether the expectations were reasonable or not. This is a tough proposition that makes the morale of service employees key to success, and quality measurement in service industries difficult.

Quality measurement is a tough proposition. Many have tried and failed, especially in service businesses where it is so difficult to achieve. One lesson that has been learned from other people's mistakes is that the measurement of quality as a percentage of totals is an obsolete measure and should

FIGURE 4.4 The Ritz-Carlton Interactive Team Pyramid

not be employed. Here are some startling facts. At a 99.9% quality success rate the following will still take place:

- The IRS would lose 2 million tax documents daily.
- Within the next hour, 22,000 checks would be deducted from the wrong accounts.
- 1,300 telephone calls would be connected to the wrong number within the next minute.
- 107 incorrect medical procedures would be performed each day.

The conclusion: Quality as a service excellence tool must be measured as an absolute in order to reach and exceed customer expectations. You must know how many customers you are negatively impacting daily, in absolute numbers. Each customer is important. Customers are the source of the franchise value as well as referrals, future business, and core responsibility. Therefore, in order to measure quality properly and to implement it as a way to achieve relationship orientation (which is so important in the context of supercommunity banking), one must

FIGURE 4.5 TQM Differences Between Manufacturing and Service Industries

products	service
• The customer owns an object.	• The customer owns a memory. The experience cannot be sold or passed on to a third party.
• The goal of product producing is uniformity—all widgets are alike.	• The goal of service is uniqueness; each customer and each contact is "special."
• A product can be placed in inventory; a sample can be sent in advance for the customer to review.	• A service happens in the moment. It cannot be stockpiled.
• The customer is an end user who is not involved in the production process.	• The customer is a coproducer who is a partner in creating the service.
• One conducts quality control by comparing output specifications.	• The customer conducts quality control by comparing expectations to experience.
• If improperly produced, the product can be pulled off the line or "recalled."	• If improperly performed, apologies and reparations are the only means of recourse.
• The morale of production employees is important.	• The morale of service employees is critical.

choose a quality target and measure it in absolute terms. The measurement process

> *Focusing on the customer's view of superior performance . . . spells out what superior competitive performance is.*

is the bridge between the overall system of quality and service, and the customer.

Without that measurement of progress one cannot improve. Improvement, by definition, is a reduction in the absolute num-ber of negative customer impacts. The measurement of quality provides a focus and a purpose to the bank's actions that are directed toward quality. Focusing on the customer's view of superior performance (the attributes of quality) spells out what superior competitive performance is (benchmarking). If the quality is properly measured and the results integrated into a continuous improvement process, one does not only exceed customer expectations relative to the bank and its competitors but also reduces errors and cycle time, increases efficiency, and increases the responsiveness of the bank to customer needs.

The measure of quality also helps identify the effectiveness of the bank as a quality service producer and a relationship builder, as well as the effectiveness of specific vendors and suppliers: Do they give us the quality delivery we are looking for? It also helps identify whether the employees are indeed committed to service quality

---

You can make the vendor a partner in the relationship commitment. Require it. It will improve your results significantly.

---

and relationship building and whether they have ownership over the process. Measuring the results of quality service can enhance bank effectiveness, vendor effectiveness, and employee effectiveness to bring about improved customer retention, improved market share, and the ultimate result of improved profitability.

The top scoring companies under the Malcolm Baldridge application have raised their market share 13.7% after implementing the quality measurement program. That is a significant figure. The key, of course, is to use the right measurement for the banking business. The Baldridge program measures quality along the following characteristics:

- Result orientation
- Customer-driven quality
- Leadership involvement
- Total employee participation
- Continuous improvement
- Reduced cycle time
- Management by objectives

The program also has a future orientation and expects vendors to participate in the program. Vendors participate by building performance criteria into their contracts. Their actual performance on site is then sampled and monitored through a quality measurement program by bank personnel. The vendor's process is continuously reviewed, using the same quality measurement process as the bank. Supercommunity banks and relationship-oriented companies look at vendors and other constituents as partners. You can make the vendor a partner in the relationship com-

---

The top scoring companies under the Malcolm Baldridge application have raised their market share 13.7% after implementing the quality measurement program.

---

mitment. Require it. It will improve your results significantly. Assign responsibility to the vendor through a single internal management point and establish clear performance criteria. Performance will improve.

Summary: What gets measured and rewarded gets done.

In order to manage and implement quality properly, develop a solid management process:

- Manage rather than administer
  - Anticipate instead of react.
  - Prioritize.
  - Focus.
  - Measure and give feedback.
  - Develop meaningful management information systems.
  - Develop an obsession with details.
- Demand excellence
  - Lead by example.
  - Own your success and failures, no excuses.
- Communicate
  - Expectations to employees.
  - Status (good and bad)—how things are going.
  - Establish high esteem.
- Mind set
  - Develop a "can do" attitude.
  - Fix it now—forever.
  - Develop action bias.
  - Good, fast decisions produce better results than excellent, slow decsions.

The service quality process incorporates the following components:

- Establish a service quality program (proactive).
- Communicate the standards.
- Reward/recognize achievements and service quality.
- Continuously review service quality standards for customer responsiveness.

- Establish service quality standards that exceed customer expectations.
- Monitor and sample all customer service contact/relationship points.
- Provide immediate feedback on all quality samples.

The Ritz-Carlton—An Example of Quality Measurement

The Ritz-Carlton, the winner of the Malcolm Baldridge Award, has done an excellent job in measuring quality. They

---

Vendors participate by building performance criteria into their contracts. Their actual performance on site is then sampled and monitored through a quality measurement program by bank personnel. The vendor's process is continuously reviewed, using the same quality measurement process as the bank.

---

demonstrated that even the service business can effectively measure service quality. The following are some examples of their experience.

The Ritz-Carlton has a very structured, highly quantitative process to achieve and integrate quality throughout its employee corps. Every day all employees of each hotel gather to discuss commitment of quality. Each week a specific department is chosen and its basic function is described.

Management does not stop at reciting the objectives in the corporate values. It makes sure that every employee knows them by heart and lives them day to day. The hotel surveys all employees twice a year to find out whether they are satisfied and happy.

Throughout the week, the key players of the department are described and their needs from other departments highlighted in order to assure that other suppliers within the company are giving this department what it needs to provide the quality service it is expected to generate. The strategic goals of the department are discussed, as well as the number one defect they are trying to eliminate. Also, one good idea from the department, which has improved the operation of the department or of the total company, is reviewed.

In addition, one of the twenty basic values of the company is reviewed daily, a process that takes ten minutes every morning. This process is transferrable to a supercommunity bank where each department has discrete strategic goals but whose operation and success depend on the col-

laboration of departments and of other banks within the holding company. Learning from each other (reviewing one good idea) is also key to making the whole greater than the sum of its parts.

The quality process is implemented further by ascertaining that every employee knows the corporate credo (values), the meaning of quality, the "gold standards" of the company, and its credo.

Management does not stop at reciting the objectives in the corporate values. It makes sure that every employee knows them by heart and lives them day to day. The hotel surveys all employees twice a year to find out whether they are satisfied and happy. They have six ways to get the employees involved, including training certification, goal setting, and hotel decisions. They have extensive training programs, including eight skill-building classes: certification, orientation, philosophy, coaching class, the quality engineer, educational class, interpersonal communications, and encouragement to quality. Career path and goal setting are also addressed by highlighting the success factors of the employee in setting long-term goals. All employees are made aware of the hotel's current events and its goals beyond their department. In the supercommunity bank context that translates to understanding the ins and outs of the holding company and the current status and performance of the holding company, even if it is outside the specific bank subsidiary. Learning more about the holding company and how the subsidiary's performance affects it provides a context for individual employee performance that promotes camaraderie and a sense of belonging, as well as corporate commitment.

The Ritz-Carlton also has many recognition facets, including five-star awards,

---

Guest satisfaction, employee satisfaction, and owner satisfaction are quantified with great precision. Benchmarks range from ten specifics, such as 85% on-time delivery, to ten conceptuals, such as 90% gold standards, which are the hotel's values and principles.
With thought and creativity, all of these standards can be transferred to the banking environment.

---

certificates, receptions, pictures, hand shakes, prizes, department plaques, graveyard breakfasts, management and leaders' roundtables (leaders are the senior executives), the notion of promoting from within, and the team. Finally, quarterly general assemblies are an integral part of the system ranging from parties to health fairs, trades shows, and talent shows to ensure that all employees interact with one another and benefit from each other's ideas, companionship, sense of team, and sense of belonging. Again, supercommunity

banks can learn from these recognition and team-building efforts and translate them into their corporate culture.

The Ritz-Carlton measures performance for quality by points. Performance rating is based on a 1-5 system, and each leader (manager) has the opportunity to be reviewed three times a year against specific criteria.

The hotel also produces a daily quality production report where every day the number of occupied rooms plus covers (restaurant contacts) less customer complaints is measured to yield total production. Then, guest complaints are categorized along five variables: facilities reliability, supplies/food and beverage reliability, lady/gentleman reliability, services missing, and guest security. (For a super-community bank, these may be translated into operations reliability, service reliability, product reliability, services missing, and loss). In addition, internal customer complaints are being plotted. Both figures are subtracted from the total production to identify total internal defect, timeliness defects, and total system reliability. The net figure is total quality production, which is identified by quality percentage.

Guest satisfaction, employee satisfaction, and owner satisfaction are quantified with great precision. Benchmarks range from ten specifics, such as 85% on-time delivery, to ten conceptuals, such as 90% gold standards, which are the hotel's values and principles. With thought and creativity, all of these standards can be transferred to the banking environment.

The Ritz-Carlton Hotel company went even farther to identify the three goals it wishes to achieve by 1996:

- 100% customer retention
- 50% cycle time reduction
- Six sigma (3.5 defects per million)

In order to achieve the above, The Ritz-Carlton has the inverted pyramid described previously in this chapter (Figure 4.3). The pyramid reflects the company's relationship-building objective: One hundred per-

---

Community banking is under siege. Its very existence is being threatened on all fronts.

---

cent retention, which means that every hotel guest will come back. This is a most ambitious objective by anybody's standards. However, the organization of the Ritz-Carlton's interactive team is designed to accomplish it. The guest is at the top of the pyramid; the corporate steering committee, which is the most senior level of management, is at the bottom. That, by itself, is a telling story (Figure 4.4).

Summary

Total quality management is a management approach that includes total employee involvement, customer requirements, and continuous process improvement.

Forming a Supercommunity Bank—A Solution to the Stategic Woes of Small Community Banks

Community banking is under siege. Its very existence is being threatened on all fronts. The regulatory burden is greater than ever, with 30 basis points FDIC premium plus escalating compliance costs, which significantly impede their ability to compete. Megabanks are creating economies of scale that attempt to use cost advantage to appeal to and acquire the community bank's customers. Nonbank competitors, which are altogether unimpaired by the regulatory burden, are also active competitors for both deposits and assets in the community banking markets. Mutual funds and investment management firms are looking for the savings and investment dollars of consumers across America, while nonbank lenders such as mortgage banks, investment banks, credit card companies, and finance companies are trying to do the same, competing for the credit dollars of American consumers. All these institutions enjoy competitive advantages relative to the community banks.

Other factors are further impeding the small bank's ability to compete. The critical mass required to implement new technology is increasing in many volume-sensitive businesses, ranging from credit card receivables to mortgage banking to investment management. How can the small bank compete in the face of such formidable competition and adverse conditions?

The community bank does have significant assets. It typically has incomparable customer relationships. Community banks

> *(The supercommunity bank) . . . strategy is unique in that it provides defenses against large and small banks, builds value in the franchise, and generates strong profits.*

are the most trusted financial institutions by consumers. They typically enjoy long-term customer retention, which often is directly correlated to profitability. They have a loyal customer base, whom they serve with great personal care and attention, something with which larger banks cannot compete effectively. Although the product line is limited, it is not a major handicap because most of their customers do not need the "bells and whistles" larger banks have to offer.

Community banks do occupy a unique position in today's banking industry. But with the changes and reconfiguration of the financial services industry, can they survive as the adverse circumstances negatively impacting their ability to compete persist? One solution to the community bank's problems is the supercommunity bank. This strategic position attempts to marry the best of both worlds. On the one hand, the supercommunity bank seeks to offer the best of what small banks offer:

intimate service levels, management availability, and personal, caring service. At the same time, the supercommunity bank strives to compete effectively with the megabanks by offering a broader product line and by taking advantage of some cost efficiencies that do not diminish the level of customer service. As we stated in Chapter 2, in order to achieve these, the supercommunity bank relies on a three-pronged strategy: strong community orientation, customer-transparent cost savings, and a broad product line. This strategy is unique in that it provides defenses against

> *Community banks do occupy a unique position in today's banking industry. But with the changes and reconfiguration of the financial services industry, can they survive as the adverse circumstances negatively impacting their ability to compete persist?*

large and small banks, builds value in the franchise, and generates strong profits.

Grow a Supercommunity Bank: Mergers and Acquisitions

Having defined the supercommunity bank, the question is: *How do you get there?* Experience indicates that an active targeted acquisition program is the most effective way to grow a supercommunity bank. We can learn from the experiences of Keystone, Integra, Community First,

---

Because community orientation is of paramount importance to supercommunity banking, the banks should retain the sales, marketing, and distribution arms of the organization. The banks are charged with maintaining local market dominance, community development, and high-quality customer service.

Florida Community Banks, and others that have put together a supercommunity bank through merges of equals or an acquisition program, and can share some of the successes and the mistakes to be avoided. For example, a $250 million bank in a major metropolitan area determined that the most effective competitive position in a market where all other banks were owned by large, out-of-state financial institutions was to become a home-grown supercommunity bank. The bank prepared a prospectus describing its objective, strategic direction, and benefits incurred to itself as well as the potential merger partners. Several targets were identified, pro forma financials calculated for the new entity, and merger part-

ners found. The bank was Sterling Bank in Houston, Texas.

Another example, and the most typical, is when one flagship bank typically embarks on an acquisition program that adds community banks to the holding company at a fairly fast pace. Many supercommunity banks that select this building strategy double their size every three to four years. The strategy makes the absorption of the new institutions less traumatic than the absorption process in centralized institutions because management is typically retained and the integrity of the acquired institution is not violated. That typically makes for a smooth transition, particularly if the corporate culture and values of the two institutions are compatible. In situations where the culture is not consistent, the supercommunity bank strategy dictates that the acquired institution must adopt the supercommunity bank philosophy in order to make the whole, indeed, greater than the sum of the parts.

Below are some of the lessons that have been learned:

- *Agreeing on this vision* is the first step in converting a conglomeration of banks into a supercommunity bank.
- *Establishing the new identity and communicating* the vision calls for a redefinition of the company's operating philosophy and a structure that converts that philosophy into reality. Because community orientation is of paramount importance to supercommunity banking, the banks should retain the sales,

marketing, and distribution arms of the organization. The banks are charged with maintaining local market dominance, community development, and high-quality customer service. This emphasis and structure encourages the

---

The bank's ability to create managerial efficiencies may be even more important than its ability to achieve economies of scale in the consolidation process. This new structure is a much more effective structure as compared to the loose federation concept.

---

bank presidents to manage their local markets free of holding company control. Although the banks typically offer common products and operate under consistent policies, each one is responsible for its own asset and liability pricing as well as credit underwriting. The goal is to deliver common products and services with a very local and personal touch.

- The holding company is charged with *setting overall corporate strategic direction* and also becomes the organization's manufacturing arm, responsible for providing all support services to the banks. These services typically include back-room areas such as opera-

tions, finance, data processing, and human resources. The first challenge to the holding company in this regard is to develop economies and efficiencies by consolidating all the support areas that do not directly touch the customer.

- A second holding company goal should be to create a high level of *professionalism* in the technical and support areas that could be leveraged throughout the organization. The larger responsibility and increased professional opportunity, in turn, enables the holding company to attract and retain top-quality performers in those areas. The bank's ability to create managerial efficiencies may be even more important than its ability to achieve economies of scale in the consolidation process. This new structure is a much more effective structure as compared to the loose federation concept. The holding company is fresh and effective.

- Another important aspect of this structure is *assigning specific responsibilities and providing the authority commensurate with it.* All support personnel report directly to a holding company employee, not to the banks. Holding company executives not only are responsible for the performance of their groups, but also are held accountable for cooperation between the groups and the banks.

- A successful transition to a supercommunity bank entails the realization that *certain elements of the business should not be changed.* The company need not sacrifice the community banking orientation and quality service obsession that are essential to a supercommunity bank's success.

The banks need to operate with a great deal of freedom in their local markets; all customer-related decisions should be made at the closest appropriate level of customer contact.

At the same time, a commitment to consolidating (to the extent possible) all support services that do not directly touch

---

The banks need to operate with a great deal of freedom in their local markets; all customer-related decisions should be made at the closest appropriate level of customer contact.

---

the customer is made. This drive for economies and efficiencies is coupled with an equally strong emphasis on providing top-quality service to the banks, so that they can serve their customers effectively.

An agreement that certain cultural elements of the company are *nonnegotiable* needs to be made. The ability to steadfastly hold to values such as maintaining high asset quality, retaining strong cost management, and treating customers and employees fairly is vital to keeping the company focused on the truly important issues.

Finally, *executive leadership* is critical to putting a supercommunity bank together

successfully. The best people available, regardless of which bank they are from, should work together in an atmosphere of sharing and mutual interest. Personalities are put aside to the extent necessary to bring banks under the holding company's umbrella. At the same time, sufficient individual entrepreneurial freedom is encouraged to properly manage each bank, preserve the community integrity of the institution, and retain the strong emphasis on the customer.

The Acquisition Process

A well-structured acquisition process is essential to an effective and efficient acquisition program (Figure 4.6). Without such a process, the company ends up spending a lot of time, money, and effort on acquisition candidates that are unlikely to materialize into transactions. It is only when a set of screening criteria and clear strategic parameters are assigned to the acquisition process that companies can be acknowledged as good candidates or turned away due to lack of strategic fit.

The acquisition process includes the following components:

1. *Prospect Identification.* A proactive and clear acquisition program is the most efficient way to achieve quality growth. In order to do that, prospects need to be identified and screened against the acquisition criteria identified as a part of the acquisition planning process. In some cases, potential acquisition candidates are classified into several cate-

FIGURE 4.6 Acquisition Process

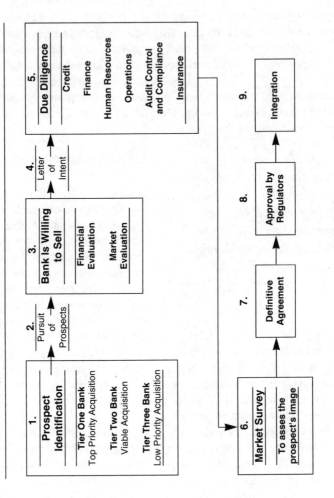

gories. For example, a tier-one bank would be a top priority acquisition that fits all the criteria specified. A tier-two bank is a viable acquisition that can be pursued but not as aggressively as the

---

Experience indicates that an active, targeted acquisition program is the most effective way to grow a supercommunity bank.

---

highest priority targets. A tier-three bank, although meeting the criteria, is not as attractive.

2. *Pursuit of Prospects.* Once prospects are identified and prioritized, an organized effort should be mounted to pursue them. It is typically the chief executive or a board member that approaches the prospect. If there is a personal contact, she or he should be identified and pursued. If not, the senior executive and the person in charge of the acquisition should approach the prospect and assess interest. At this stage, additional fallout will occur since some banks may not be interested in selling.

3. *Assessment of Banks that are Willing to Sell.* The first two stages created two waves of fallout from the initial universe of potential acquisition targets. At this point, we have a short list of banks that are willing to sell. The valuation at a distance should be performed at this

stage to identify the best prospects of the short list. This evaluation includes a detailed financial valuation of the company and its performance to ensure that it fits into the screening criteria initially identified as well as into the overall performance and dilution characteristics of the holding company.

A second evaluation should be performed on the market to ensure that it indeed conforms with the depth, fragmentation, growth, and other characteristics identified in the acquisition criteria. For example, if the market is totally dominated by another company and our acquisition criteria involves a first, second, or third position in the market-

---

In situations where the culture is not consistent, the supercommunity bank strategy dictates that the acquired institution must adopt the supercommunity bank philosophy in order to make the whole, indeed, greater than the sum of the parts.

---

place, the market evaluation will knock this acquisition candidate off.

4. *Letter of Intent.* Once the initial screening is completed, some companies will constitute, on the face of it, good acquisition targets. Their financial performance and profitability dynamics are consistent with the acquisition criteria

in the market in which they operate, and their position in that market complies with the hurdle rates as well. At this point, it is time to issue a letter of intent. It is wise to keep the letter of intent quiet through the due diligence process and not advertise the transaction before a definitive agreement is signed. The due diligence and market survey steps may eliminate this candidate; therefore, revealing the letter of intent may prove embarrassing. At the same time, depending on the relationship with the regulators, a bank may elect to discuss the possibility of a merger with the regulators and prepare them for the possibility of a definitive agreement.

5. *Due Diligence.* Due diligence is the "nonnegotiable" of acquisitions. The quality of the acquisition and its success depend on the quality of the due diligence process. It is at this stage that the prospect's attractiveness must be verified to ensure that the price paid is appropriate and that the acquisition candidate will fit into the holding company.

The first step in the due diligence process is, of course, assessment of credit quality. If the credit quality of the institution does not fit with the profile developed in the acquisition criteria, the transaction will be canceled. Accordingly, a quick and dirty due diligence on the loan portfolio of the target is advisable. If the results are positive, the time was not wasted. If the results are negative, the acquiror avoids spending additional time on other functions of

the company that will, in the long run, be wasted since the company's credit profile will not fit the target acquisition requirements. (Appendix 4 depicts a due diligence list that starts with the credit process as described.) Once the quick and dirty step is completed, detailed due diligence needs to be performed on the rest of their loan portfolio as well as on other key functions in the company, including finance, human resources, operations, audit control and compliance, and insurance.

There are many ways to accomplish a due diligence process. Many companies, including intense acquirors, do not have a special acquisition team that conducts the due diligence. Instead, they use line personnel who are familiar with all phases of bank operations to conduct due diligence on their counterpart area in the target candidate. At Community First, for example, the

---

The best people available, regardless of which bank they are from, should work together in an atmosphere of sharing and mutual interest.

CEO and CFO constitute the acquisition screening and pursuit team. The due diligence team is composed of the heads of credit, finance, human resources, operations, audit, and assurance at the holding company.

In other situations, particularly in acquisition-intensive companies that are large enough, a specialized team is formed to conduct due diligence on all potential targets. In many situations this is not necessarily the most effective way to proceed, however, especially when there are no clear acquisition criteria identified up front. In those cases, due diligence is conducted on companies that clearly do not fit the profile of the acquiror yet. Since such a profile does not exist in unequivocal terms, the due diligence process is conducted anyway.

6. *Market Survey.* Understanding the internal operations of the company, although a critical condition, is not sufficient. An acquisition candidate for a supercommunity bank must possess a certain market image. It must be linked to the community, be well-respected, and be perceived as a strong service provider. Therefore, a market survey needs to be conducted either in a formal or an informal fashion to assess the prospect's image. The survey can be conducted in a formal way through questionnaires, or in an informal way by contacting prominent business people in the community and selected customers to form a picture of the prospect's image, service level, and philosophy as perceived by the marketplace.

7. *Definitive Agreement.* Once an acquisition target passes through the hurdles described above, it is time to strike a deal. A definitive agreement is formed and signed. The price identified in the

---

An acquisition candidate for a supercommunity bank must possess a certain market image. It must be linked to the community, be well-respected, and be perceived as a strong service provider. Therefore, a market survey needs to be conducted either in a formal or an informal fashion to assess the prospect's image.

---

letter of intent may be changed to reflect knowledge gathered during the due diligence and market survey process. However, it is recommended that one create enough latitude within the letter of intent pricing to avoid major changes. They may be perceived by the acquisition target as a cat-and-mouse game played by the acquiror. One way to avoid surprises is to price the transaction in the letter of intent conditional upon the performance of the nonperforming loan portfolio. If loan workouts do not take place in a projected manner, the loan amounts will be added to the price. This protects the acquiror but also does not create the impression that once the transaction gets close to closing, the acquiror is going to play games with the price.

8. *Approval by the Regulators.* Once the regulators review the application and

---

Once an acquisition is made, the acquired company should be integrated into the super-community banking structure rapidly. Integration is often the most difficult part of the acquisition process. It involvescontinuing to implement the strategic prescriptions consistent with the supercommunity bank strategy.

---

approve it, the deal is ready to be consummated. It is helpful to discuss the transaction with the regulators in advance, as mentioned, as well as to have an appropriate CRA rating. Companies that do not have good CRA ratings have been penalized in the acquisition process. In many cases, the acquisition has been stopped by one or more consumer groups, which eliminated or significantly delayed the transaction. For example, in one case, a Native American group blocked an acquisition of a small bank by a large supercommunity bank for over eigh-

teen months, demanding cash money up front. The agreement that was finally negotiated included $5 million in loans, the installment of an ATM machine on the reservation, and the use of Native Americans in the bank branch on that location. In other cases, consumer groups held up transactions for things such as board membership for Hispanic or African-American consumer groups, feature in advertising for customers with disabilities, or actual cash gifts for several advocacy groups. Strong relationships with regulators can prevent such occurrences or diminish their impact on the transaction and its timing.

9. *Integration.* Once an acquisition is made, the acquired company should be integrated into the supercommunity banking structure rapidly. Integration is often the most difficult part of the acquisition process. It involves continuing to implement the strategic prescriptions consistent with the supercommunity bank strategy. The same strategic prescriptions that have already been effectively imposed on existing subsidiary banks should also be imposed on acquired companies. For example:

- Centralized customer-transparent functions such as bank operations, human resources, internal audit, policy-making, data processing, regulatory affairs, legal services, accounting, and credit review.
- Investment in centralized technology such as data processing and account-

ing functions to achieve economies of scale.
- Enhanced non-interest income by distribution and cross-selling of centrally managed products through subsidiary banks.
- Maximized strength of customer relationships through stability of line personnel and delegation and decentralization of authority.
- Improved credit quality through decentralized credit decision making and utilization of community knowledge.
- Maximized net interest origin through reliance on a stable core deposit base in community-oriented lending.

In order to ensure implementation of an acquisition strategy, the acquisition process should be institutionalized. In addition to the development of a structured plan and acquisition criteria as described above, other steps toward institutionalization can include the following:

• Appoint a specialist for actively identifying analyzed acquisition candidates. Once prospective targets are ranked in terms of desirability, the chief executive officer of the bank should contact the chief executive of the prospective target to informally discuss opportunities.
• The chief executive officer should be closely involved in the identification of acquisition candidates through meetings and informal discussions with regional industry members. (Cor-

respondent banking is most helpful in identifying prospective targets for acquisition.)
• Identify appropriate legal and investment banking advisers to rely on in any future acquisition transactions.
• Develop necessary procedural and operation infrastructure in areas such as due diligence procedures and teams,

While the bank industry consolidation is expected to continue throughout the nineties, the approval process for bank merger transactions can be enormously complex and time consuming. It is fraught with obstacles, any one of which might delay, disrupt, or terminate the process.

data processing integration, credit control, and marketing planning for streamlined acquisitions.

As one contemplates acquisitions, one cannot forget the regulators. They keep on changing their minds as to what constitutes an approvable, legitimate acquisition. The situation is particularly confusing since over the last two years the Federal Reserve Board and the Justice Department have publicly disagreed as to whether the cluster market definition was valid as well as other acquisition-related matters. While the bank industry consolidation is expected to continue throughout the nineties, the approval process for bank merger transactions can be enormously complex and time consuming. It is fraught with obstacles, any one of which might delay, disrupt, or terminate the process. Moreover, as consolidation continues, it will become increasingly difficult to affect in-market mergers, which are a popular way to realize immediate profits through consolidation of back-office and other cost-reduction measures soon after the acquisition.

The Federal Reserve Board generally has approved mergers that appear to make

---

The most probable battleground for merger approval and consummation focuses these days on the possible anticompetitive effects of the transaction, if consummated. Careful planning, including a realistic assessment of the potential costs involved, is key to maximizing the chances for an early and successful approval for an acquisition.

---

economic sense and contribute to the orderly consolidation of the industry. The Department of Justice, however, recently has shifted from a passive enforcement agency to an active regulatory agency by its assertiveness in defining acceptable

bank mergers. State regulatory authorities, community, and advocacy groups also mount challenges to merger transactions

---

The Department of Justice, however, recently has shifted from a passive enforcement agency to an active regulatory agency by its assertiveness in defining acceptable bank mergers. State regulatory authorities, community, and advocacy groups also mount challenges to merger transactions on anti-trust grounds.

---

on anti-trust grounds. The most probable battleground for merger approval and consummation focuses these days on the possible anticompetitive effects of the transaction, if consummated. Careful planning, including a realistic assessment of the potential costs involved, is key to maximizing the chances for an early and successful approval for an acquisition.

Acquisition Criteria

Attractive acquisition targets should be specified in terms of the characteristics they should possess as well as the parameters within which the transaction should occur. Location, financial condition, strategic position, expected operating results, and size are examples of acquisition criteria. It can be clearly implemented for each specific institution. For example:

- *Location.* In the case of a supercommunity bank seeking an acquisition out of market or in contiguous market areas, given the strategic position, the target bank's management will typically be less intact. Therefore, in a transaction involving the acquisition of a franchise in a contiguous or new market area, it will not disturb the community roots and franchise value of the acquired institution. In addition, the economic profile of acquisitions made in contiguous market areas may present superior growth and profitability opportunities as well as economic diversification. At the same time, the logic of cost savings typically attributed to transactions in

---

Suitable acquisition candidates should have management teams with extensive personal contacts and community roots, which are core competencies of supercommunity banks.

---

existing market areas is not often consistent with the requirement that subsidiary banks maintain strong and positive local roots. Therefore, in-market acquisitions can be made if they are not

destructive to the existing institution franchise and where they augment the total franchise through greater leverage of back-office functions.

Strong management and customer service teams will allow the acquiror to maximize the value of the acquired franchise and to minimize disruptions arising as a result of the acquisitions.

- *Management.* Capable local management teams are the ideal management for a supercommunity bank acquisition. They facilitate rapid integration into the supercommunity bank strategy. Because of the importance of personal contacts, changes in management and customer contact and staff are especially disruptive in the case of community-oriented service institutions. Therefore, both the quality of existing management and the continuing commitment of that team are important to the success of a supercommunity bank acquisition. Strong management and customer service teams will allow the acquiror to maximize the value of the acquired franchise and to minimize disruptions arising as a result of the acquisitions.

- *Strategic Fit.* Supercommunity banks typically seek to make acquisitions of companies that have strong community roots and core banking franchises. Suitable acquisition candidates should have management teams with extensive personal contacts and community roots,

---

Some look for troubled institutions that they can turn around and integrate into the supercommunity bank philosophy. Others look for non-dilutive transactions that allow the acquiror to maintain adequate levels of capital and effective deployment of deposits. Each bank should determine its own strategy when it comes to the financial condition of target acquisitions.

---

which are core competencies of super-community banks. Local funding and a stable core deposit base are also helpful.
- *Financial Condition.* Different philosophies apply to different supercommunity banks. Some look for troubled institutions that they can turn around and integrate into the supercommunity bank philosophy. Others look for non-dilutive transactions that allow the acquiror to maintain adequate levels of capital and effective deployment of deposits.

Each bank should determine its own strategy when it comes to the financial condition of target acquisitions. There are benefits to weak and strong institutions as well as disadvantages. Position of the acquiring institution will determine the appropriate financial profile of target institutions.
- *Asset Size.* Smaller institutions are more easily assimilated into the supercommunity banking culture. Generally, they are companies with total assets ranging from $50 million to $1 billion. By the same token, merger equals of supercommunity banks that are larger than $1 billion in assets have been proven effective. The target size depends on the size of the holding company and on its acquisition philosophy. As we saw in Community First's case, they acquire only small banks for a certain price range, and the acquisition strategy has been extremely successful. Novices in the acquisition game would be better off targeting smaller companies for the following reasons:

- Smaller banks can be assimilated into the acquiror's organization structure and operation system much more rapidly than larger institutions with greater organizational operational inertia.
- Smaller banks are much more likely to obtain significant benefits from the centralized back office of the supercommunity bank.
- Smaller banks are more likely to benefit from the expanded product

portfolio available through the holding company and, therefore, greater value will be added to the acquisition target.

- Smaller banks are more likely to be priced between 1 and 1.5 times book value and are therefore more likely to be non-dilutive transactions.

• *Pricing.* Transaction pricing should be determined based on the strategic objectives of the supercommunity bank and the importance of growth in the strategy, as well as the value of the acquisition targets. To ensure immediate payback, some companies set pricing parameters beyond which they will not negotiate. Others are prepared to look over a longer time horizon and fix pricing objectives that are more flexible.

There are many benefits to pricing parameters, especially when they take

There are many benefits to pricing parameters, especially when they take into account the dilution effect of the acquisition.

into account the dilution effect of the acquisition. For example, transactions that are consummated at price levels ranging from 1 to 1.5 times the targets book values are non-dilutive yet realis-

tic in many cases in today's market for the following reasons:

- As the supercommunity banks are viewed by many targets as a more

Many super-regionals known to pay up for acquisitions have been seeking targets with at least $1 billion in assets. Therefore, a strategy of acquisitions targeted at smaller institutions should be less competitive in terms of pricing.

attractive buyer than institutions that fully centralize controls, assets, operations, and marketing, the continuing and important role of local management and directors in the supercommunity banking strategy should be viewed as a major selling point for acquisition proposals made by supercommunity banks.

- Completed acquisition transactions involving smaller banks are typically priced significantly below transactions involving larger targets. Many super-regionals known to pay up for acquisitions have been seeking targets with at least $1 billion in assets.

Therefore, a strategy of acquisitions targeted at smaller institutions should be less competitive in terms of pricing.

- Small institutions are more likely to have considerably less liquid stock and therefore are more likely to value the liquidity that would be obtained through a sale to a supercommunity bank.

Specific Acquisition Criteria—An Example

Alpha Bank has been successful with its in-state acquisitions due, in part, to the bank's strong corresponding banking group and executive management's knowledge of banking within the state. Some of the challenges for the bank as it moves out of state in its acquisition philosophy will be:

- How to develop the relationships
- How to enhance their knowledge of the market areas
- How to inform banks that they are a potential acquiror

One approach to building an out-of-state franchise is to identify a key person in the state capable of establishing an organization of at least $500 million in assets. The alternative strategy would be to seek a core organization of at least $250 million in assets and then acquire entities with at least $100 million in assets. This could be done by a banking executive in that state, a broker/consultant, or a bank employee.

The methodology to identify potential prospects is as follows:

1. *Market attractiveness.* The following procedures will be used to identify the markets in which the company wants to acquire the bank:

- Determine the region that management deems appropriate for a contiguous state.
- Identify the rapid growth counties for that state. Rapid growth is defined as a population growth rate of at least X times the state as a whole.
- Identify the rapid growth cities with a population of at least 5,000 within the rapid growth counties.

2. *Acquisition Targets.* The following methodology will be used to determine banks that are attractive potential affiliates:

- Eliminate banks that are a part of a large multibank holding company.
- Consider banks that have at least $100 million in assets, a return on assets of 1.2%, and a return on equity of 15%.
- Eliminate banks that were within a declining population area in the last ten years.

Once a list has been established that meets the above criteria, a list of prospects will be prioritized based on asset quality, sustained financial performance, and growth potential.

In summary, as community banks face the problem of survival in a restructuring industry, building a supercommunity bank offers a viable, proven strategic alternative for prosperity in the future. Those community banks that elect to embark on this strategy should bear in mind the commitment they need to make to service excellence, cost efficiencies that are transparent to the customer, and a broader product line. Underlying these three is a corporate culture emphasizing teamwork, service orientation, and closeness to the customer.

CHAPTER FIVE

Customer-Transparent Cost Savings

Supercommunity banks are cost-conscious, like every other bank in the country. However, their cost-consciousness is unique. They recognize the need to focus on costs, but only within their strategic context of high-touch, service-intensive delivery system. That, in turn, implies that service levels cannot be compromised through cost-reduction efforts, which makes for tough decisions throughout the strategic cost management process. However, cost management is still the key to profitability and to resource allocation and cannot be ignored. Many supercommunity banks recognize this and implement strategic cost management successfully, as evidenced in this segment's cost performance numbers relative to the industry as a whole. This chapter offers some of the proven techniques for effective cost management in supercommunity banks.

Effective Cost Management

Several elements enter into an effective cost management program.

Planning and Control Structures

The chief executive must lend strong support to cost containment and profitability enhancement. Without the CEO's lead, the troops will not follow. The CEO also leads the effort in supervising the development of operations plans and operations controls toward strategic cost management. Figure 5.1 depicts an example of cost control structure. Once the objectives for the a cost control process are established by the CEO (for example, if $1 million worth of expense savings is identified as the goal), management communicates the decided-upon actions to the different operation centers and functional units, which, in turn, attempt to achieve the desired results. Subsequently, those results are measured, and feedback to management generates additional action. An example of this process is a recent memorandum in a supercommunity bank entitled, "Project $1 Million" (See pp. 120-121.)

Project $1 Million is an example of one process. There are others. But the intent is all the same: to achieve cost efficiencies that come from the bottom up from the people who know best how to implement them—your employees—and that stay within the parameters of the supercommunity banking strategy.

Strategic Objectives

Profitability measurement and cost containment should be guided by the strategic objective of the organization, both bankwide and departmentally. Examples of strategic objectives within the supercommunity bank context can be:

Bankwide:
- Improve ROE to reach 17%.
- Expand market share to reach 20%.
- Reduce overall cost by $1 million.

Departmentally:
- Improve productivity by 10%.
- Reduce staff by 25 people. Reduce errors per 1,000 items.
- Improve response time by 15% without additions to staff.

These objectives provide the context within which cost efficiencies should be evaluated.

FIGURE 5.1 Structure for Cost Control

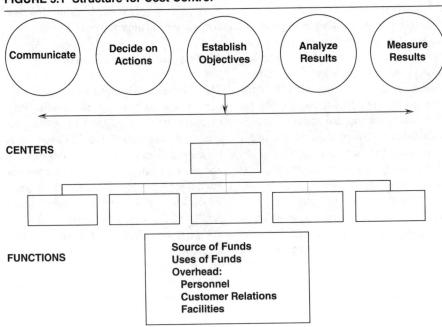

Identify Areas of Effort

Because cost management efforts range from bankwide to departmental levels, activities may overlap, making the costing measurement process, which is essential to effective management, more complex. Individual responsibility for different areas of effort or different projects must be identified. Examples of clearly delineated areas of responsibility include:

- Bankwide
- Each affiliate
- Customer service
- Human resources
- Investor relations
- Consumer loans
- Mortgage loans
- Branch banking
- Small business lending
- Trust
- Auto loans

Organization

Proper organization is important to effective cost management. The right organizational structures will facilitate proper deployment of resources and help optimize cost efficiencies. Clear organizational structures and clear lines of authority and responsibility are necessary for an effective cost-reduction program. Without them, one cannot pinpoint accountability.

Action Plans

Action plans are the guides that allow management to understand the implications of the proposed cost-containment effort and its progress. They must be concise, practical, and clearly outline individual and time accountability. Following are some important components of an action plan:

- Tasks
- Milestones and respective dates
- Individual responsibility
- Anticipated results/benefits
- Required resources/investments

Such action plans can be used by senior management to prioritize objectives and actions as well as to develop a monitoring device for cost containment progress.

Communications and Control

Cost management, like other bankwide initiatives, depends on effective cooperation and resource sharing; hence, communication is key to success. Senior management should specify requirements for cooperation and goal attainment to ensure that all employees are moving in the same direction and working together to maximize cost efficiencies throughout the system and across the board.

Cost Measurement and Reporting

One needs to know how much activities cost in order to accurately assess product profitability. Reams have been written on costing. Below is a brief description of the process.

The costing process is composed of five basic steps:

1. *Define the purpose.* The purpose of cost measurement will determine the level of depth and the methodology to be uti-

Memorandum
To: Management
Re: Project $1 Million

Corporate senior management will be introducing Project $1 Million to all bank employees. This project is an attempt to encourage all employees to submit ideas for cost savings with a goal of identifying $1 million reduced costs by December 1993. In order for our bank to achieve the goal, we need your support of this project. Project $1 Million's success depends on you to motivate your team. We need our bank leaders like you to challenge and encourage members of the team to think about and submit ideas. As a role model, you can set an example of controlling expenses and generating ideas to decrease costs.

- Any employee may participate.
- To submit an entry, an employee should complete a Project $1 Million form (Figure 5.2) and send it to Jim in cost accounting.
- All ideas submitted will be reviewed for approval by the Advisory Committee.
- Any idea that is approved will be assigned to a sponsor from Corporate Services Group who will implement the idea.
- Ideas that do not qualify for Project $1 Million will be submitted to the appropriate Ideas Count Committee.

The Project $1 Million Committee seeks ideas which save significant amounts of money. The more money the idea saves, the higher the reward to the employee who submitted the idea.

Some general questions to direct your team members' thoughts and help them identify specific ways that our bank can save money are listed below. Please use them as you deem appropriate:

- Are expenses or tasks duplicated when they could be shared?
- Are procedures performed or reports generated unnecessarily?
- How could total costs be reduced by automation?
- How could space be better utilized or procedures be changed to increase efficiency or production?
- How could vendor or customer service costs be reduced?
- How could inter- and intra-departmental cross-training be maximized so that work flow can continue during peak periods, illness and vacation with a minimal amount of additional part-time/overtime expenses? [This is where service level requirements are superimposed on the cost initiative.]

The following are some general classes of ideas which probably will not be accepted:

- Increase in existing fee or service charge.
- Non-specific ideas, such as reduce overhead.
- Changes to the organizational structure.

Remember, a small savings by each employee will add up to a material savings overall. Thank you again for your support. If you have any questions regarding the project criteria incentive, please call. We look forward to your great ideas.

This memo was submitted to all bank presidents and department heads. Another memo followed to all bank employees:

The April issue of the United States Banker lists our bank as one of American's 60 most profitable banks. This is a great tribute to the effort and dedication of all our employees. However, to remain a high-performing bank, we must continue to seek opportunities for improvement. As described below, we have established a corporate goal to reduce expenses by $1 million annually. To accomplish this, we are introducing Project $1 Million in which we are asking all employees to consider how the company can reduce or eliminate costs without adversely affecting our customers or employees [i.e., within the supercommunity bank context.] Project $1 Million is different from Ideas Count in that it is a corporate-wide project with a defined monetary goal to be reached within a specific timeframe. The purpose of Project $1 Million is to:

- Make our company more competitive by decreasing operating costs.
- Increase shareholder value.
- Respond to the employee opinion survey concern regarding cost control.
- Recognize and reward employees for contributions.

The Project $1 Million Plan:

Goal: Identify ideas to decrease annual expenses by $1 million. Who? All bank and corporate employees? When? Now to December 31. How? Complete and submit a Project $1 Million idea form to Jim in Corporate Accounting. Incentive? Special incentives for qualified Project $1 million ideas.

Incentive Schedule:

Size	Ideas Count	Project $1 Million	Total Incentive
$0 to $9,999	$100	$-0-	$100
$10,000 to $19,999	$100	$200	$300
$20,000 to $29,999	$100	$300	$400
$30,000 to $39,999	$100	$400	$500
$40,000 to $49,999	$100	$500	$600
$50,000 Plus	$100	$600	$700

We look forward to reviewing your ideas. In closing, we again want to express our thanks for your fine efforts and commitment to our bank.

lized. If the objective is to analyze alternatives or to communicate plans, precision in costing is less important. On the other hand, when costing is used to measure results, precision is critical. Examples of purpose definition include:

- Considering alternative uses of excess funds.
- Most effectively using MIS budget.
- Measuring profitability of lending function.
- Measuring profitability of each branch.

FIGURE 5.2 Project $1 Million Idea Form

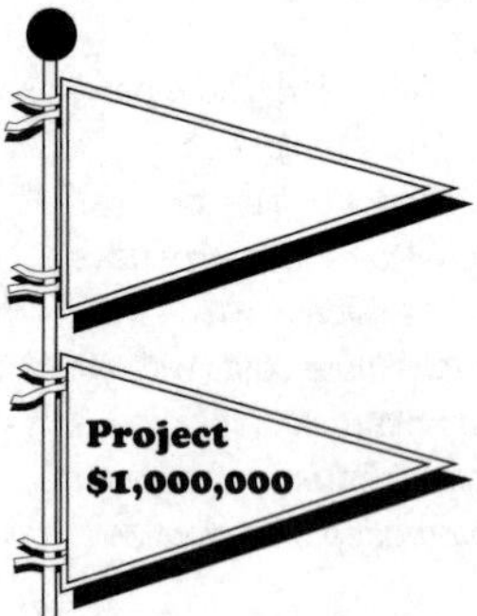

Please Review the criteria for PROJECT $1,000,000 and complete the questions below. Completed forms should be submitted to Jim in Corporate Accounting. If you have any questions, please call ext. 9341.

Project $1,000,000

CRITERIA:

- Specific and Identifiable
- Reasonably Measurable
- Approved and Date Established for Implementation

Name _____   Bank/Department _____

Estimated Savings _____   Your phone number _____

Summarize your suggestion _____

_____

Explain how your suggestion will reduce expenses for First Michigan Bank Corporation. _____

_____

_____

_____

_____

_____

_____

My foregoing suggestion is submitted for consideration under the terms and conditiond of the program. I understand and agree that upon submission this suggestion and all ideas embodied will become the exculsive property the Bawr. I also agree that the advisory committee has the sole responsibility of approving ideas and awarding the incentives

Date Received   _____

Suggestion Number   _____

Signature _____

* Please attach any calculations you made to estimate the savings. Estimated savings are subject to review and verification.

FIGURE 5.3 Costing Object: Credit Card

		PURPOSE						
		Expand	Contract	Add	Drop	Determine Profitability	Evaluate Prices	Control by Center
COST GROUP	Costs added	X		X				
	Cost eliminated		X		X			
	Directly related costs						X	X
	Allocated portion of cost of EDP or other bank services used						X	X
	Allocated portion of general overhead						X	
	Controllable expenses							X

FIGURE 5.4 Define Object

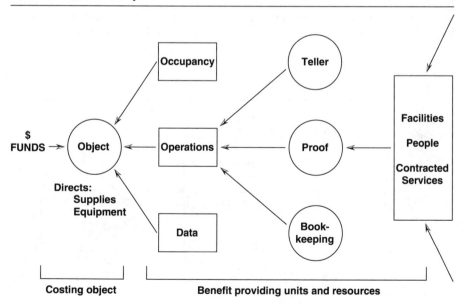

Costing object   Benefit providing units and resources

FIGURE 5.5 Eliminate Irrelevant Facts

Purpose	Object	Data	Relevancy
Decide to close branch	Branch	Rental cost	Relevant
Decide to close	Branch	President's salary	Irrelevant
Decide to open branch	Branch	Head office proof cost	Relevant incremental add-on

2. *Define the costing object.* Having defined the objective, one must define the costing object. An example of a definition is provided in Figure 5.3, which uses a credit card as a costing object. That is a fairly complex costing objective. It involves funds, people, facilities, and resources. On the other hand, an ATM machine is a very simple costing object. The simple elements associated with it are the model, size, power, and speed. Figure 5.4 outlines the process by which an object for costing can be defined.

3. *Specify the Data.* In order to cost, one needs information. Identify the data from the resources that make up the costing object. Identify the sources of data, screen out the irrelevant data, and determine the degree of precision required. For example, when interest on deposits is under evaluation, small changes result in big changes in the cost of funds. On the other hand, pencil expenses are such that a 100% error would not change the decision in any significant way. An example of eliminating irrelevant factors is provided in Figure 5.5.

FIGURE 5.6 Allocation Flow

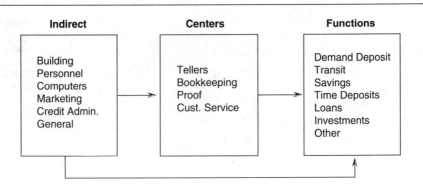

4. *Determine the Allocation Process.* The cost allocation process is key to effective cost measurement and subject to much debate. Internally, cost allocation is a real issue in supercommunity banks, where subsidiaries invariably bemoan the excessive allocations from the holding company. Consequently, a precise allocation process is helpful in alleviating internal disagreements.

The allocation process needs to accomplish the following:

- Determine the basis for cost (such as area occupied, transactions handled, or time spent).
- Determine transfer units (such as square feet, transaction, person hours, or loans).
- Determine the method, such as direct, compound, or complex. An example of an allocation flow is presented in Figures 5.6 and 5.7.

5. *Calculate and Report.* Measuring activities is a tougher proposition because it is less specific. One needs to define the units of measurement as well as the methods of counting and the measurement process that will allow the bank to associate time with activities. Activity units could be highly specific or more general. The first one should measure only significant activities. For example, in a teller situation, perhaps counting cash should not be measured, but taking deposits should be. Second, activities should be susceptible to measurement. For example, the difficulty of phone inquiry or ease of withdrawal are tougher to measure. Different methods of counting are presented in Figure 5.8.

Once the cost of activities and objects have been measured, the cost performance needs to be assessed; cost by itself is less relevant. This concept is of particular importance to supercommunity banks,

FIGURE 5-7 Allocation Calculations

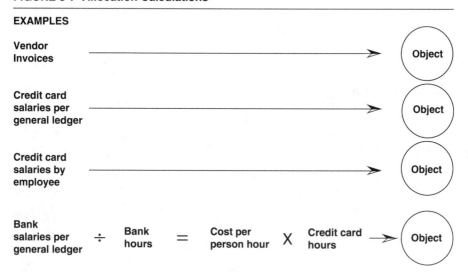

FIGURE 5.8 Methods of Counting

- First and last in sequence
- Length of adding machine tape
- Counters attached to machines (proof, microfilm)
- Hand counters
- Height of document stacks
- Weight of documents
- Logs and tallies

where certain costs (e.g., subsidiary bank presidents and boards) produce revenues that significantly outweigh the expenses. Revenue-producing costs should not be cut if the revenue exceeds the cost to produce an acceptable return on equity. Remember, it is cost in relation to revenues that counts.

Cost management is designed to accomplish these objectives:

1. *Maximize the use of resources* as depicted in Figure 5.9. In other words, the resources themselves should be used in the most efficient and effective manner. Total quality management and re-engineering are designed to do that.

2. *Minimize resource cost.* Figure 5.10 depicts the alternatives of minimizing the resource cost. The easiest way to reduce resource costs is to cut the resources themselves. However, strategic cost management goes beyond that. The idea is to change both the location and the slope of the cost curve, as depicted in Figure 5.11. Changing of the slope (efficiency) and location (amount of resources invested) of the curve is what reengineering is all about. Strategic cost cutting is designed to achieve sustainable cost efficiencies without mortgaging the future or penalizing profitability. For example, changing location of the curve can be accomplished through technology, which can affect a one-time permanent change. Technology can also be used to change the location of the curve by permanently changing the way things are done to make the same process more efficient and less costly.

FIGURE 5.9 Maximizing Use of Resources

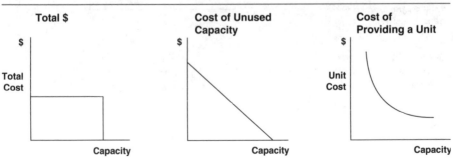

FIGURE 5.10 Minimizing Resource Cost

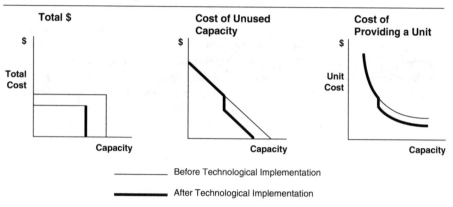

——————— Before Technological Implementation

————— After Technological Implementation

Downsizing is another alternative that uses only the concept of reducing resources in order to reduce resource costs. Re-engineering, on the other hand, is designed to improve cost performance within the same cost structure, or to maintain performance levels within a reduced cost structure (changing the slope of the curve).

Re-engineering is a creative, expansive, and difficult process to implement. Occasionally, it can get too tough, expensive, impractical, painful, or scary. When that happens, one can use incremental change to bring about an effective, albeit partial, cost reduction. However, even when incremental and smaller strategic cost-reduction efforts are undertaken, a strategic perspective is essential to achieve sustainable results in cost management.

FIGURE 5.11 Technology Can Change the Location and Slope of the Curves

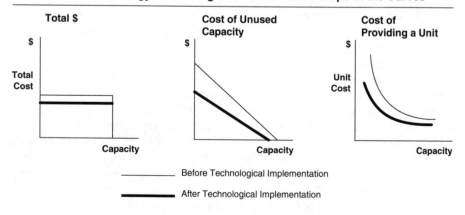

——————— Before Technological Implementation

————— After Technological Implementation

Six Points to Keep in Mind

Creating an effective, strategic cost-reduction program requires that you do the following:

1. *Start early.* The process is going to be difficult and require change. Anticipating change allows for less friction by carefully preparing for bringing about that change. Being reactionary and respon-

---

Using a successful affiliate as an example and a leader for others to follow is an effective way to bring the supercommunity bank concept to bear.

---

sive is not as effective as being pro-active. Therefore, initiate the process before problems occur. Whatever you do, fix it right the first time.

2. *Take the long view.* Making a strategic change takes a long time. If you expect results right away, you are setting yourself up for failure. Immediate payback is not going to take place. Also, short-term, quick-fix solutions may not be the best. Structural solutions, despite taking longer to implement, are more likely to bring you a better return on your investment. Employees and management alike will need time for training and adjustment. Give them that time.

3. *Take the bankwide view.* Look at cost savings locally by subsidiary, department, task, or project, but act globally, using the concept that the whole should be greater than the sum of the parts. Examine closely the impact of changes in other departments and banks resulting from improvements in one particular unit. Using a successful affiliate as an example and a leader for others to follow is an effective way to bring the supercommunity bank concept to bear. Using an idea generated in one area that created cost savings all across the board will help bring about not only consistency, but also greater cost efficiencies throughout the system.

4. *Look outside, not only inside.* Examine the cost structures of your competitors and other supercommunity banks. Do not try to be the low-cost provider of a service if you cannot hope to compete in a commoditized fashion or when it is clearly inconsistent within the supercommunity bank's strategy. It does not make sense to cut to the bone when cost is not a competitive variable. This is particularly true for supercommunity banks. They need to set their sights on enhancing strengths, raising customer service levels, and improving overall performance through revenue enhancement. Cost reduction is important to impose discipline and figure out the smarter way of doing things, not as a way to achieve unachievable volume savings off the core business of community banking.

Volume savings and low-cost production *can* be achieved in those product lines that a supercommunity bank may roll out beyond its franchise to add fee income. Many supercommunity banks outperform their peers by having a single product or a couple of products that they use as revenue enhancers, such as correspondent banking, data processing, trust services, indirect auto lending, credit cards, and so on. In those segments of the business, the low-cost production philosophy prevails.

5. *Prioritize projects and track results.* Carefully pick the projects to invest in. Look at the cost, savings, and strategic impact of the alternative cost-reduction projects. Once you select the projects, use the action plans to monitor the results and demonstrate your interest in them regularly. Ask questions, talk to the people in charge, and raise the subject in management meetings.

6. *Pick an Effective Team.* Effective re-engineering depends on picking an effective team. Pick a team made up of representatives from all disciplinary areas to be affected: I recommend the following:

- Pick a visionary to plan the project.
- Pick a technician to design the project.
- Pick a manager to implement the project.
- Pick a systems person or a staff person to monitor the project.

To make re-engineering effective, the following "to do's" will help:

- Look at the old rules and question them.
- Organize around outcomes, not tasks.
- Choose those who use the output of the process to perform the process.
- Incorporate information-processing work into the real work that produces information.
- Treat geographically disbursed resources as though they were centralized.
- Link parallel structures.
- Put the decision point where the work is performed and build controls into the process.

Re-engineering is a fancy word to describe a simple task—figuring out how to do things better. The advantages are many. Through re-engineering, you will achieve sustainable results, more efficient resource usage, and high rewards in terms of enhanced profits. The disadvantages are significant as well. Re-engineering is a costly project in terms of money, management time, and frustration level, and it is difficult to implement. However, those who have done so effectively have not questioned the payback.

The first rule of re-engineering is to question all the old rules. For example, traditionally, credit decisions were made by the lending department utilizing several people. At a local level, lending officers were needed to provide good customer service and make the credit decisions. Forms had to be filled out completely, then circulated among several decision makers to ensure credit quality and process control. *If you organize the work around outcomes, not tasks,* one person could perform all the tasks and steps. The local loan officer, who is still the best person to make the lending decision and sale, can handle the loan applications through an expert system using imaging and a single point of entry. The expert system is used to clone decision capabilities and implement controls without physical proximity.

Bear in mind that special centralized departments typically encourage building a bureaucracy—something we all want to avoid. This expert system for loan applications can treat geographically dispersed resources as though they were centralized. Loans are booked locally at the point of entry, but the applications are moved elec-

FIGURE 5.12 Profile of Portfolio of Activities

Typical Portfolio of Activities in a Staff Area

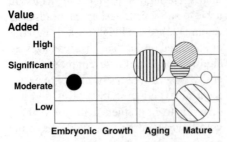

Diameter = $ expended

Most staff expenditures are typically for mature activities that are considered to be valuable. (This is a kind of ratings inflation.)

tronically with image processing to another location where credit controls are being imposed if necessary. This is a useful feature for supercommunity banks where credit consistency and quality may be perceived as in conflict with local decision making. Such a system can effectively satisfy both needs and at a lower cost, too.

Another way of making size and geographic dispersement transparent is to put signature cards on an imaging system, which will make the signature cards available to all and make the supercommunity bank's affiliates and branches capable of cashing checks for customers of other banks and branches within the holding company (state laws permitting).

Flattening Organizational Structure

An important characteristic of re-engineering is putting the decision point where the work is being performed and building con-

trols around the process at that point. There is a difference between those who do and those who monitor. In the past, accountants, control staffs, and supervisors recorded and monitored work. Managers handled exceptions. This is not an effective structure. Flattening the organizational structure is a partial solution while controls are being built into the process. The supercommunity bank structure is a personification of this approach on an organization-wide basis.

When a supercommunity bank considers cost containment, the portfolio theory may be brought to bear. The bank has a series of products and services that range on the life cycle spectrum from embryonic to mature. The added value associated with these activities is also different, as depicted in Figure 5.12. As a business or activity matures, as depicted in Figure 5.13, size and investment are directly affected. For example, in a maturing product with moderate value added, training employees and reducing costs are an inappropriate strategy. It is time to prune, not to invest. Put the life cycle phase test to the products

FIGURE 5.13 Guidelines for Managing Problems

Value Added	Embryonic	Growth	Aging	Mature
High	Moderate Growth	Expand	Monitor	Reduce Size Consolidate
Significant	Monitor	Expand	Reduce Size Consolidate	Streamline
Moderate	Monitor	Monitor	Streamline	Prune
Low	Eliminate	Streamline	Prune	Eliminate

Business or Activity Maturity

offered, and use the result to focus your resources where you get the most bang for the buck.

Flattening the organizational pyramid has been in vogue in manufacturing industries for years. Manufacturing spends 23 cents of management salaries for every dollar of nonmanagement pay. Banks, on the other hand, spend 52 cents on management talent. Although banks may use more skilled employees, the opportunities for cost reduction through organizational flat-

---

*Supercommunity banks
add at least one layer
of management to
the organization in
order to stay close
to the customers.*

---

tening abound. Re-examining the span of control is one way to assess the viability of flattening the organizational structure.

Before one changes the span of control, one needs to examine the organization. What is the average span in your bank? Those areas where the span is very high or low need to be more closely examined. Try to justify each layer between profit-center level and first-line supervisor. Then evaluate each manager's situation and adjust. Supercommunity banks add at least one layer of management to the organization in order to stay close to the customers. The question is, notwithstanding that additional layer, are there flattening opportunities within the company that will help

remove the distance between the doer and servicer, the doer and the customer?

In summary, effective cost reduction and re-engineering must be strategic, with the commitment to change coming from the very top. Permanent change through re-engineering is a worthwhile investment, but expectations for quick payback will not be met. Re-engineering helps cut the cost of resources by increasing the efficiency with which they are used, not by cutting them.

Cost Cutting Tips

There are no such things as small ideas. Every dollar counts. Below is a list of twenty-one ideas that proved effective in other companies. Use them as mind ticklers to jog your thinking process and initiate an effective cost-reduction program.

1. Convert full-time positions to part-time positions. This improves capacity planning and reduces benefit expenses.
2. Change to a lower-cost health care provider.
3. Revise procedures to streamline branch operations.
4. Reduce medical benefit programs for future retirees.
5. Establish a schedule of employee contribution to costs of medical insurance.
6. Replace old phone system.
7. Centralize subscription renewals. Establish circulation lists in the library.
8. Renegotiate contracts for security systems (30% savings achieved elsewhere).
9. Establish an accountability PC-based system for telephone expenses based on usage and charged to departments.

TABLE 5.1 Summary of Profitability of Fund-Using Profit Areas

	Interest Income	Fees	Revenue From All Sources	Cost	Profit (Loss) Amount	Rank
Commercial Loans	$1,850,000		$1,850,000	$1,464,800	$385,200	1
Real Estate Loans	550,000	$30,000	580,000	526,000	54,000	4
Installment Loans	1,050,000	40,000	1,090,000	875,600	214,400	2
Credit Card	78,000	8,000	86,000	123,300	(37,300)	5
Other Loans and Investments	724,000	10,000	734,000	633,100	100,900	3
Total	$4,252,000	$88,000	$4,340,000	$3,622,800	$717,200	

10. Stop paying interest on non-account balances under $2,500.
11. Establish equipment maintenance contracts on a time-and-materials basis.
12. Install digital data lines to computer center.
13. Install on-line signature systems for tellers.
14. Automate accounts payable.
15. Produce ATM cards in-house.
16. Provide detailed analysis of branch costs to senior management and to branch personnel by branch.
17. Close inactive checking accounts after six months.
18. Charge higher research fees for inquiries.
19. Go outside immediate local markets to shop for products and vendor services.
20. Use a vendor who can presort statements prior to giving to post office. The four cents discount is shared, two cents to vendor and two cents to bank.
21. Use bar coding on statement mailers. It saves postage.

Measuring Profit Quality

Comparing quantitative information on profitability is important to assess the true quality, sustainability, and improvement potential of the profit. As Table 5.1 demonstrates, although credit cards yielded $86,000 of revenues the cost to administer them was so high, they were losing money. Further, as Table 5.2 indicates, although commercial loans yielded the highest dollar amounts, they did not yield the highest profitability percentage. Installment loans, while much smaller, yielded the highest profits. And credit cards lost money altogether. Analysis of the profitability quality indicates where further resources need to be invested, and it will only be accurate if the cost allocations are correct and accurately reflect capital and other costs allocated to the business.

TABLE 5.2 Profitability as Percent of Invested Funds

	Invested Funds	Interest Income %	Revenue From All Sources %	Cost %	Profit (Loss) Percent	Rank
Commercial Loans	$35,935,000	5.15	5.15	4.08	1.07	2
Real Estate Loans	11,681,000	4.71	4.96	4.50	.46	4
Installment Loans	19,299,000	5.44	5.65	4.54	1.11	1
Credit Card	1,022,000	7.63	8.41	12.06	(3.65)	5
Other Loans and Investments	19,603,000	3.69	3.74	3.23	.51	3
Total	$87,540,000	4.86	4.96	4.14	.82	

Outsourcing: An Idea Whose Time Has Come?

In today's banking environment, where further industry consolidation is almost a certainty, what is the role of outsourcing in enhancing a bank's competitive posture, especially for supercommunity banks where service is king? The tremendous overinvestment in technology and real estate that banks have made over the past decade (in 1991, an Ernst & Young survey found that U.S. banks had invested $200 billion in hardware and software technology) and the creation of megabanks (which presents cost efficiencies that are available to only the largest) raises the question: Does outsourcing play a more important role in the future of supercommunity banking?

Questioning is one of the reasons for existing as a supercommunity bank and is a basic survival skill. Banks now understand that sharper business focus and attention to the question of scale are strategic imperatives. Downsizing works for megabanks, but what about supercommunity banks? The answer is rightsizing and out-

sourcing. As Peter Drucker said (Forbes, Aug. 1990–91), "The period of being big is over (for most firms. . . .) This is the time to decide which size is best. Elephants have a hard time adapting, but cockroaches outlive everything."

This metaphor is quite appropriate when considering profitability. After a decade where every million instructions per second in the data center and every blip on the terminal costs less than the previous ones, and after investing hundreds of billions of dollars to place technology on every desk top, the banking industry still finds itself in a state of low productivity. Hence, the call for a whole new tool kit, including concepts such as outsourcing and re-engineering. These new tools are now a reality. Most banks cannot afford the capital investment required to scrap what they have and start over. Effective cost management depends on rightsizing what there is now and avoiding spending one's way to a position of competitive advantage. That advantage is a fleeting moment in time, as Chase found in its custody business.

Chase was the leader in global custody for years due to the foresight of its management and the investment of hundreds of millions of dollars in global custody technology. However, as the bank reached that position and created an effective entry barrier for itself and a position of leadership, Chase rested on its laurels and did not continue investment. While Chase was reaping the cash cow benefits of its global custody business, Morgan Stanley and State Street targeted global custody for strategic reasons unique to each company. They made the requisite investment and overcame Chase's entry barriers achieved through the sheer capital investment in technology. Chase was left in the dust as these two companies outspent Chase and eliminated its competitive advantage. The lesson to be learned is that capital investment in technology is not an effective way to create a competitive advantage. As supercommunity banks already know, customer service is one effective way to create such a barrier. However, supercommunity banks, like every other bank, need to consider costs in order to stay in the game. The way to success is to develop a productivity vision that will enhance cost performance and profitability. It can be developed along the following seven dimensions (Figure 5.14).

Smarter Marketing. Retaining one's most profitable customers and truncating others seems to be basic, but the fact is that banks and brokers have not done this very effectively in the past. There is plenty of evidence to indicate that financial service firms get most of their profits from long-term customers. Some new customers are true money losers. Knowing how to segment and instill discipline with the sales

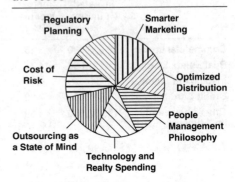

FIGURE 5.14 Productivity Risk for the 1990s

culture is key to success and financial services going forward, as well as cross-selling the customer base and acquiring attractive segments.

Optimized Distribution. Knowing and allocating one's fully loaded costs of product delivery are the starting points. (Appendix 5 offers two holding company cross-allocation methodologies especially designed for supercommunity banks.) Funneling more products and services through the system can reduce per unit costs significantly. Service quality becomes even more important because fewer mistakes mean less reworking, less management time, lower costs, and higher customer retention rates.

People Management Philosophy. Salaries and benefits, the largest non-interest expense on banks' income statements, are not considered a variable expense by many supercommunity banks. Although they wish to remain humane organizations (and should), the bottom line on salaries must be tied to business volumes and profitability. Compensation needs to be tied to performance and profitability at all levels of the work force, and benefit programs need to be downscaled as benefit costs rise. Employee retention is key to super-community banking, but it has to be based on performance.

Technology and Realty Spending. In the 1980s, there was significant overinvestment in bank technology and real estate. Not the temporary excess capacity, but permanently unneeded facilities in the form of hardware, software, communication networks, data centers, headquarters buildings, branches, and the people needed to manage this infrastructure were put on many banks' books. It is time to revisit this philosophy. Management and investment in technology and real estate can be significantly reduced using outsourcing and flattening of the organization to eliminate chief information officers, for example. Watch the net occupancy cost for employees. That ratio often varies by over 30% among banks in similar lines of business and cities. Those firms that built grand headquarters sites usually did so at the expense of future profits.

Outsourcing as a State of Mind. Almost no activity, whether operations, technology, origination, or certain types of distribution, must be retained in-house. The decision to outsource is a statement of one's willingness to try a different set of managerial tools. Outsourcing is no mere fad, but a permanent change that is reshaping the industry just like it did for manufacturing over the last twenty years. Toyota today produces only 30% of its needs in-house versus General Motors, which produces 70% internally. This statistic certainly enhanced Toyota's flexibility, customer service, and perceived value.

The decision to rely more heavily on external vendors should not rest on cost alone. Other benefits include greater management focus on strategic business issues, less operational complexity, and a tighter linkage between volume and expense—a pay-for-what-you-use approach. When a high efficiency player like NationsBank at $120 billion in assets turns its data processing over to an outsider (Perot Systems Corp.), we all better take notice and question why most banks have so far chosen not to. The reason, especially for super-community banks, is the need to control service levels and to ensure that customer interface is done in a mode consistent with the philosophy and the attitude of super-community banking. But outsourcing is not mutually exclusive with that concern. It can be accommodated through vendor partnerships and service agreements that specify quality expectations, performance benchmarks, and penalties for lack of performance. Think of outsourcing for a full range of activities, including internal audit, regulatory compliance, or loan review. Considering outsourcing will facilitate imposing market discipline on internal functions and increasing efficiencies, whether outsourced or retained in-house.

Cost of Risk. Risk management is a very important cost-control issue for all financial institutions going forward. It involves far more than control over credit and asset quality, although those are the most important nonnegotiables. The cost of risk has historically been managed in part by luck. As Robert Frost said, "Take care to sell your horse before he dies. The art of life is passing losses on." Innovative banking management attempts to forecast, allocate, and measure all costs associated with risk. A category such as actual and forecasted losses, insurance premiums, expenses associated with internal risk management, and its relevant control systems and the capital allocation to increased risk businesses needs to be better understood and managed. Even unlikely risks that involve disaster planning can be factored into a bank's strategy and measured as part of the overall cost of operations.

Regulatory Planning. Although we all recognize the burdens of regulation, not all banks have done enough to simplify the process for regulators, auditors, and others concerned with control and due diligence. Prepare for the regulators and make your systems as easily examined as possible. This will reduce the cost of your examination as well as the opportunity cost of regulatory criticism and resistance to mergers.

Summary

Cost methodologies and approaches abound. However, supercommunity banking presents unique challenges in cost cutting: How far can you cut without jeopardizing service levels? Which approaches are appropriate in a team-oriented, caring environment? Some of the important points for supercommunity banks to remember are:

- Cost structures and efficiency ratios of supercommunity banks need not exceed industry averages.
- Being a low-cost producer is an appropriate objective for supercommunity banks in volume-sensitive businesses, but not to the detriment of service levels.
- Fully understanding the cost structure is essential to accurate profitability assessment and resource allocation.

The productivity initiatives described above can help supercommunity banks enhance profitability through cost management. They are associated with a sharper focus, simpler organizational structure, and more efficient sizing for chosen businesses. These may result in cost improvements both at the holding company level and at the subsidiary level, and in the use of productivity enhancement and cost management as a profitability tool.

CHAPTER SIX

Broader Product Line

In order to compete effectively with national money centers and banks, supercommunity banks need to offer a product line that will fully meet their customers' needs, further anchor those customers to the bank, and build fee income. The key question is, of course, into which products should the supercommunity bank expand? The answer lies within the customer base. It is much more effective to offer a product to people who want to buy it. As the wise man said, "You can build the best mousetrap in the world, but in a miceless world that trap is not going to sell very well." Giving the customer what he or she wants is the secret to success.

**The Supercommunity Bank
Product Line Evolution
First Commercial Corporation**

First Commercial was established by a merger of Commercial National Bank of Little Rock and The First National Bank of Little Rock in July 1983. Like many other supercommunity banks, this was the core beginning. Today it is the lead bank of First Commercial Corporation (FCC), a $2.6 billion company. The bank has expanded its product line beyond the core business to enhance fee income opportunities as well as to create a competitive posture vis a vis other players in the market.

For one thing, the company's strategic plan incorporates the concept that a large and diverse funding base will ensure liquidity and profitability. To provide such a deposit base, the company has established an aggressive, innovative position in the consumer and correspondent bank markets that it serves. In addition, commercial banking services are available with equipment lease financing, and money market services are offered as an alternative to the traditional commercial banking services.

Of the 259 banks in Arkansas, 206 maintain a correspondent banking relationship with FCC. Services provided to correspondents by the company include complete data processing services, loan participations, money market investments, security safekeeping, check clearing services, and assistance with other banking functions. For example, the company sponsored the development of the Arkansas Cash Network, one of the first statewide networks of shared automated teller machines in the country. Customers of thirty-eight participating banks can make cash withdrawals at 128 ATMs in thirty-four Arkansas cities.

First Commercial also has a trust business. It offers personal and corporate trust services to all market segments through First Commercial Trust Company and its affiliates. As of December 31, 1992, the trust company was custodian for almost $6 billion in trust assets.

Another subsidiary is First Commercial Mortgage Company through which the company provides mortgage financing statewide. During 1992 the mortgage company acquired servicing rights to approximately $190 million in additional mortgage loans, bringing the servicing portfolio to $2.2 billion at year end. The mortgage company provides servicing for approximately 211 investors.

In summary, the product line of First Commercial includes the following:

- Core deposit services
- Core consumer loan services
- Core commercial banking services, not traditional banking services
- Aggressive consumer deposit products
- Correspondent banking
- Equipment leasing
- Money market services
- Corporate trust
- Personal trust
- Mortgage company

This product line is not atypical of supercommunity banks of First Commercial's size. Supercommunity banks typically start from a core margin business that is strong and high performing. They also often have a trust department with assets under management equal to or greater than the bank's assets. However, as the company grows and fully implements the supercommunity bank concept, the product line broadens as well. The purpose of broadening the product line is twofold:

- To fully anchor the customer, both commercial and retail
- To enhance fee income

Equipment leasing and money market services are examples of alternative products that were added to fully capture commercial customer business. The Arkansas Cash Network, on the other hand, is a product innovation designed to generate fee income as well as to augment the corresponding banking business. First Commercial has four major fee-income-producing services: trust, the cash network, mortgages services, and correspondent banking. The fee-income-producing services enhance the already strong core margin business to create a super performer.

Many supercommunity banks embark on a path of product expansion much like First Commercial. There are many opportunities, and the value of broadening the product line is tremendous. The selection is the difficult part: where to go for more fee income and for better meeting the customer needs.

The key to the answer is in identifying the customer needs and other market voids where the bank could capitalize. The answer to the product question, therefore, is very individualized and depends on the customer composition of each supercommunity bank, the competitive profile for each product in the marketplace, and the leverage point within the company (distribution network, expertise, and technological capability). The product evolution is not dissimilar from one supercommunity bank to another, however. Most companies start with a strong core margin business and a trust service. They then expand into one additional major fee-income-producing business. Some, like First Commercial and BankNorth, move into mortgage banking; others, like Bank Four and Synovus, move into credit card processing. Many choose correspondent banking, which is a leverage business that builds upon existing capabilities and has an additional side ben-

efit of getting close to other banks and identifying appropriate acquisition candidates. On the retail side, the trust department is often a springboard to mutual funds, management, and sales; leveraging equity management skills within the trust company; insurance; and annuity sales, another product expansion that is very popular in today's environment due to its intense profitability.

Let us examine in greater detail the fee income opportunities associated with one product family—mutual funds and annuities. The same analysis can be used to examine other business line opportunities that will help a supercommunity bank improve performance and fully implement the relationship-capturing strategy.

Mutual Funds and Annuities—An Example of Product Line Expansion

Supercommunity banks look for products and services to meet their primary customer bases, which often involve retail customers as well as small businesses in middle-market companies. The hottest products on many supercommunity banks' drawing boards are mutual funds and annuities.

There has been a 269% growth of investment assets such as mutual funds, but much less growth in nonbank sources of assets. This implies what we already know: there has been significant loss of deposits on the retail side of the business. These banks are vying for a position in the investment services segment of the business.

Speculation abounds that second-tier mutual funds will joint venture with banks to capture the market. Some believe that mutual funds and annuities are the biggest profit opportunity in the area of changing the mix of deposits and investments. At Marshall & Ilsley, for example, distribution of mutual funds is becoming increasingly important within and outside of the trust department. A dedicated sales force focuses on the distribution of complex securities such as mutual funds and annuities. The company opted for establishing the dedicated sales force because of the high percentage of problems that arose when selling these products was handled by branch staff, who could not successfully explain the products to the customers. Successful distribution of mutual funds and annuities has brought the following results to the banking industry:

Size of Bank	New funds (6 months)	New funds (2 years)	Net Contribution
$8 billion	45%	25%	$2 million
$8 billion	50%	25%	$4 million
$10 billion	60%	–	$15 million
$20 billion	60%	–	$5 million

When considering starting up in mutual funds, banks should assess entry attractiveness for five years out, because the market may very well become commoditized. If competition intensifies and some low-cost providers enter the market, profitability and a defensible market position may be difficult to achieve.

After years of resistance, many banks have begun to view fee income as a cornerstone of future profitability. That does not necessarily mean it would be a quick earnings fix. Although most supercommunity banks recognize the need to offer mutual

funds to reduce the risk of losing long-standing customer relationships, without the product, it is still unclear what the potential impact of alternative investment products on core deposits and earnings would be. Supercommunity banks need to offer mutual funds, at minimum, as a defensive move (Figure 6.1), as mutual funds eat into banks' share of the total U.S. household financial resources.

Our most recent supercommunity bank survey showed a widespread expectation of growth in alternative earning streams. For 1992, brokerage was listed only by 15% of the respondents as one of their three biggest income sources, and annuities by only 9%. But looking five years out, the supercommunity bankers' answers became more diversified. Trust was named by 80%, loans by 54%, transaction accounts 47%, annuities 39%, brokerage 28%, and insurance 24%. Why the optimism? As consumers become more financially sophisticated, they

FIGURE 6.1 A Big Bite

Sales of stock, bond, and money market funds, first six months of 1992

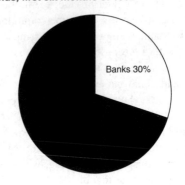

Banks 30%

Total = $1.347 trillion

FIGURE 6.2 Changes Expected in Income Stream

Services listed among top three income producers . . .		*. . . and what bankers project over the next five years*	
Transaction Accounts	81%	Trust	80%
Trust	78%	Loans	54%
Loans	78%	Transaction Accounts	47%
Brokerage	15%	Annuities	39%
Insurance	12%	Brokerage	28%
Annuities	9%	Insurance	24%

Sources: *American Banker;* BDO/Seidman 1992 survey of supercommunity bank executives.

are demanding a wider array of services than banks historically have offered. While brokerage houses and mutual fund providers have the product advantage, supercommunity banks own the customers. The vast majority of consumers at all income levels identify a depository institution as their primary financial institution, and research shows that they have more trust in the depository institution than in its competitors (Figure 6.2).

Supercommunity banks should be able to capitalize on that trust and loyalty more than other banking companies due to their relationship orientation. If they do so successfully, they will be able to earn mutual fund commissions of from 1%–5% of sales. The mutual fund business, with assets of more than $1.6 trillion by year end 1992, is expected to double or even triple by the end of the century. Although a well-designed program can have a contribution of as much as ten basis points on assets pretty quickly, some banks look at mutual funds and annuities as the "flavor of the month." They tend to overlook the need for a fundamental shift in their profitability dynamics.

The opportunities for supercommunity banks to look at mutual funds and annuities as a core product are significant, especially if they get the trust department and the retail branch network to work well together. The profit potential is enticing. In 1991, the pretax operating margins averaged 33% at eleven publicly traded mutual fund companies in a study done by Strategic Insight Company. Average return on equity was 2%. At the same time, we all recognize that banks are latecomers into a very competitive environment. Nevertheless, banks captured 14% of all mutual fund sales last year and 17% of sales in the first quarter of 1993. The potential for growth is clearly there.

Let's examine mutual funds and annuities from a customer need standpoint. The industry is witnessing changing markets and demographics. The baby boomers are aging; many are reluctant to be as credit-intensive as they were in the past and are moving into more of a savings orientation. At the same time, the current low-interest environment makes bank deposit products unattractive and lowers the opportunity cost of switching into a nonbank deposito-

FIGURE 6.3 Mutual Funds Growth

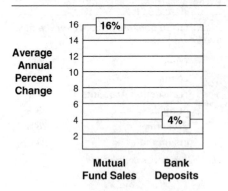

ry product, as many banks offer 2%–3% on the savings. Furthermore, baby boomers as savers are sophisticated individuals and are looking for varied financial products to put their money in. They are going beyond traditional investment products and seeking services such as annuities, mutual funds, municipal bonds, common stocks, and sweep accounts in an effort to seek diversification and create capital gains as well as an income stream.

Over the last five years, total mutual fund sales have grown at an average annual rate of 16%, while bank deposits have grown at an average annual rate of 4% (Figure 6.3). Banks are expected to take a significant share of that growth. Bank sales of mutual funds were at approximately $10 billion in 1990 and are expected to reach $40 billion by 1995 (Figure 6.4). Banks are already contributing to the sale of mutual funds as their CDs convert into funds. Between 1991 and 1992, more than $179 billion moved out of banking CDs, with approximately $100 billion of that going toward the mutual fund markets (Figure 6.5). Annuities provide a similar

picture. Bank sales of annuities have doubled in volume from 1987 to 1991 and are expected to grow to $40 billion in 1995 (Figure 6.6).

There are many benefits of introducing mutual funds and annuities. They generate more fee income and help the supercommunity bank expand the product line and strengthen the customer relationship. When a customer comes into the bank to close a CD, the bank improves its chances of capturing the money if it has in its quiver more arrows to better meet the customer's needs in the form of a variety of mutual funds.

These alternative investment products give the bank the opportunity to capture additional investment assets as well as attract new customers. This is especially relevant for supercommunity banks in aging markets where they find it difficult to attract younger customers, yet must do so in order to continue to infuse fresh blood into the customer base.

In addition, mutual funds and other alternative investment products also meet the customer needs by:

FIGURE 6.4 Bank Sales of Mutual Funds

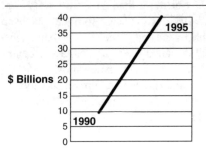

FIGURE 6.5 Bond CD Erosion

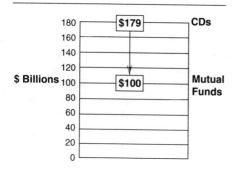

- Providing tax benefits
- Meeting a broader range of investment needs
- Offering safety of principal (secondary to FDIC insurance, but superior to more risky instruments)
- Supplying improved income stream/ higher returns
- Offering portfolio diversification
- Requiring a small initial investment
- Providing liquidity

As a supercommunity bank considers the introduction of mutual funds, it should bear in mind those benefits to the customer and look at that introduction as a customer service feature. There are several critical success factors associated with the introduction of mutual funds.

Senior management commitment. Much like in the other new product initiative, the interest of senior management in the product will make a tremendous difference in its success. If bank staff perceive senior management to be fully behind the introduction of alternative investment products, they will treat them as a high priority. Otherwise, they will revert back to a deposit-gathering mode and ignore the competing alternative investment products.

The sales culture. This is one of the tougher balances to meet. On the one hand, you want employees who are customer-needs oriented and who will not sell the customer products for which they have little use. On the other hand, you want to be able to expand the alternative investment products line, thereby meeting a broader range of customer needs. For that you need a discerning sales force that is both knowledgeable about the product and also able to problem solve and therefore capable of offering alternatives to customers that are in their best interest as well as in the best interest of the bank.

Product mix. The variety of mutual funds to be offered is important. The only way to know which is the right mix is to ask your customers. Include a survey with the introduction of alternative investment products so you will understand the customer's current investment behavior, perceived future investment needs, current service providers, what they like and don't like about them, and so on. By surveying

FIGURE 6.6 Bank Sales of Annuities

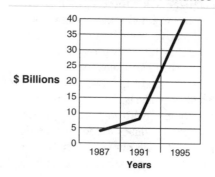

the customers, you not only pre-market them by informing them of your intent to offer alternative investment products, but you also find out what their preferences are in terms of product features, mutual fund types, marketing programs, delivery mechanisms, and so on.

Training. Your sales force must be educated. Mutual funds are not highly complex products, yet they require more

---

Your sales force must be educated. Mutual funds are not highly complex products, yet they require more knowledge than traditional deposit products.

---

knowledge than traditional deposit products. The sales force and all platform people should know what the funds do, how they are structured, the risks and benefits associated with them, and the answers to the ten most frequently asked questions by customers.

Cross-selling incentives. Your sales force, i.e., the branch network, as well as a specialized sales force (which is often associated with the sale of mutual funds), should receive incentives for performance. Although relationship orientation and meeting customer needs are the primary motivator behind the sale of alternative investment products, incentives are necessary to motivate effective sales personnel. If the bank continues to look for the right way to distribute mutual funds, the need for a sales force is undeniable, although

you want to avoid a sales force that behaves like a brokerage firm's sales force. You still need people who are motivated by closing transactions and whose compensation is dependent to a significant extent on incentives.

Delivery systems. There is an ongoing debate about whether the sale of alternative investment products can be effectively made through the existing distribution network or whether a dedicated sales force needs to be developed. Most successful companies do have a dedicated sales force at the initial product introduction stage. Many use third-party vendor sales forces to introduce the product. That helps create momentum for product sales as well as teaches bank personnel how proper sales are made. Once internal staff develops a good understanding of the sales process and the product features, the external sales force is gradually phased out. In a sense, this process allows the bank to piggyback on someone else's intellectual capital during the initial product introduction phase before it becomes incorporated into the day-to-day product sales.

Customer relationships and trust. A supercommunity bank is focused on customer relationships. That should not be forgotten by anyone who touches the customer, including the alternative investment product sales force. Customers still trust their primary depository institution more than any other financial institution, and certainly more than brokerage firms and mutual fund companies. Supercommunity banks should take great care not to abuse that trust and to continue to strive to fully meet the needs of their customers. Alternative investment products could be a double-edged sword. If the customer needs them, selling them to the customer is a service enhancement and a way to strengthen the customer relationship. However, if the customer does not perceive a need for them but is aggressively sold, that could threaten the customer relationship. Further, a poor product quality could significantly hurt the customer relationship.

We have so far seen the introduction of mutual funds only through a low-interest rate environment. Let's see how they make it through an 800 point drop in the Dow Jones. At that point, many customers will be disappointed. A bank should take care to anticipate such events and try to insulate the customer relationship from product performance. That is why, if the bank selects outside vendors for mutual funds and annuities (and the vast majority of supercommunity banks making product introductions will, given the critical mass considerations of a product introduction, which will be discussed later), vendors should be very carefully checked to ensure that the product quality is indeed superior and that the introduction of this product will not reduce overall customer satisfaction.

Proper pricing. Banks, especially supercommunity banks, tend to leave money on the table in the name of relationship maintenance. A tendency of many banks is not to fully account for the cost of providing the service to customers over time, especially in the trust department. Banks' pricing should be on a par with mutual funds, especially for supercommunity banks. These banks compete on relationships in service levels, not on price. Discounting is not necessarily the best way to achieve sustainable share. You can buy

shares for discounting, but it is also associated with price shoppers who will switch relationships for ten basis points just as easily as they switched into the bank for the initial discount. Supercommunity banks offer superior service and are relationship oriented. Most customers are prepared to pay for that; accordingly, supercommunity banks should not discount their services, including mutual funds, unnecessarily. This is not to imply that they should not be price-competitive, but they certainly should be on par with the competition.

Cost efficiencies. Mutual funds are a scale business. On the management side, it takes one person to manage a hundred thousand dollars worth of stocks or a hundred million dollars worth of stocks. The management side of mutual funds is therefore intensely scale sensitive. This is especially relevant to supercommunity banks that have strong trust departments with equity management capabilities. The capacity imbedded in these people can be leveraged to manage mutual funds, particularly if the common trust pools from the trust department are used as the basis to achieve a critical mass boost into the mutual funds. On the distribution side, leverage can be achieved either through an effective sales force that has geographic designation or through the branch distribution network. Many banks do not find current branch personnel the most effective way to sell mutual funds even when they are fairly advanced in the introduction of a sales culture into the system.

An effective solution that takes advantage of scale efficiencies is a centralized sales force where each salesperson has geographic responsibility for a cluster of branches. In major metropolitan areas where the branches are large, there might be one salesperson for three to five branches (when the branches have at least $100 million worth of deposits). In other areas where branch size is between $30 million and $60 million, typical sales coverage ranges between five and ten branches per salesperson. The importance of geographic designation is that the salesperson then becomes an integral part of the distribution network in that region and can effectively leverage the relationships represented by the branches in his or her territory. This is key to taking advantage of the supercommunity bank relationship orientation. It will not be effectively accomplished without close collaboration between the sales force and the branches.

The potential profitability of mutual funds is significant. A rule of thumb is that for every $100 million of retail deposits, you can expect sales of about $2 million and fee income of between $20,000 and $40,000 per $1 million in sales.

Distribution Alternatives

As one contemplates the introduction of alternative investment products, the three primary distribution alternatives are available.

Platform People

Figure 6.7 shows the advantages and disadvantages of using platform staff to market alternative investment products. By using platform staff, no incremental costs are incurred for product introduction—the ultimate leverage. Also, it allows for a strong linkage to customer relationships, which are represented through the bank staff. And it also facilitates the transition of platform personnel into a financial adviser role, thus more fully meeting the customer's needs. At the same time, there are some significant disadvantages. Many traditional bankers are simply not sales oriented and find it very difficult to change. Some are not convertible into the sales attitude necessary to be successful in the distribution of mutual funds and annuities. In addition, current personnel may not have the expertise needed to sell mutual funds and annuities, and not all can absorb the knowledge necessary to do so effectively. Typically, traditional branch people have been compensated for generating deposits. As a result, most retail distribution personnel are heavily deposit- oriented and resist the marketing of new products, especially when they are competing with their bread and butter, the deposit generation. Many are concerned about the impact of the sale of nontraditional investment products on their core business and are reluctant to sell it explicitly or implicitly. Last, branch per-

FIGURE 6.7 Using Your Platform Staff

Pluses	Minuses
Leverage	Often not sales oriented
Linkage to customer relationships	
	Expertise needed
Advisory role	Tendency to market more familiar products
	Relationship to product manager potentially problematic

FIGURE 6.8 Using Your Dedicated Sales Staff

Pluses	Minuses
Sales culture	Little leverage
Lead generation	Greater overhead
High motivation	Broker syndrome
Expertise	Linkage to overall
Commitment	relationship questionable

sonnel are branch oriented, not product oriented. As a result, their relationship to the product manager could be potentially problematic since it may require matrix management, which is not an effective way to manage within most supercommunity banks.

A Dedicated Sales Force

A dedicated sales force has many benefits associated with it (see Figure 6.8). The sales culture is already imbedded into the sales force, and they know how to go about selling a new product. The sales force is typically highly motivated and has the requisite expertise to sell the product. They know how to generate leads and go after the customer with a vengeance. Their commitment to the product is unwavering since their livelihood depends on it. The very benefits of a dedicated sales force represent the downfall of that mode of distribution. A dedicated sales force may turn into a transaction-oriented rather than relationship-oriented distribution vehicle, which is destructive to supercommunity banking and inconsistent with its fundamental philosophy. The salesperson may

be much more interested in churning the account and getting their commission than in the welfare of the customer. Just as it is difficult to convert branch staff into a sales force, it is difficult to convert sales people into relationship people. The downside of the transaction orientation is very significant in supercommunity banking, more so than in other types of banks. Finally, a dedicated sales force does not provide any leverage, and it represents overhead to the organization.

Third-Party Managed Program

As seen in Figure 6.9, third-party vendors have one major benefit: They reduce the uncertainty associated with the product introduction. They have effectively introduced mutual fund and annuity programs before and they have a track record. Therefore, start-up becomes an easier proposition than doing it all yourself. In addition, the start-up cost associated with product introduction is minimal, and the approach allows the supercommunity bank to piggyback on someone else's research

FIGURE 6.9 Third-Party Managed Programs

Pluses	Minuses
Minimal incremental cost	Lower profitability
Piggyback on someone else's experience and expertise	Little cross-selling of other bank products
	Broker mentality
Start-up easy	Separation from bank staff
Effective, proven	

and development expenses, experience, and expertise. The downside is that using an intermediary takes away some of the profits. It also makes it more difficult to be relationship oriented and cross-sell other bank products. The total separation from bank staff can reduce the cross-selling potential and increase the risk of a broker mentality, a nonnegotiable for supercommunity banks.

Which is the best approach for you? That depends on the extent to which you have successfully incorporated a sales culture throughout your supercommunity bank and their level of comfort with product features of alternative investment products. As already mentioned, many supercommunity banks opt to introduce the program with a third-party sales force working side by side with bank personnel and educating them so that a transition can take place within one year of product introduction.

Product Ownership Issues

Another structural issue is where to house and control the mutual funds. Most successful supercommunity banks that have mutual fund operations and other alternative investment products appoint a holding-company-level product champion who sponsors the product and provides technical support. At the same time, the ultimate control should rest with the retail side of the organization, consistent with the supercommunity banking approach. It is the product champion's job to mobilize the distribution power of the branch and affiliate network behind the product, and to create a cooperative team between his or her sales force and the CSRs throughout the

system. This is a significant challenge in many cases, since bank presidents do not want their branches to be treated as "space for rent" by different product managers at the holding company. A supportive incentive system, a corporate culture that fosters teamwork, and a strong CEO who stands behind product standardization and distribution are all helpful in achieving the delicate balance between product management and geographic or customer ownership.

The Use of Incentive Compensation

Incentive compensation is an important way to motivate employees to sell. But it could be devisive and have some negative implications to the relationship manage-

---

*The important factor
. . . is not how much you pay,
but the ability to use incentive
compensation to motivate without creating the mentality of a
commission-based sales force.*

---

ment so important to supercommunity banking. Some supercommunity banks pay little incentive compensation since they perceive they already have the captive customer base and, therefore, should not reward employees for cross-selling a relationship-oriented customer. In other words, it is not how much you pay, but the ability to use incentive compensation to motivate without creating the mentality of a commission-based sales force that becomes the ultimate goal. Incentive compensation is essential to transform the bank into a sales culture shop. At Norwest, for example, the bank has done this by using incentives as well as calling its branches "stores." Introduction of a sales culture is important to the future of supercommunity banks as they seek to anchor their relationship further. However, as incentive compensation is being used, it should be done with caution, trying to avoid the broker mentality and continuing to foster relationship orientation.

Marketing Mutual Funds

The following are among the key issues to be considered in the marketing of mutual funds, annuities, brokerage, and other alternative investment products:

1. Should the sales force be handled by specially trained bank employees, or by specialists employed by a third-party vendor or joint venture partner?
2. Should control of the sales force be centralized at the holding company level, regionalized, or handled by individual banks?
3. What should be the relationship between product managers and the business line managers?
4. How can you effectively encourage cross-referrals and cooperation between sales personnel and other bank personnel?
5. What is the most effective way to ensure that compliance issues are handled completely and correctly?

Many banks use third-party partners and use the geographic cluster assignment as an effective way to introduce mutual funds. The sales can then become an important measure of performance, especially when there is some fear that the sales force would aggressively take business away from deposit products. In many cases, this fear has proved to be unfounded because the incentive systems help encourage teamwork. Other banks developed their own dedicated sales force after starting with a third-party partner. In some companies, the sales force reports to the capital markets area, which makes it difficult to ensure that the subsidiaries will still have referral control.

Affiliate banks do not like to be perceived as "space for rent." They want some say in who distributes what within their market area and to their customer base. The supercommunity bank does not want to deny the affiliates that control, at least to some extent, because their relationship orientation is an important ingredient in the strategic direction of the company. At the same time, they need to cooperate when a corporate-wide initiative is launched, especially with the introduction of new products.

One bank found an effective solution to that tension by shifting deposit-generating branch managers into net worth managers, and measuring their effectiveness by the total assets brought into the branch, rather than deposit products only. In addition, the bank required the sales force to cross-refer business to the branches, not only the other way around. This reciprocity was important to enhance the linkage between the two in order to maximize customer relationships. At another bank, compensation and incentives are controlled at the subsidiary bank

level. The bank presidents have the autonomy to manage their sales force, and it is up
to them to fully meet the customers' needs
with broader product lines. To do so effectively, a dedicated sales force was developed through a security subsidiary of the
bank. The salespeople are employees of the
security subsidiary, but they report to the
individual bank presidents, thereby ensuring local control over their activities and
enhancing the likelihood of cross-selling.
The sales force distributes a host of alternative investment products ranging from
annuities to securities.

Yet another bank split the product line
between simple and complex products.
The branch personnel sells the simpler
product line, including annuities, CDs,
Treasuries, and money market funds. The
complex products are sold through a dedicated sales force with the support of a
product manager at the holding company
level.

Although there is no one right way to
introduce alternative investment products
to supercommunity banks, the experience
of the companies described above may be
helpful in identifying an appropriate path

Concerns About Liability

Among the concerns associated with the
introduction of non-traditional investment
products is the sense that fund sales, while
profitable, are not in the best interest of
bank customers. Some suggest that banks
have been preying on unsuspecting consumers by making misleading claims
about the safety and return potential of
these products. Many customers do not
realize that when they buy mutual funds

they expose themselves to capital reduction during downturn times. The concern is
that banks have created a customer satisfaction together with a financial liability
time bomb that will be triggered by the
next severe downturn in capital markets.
While one may focus on the potential
downside of this product introduction, one
should not neglect to examine the potential
value mutual funds and other alternative
investment products can add to the bank's
relationship with its customers based on

---

*The concern is that banks have
created a customer satisfaction
together with a financial
liability time bomb that will be
triggered by the next severe
downturn in capital markets.*

---

the ability of these investment products to
enhance the consumer's overall financial
well-being.

One way to allay the fear of liabilities is
to aggressively manage the compliance
process to protect both the customers and
the institution from unnecessary risk while,
at the same time, increasing sales effectiveness. Mutual funds provide individual
customers, first-time investors, and small
savers access to features such as diversification, professional management, liquidity,
and other features that otherwise might not
be available to them.

When considering regulatory compliance and meeting customer needs at the
same time, new account opening guidelines and suitability tests for specific

investments are insufficient. Super-community banks should go beyond the routine securities industry practices and face a higher standard. Customers often assume FDIC insurance on the funds, especially for a bank's proprietary funds, which are sometimes confused with bank deposits. In order to avoid customer dissatisfaction with the bank's investment services during downturn times in a way that will damage the broader banking relationship, certain steps can be taken:

- *Educate your bankers on effective customer profiling and referral techniques.* Personal bankers often have in-depth knowledge of the customer's financial position and sophistication given their long-standing relationship. They are in an ideal position to prequalify mutual fund prospects from both a sales and an initial suitability prospective without crossing regulatory boundaries and engaging in securities sales. Some banks train their CSRs in making investment referrals with a strong emphasis on profiling customer needs and assessing previous investment experience. While final responsibility for suitability will always rest with licensed specialists, the personal bankers are the first line of defense.
- *Document and make appropriate disclosures during the sales process.* Customer financial information, often already available within the bank, should be documented as part of the sales process. Certain items associated with the sale must be acknowledged up front and in writing by the customer. The most important items include the

absence of deposit insurance, the potential for price fluctuation and loss of principal, and a review of the sales loads, especially bank and/or contingent deferred charges. Although product disclosure can be disruptive, it can be used as an educational tool as well as a compliance activity and become an integral part of the sales process.

- *Create an actively managed and approved fund list.* Many banks sell too many funds from too many funds companies. The institutions that hire experienced investment sales staff from the outside often allow them to bring their product and vendor preferences with them. As a result, a bank's fund offering can be too broad and potentially uneven in quality. An approved fund list should be created and updated periodically. Outside evaluation services can be employed to track investment performance and asset composition of the funds sold through the bank. Fund management fees, loan structures, and exchange privileges deserve special attention, and effort can be made to identify funds that are more appropriate for a relationship-oriented bank environment. For example, bond funds that consciously manage for current income and stable net asset value, as opposed to total return funds, will reduce the potential for customer dissatisfaction due to principal loss. A bank's proprietary funds must measure up as well.
- *Test your sales force.* Use mystery shoppers posing as unsophisticated investors to test the branches and the sales force with a hypothetical invest-

ment opportunity. Test answers to sensitive issues such as deposit insurance and sales charges.

Product Offering Risk

There are risks associated with the offering of alternative investment products beyond the ones already described. In annuities, for example, vendor failure is a primary risk. Banks that offered annuities underwritten and managed by Executive Life faced many irate customers who lost their life savings with the demise of the company. Other risks, such as potential bank liability and the intensive competition, have been addressed above but should not be neglected. Managing those risks should become an integral part of the management of this product introduction.

Another risk very much on the minds of bankers is the displacement of the deposit base. There is a perception that significant cannibalization of the deposit base takes place when mutual funds and annuities are introduced. Experience indicates that although some disintermediation does occur, it is fairly limited and rarely exceeds 15%. Typically, within the first six months, 80% of the funds brought in will represent new money. As time goes by, that figure declines to 25–40% within two years. The decline in deposit funds is often temporary, and dollars shifted from CDs to mutual funds are replaced by a deposit reflow within 6–12 months, netting an increase in total investment assets for the bank.

Customers shift funds between deposit instruments and other investment products within the bank once they establish both accounts. This is because customers do not perceive all money to be direct substitutes until refundable. Every deposit product and investment product has features associated with it, which, in the customer's mind, imply a different bucket of liquidity. For example, all customers want to keep a certain amount of money in a totally liquid and safe state. They put the money in an FDIC-insured checking account. Some want to get a modest return on liquidity, therefore putting the money in a money market account or in money market funds, although a portion of the liquid funds will

---

Customers' risk propensity and the need for capital gains versus current earnings change as they get older.

---

go to a money market fund because of the different safety perception associated with funds relative to FDIC-insured products. Shifting to the next bucket in many customers' investment pool will typically involve funds that give a superior return and though frozen for a certain period of time also have superior safety features. Those monies are allocated toward CDs.

Additional buckets with high-risk, high-return profiles are also allocated within every customer's investment pool. These can range from stocks, bonds, and stock and bond funds to high growth funds, options, futures, and so on. Each product has its own risk/return profile. For example, many people have funds they are prepared to lose, in which they invest in high-risk, high-return instruments such as options or small business, high-growth funds. Customers' risk propensity and the need for capital gains versus current earnings change as they get older. A 28-year-old couple will require much less current income but are prepared to take a risk on capital appreciation. A preretirement couple, on the other hand, will try to strike a much better balance between current income and capital gains through expansion of their stock and bond portfolio and reduction of their high-risk, high-return portfolio. All this is by way of explaining why the introduction of alternative investment instruments does not necessary incur significant deposit cannibalization. Investment instruments are not direct substitutes; therefore, monies will not flow without limit from the deposit accounts to the investment products.

Yet another risk involves critical mass considerations. To profitably run a money market fund, you will need about $100 million in assets to break even. An esoteric fund can be as small as $25 to $30 million in assets. Fund management is profitable, but the price to be paid is high. Customers buy funds based on track record and performance, and brand new funds typically do not have that information. Therefore, the lag between start-up and critical mass achievement could be significant.

Other risks associated with mutual funds range from potential bank liability to the need for outside vendor involvement and the disintermediation of the deposit base, as discussed above. Due to these risks, some start-ups of internal fund management have failed, particularly due to the lack of investment track record. But those that have introduced the product successfully generate significant bottom-line profits. A $10 billion supercommunity thrift, for example, generated $18 million in fees in 1992 using existing branch staff as a sales force.

One way to reduce the risk associated with third parties in mutual funds and annuities is to carefully select the vendor partner. The following are some of the vendor selection criteria in annuities:

• Publicly traded
• Rated
• Diversified investment portfolio
• Good asset liability management

In mutual funds, vendor criteria include the following:

• Reputation
• Financial strength
• Broad product offering
• Training in management support
• Performance track record
• Compliance track record

The pitfalls associated with the introduction of alternative investment products could range from lack of full commitment from senior management, ineffective leverage of the distribution system, insufficient pool to achieve critical mass, or weak investment management skills, to the inability to leverage employees or customers.

To be successful, you need to do the following:

• Know the risk profile and product needs of the customer base.

- Ensure that critical mass achievement is feasible.
- Effectively leverage the customer base and distribution system.
- Retain a strong relationship orientation.

The Trust Business—Another Product Line Expansion Example

The trust business has grown dramatically over the past decade. Total trust assets have grown at an annual rate of nearly 28%, hitting $7.9 trillion in 1989. In contrast, bank assets have grown at only 9% yearly over the same ten-year period. Much of the trust growth has occurred on the institutional side of the business. After all, it's hard to pass up the fees involved when huge pension plans come calling. But as the institutional business continues to consolidate into the hands of fewer and fewer large players, more banks are turning their attention to the lucrative field of personal trusts.

The trust department has evolved into three distinct businesses. The heart of trust banking is personal trust, which provides individuals with services such as estate management with the trust department acting as fiduciary. The second business, corporate trust, provides custodianship and recordkeeping for bond issues. The third and newest portion of the trust business is the employee benefits or institutional segment. This has been the fastest growing of the three sectors, in part because of the huge assets managed by master trustees. A master trustee provides recordkeeping and custodial services for pension plans. Large pension plans usually employ several fund managers but only one master trustee. This is a highly computer-intensive business that has evolved to the point where the trustee not only keeps records but competes with other trustees to offer the most timely information in a format compatible with the performance-reporting criteria of the pension fund sponsor. Institutional business has become intensely competitive and less profitable. Over the last few years, Citicorp, Chemical Bank, Manufacturers Hanover, and First Chicago have sold all or part of the institutional asset management businesses. Many observers attribute these sales to the bank's need to build capital, but there is another explanation. A lot of banks got into institutional trust in the mid-1980s, but as pension funds became overfunded, price competition became fierce, and the business became unattractive.

Personal trust, on the other hand, continues to be a relationship-oriented business and lasts longer than institutional relationships. There are more opportunities to cross-sell banking services and products to retail bank customers, and profit margins for personal trusts are equal to or better than margins in the institutional business. Personal trust departments can also be used to manage mutual funds that are originated and distributed by third-party vendors. Some banks are also selling stocks and bonds through full-service brokerage units as well as discount brokerage units. These products often require expensive technology and highly paid portfolio managers.

The vehicle of trust banking is attractive to supercommunity banks of all sizes, but the bank size can also determine how it approaches the trust market given the economies of scale of the business. Size makes a difference, especially as more and more clients are demanding sophisticated investment products. If a bank is not big enough to support its own research staff and investment managers, it's going to have to hire a medallion. (A medallion is a separate investment subsidiary of another bank with its own chief executive officer and an investment style that offer various mutual funds—ranging from plain vanilla to index funds and global investment funds—to other trust departments.)

Many see mutual funds as the investments of the future even within the portfolio of trust departments. We are beginning to see a significant investment transition to asset allocation. It used to be that wealthy clients wanted to own portfolios of individual stocks, but they are beginning to see they can do much better if they own several mutual funds and use a trust officer to advise them on the allocation of their money among various types of funds. Here is a case in point.

In all likelihood, Banc One Texas would not have been able to enter the trust market as quickly and as cheaply were it not for the support of its parent company in Columbus, Ohio. When Banc One Corp. took over MCorp from the Federal Deposit Insurance Corporation in 1989, it received a bank stripped of its trust department, which had already been declared insolvent and had been sold to Ameritrust Corp of Cleveland (subsequently sold to Society). According to Richard Hart, who heads Banc One Texas Trust Division, the board never even considered running the bank without a trust department. "Not to have a trust department would be like not having

a couple of fingers. You can't tie customers closely without trust," says Hart.

Banc One Texas proceeded to utilize the supercommunity bank concept at its best. While Hart was working to position the bank's trust operations, Banc One Texas was able to get into the market quickly by using Banc One Indianapolis for back-office operations. Further, Banc One investment advisers were investment professionals. "We do not use common trust funds," says Hart. "They are dinosaurs." Instead, Banc One Texas uses the mutual funds managed in Indianapolis by Banc One investment advisers. Mutual funds react more quickly and are traded more frequently than common trust funds and can be a more flexible an investment tool for the customer. Banc One Texas provides, through its trust department, in-depth analysis of asset allocation strategies, which are then translated into a portfolio of mutual funds for each customer. To avoid "double dipping" the customer in management fees, Banc One's mutual funds unit waives the fees when the trust department is involved.

This is a perfect example of making the whole greater than the sum of the parts for supercommunity banking. Other supercommunity banks that do not have a deep-pocket parent like Banc One Corp. can still use the same principle to support their position in a competitive trust marketplace.

The trust business can be very profitable because it requires the least capital for every dollar of fee revenues, the least funding per dollar of revenues, and the least credit risk for every dollar of fee revenues in the banking business. By relying on return on assets and return on equity measures that banks use to analyze their other business for the trust department as well, bank managers and directors are comparing apples to oranges. To counter this, measuring trust department profitability can be done using net operating profit margin and return on required investment. The first measure is calculated by subtracting direct and indirect costs for total operating revenue and dividing the resulting profit by operating revenues. The second measure is more difficult. It is computed by capitalizing the investment in systems and other fixed costs and dividing this by after-tax net income. The profit margin measure not only puts the trust department on an equal field with other bank departments, it bridges the gap between banks in other types of businesses. With these measures in place, it is easier to scrutinize the various aspects of a bank's trust department. For reference, below are some benchmarks:

- Trust and estates range between 20% and 25% profit margins (estates are less profitable).
- Investment management and advisory services for individuals is the more profitable trust business, while employee benefits business is the least profitable, because competition is cutting fees and margins to buy share in this high-volume business.
- Recordkeeping, including master trust, is also a low-profit business, with margins in a 10% to 15% range.

- Other processing businesses, including custody, stock transfer, and bond recordkeeping, are quite profitable, with margins in the 30% to 50% range.

Since trust is a relationship-oriented business, it fits exceptionally well into the supercommunity banking strategy. It is enhanced by the scale economics of the business, which make it ideal for supercommunity banks. The service is offered by the individual banks in a relationship-oriented, high-touch, high-feel style, but the operations and processing are done in a centralized location, thereby taking advantage of the full asset range of the company. Not surprisingly, trust is typically the first fee income product line offered by supercommunity banks beyond the core margin business.

Summary

A broader product line is an important competitive advantage for supercommunity banks. A full product line will permit the bank to better meet a broader range of customer needs as well as generate fee income. The answer as to which products to incorporate and the best way to introduce them varies from bank to bank and from customer base to customer base. The key to successful introduction, however, is uniform and involves understanding the needs of customers and giving them what they want, with a strong backing from senior management.

CHAPTER SEVEN

Growth Through Acquisition

The banking industry in the United States is in the midst of a consolidation process driven by the need to reduce costs and create more efficient organizations. Supercommunity banking is one answer. It requires growth to succeed. The very formation of a supercommunity bank is the growth answer to any small community bank that realistically acknowledges it cannot make it on its own. The following examples illustrate the three ways a supercommunity bank can be formed:

- By a merger of equals of several large companies. Keystone is a prime example of such a bank. Its formation is described in Chapter 3.
- By the coming together of small banks into one large supercommunity bank.
- By the initiative of one small bank which sees the writing on the wall and recognizes a market void.

Florida Community Banks— Fifteen Small Banks Come Together to Form a Supercommunity Bank

With their stock prices stagnant, enticing few buyers, Central Florida community banks have mergers on their minds. Investment bankers have been telling them for more than a year that their stock would be worth more if they pooled their resources and formed bigger companies. In the banking business, market share is one major secret to profitability. A network of many banks is therefore worth more to a potential buyer than a small community bank with one or two offices. Fifteen small banks from Titusville to Tampa realized that supercommunity banking may be the answer to their stock illiquidity and share value woes, and are now talking about forming Florida's next $1 billion banking company.

The group is built around a core of five banks whose presidents have been meeting monthly (and boards, quarterly) to get to know one another and work out the logistics of forming a holding company to provide a single stock for all the banks. The five banks that have publicly declared their involvement are First National Bank of Osceola County, First National Bank of Polk County, Community National Bank of Pasco County, First Mercantile National Bank of Longwood, and the Bank of Tampa. None of the banks has been asked to put up any money yet, but each is expected to contribute about $20,000 to cover such costs as hiring an appraiser and a consultant to evaluate each bank and guide the deal through the regulatory process. The new supercommunity bank also has a trademarked name, Florida Community Banks, for the future holding company, and it would like to have the merger completed by the end of 1994.

The idea was hatched by James H. White, retired president of Flagship Banks, Inc., of Miami. Observers say his involvement is the glue that is likely to make this deal stick. A strong leader is needed to put the banks together and make them one company. Nine of the fifteen bank presidents worked for White as senior executives or presidents of Flagship subsidiary banks before the chain was sold to Sun Banks in 1984. Most consider him a mentor and are willing to defer to his judgment.

Within the group there is a camaraderie that dates back to the Flagship days when they were rising stars under White's leadership. The structure proposed by White would be very similar to Flagship's structure, a classic supercommunity bank, in which the holding company acts as a back office for a network of community banks. Sun Trust, the acquiror of this company, is also a supercommunity bank. Analysts also believe that White's ability to get the presidents to put aside their personal interests and work as a team will be vital. "It's an idea that a lot of us around the banking scene have kicked around for a while," says Tim Rayl, a bank analyst with Southeast Research Partners in Boca Raton, "but it always has to get down to a point where somebody has to be the boss and somebody's ego has gotten in the way of that. These bankers all know and respect Jim White and trust him. Clearly, you should negotiate with a colleague you trust. You may still want to be tough, but it makes the negotiations much easier."

At 67, White does not plan to run the company. He wants to adopt a mandatory retirement age of 65. He has picked A. Gerald Divers, Chief Executive Officer of the Bank of Tampa, to be president. The others have accepted that decision. "Jim is a natural leader," says Dennis Courson, President of First Seminole Bank and the former Flagship banker who is not involved in the merger talks. "Most of these people are people Jim hired in the beginning of their banking careers. They have worked together successfully before, and they share a mutual respect for each other personally and professionally."

Geoff Longstaff says he has dreamed of such a combination since he started the First Mercantile in 1988. He has kept in touch with White since Flagship and frequently turns to him for guidance. There are no promises, Longstaff said, but comparative analysis has led him to believe that if the holding company comes together as planned, First Mercantile shareholders will see their investment increase to as much as 1.5 times book value from its current range of .95 times 1.1 times book. With an estimated 7,500 shareholders, he said, he should be able to eliminate the existing list of sellers waiting for someone to buy their stock. "We can't commit the bank because obviously the shareholders have to do that," he said, "but our board has taken an action that says we think this is something we want to explore and we want to be involved in, and we don't mind having our name used in conjunction with it."

Supercommunity banking is indeed the answer to many community banks that realize they cannot weather the changing marketplace in their communities, and that believe that it is the answer to enhancement of shareholder value.

In the Flagship days, White circulated monthly reports of key financial ratios so that managers at each subsidiary bank could see where their numbers ranked in relation to their peers. Longstaff said the reports were a great resource and led to good-natured competition among bank presidents trying to rank highest in as many categories as possible. Bank One, for example, has adopted a rigorous financial reporting system and a shared information network of ranking as a major motivator for all 60-plus banks in their system. Each bank president gets a monthly list of all banks ranked by various performance categories. Obviously, no one wants to be last on the list. What has worked for Bank One may indeed work for other supercommunity banks, including de novo ones. Financial reports are already circulating among the fifteen proposed merger partners, and Longstaff said he can feel the old competitive instincts resurfacing. "We've already put out a couple of those reports, and I've got a ratio that's out of whack," Longstaff said. "I've called four of the other banks that have a better ratio, found out what they're doing, and we're going to see what we can do to fix our problem." This is precisely the value of shared information that holding companies can bring to the table to enhance individual bank performance within the affiliate system.

If the merger comes together, the ownership change would probably be invisible to many customers. The banks plan to keep their names. One difference: shareholders would own in the parent company instead of in the individual banks. Management plans to list the stock on the National Association of Securities Dealers Automated Quotation System (NASDAQ), which will free bank presidents from the delicate chore of brokering stock for shareholders and will increase the liquidity of the stock for current and prospective investors. Analysts say White's proposal offers managers a good way out of a stressful situation. The banks involved are all profitable but, alone, their growth prospects are limited. In addition to relieving pressure from shareholders anxious to sell, the combination would likely help the banks attract new management talent.

White says there are also cost-cutting opportunities. The holding company, for example, could hire one auditor for all its banks instead of each bank president having to recruit and pay for one of their own.

The holding company would also have leverage when it came to negotiating for office equipment and data processing services. This is one of the core premises on which supercommunity banking is based.

There is also a benefit for shareholders who choose to hang on to their stock. White cannot promise that the stock will increase in value, but it is a likely occurrence, as evidenced later on in this book. Other bank chains of similar size that are supercommunity banking oriented traded at much higher multiples than small banks or rolled-up, non-supercommunity banks. Further, shareholders benefit from enhanced stock liquidity in addition to the site and franchise value premiums typically associated with supercommunity banks.

Sterling Bankshares—a Small Bank's Initiative to Become a Supercommunity Bank

Sterling BancShares is a one-bank holding company, with roughly $200 million in assets, located in Houston, Texas (see Figure 7.1). Its primary asset is Sterling Bank, which has six community bank offices, serves in Northwest and West Houston markets, and is a firm believer in supercommunity banking. Even within the bank itself, a decentralized philosophy of banking reigns where the local offices have significant autonomy over credit pricing and other decisions. The management of Sterling Bank reached the conclusion that the long-term viability of the bank depends on its ability to grow. George Martinez, the CEO, envisioned building a supercommunity bank in the greater metropolitan Houston market, and the compa-

ny set out to do it in a very deliberate manner. They identified several banks within their market that would be good partners with Sterling as the foundation of a new supercommunity bank. They looked for strong performers that would not dilute Sterling's already strong performance (1.3% return on assets). And they looked for a bank with a compatible philosophy, and that was located within the target market—the great metropolitan Houston area.

Martinez realized that other major independent banks in Houston were sold to out-of-state acquirors during the banking crisis in Texas, which left a huge market vacuum that needed to be filled. In addition, his own shareholders did not have much liquidity to their stock, much like many other small banks. The solution? Capturing the market opportunity with a supercommunity bank. Martinez set out to find a merger partner. There were many benefits:

- A stronger combined entity
- Improved stock liquidity
- Enhanced profitability
- Operating efficiencies
- Opportunities for expansion to reach the necessary critical mass for the future

Martinez identified the benefits of the supercommunity bank concept and communicated the concept to his potential merger candidates. The broader product offering would allow the new company to leverage existing customer base and distribution networks as well as enhance fee income. The greater sophistication represented by the new products would create a

EXHIBIT 7.1 Sterling Bank

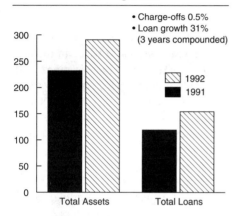

• Charge-offs 0.5%
• Loan growth 31%
(3 years compounded)

1992
1991

competitive advantage relative to other community bank competitors in the market. At the same time, cost savings opportunities would exist for the new entity through standardization of product offers further consolidation of functions, the use of technology across the system, and the concept of re-engineering.

Sterling Bank then described what it could bring to the table:

• Stock liquidity and dividend policy.
• Company stock privately traded on NASDAQ stock market, with average weekly trading of 43,000 shares.
• An annual dividend of 36 cents per share, paid quarterly.
• Independence. As a supercommunity bank, Sterling offered its merger partner the opportunity to keep their name and charter, the senior management team and board of directors, and decision-making authority.

• Economies of scale. Sterling already centralized functions such as data processing, bookkeeping, regulatory compliance, internal auditing, and investment portfolio management. It planned to further centralize the mortgage loan operations and the trust services. It offered the benefits of that experience to its potential merger partners.
• Established infrastructure to support ongoing effective management. Sterling already had in place an effective infrastructure, including processes such as the following:

- Strategic planning
- Credit policy and administration
- Human resource and benefit plan administration
- Profitability management
- Asset liability management
- Marketing
- Investment portfolio management

Sterling also had the following readily leverageable assets:

• *Financial resources and strength.* Sterling is a well-capitalized company with a somewhat liquid stock and access to the capital markets.
• *Franchise value.* Sterling recognized the value of relationships and community banking in creating franchise value. It also recognized the importance of critical mass to get the true multiples for the franchise. Assets to enhancing the franchise value of supercommunity banking in the Sterling context were:

- Liquid stock
- Maintaining the corporate culture of both Sterling and its merger partner
- Enhancement of the competitive position and market coverage
- Risk diversification
- Enhanced service levels
- The ability to handle larger transactions

• *Effective employee compensation plans.* Sterling already had in place an incentive compensation plan, an incentive stock option plan, an employee savings and profit-sharing plan, and a stock purchase plan. These could serve as powerful motivators to a merger partner's staff where such plans may not exist.

• *Strong credit environment.* Sterling has an excellent credit track record. The underwriting controls are effective and well established, and delinquency rates are exceptionally low. Sterling's loan portfolio was profitable and well seasoned, and it looked for merger partners that shared a compatible emphasis on small businesses and professional lending.

• *Enhanced fee income through product line expansion.* Sterling Bank already offered product variety beyond its size. It had merchant card services, cash management services, discount brokerages, mutual funds, and letters of credit. Sterling used vendor partners to introduce some of these products into its product lines and also planned to offer trust services and insurance. These products and services could be used by a merger partner to better serve its

existing customer base and expand the franchise.

• *Experience with office expansion.* "Sterling opened five offices in the past nine years and two offices in the last two months," George Martinez told potential merger partners. "We know how to do it and we can do it together," he said, thereby offering to leverage the intellectual capital Sterling garnered throughout the years.

Sterling targeted potential merger candidates that, together with Sterling, would

FIGURE 7.2 Loan Loss Reserve as a Percent of Total Loans

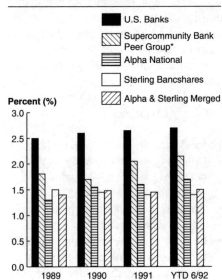

* 83 supercommunity banks who responded to the 1992 BDO Seidman and American Banker Supercommunity Bank Survey

Source: Sterling

FIGURE 7.3 Return on Assets

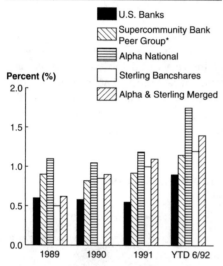

* Comprised of 83 supercommunity banks who responded to the 1992 BDO Seidman and *American Banker* Supercommunity Bank Survey.

merger partners. It painted a powerful picture of what the new entity would look like, including stock price, loan composition, loan loss reserve, and so on. (Figure 7.2 is an example of the loan loss reserve as a percent of total loans.) It showed how the two companies will complement each other on a variety of levels (Figures 7.2 through 7.6).

The epilogue is that Sterling Banc-Shares is in the process of merging with one of the partners it considered, Alpha National, and has plans to continue to build the company beyond this merger, with the goal of creating a critical mass and the largest independently owned supercommunity bank in the greater Houston marketplace. Its asset site after the merger will exceed $570 million.

all become a stronger entity, and that could offer the following:

- Enhanced stock liquidity
- Unique market position in greater Houston
- Experience with a broad product line
- Enhanced profitability
- New markets/marketplace augmentation
- Special relationships with customer base
- Combined cost savings
- Strategic synergy
- Expanded franchise

Sterling then proceeded to project the income statement and balance sheet as well as the stock conversion price for several

FIGURE 7.4 Return on Equity

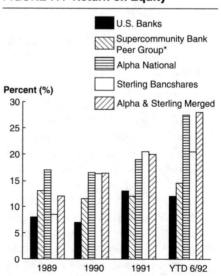

* Comprised of 83 supercommunity banks who responded to the 1992 BDO Seidman and *American Banker* Supercommunity Bank Survey.

FIGURE 7.5 Nonperforming Loans & ORE as a Percent of Total Loans & ORE

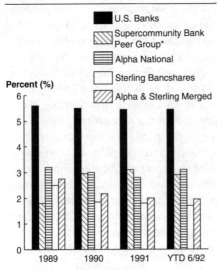

Legend:
- ■ U.S. Banks
- ▨ Supercommunity Bank Peer Group*
- ☰ Alpha National
- □ Sterling Bancshares
- ▨ Alpha & Sterling Merged

* Comprised of 83 supercommunity banks who responded to the 1992 BDO Seidman and *American Banker* Supercommunity Bank Survey.

Community First—Born Through Acquisition, Growing Through a Deliberate Acquisition Program

In 1985, First Bank Systems made a decision to divest itself of $60 million in assets in twenty-one offices in North Dakota. A group of investors bid for the entity, which included three multibank holding companies. The purchase was completed on September 30, 1987, and Community First was born. The company was committed to supercommunity banking from the start. It also devised the unique acquisition strategy to achieve growth since most of the markets in which it operated were fairly stagnant. Through venture capital financing, Don Mengedoth created a supercom-

munity bank out of a divestiture of a larger super-regional. Among the unique things about Community First, in addition to its acquisition strategy of small banks in the market, is its commitment to lead a minority interest in all the communities and banks it acquires. That minority interest ensures the continuing commitment to the community by the bank and the linkage that is so important for future growth and

FIGURE 7.6 Deposit Composition June 1992

Sterling Bancshares

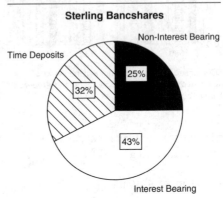

Alpha Bank

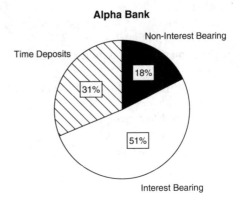

Source: Sterling.

FIGURE 7.7 Deposit Composition
June 1992

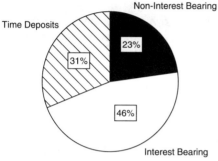

Sterling & Alpha Merged

asset quality. Credit quality was another nonnegotiable at Community First. In 1988, the company fully implemented the supercommunity strategy, which involved a data processing conversion that put all banks on the same system, the introduction of common policies and practices throughout the affiliates, and a merger of the three multibank holding companies that constituted Community First when it was divested from First Bank System.

Community First also has a unique attitude toward the regulators. They look at them as partners that need to be involved on an ongoing basis in the acquisition process of new entities. The company achieved credibility with regulators with its superior performance and prudent acquisition process. It established common policies throughout the system to ensure regulatory compliance of all the subsidiaries. In addition, if the company contemplates new acquisitions, it approaches the regulators in advance and describes the transaction to them so that they know what is in management's mind and how the acquisition will improve the financial condition of the holding company.

Community First's acquisition program is unique. The company purchases small banks that are very carefully targeted through the standardized acquisition process, which makes the program efficient and allows Community First to make acquisitions as small as $27 million in assets without a costly bureaucratic process. Since July 1990, the company completed ten acquisitions and doubled its size to $1.2 billion in assets, thirty-three offices, and twenty-one unit banks.

Community First has a healthy capital base and has access to additional capital through the public markets. The company has extensive experience in operating com-

---

Community First's owner-ship structure—which allows bank managers to retain a portion of the equity in the bank—may have some special appeal as an alternative to selling to a large holding company or to an individual buyer.

---

munity banks and in negotiating acquisitions with the owners of small and medium-sized banks. Systems and procedures for a multibank organization are already in place and working. In addition, Community First's ownership structure—which allows bank managers to retain a portion of the equity in the bank—may have some special appeal as an alternative to selling to a large holding company or to an individual buyer.

There is no shortage of acquisition opportunity in the region Community First has targeted for expansion. The states in which the company already operates—Minnesota, North Dakota, and South Dakota—have about 900 banks owned by individuals or by holding companies with less than $1 billion in assets. In addition to those three states, the company has targeted the contiguous states of Montana, Wyoming, Nebraska, Iowa, and Wisconsin, together with Colorado and Kansas—a ten-state region whose economic composition is similar to that of Community First's current territory. This region contains about 3,000 independent community banks that are possible acquisition candidates (see Figures 7.8 and 7.9).

Acquisition of deposits from institutions being liquidated by the Resolution Trust Corporation provides another opportunity. Community First will acquire such deposits only to improve market share in communities where the company's banks already operate.

When seeking acquisitions, the company applies a number of parameters they have established as the result of past experience. Among these are market factors such as the size and long-term viability of the community, dominance of the acquisition candidate, and the proximity of other Community First banks. In looking at new market areas, Community First seeks to acquire banks in areas with cultural and economic bases similar to those of communities already served.

Strict financial criteria are also applied, with only profitable banks considered. The company seeks to purchase banks on terms that will enable Community First to meet its target for return on equity over the long term.

Many owners of community banks are currently seeking buyers. Shareholders' liquidity is frequently a driving force, but difficulties in complying with increasingly demanding regulatory requirements are also a factor, as are increased capital requirements. As a result of its unique position as an acquiror in its target markets, Community First is approached by approximately seven institutions a month. The company quickly applies its acquisition parameters to the suitors and screens accordingly. Those that are consistent with the acquisition criteria are passed through a quick due diligence of asset quality before any significant resources are invested in the due diligence process.

Community First is another example of the formation of a supercommunity bank. In this case, the company was created out of a divestiture and has committed to supercommunity banking from the start. This approach, coupled with a highly focused and routinized acquisition program, resulted in a doubling of the company's assets while maintaining a profitability level of 22% on equity.

Community First—Alive and Growing Through Non-Metropolitan Area Growth

Community First examines as many as 120 opportunities each year as it is approached by seven to ten companies a month. It has developed the reputation of being a friendly supercommunity acquiror. In most cases, Community First is seeking small community-based acquisition targets with assets from $20 to $200 million. Target population size ranges from five to ten-thousand people. The deals are usually completed in a noncompetitive environment at prices that do not exceed 1.5 times book value. Transactions are friendly. The company expects to have virtually all directors of the target buy into the deal. This is part of the community-based strategy and the need to maintain good relationships among business leaders in the market area. Although the transaction price is designed to meet competition if there is any, pricing is based on the analysis of the earnings opportunity, and an understanding of the acquisition impact on the financial ratios. The pro forma benefits from effective deployment of an acquired institution's assets, particularly the securities portfolio, could represent as much as 50% improvement. Prior to acquisition, on a pro forma basis, a target return on the invested capital is set and, after conducting an analysis of the acquisition, a pro forma income statement is developed to evaluate the return on equity of the new institution. Community First has lost some opportunities for price reasons and they are proud of it. One should not pay up beyond one's preset parameters barring extraordinary circumstances.

Community First's strategy, like many other supercommunity banks such as Sovereign, Banc One, Michigan, and others, is to avoid major metropolitan areas. They enter rural areas for small-town locations. In 70% of their market areas, they are the dominant bank in town.

FIGURE 7.8 Community First's Target Market
Number of Independent Community Banks is Shown for Each State

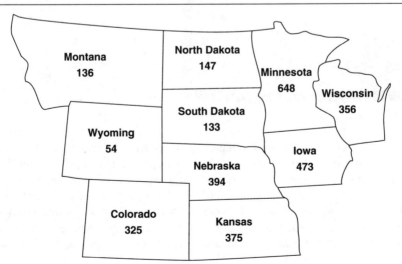

FIGURE 7.9 Community First Community Banking Locations

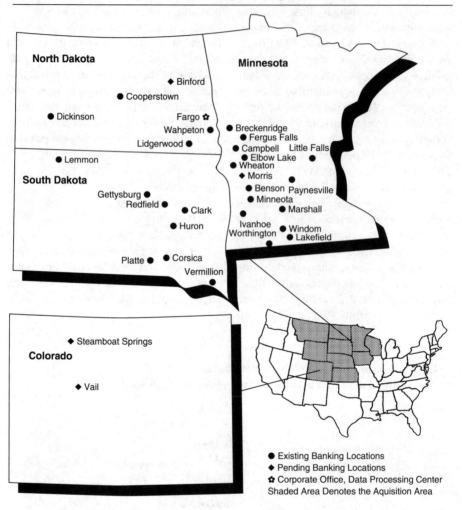

The supercommunity bank concept makes Community First a much more attractive buyer to many small banks that have been family owned for generations and do not want to lose their heritage. While interested in liquifying their stock, and perhaps in retirement, they want the institution to continue, particularly with its community orientation. The supercommunity bank strategy allows for such continuation.

It typically takes nine to twelve months from the point of identifying a bank wanting to sell to such time as an acquisition is complete. This period of time includes four to six months from signing the letter of intent through transaction completion. This time frame could be somewhat shortened if the process is routinized and due diligence is conducted effectively.

First Commercial Corporation— An Example of a Deliberate, Successful Acquisition Process

First Commercial Corporation (FCC) is a successful supercommunity bank. Its market, however, is economically stagnant. Therefore, growth has been achieved through acquisition. Barnett Grace, the company's CEO, set forth an extremely detailed and deliberate acquisition process to ensure quality acquisitions for FCC. The careful selection of suitable commercial bank candidates for acquisition has established the company as a leader within those Arkansas markets, which it targeted for future growth. The consistent stability of management within an acquired affiliate is an indicator of the viability of not only focusing on acquiring profitable market leaders in growing markets, but also of acquiring institutions that fit well into the FCC corporate culture of supercommunity banking. The acquisition of Arkansas Bank & Trust during 1990 illustrated the harmonious fit of a new affiliate that quickly became an active participant in both the formation of the new trust company and the standardization of data processing. The existing Arkansas Bank & Trust management was instrumental in providing the continuity of management and name recognition to the trust function.

The growth of First Commercial's Mortgage Company mortgage servicing portfolio is also an example of conservative entrepreneurship. During 1992 the mortgage company opened a retail office in cooperation with a bank affiliate to place mortgage professionals closer to the regional Arkansas market. This prudent expansion follows the successful establishment of a satellite mortgage company office in another location in 1991, and the opening of the regional mortgage office in Memphis, Tennessee, during 1990.

Reaching back into the 1980s, a consistent pattern of deliberate, mutually beneficial acquisitions became a visible FCC trademark. Six acquisitions since 1980 clearly indicate that FCC has concentrated its growth within areas having diversified, growth-oriented economies. FCC targets markets with rapid growth and low unemployment that are within its geographic target market. FCC has an ongoing program of exploring the economic viability of contiguous areas to Arkansas that are a prospective site for future acquisitions to ensure that any acquisition location has a local economy consistent with the diversity critical for sustained growth.

The company is careful, deliberate, and highly successful in acquiring banking and other assets, including mortgage servicing portfolios, trust companies, and a credit card operation. They have successfully integrated these assets and leveraged them through combinations with other similar assets. In effect, purchasing another trust company and/or mortgage servicing and/or credit card receivables is used to produce greater economies of scale. First Commercial Corporation supports its acquisition program of banks in high-growth markets with the acquisition of compatible assets and volume-sensitive businesses which allow it to achieve economies of scale unique to those businesses.

Key Elements of the Acquisition Process

To summarize, the following are the key elements in the acquisition process:

* Have a sound *due diligence* process. Asset quality is the primary focus. Successful institutions review at least 60% of the loans during due diligence, which is expensive. Some go as high as 80% of the loans. The good benchmark of an effective institution is that it takes five people one week to conduct due diligence on a $60 million bank. The due diligence efforts should go beyond asset quality into other areas of concern, such as employment contracts and problems of discrimination. All contracts that are committed to by the target institution should be examined. An effective way of doing that is to assign each functional area examination of the target institution to a person from that same functional area at your bank.
* Leave enough *latitude in the letter of intent pricing.* It may threaten the deal and the spirit of the transaction if you appear to be nickel-and-diming the seller in the final stages of negotiations.

* Leave *latitude in the merger agreement* for uncertain credits by scheduling them so that adjustments to the price can be made based on the final outcome of review of those credits, their workout, or collection. This way, the acquiring institution can hedge their bets on the asset quality of the acquiree without changing the price.
* Always try to get the seller to *retain knowledgeable counsel.* This way, you won't have to waste time explaining representations and warranties and other deal terms that are standard to the industry.
* Have a *satisfactory or better CRA rating.* Otherwise, you may be held up for even simple or small transactions. At Community First, for example, 38% of the banks are rated "outstanding."
* Start *talking to the state regulators in advance* of making applications. This way, they know what to expect and feel as though they are part of the process. In general, getting along with the regulators is highly conducive to a smooth approval process.
* *Wait until the signing of the definitive merger agreement before going public* with the deal. Too many things could go wrong between the signing of the letter of intent and the signing of the definitive merger agreement. Premature announcements can prove an embarrassment.

CHAPTER EIGHT

Corporate Culture

Learning From the Geese— Boundarilessness as a Team

I have learned some interesting facts about geese. In addition to mating for life, geese have figured out key elements about corporate culture and teamwork that we have yet to learn. Here are the facts:

- As each goose flaps its wings, it creates an uplift for the bird following. By flying in a V formation, the flock has 71% greater flying range than if one bird flew alone.

Lesson: A company whose people share a common direction and sense of belonging can get where they're going more quickly and easily because they're traveling on the strength of the whole group.

- Whenever a goose falls out of formation, it suddenly feels the drag and resistance of trying to fly alone and quickly gets back into formation to take advantage of the lifting power of the bird immediately in front.

Lesson: If we have as much sense as geese, and if the leadership of the company provides as much lift as the goose in front, we will "stay in formation" with those who are ahead of us to get where we want to go, and be willing to accept their help as well as give ours to others. There is nothing altruistic about it. Making your boss look good is an effective way to get ahead, and if your boss indeed is supportive of you she will bring you along with her. This is true for whole departments and the bank as well, but it assumes that there is a corporate value placed on cooperation and that back stabbing does not get rewarded.

- When the lead goose gets tired, it rotates back into the formation and another goose flies at the point position.

Lesson: It pays to take turns doing the hard tasks and to share leadership. Sharing power is an effective way to mobilize support and get the most out of your people.

- The geese in formation honk from behind to encourage those up front to keep up their speed.

Lesson: When a colleague is doing a good job, the culture should encourage employees to support him and not be envious. In such a corporate culture, if we support him, he will support us when we're in front.

- When a goose gets sick or wounded or shot down, two geese drop out of formation and follow it down to help and protect it. They stay with it until it is able to fly again or dies. Then they launch out on their own or with another flock until they rejoin their own.

Lesson: Cooperation and standing by each other in good and bad times sounds very idealistic, but it pays off in overall employee satisfaction and in effectively using and motivating employees.

The geese tell us that strong identity and clear strategic direction are the secrets to making the most out of each member of the organization. An explicit, unifying mission creates organizational leverage and builds momentum. When all employees know where the company is going and believe they will be taken care of by their bank when times are bad, they will give 110%. The gains in productivity and customer satisfaction could potentially outweigh the cost of time and money invested in employee motivation manifold.

Banks that have made a commitment to a clear strategic direction and have communicated that to their employees have done well. In addition to Banc One, companies such as First Empire, Barnett Banks, SunTrust, and others are evidence to the benefits incurred by a well-defined strategic vision, corporate culture, and taking a caring attitude toward employees.

Many supercommunity banks, for example, rarely hire from outside. Such banks have a very clear idea of their unique way, and its employees fit the profile. Promotions take place mostly from within, and performance is rewarded both in monetary and power terms. The result—corporate loyalty, minimal defections, and a company that is well-known for excellence.

Other banks committed to community banking exhibit similar characteristics. They care for their people and are interested in the human side of the business. They realize that people are their most important asset and invest in them accordingly. Even their acquisition programs are humane and attempt to create economies of scale without blood baths. Their employees recognize that and respond with greater commitment, minimal turnover (which, in turn, enhances customer retention), and productivity.

Banks that opted for a "barracuda" culture, such as Citibank, are now reaping the bitter fruit of that corporate value. Fostering internal competition works to a degree. However, when all bets are off and corporate commitment is uncertain, customer service and overall quality of service and product suffer greatly—the result is many irate customers.

We should all learn from the geese: there is strength in team playing. Working together does not necessarily mean sinking to the lowest common denominator. It could mean raising everyone's performance to a higher standard and working in unison toward a common goal. Today's successful supercommunity banks (and the geese) demonstrate teamwork in action.

Making Teamwork Happen—The MasterCard Experience

In 1988, a new management team took over the MasterCard Automated Point of Sale Program (MAPP). MAPP was an unprofitable division of the company. Its product line was electronic transaction processing services for the financial services market. Within two years, MAPP became one of the most profitable MasterCard departments, returning 40% on equity. Revenues increased 65% in 1991 over 1990, while the number of employees increased only 33%. All this occurred, as well as volume growth of 20% over 1990, despite the economic recession.

In addition, a recent survey of MAPP employees conducted by an independent consultant found that the employees like to work at MAPP. They were proud of their company and rated it an above-average place to work. 92% of the employees rated the MAPP senior management team as good or very good—a 49% positive variance from the industry norm.

These stellar results show that no matter how difficult the challenge, quality initiatives and teamwork can help. Happy, proud employees translate into bottom-line performance. What did Senior Vice President Heidi Goff and her team do in order to bring about this remarkable change?

MAPP's first-year goal was to get the organization functioning from a management standpoint and to empower employees to help fix problems instead of feeling victimized by them. Contrary to the advice of their facilitator, the new management team established more project teams to tackle different issues. Predictably, this was overkill. MAPP people became lost in attempting to define the objectives of each team and struggled to break up the work into manageable chunks. At the same time, by simply starting the quality effort, MAPP realized some initial benefits. Individuals began to feel they could make a difference and took initiative to begin fixing pieces of the problems. Some small victories were achieved, and people began to invest more time in the process. While no overwhelming successes were achieved, a lot of small work efforts created a better feeling and work atmosphere in the division.

In the second year, MAPP scaled back to five projects and acknowledged that some would take more than a year to complete. During the second year, employees brought one-year projects to a successful conclusion, but tended to give up on multiyear projects. The project teams worked well at defining but not fixing the problems they faced, but, once again, the partial success and the process of trying led to improvement regardless of whether the division succeeded on any particular project.

In year three, the division inaugurated its Total Service Quality (TSQ) program, which was a major success. By giving the program a name, people could sign up for it and could discuss it. The name brought the reality of the program home. As a result, it became much more focused. Quality became 10% of the bonus structure for all functional unit heads. Quality measurements were installed for each direct report area. Enormous progress was made in year three, so much so that in that year MAPP exceeded the plan in every corporate measurement. Using the right techniques and getting people involved in the planning cost money, but doing so paid off in big dividends.

MAPP's year four off-site planning conference included twenty-one top employees, as well as the division's internal vendors and process customers. Departments that report to different senior vice-presidents attended and participated in the planning process. In a year or two, MAPP hopes to include external customers as well.

Because MAPP staff members were not trained to facilitate workshops focusing on connecting with a customer, total quality management, and functional strategies, a special facilitator led MAPP personnel through outdoor team-building exercises that broke down barriers, strengthened col-league relationships, and provided participants with new insights into the people they work with each day.

MAPP's quality experience in a brief period of time has been truly energizing. Challenges yet to come do not seem so enormous anymore. Step by step, the division is moving forward, reaping tremendous rewards along its path to quality. MAPP is but one of the many institutions discovering that placing high value within the company or the division on cooperation, teamwork, and goal-setting is an effective way to bring about bottom-line turnarounds. By bringing together the key participants, including internal vendors and service providers, clarity and focus result. Success can be more easily defined and quantified. In addition, by humanizing all members of the team through team-building processes away from the typical day-to-day interaction environment and transaction orientation, interpersonal relationships are enhanced and a more complete understanding of each member of the team is reached. Although leadership is clearly defined, individual leaders exchange positions depending on the topic at hand and their personal experience with that topic. If one unit falters, the rest come to its assistance as part of the win-win strategy. The same principals that guide the flocks of geese we discussed are brought to bear in the financial services environment to enhance effectiveness and job satisfaction.

In a highly quantifiable business such as banking, where dollars and cents are at the bottom line of each statement every day, it is difficult to assign value to the touchy-feely aspects of business management. The MAPP story and many others like it are an example of the value that attending to the intangibles can bring. Those geese do know what they're doing; those of us who are following their example are much more effective in tackling today's and tomorrow's problems.

The Importance of Corporate Culture to Supercommunity Banks

Corporate culture is an intangible. It is not the numbers, balance sheets, and ROA figures that bankers are accustomed to. At the same time, corporate identity, values, and culture have been identified as a cornerstone of successful companies for the past decade. Tom Peters' *In Search of Excellence* highlighted the critical role of corporate culture, and manufacturing companies have been focusing on that as part of their business for years.

Service industries have traditionally lagged behind manufacturing in management discipline. Strategic planning, for example, was a well-integrated concept in the manufacturing sector long before it was considered by service businesses, including the financial service industry. It certainly appears that corporate culture and values are next in line. More and more financial services companies are turning their attention to the intangibles of management. In addition to managing by the numbers, they are starting to define the values central to their corporate identity and to integrate these values into their management style, acquisitions strategy, and reward system.

One interesting example is Sovereign Bancorp, a $4 billion thrift headquartered in Pennsylvania. Sovereign has a crystal-clear strategic focus; its overwhelming asset emphasis is residential real estate lending, and its funding is composed of

---

Strategic planning . . . was a well-integrated concept in the manufacturing sector long before it was considered by service businesses, including the financial service industry.

---

deposits generated through strategically located branches outside major metropolitan markets. The multi-bank company is patterned after the supercommunity bank with three distinct thrifts in well-defined markets.

Sovereign has clear performance targets, and its number one driver is shareholder value. At the same time, Sovereign puts a tremendous emphasis on its people and the values that guide their behavior. "Making the numbers" is not enough. How they were achieved is of critical importance. Accordingly, Sovereign does not have employees. It has team members. It does not have a human resources department. Instead, it has team member services. Managers are leaders. Each of the company's fifteen departments has developed its own mission, vision, and strategies. All are consistent with an extremely concise, corporate-level vision statement and an unerring commitment to customer service.

Sovereign boasts over 1.00% return on assets and over 16% return on equity.

These numbers were achieved not only through astute financial management and clear strategic objectives, but also through an extraordinary emphasis on company values and culture. It is the motivators beyond money that make the difference and seem to be most effective. All team members are shareholders at Sovereign, and bonuses used to buy stock are matched by the company. Sovereign goes well beyond the garden variety 401K plan to share the company with the team members. For example, the best parking spot is reserved for the company's employee of the month. The CEO doesn't even have his own spot. The result—high profitability and $4.2 million in assets per employee, more than double the industry average.

Sovereign is not alone in its focus on corporate values. Many other banks, most particularly those that put special emphasis on service levels and relationship to the customer, rely on company values to enhance service levels and employee responsiveness to customer needs. At First Michigan ($2 billion), for example, all employees have a customer, whether internal or external. Service orientation and accountability are expected from all— staff and line personnel alike. Internal customers deserve the same service levels, efficiency, and courtesy as do external customers, and FMB is committed to integrate that value into its day-to-day life. As the company strives to make the whole greater than the sum of its parts, to create synergy, it communicates to its people the values that will facilitate such achievement—ranging from honesty and fair dealing to a partnership concept with all its audiences—customers, communities, vendors, and shareholders.

FMB's extraordinary success is evidence to the effectiveness of combining clarity of rational financial expectation and rigorous financial management with corporate identity and values.

Well-defined values contribute to employee creativity in devising innovative ways to achieve corporate goals. At Georgia Federal, ($5 billion) service values were translated into employee creativity at the branch level. The company's "corporate heroes" program highlighted the importance of going the extra mile and emphasizes dedication and service orientation. Dick Jackson, the CEO and a former Marine, used leadership by example to inspire his people. He supported the value drive with incentives to reinforce the program. The result: unique branch-originated service programs and another 1%, 16+% ROE.

US Bankcorp is one supercommunity bank that clearly identified its core values: integrity, quality, performance, caring, cooperation, and trust. These core values are applied in a wide variety of situations, including senior management meetings, to ensure that decisions are consistent with the corporate culture. When conflicts arise, corporate values are raised as the test against which the decision is being made. Similarly, Old Kent implemented a corporate values program over a decade ago. The change was subtle, but important, and the values have come to exert a big influence on all employees. All employees are conscious of Old Kent's service orientation and other values and conduct themselves consistently with those values on a day-to-day basis. The values serve as guidelines for daily contact and decision-making.

In many acquisitions, one of the more difficult parts is to meld the companies together from a cultural standpoint as opposed to sheer operations issues. Corporate culture can be used as a vehicle to facilitate such integration through the explicit documentation of values, vision, and behavior norms that make clear to the newest affiliates the themes that are expected throughout the company. Integra, for example, used corporate values as a vehicle to blend cultures of disparate institutions into a supercommunity bank. Clear corporate culture by the Integra facilitated acquisition and integration. Its expectations were clear, values were nonnegotiable, and its style of interaction was explicitly defined.

These stories are but a few of the success stories where corporate culture and values were formatted, clearly communicated throughout the company, and rewarded with a well-thought-out, motivational program. Talking to the employee of these and other financial services companies committed to a culture, I am impressed with their clear understanding of what the business is all about and its objectives, and with the style and mode of behavior we observed. The people are happier—for they have a sense of belonging and contribution.

The numbers speak for themselves. The intangible of corporate culture is a direct contributor to highly tangible financial success as expressed by profitability and market capitalization (all these companies are trading at 150% or more of bank value).

Corporate culture may sound like voodoo economics, but the results indicate it is another management tool for overall organizational success. The specific values used by supercommunity banks are quite familiar. They are statements such as the following:

- **Innovation.** We seek and encourage appropriate problem-solving programs and innovative solutions that deliver results to our customers.
- **Excellence.** We create value for our customers by providing quality in all that we do and the way that we do it.
- **Participation.** We work together in teams with each member contributing to the best of his or her capabilities.
- **Honesty.** We expect honesty and fair dealing in interactions with all our constituencies and with each other.
- **Accountability.** We are each held accountable for our performance and share in the results.
- **Ownership.** We each have a stake in the company and share its risks and rewards.

As you read these values, you may find them quite "ho hum" and classify them, together with "synergy" and "total quality management," as another invention by consultants designed to generate fees and buzzwords.

But the values described above—and others—have made a significant contribution to the success of the companies committed to them. The key to that success, however, is selecting the values that best fit your company and its objectives, clearly defining them, and incorporating them into your day-to-day management. It is not only the values that make a difference;

success hinges upon their successful integration into your bank.

Although the values may be similar across companies, their meaning and integration may be quite different, reflecting the personality of the CEO, the company's strategic position, the employees, and so on. For example, while "service" at a community bank may be translated into community orientation, relationship longevity, or in-person visits, it may also be translated into need anticipation and proactive technology installation in a centralized, scale-driven organization. The meaning of "service" is different for Citibank and First Valley National Bank.

As the CEO and senior management might ponder the relevance of corporate culture to their organization, the point of departure for identifying corporate values should be "who are we today?" The intangibles that already govern the institution should be identified, and management can then determine whether change is needed. Incongruity between the organization and its values implies change. Such change needs to be carefully monitored, as it is difficult to bring about.

Values should be as unambiguous as possible. In addition to being clear, values should be specific to your company. "Motherhood and apple pie" is not meaningful enough to your audiences—employees, customers, communities, vendors, or shareholders. If, for example, you are a close follower, do not put "innovation" as a corporate value. Although creativity is always important, innovation is costly and may not be a top priority for you. As you consider the four to six words that describe your culture, try to describe what it is that

is different about them at your bank. What makes "service" a special value for you, beyond perfunctory lip service? It is the recognition of the unique values and their meaning in your company that will integrate them into your culture and give them a special meaning in the context of your bank. Differentiation and focus are the name of the game in banking today. You can use corporate culture and values to achieve and sharpen both.

Developing Corporate Values—An Example

First Commercial Corporation— An Organized Approach to Corporate Culture

First Commercial Corporation, a $2.6 billion supercommunity bank headquartered in Little Rock, Arkansas, owns nine affiliated banks, 50% ownership of a tenth affiliate bank, a mortgage company, and a trust company. First Commercial has done an outstanding job of defining and subsequently communicating the corporation's identity. Senior management and the board realized they had a clear understanding of the objectives the company wanted to accomplish—strength, profitability, and growth. However, these objectives and how they were planning to accomplish them needed to be communicated to the organization, not only by the executive management but also by line managers to their employees. Everyone in the entire organization, management felt, should be able to state and understand the company's three simple objectives.

They felt there was a communication

gap between the management team and the other bankers in the company. Therefore, they structured a planning conference whose purpose was to communicate to the management team the corporate vision, values, objectives, and strategies, as well as to develop a sense of camaraderie among the management team. Management also used that opportunity to recognize and reward staff throughout the organization and to educate management on topics such as sales, quality management, new competitors within the market, and so on.

In addition, First Commercial established the FCC College in 1991. It is designed to provide company managers with the direction and knowledge that will enable them to perpetuate and live FCC's mission statements. Three sessions of twenty participants per session were held in 1991 and 1992. The same is planned for 1993 and beyond. In the first college session, the bank CEOs developed the following vision for the company: "The corporation is recognized for its strong financial performance, impeccable ethics, capable and caring bankers, competitive services, and modern technology." In addition, the CEOs formulated the following values, taken from First Commercial Corporation, Value Statement, 1991:

A. We must be honest and ethical with ourselves, our customers, and our company.
  1. We will not mislead.
  2. We will share information when possible.

B. Dedicated to excellence.
  1. Hire the best bankers
  2. Train them
  3. Offer quality customer service through quality product and modern technology
  4. Maintain high asset quality
  5. Maintain strong capital position

C. Commitment to bankers, customers, and shareholders
  1. Balance our obligations to meet our needs
  2. Do the right thing

D. Open communications. We will listen, hear, and try to keep an open mind within the chain of corporate, affiliate, department, and customer.

E. Reinvest in our community
  1. Loans (support economy)
  2. Contributions (dollars plus time)
  3. Image creation - solid corporate citizens

F. Reward performance. Performance (objective) to measurement system to gage results.

G. Respect
  1. Ideas
  2. Others

First Commercial recognized that companies that communicate their values have more success in their marketplace than companies that have not done so. Therefore, said management, we need to ensure that FCC bankers know and adhere to these values, not only because it will help us achieve our objectives but also because these values reflect the type of organization FCC wants to be. It is such awareness and clarity of commitment that made FCC a super performer, with a 1.29% return on assets and a 15.72% return on equity (reflecting a capital ratio of 8.42% and a risk-based capital ratio of 15.48%). First Commercial is among the strongest banks in the country when it comes to capital ratios, reflecting its commitment to a fortress balance sheet and the value of strength as a major differentiation factor.

The FMB Partnership—One Plus One Equals Three

David Ondersma, the chief executive of First Michigan Bank (FMB), has been leading the company along the supercommunity bank path for several years. The company's superior results, including doubling its size within four years without sacrificing one basis point in return on equity, speak for themselves. But Ondersma did not rest on his laurels. He wanted to go one step further and created the concept of the FMB partnership. "Everyone at FMB has a partner," says Ondersma. And those partnerships are designed to help achieve the bank's mission: "To be a profitable, progressive company of the highest quality, offering financial services to communities in Michigan. The FMB team is dedicated to seek out customer needs in a caring, responsive way. Our commitment to provide customers with superior service is unwavering. All partners—customers, employees, communities, vendors, and shareholders—will benefit from FMB's success."

He adds, "FMB's success hinges upon working effectively with others." "We must make the whole greater than the sum of its parts; hence, one plus one equals three." The concept of the FMB partnership, as depicted in Figure 8.1, is designed to create relationships consistent with the company's mission. The FMB team, at the core of the partnership, creates partnerships with shareholders, vendors, customers, and communities to achieve mutually beneficial relationships. The company combined its vision—which describes its strategy and its desired position in the outside world—with the corporate values—which describe the desired culture for FMB and guide internal interactions among corporate employees and the rest of the partners—to explain its mission in a more detailed way and provide a strategic direction expected through seven strategic initiatives (Figure 8.2).

In summary, the FMB partnership is directed strategically by the corporate mission and vision. Each individual partner is expected to work toward attaining the mission and vision of the company using the corporate values as the guidelines for such interaction. The corporate values are as follows:

- Honesty—the way you conduct yourself.
- Service—the way you treat others.
- Excellence—what you strive for.
- Participation—the way you interact with others.

FMB's corporate values clearly outline the kind of a company FMB is committed to becoming and the type of people it

Figure 8.1 The FMB Partnership

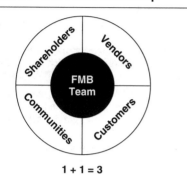

1 + 1 = 3

expects to employ. It describes a give-and-take relationship between the company and its partners that sets the tone for the way employees deal with each other, with customers, and with other partners.

Developing Your
Corporate Culture

Developing your corporate culture needs to be a consistent and well-thought-out process. The following tasks are typically associated with the process:

1. *Develop a vision statement.* Develop a statement that describes your company

the way you would like it to be, not necessarily the way it is today. It is an ideal to strive for.

Avoid motherhood and apple pie. Use the vision statement to distinguish your bank from others; to make it special and understandable to your employees. Therefore, the vision has to be clear and brief and as specific as possible. That does not mean it needs to be complex. For example, Sovereign Bank, a $4 billion supercommunity bank headquartered in Pennsylvania, states: "Our vision is that when homeowners think of a bank they choose Sovereign." It is simple but very specific and makes it clear that Sovereign's business is homeowner financing, and its expectations are to create pull demand across the marketplace by its excellence, reputation, and so on. Sovereign's vision is only one sentence. The next sentence, however, explains the role of every employee in that vision: "It's up to every team member to make that vision a reality each and every day. If homeowners do not choose Sovereign, either they are misinformed or we haven't done our job." This is certainly not moth-

FIGURE 8.2 Strategic Direction
Translating the Mission and Vision into Reality

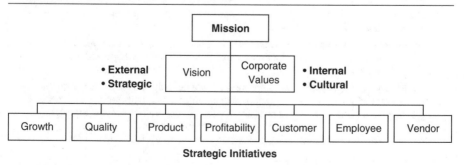

Corporate Values—A Supercommunity Bank Example

Below is an example of typical guiding principles for supercommunity banks. The were used by a $5 billion company to convert into a supercommunity bank.

Our vision will be accomplished within a set of fundamental operating principles. These principles will guide our strategic decisions and actions and form the basis upon which accomplish our primary objectives:

1. We believe that sustainable long-term shareholder value will be achieved by remaining a strong, locally oriented independent banking organization. We will retain our independence through developing and retaining a loyal customer franchise and building a strong capital base while generating superior financial performance.

2. We will standardize those functions, tasks and responsibilities that provide significant operating efficiencies at value to customer relationships or control risk. Specifically, standardization will be pursued in the following areas:

   - Product line and product features
   - Operating policies and procedures
   - Data processing, management information and financial systems
   - Risk management and financial control systems
   - Credit policies and processes
   - Marketing systems
   - Human resources policies and procedures

3. We will centralize those responsibilities and decisions that do not have a direct impact on customer relationship management. We will retain local flexibility in those areas that increase market responsiveness, encourage community involvement, enhance sales and service effectiveness, and maximize value of our local identity.

4. We will consolidate our three banks into one organization. During the transition from three banks to one, we will centralize and standardize as many functions as possible and will coordinate activities within defined lines of business.

5. After consolidation into one organization, we will retain original areas of responsibility to promote local flexibility, responsiveness, decision- making, and community involvement.

6. We will achieve incremental steady improvement in our operating and financial performance. We will take advantage of opportunities to improve our performance but will not engage in high risk ventures to generate short-term profitability.

7. We will invest in proven technology to increase efficiency and productivity, reduce expenses or enhance sales effectiveness of customer service. We will not pursue technologies that do not have established performance histories and significant economic justification.

8. We will continue to explore opportunities to improve our expense structure and consider outsourcing those functions that can be performed better, faster, or at a lower cost and ensure the development of internal capabilities.

9. We will make strategic capital investments in those projects and initiatives that have a clear measurable potential to enhance the corporation's profitability. Expected levels of risk and reward will be clearly defined.

10. We will invest in our employees to ensure that they have the skill and knowledge necessary to perform effectively in their current positions and advance to higher levels of responsibility. Whenever possible, we will fill positions from within but will supplement our capabilities by recruiting highly qualified experienced personnel from outside the organization in those instances where specialized expertise or a new perspective is required.

FMB Corporate Values

Excellence

- Honest, ethical, and moral behavior—Deal with each other and with our external partners in an honest and ethical way. There are standards outlined in the FMB Business Ethics and Conflicts of Interest policy.
- Mutual trust—Trust and respect each other, treat our external partners and each other with dignity.
- Loyalty—Our people's commitment to FMB as a company is essential.

Service

- "We want to help"—All of our jobs depend on working with others, those who are both internal and external to the company. Be willing to give a helping hand to everyone with whom you come in contact.
- Partnership with others—Our customers, employees, directors, communities, vendors, and share-holders are all our partners; recognize the value that a partner brings to your job and to the company; search for ways to enhance your relationship with partners in order that our customers can be better served. Working together and sharing values will make the whole greater than the sum of the parts, and help us realize our vision.
- Commitment to the customer—FMB's customers are our most valued partners. We are committed to provide them with a superior level of service. Existing customers will be treated with the same degree of attention and diligence as new or prospective customers. Proactively seek out your customers' needs and expectations, and be responsive to them.
- Long-term relationships—Adopt a long-term view of relationships, thereby maximizing the profitability of that relationship over time; involve partners' considerations in developing and delivering products and services.
- Friendly, caring attitude—Treat all our partners with a high degree of friendliness, care, and personal attention.

Excellence

- Quality in all that we do—It is up to all of us to maintain FMB's excellence; continually apply high-quality standards to all company activities—assets, operations, service, technology, etc.
- Hard work and dedication—There is no substitute for hard work to achieve our objectives. Dedication to our jobs and our willingness to invest the necessary time and effort sets our team apart.
- Creative thinking, seeking continuous improvement—Be creative in thinking and constantly seek ways to improve; be innovative. New ideas and better methods are expected in every area.
- Positive attitude and self-improvement—Continuous self-improvement and a positive attitude are key ingredients to our success. Training, professional development, and an expanding knowledge base will ensure continued excellence in our performance.
- Accountability—Taking accountability for our performance also means having pride and ownership in the results of our work; taking responsibility bears its rewards.

Participation

- Team work and common purpose—Mobilize our people and work within the team that will better lead FMB toward obtaining its objectives. Recognize the contribution of all team members to achieving results.
- Initiative—Take initiative to get involved; participate; volunteer; when involved, go the extra mile.
- Community involvement—Actively support and participate in community activities, charities, and civic events. Take leadership roles as ambassadors of FMB.
- Open communication—We want FMB to remain a warm, caring place where people can freely share opinions and be supportive of one another.

erhood and apple pie but rather an ambitious, specific, and understandable vision.

Norwest also has a clear, uncompromising, brief yet ambitious vision: "We share a vision throughout the community banking group to be the premier financial institution in each of our marketplaces . . . number one, second to none. Service is our primary product. We differentiate ourselves by delivering a superior level of service and by being innovative and responsive to both customers and to community needs."

First Interstate of Montana's vision is "To maintain and enhance our leadership in the financial and social fabric of the community we serve—for a commitment to customer satisfaction, creative management, productive employees, shareholder value, and community involvement. That is First Interstate's strategic vision for today . . . and for tomorrow."

At First Michigan Bank Corporation "The vision of our company takes the attributes of smaller, community-oriented banks . . . and adds to it a number of the advantages and efficiencies that large banks provide. Together, the result is FMB Banking."

The vision statements presented above all describe distinct companies. They differ from one another, yet they are all supercommunity banks. That commitment comes through loud and clear in their statements. The implementation of that vision for all these companies is supercommunity banking.

In summary, a vision statement should be:

• Clear and brief
• As specific as possible .
• Distinct for your bank

2. *Identify the "nonnegotiables."* Every company has corporate values that are the backbone of the company, that are critical to the company's future. These values need to be explicitly identified. Although the CEO and senior management live them every day, you cannot assume your employees and other partner groups know those values. They may have a sense of your guiding principles, but they may not be fully familiar with them and with the way you personally interpret those values. Therefore, it is important to identify the nonnegotiables in clear, unequivocal terms. The corporate values described above are such nonnegotiables. Others may be asset quality, service level, and so on. The purpose of the values is to clearly send signals to all employees of what really counts and to focus their attention on those specific elements that should be incorporated into their day-to-day behavior.

3. *Communicate.* It is not enough to put a corporate culture on paper. It has to be communicated and then lived every day. The communication must be initiated by the chief executive, but involvement of all managers is essential. It's a corporate-wide activity where value and other statements are communicated on paper, videos, slides, and verbally from the chief executive to the management team, and from the management team to the officer core and the entire employee regiment. The communication need not be hypothetical; rather, management must walk the talk throughout the company and continue to reiterate the corporate values and corporate culture expectations. Start with the trainees and end with the board.

At Sovereign, a value, critical success factor, or a mission element appears everywhere you go—in the elevator, on bulletin boards displayed on every floor of the building, and in every form of corporate communication from the newsletter to awards. Every time you talk to the chief executive, Jay Sidhu, he himself walks the talk, and others do, too. And he can recite, and does, the corporate values and vision regularly. All employees are expected to be able to do the same. Jay immersed his company in building the corporate culture (Figure 8.3). (See also, Appendix 6.) Other supercommunity banks do the same. Blanketing the company one time is not

FIGURE 8.3 Sovereign Bank Values

OUR VISION
When homeowners think of a bank, they choose Sovereign.

OUR VALUES

CUSTOMERS. Our goal is to always put customers first at Sovereign and consistently exceed customers' expectations of service from the Company.

TEAM. We expect nothing but the best from our team and in return show extreme respect for the individual team member. We encourage open communications and an entrepreneurial spirit, always seeking and implementing ideas and innovations which help us to excel.

SHAREHOLDERS. Keeping the expectations of our owners in mind, we will continually seek to outperform the market in terms of quality of earnings, growth in earnings and return on equity.

COMMUNITY. We are a committed, socially responsible, corporate citizen, supporting worthwhile community activities through our Foundation and encouraging our team members to be actively involved in our communities.

OUR MISSION
Sovereign Bank is a highly focused, market-led and results-oriented company, primarily serving homeowners and mature customers for loans and deposits. Our differentiation is based upon quality and excellence in service through people, while maintaining a low cost, low risk profile.

OUR STYLE
We achieve our mission and practice our values in an ethical, moral and legal atmosphere, where mutual trust and understanding are practiced. Our ethics are based upon being honest, fair and up front with all people and we follow through with our commitments.

OUR MOTTO
Quality Service Through Quality People.

CRITICAL SUCCESS FACTORS
❑ Superior asset quality,
❑ Low overhead and high productivity,
❑ Low interest rate risk,
❑ Emphasis on sales, service and growth of our team members.

⛫ Sovereign Bank
The HomeOwners Bank

Reprinted with permission of Sovereign Bank

going to do the job. The secret is to communicate, communicate, communicate at all levels, from employees to board members, and to continue reinforcing on an ongoing basis. Otherwise, the initial enthusiasm will peter out and the culture and values will remain on paper, as opposed to a live concept.

4. *Offer rewards and incentives.* Integration of the corporate culture should be rewarded. Reward a nonnegotiable performance first; it is the most important behavior to the company, and that signal has to be sent to every employee. Interestingly enough, to some, bonuses are less important than corporate-wide recognition. Tailor the incentives to the appropriate motivator; not everyone is motivated by cash. In one supercommunity bank, for example, when incentives were accompanied by a personal assessment and feedback session with the manager every month, employee satisfaction and productivity increased exponentially. It wasn't the money that was motivating them; it was the attention and feedback provided by their manager. That had a dual effect. On the one hand, it showed people that management was paying attention and, therefore, employees had better perform; on the other, it provided a nurturing feedback, both positive and negative, that motivated the employees to go the extra mile.

At Sovereign, Keystone, Old National, and many other supercommunity banks, corporate recognition is an important component of the motivation system. They have corporate heros, president awards, monthly president lunches, plaques, contests, and corporate-wide recognition and officer meetings for employees. Providing company-wide forums to recognize performers is a most effective and rewarding incentive, motivating employees toward reinforcing corporate culture behavior. Last but not least, as a supercommunity bank, use overall corporate performance in bonus programs as you go up the individual subsidiary bank's ladder. Although bank subsidiary presidents should retain their pride and performance measurement, they should consider themselves a part of the total company. Monetary and other rewards can be used to reinforce that concept.

5. *Lead by example.* Your behavior and message must be consistent. By so doing you will demonstrate the chief executive's commitment to the values he or she endorses. CEO actions speak louder than words.

In summary, a strong corporate culture mobilizes all resources in one direction. It is of critical importance to service organizations in general, and to supercommunity banks in particular.

CHAPTER NINE

Quality Management— A Cornerstone of Supercommunity Banking

Total Quality Management— A Critical Factor in Supercommunity Banking

Quality service is a key component of the supercommunity banking strategy. This strategy is predicated on higher levels of personalized service. Without those service levels, a supercommunity bank cannot effectively compete against small banks that offer highly personalized service, nor can it compete effectively against large banks that can offer a greater product diversity. In supercommunity banks, decisions are made closer to the customer. It is very different from the centralized decision making at large bureaucratic organizations. At least one more layer of management is added as compared to rolled-up branch systems, and an extra layer of presidents and board members are retained in order to enhance the community orientation of the company. This could become a more expensive strategy to implement relative to rolled-up branches in other strategic alternatives, yet successful supercommunity banks do not have higher costs as compared to other similarly sized companies. One way to enhance cost performance and to drive costs down while continuing to meet and exceed customer expectations is the quality program, which enhances revenues, increases savings, and improves full employee participation and sense of ownership.

Total quality management seems to be the buzzword for the 1990s. Many people tout it, but few implement it well. Quality service is the cornerstone of the supercommunity bank concept: it is one of the major competitive advantages that a supercommunity bank has over its larger and smaller bank competitors. Service levels are key to customer retention, which, in turn, is key to profitability. The story below illustrates the importance of quality service and its impact on customer retention.

When customer John Smith first moved to this small town thirty years ago, he was beginning his career at a good salary. His wife was pregnant and they had found a house they could afford. John's boss did business at First National Bank, which had an office just down the street. So, armed with an introduction, John dropped in and came away with a checking account and a mortgage application. His wife added a savings account. The $12,000 mortgage at 7% was approved. They rented a safety deposit box to put the documents in, and they were launched financially. A few years later, they inherited some money from grandparents and wanted to start thinking about investing. They met with a trust officer at First National Bank who outlined a growth investment plan, and they entered the stock market. From then on, they met once a year with the trust officer to review the portfolio, which eventually grew to $75,000. When their first child was born, they opened a savings account in her name to save for her college education. They did the same for their son a few years later. Both accounts grew over the years to about $15,000 apiece.

As the family grew, the first house was getting small. So they looked around for a dream house. The Smiths always wanted to live in the country and have lots of space—a big garden, room for the dog to run, maybe even a tennis court someday. Together with three other couples, they bought seventy-five acres of farmland, mapped it out in large parcels, and put in a road. They borrowed $10,000, their share for the land and the road, from First National. Then came the new house with the $30,000 mortgage. A few years later, the family invested in a working farm and got a second $50,000 mortgage from First National. John really liked First National. It was small enough to be friendly, but big enough to have the services the family needed. The chief trust officer handled the portfolio himself. The tellers knew the family members' names and so did the president and chairman of the board. This was one of the reasons why the Smiths bought the bank's stock whenever they had a little extra money. They bought stock for the children, too. It was a good investment and grew to over $60,000 before the kids were through college. When credit cards became available, John's family got theirs from First National, and even though they suffered through some computer glitches, they never thought of going elsewhere. As John said, "We just called Gary, the credit card officer, and he straightened things out."

Another mortgage came when the family bought a student rental house convenient to the nearby university where their daughter was enrolled. First National put up the $25,000.

Things began to change when the bank was acquired by an out-of-town bank holding company. The holding company was not a supercommunity bank and therefore did not apply the supercommunity bank philosophy, which would not have changed quality of service at all for John and his family. At first, they didn't notice much difference, even though the name on their checks and statements changed to First Commercial, nor did the family expect things to change, because First Commercial told the shareholders that there wouldn't be any changes. In addition, the new entity repeatedly advertised that it was really a community bank dedicated to the people and businesses of the communities. The Smiths believed it at first.

Then, their trust officer took an early retirement. John went to his retirement party, and the officer didn't look happy. It seemed more like a wake than a party. The trust officer was not the only somber face. His contemporaries at the bank looked worried and, in fact, during the next few years, most of them retired or left the bank. The tellers were different, too. Many of them now asked John for his ID, which he didn't like very much. Just when he would get to know a teller, a new one would take her place, and he would have to start all over again. Although the bank continued to proclaim that its subsidiaries were community banks, it didn't act as though this were true. Within five years of the merger, the Annual Report revealed that twelve of the twenty-nine bank subsidiaries had been absorbed into other subsidiaries, and the boards of directors eliminated. John talked with one director who had been marched out of office. He said that he had been told one year after his bank became a branch that he would be put on the board of directors of the parent bank. But he never was.

On a more personal level, the service at the bank gradually deteriorated. John and his wife decided to put an addition on the house and refinance it. The original mortgage was almost paid off. The tax laws had

changed to make only mortgage interest deductible, so it seemed sensible to enlarge the $5,000 mortgage to an $80,000 mortgage to pay for the addition. By then the house was assessed at well over $200,000. So, given the long relationship (including three mortgages, a good-sized IRA balance, and a profit-sharing plan of over $400,000 with the trust department), John's family figured the bank would treat them differently than a stranger who just walked in. Wrong. The bank quoted the usual rates, points, and fees, and acted as if it didn't care whether they got the mortgage there or not. For the first time, John checked with another bank and found that their rates and terms, including closing fees, were similar to, or a bit better than those at their bank, even though they had no other accounts with them. Also, they said that they would really like the Smith's business, called several times with various options, and mailed John information. So the Smiths said good-bye to the old bank and took the mortgage with another bank. They expected that someone at First Commercial would ask why they hadn't gone ahead with the new mortgage, but no one did.

About the same time, they got a form letter from the bank saying that it was adjusting the credit card fees. "The annual charges on your credit card with us may or may not be increased this year unless you qualify for one of our special programs." John's wife Lisa called the toll-free number given on the letter to find out what the new fees and special programs were. She figured a twenty-five-year customer would qualify for something good. "What bank are you calling you about?" the operator asked. Lisa told her. Then the operator wanted to know what city and state the branch was in. With that out of the way, Lisa said, "I'd like to know what our annual credit card fee will be and whether we qualify for your special programs."

"You will have to ask your own bank about that," replied the operator, "We don't have that kind of information here.

"Where are you located?" asked Lisa. The operator named a large city 1,500 miles away. Some community bank!

Dismayed but undaunted, Lisa called the bank. But there also, people didn't know whether the fees had been increased and they did not believe the Smiths qualified for the special program since neither was over 65. They did not qualify even though they had been customers of the bank for more than twenty-five years and had accounts that by then totalled about $750,000 (without the $80,000 mortgage). When the credit card came up for renewal, the family canceled it. A few weeks later, when several of the certificates of deposit matured, instead of automatically renewing them, John checked the rates at other banks. First Commercial was lower than most of them by two points or more. John transferred about $60,000 in CDs to the higher paying banks. No one at First Commercial said a word. Sometime later, the bank that held the new mortgage contacted John about a special program. If they opened a $1,000 balance checking account and a savings account, it would give John a free safety deposit box, and since they were over 50, it would pay interest on the checking account and not charge for check printing. John closed the First Commercial safe deposit account

(then costing $60 a year) and stopped writing checks on the account so that they could close that, too.

A month or so after closing the checking account, John received a statement from First Commercial showing an overdraft and a service charge. He figured it was a computer error since the account had been closed for more than thirty days and there were no checks outstanding. He ignored it. But the next statement had another service charge added to the first. He went into the bank fuming. But he had failed to close the overdraft protection on the defunct account. Since First Commercial considered that the account was still open and had zero funds, it billed John $6 for the monthly statement and also lent $100 to cover the $6 overdraft created by the statement charge. John was now two statements into this process, and the negative balance was growing. The bank made it clear that it was John's fault for not knowing to cancel the overdraft protection when he closed the account. But they generously offered to forgive the charges. After that, John felt no guilt about closing First Commercial accounts. They still had two mortgages there, but when the properties were sold, they put the proceeds in the new bank. Finally, the only thing left was the profit-sharing plan, which had grown to about $500,000. The trust officer who had replaced the original adviser called one day and suggested that John roll the plan into an IRA deposit account to save annual fees. First Commercial was charging about $900 a year to send out the account statements. That seemed stiff, but the account was growing and inertia kept John from looking around. Now, his own trust officer suggested that he leave the trust department where he had been doing business for thirty years.

So John looked around, and what he found was an investment officer at another bank who sketched out a program of growth and income substantially exceeding what he had been getting at First Commercial. Barring an original broker's fee, there were only nominal annual

---

Supercommunity banking is a valued concept, but not by lip service alone. Quality service must follow.

---

charges. The broker's fee was earned back during the first year's increased earnings, and the account still grew by more than it had at First Commercial. So that's the end of a long relationship. And the lesson to be learned is clear. Supercommunity banking is a valued concept, but not by lip service alone. Quality service must follow.

Here is an another example of how quality counts with a small business. A large heavy equipment manufacturer with sales of over $50 million was banking with one of the largest institutions in town. Due to the recession at this time, the manufacturer experienced decline in financial performance and went through some tough times. As a result, the bank put a lot of restrictive covenants on the manufacturer. For example, all capital expenditures over $50,000 required bank approval. Within a short period of time, things started turning around for the company, and they became

highly profitable. The company approached the bank and asked to have the covenants loosened. The bank was unwilling to make any changes to these restrictive covenants. The company felt that the bank was being unreasonable and decided to move the relationship to a financial institution that would be more flexible. The company moved to another large institution in the same town.

Things went well for a couple of years until the institution decided to restructure. The responsibility for this loan was transferred to another division. The officers assigned to the account were inexperienced and did not have a good understanding of the business. Further, officer turnover occurred, and the new loan officer established very restrictive covenants on this borrower despite the fact that the company was continuing to make good money. Despite the company's pleadings, the bank did not agree to lessen restrictive covenants.

About the same time, the company's leasing subsidiary established a deposit relationship with a supercommunity bank in a neighboring town. Because of the good service they received there, the company made the decision to move the overall relationship to the supercommunity bank two years later. When asked about their experience with the bank, the customer said, "There was no lending turnover. The lending officer took the time to fully understand our company and its financial condition. As a result, the covenants established were reasonable and appropriate to our financial condition. Further, when we needed a decision, turnaround time was quick." Recently, the customer had an opportunity to buy assets of a competitor and needed money quickly. The supercommunity bank delivered. The company's financial needs were met quickly and efficiently. To make a long story short, the supercommunity bank developed a closer relationship with the customer than his previous bank had, and they had all the products and services required to meet this particular customer's needs.

Total quality management is an accepted buzzword today. However, as more and more companies adopt the TQM banner, more criticism and cynicism are heard from top executives. Due to the faddishness of the concept and its fuzzy, intangible nature, many corporate leaders ask the question, "Does quality management really pay?" As CEOs point the finger at companies that are undertaking quality programs but losing money, it may be helpful to provide some specific examples of the implementation of quality management around the country and the relationship between that program and the bottom line.

What is Quality?

The concept of quality came to the limelight as quality management became more successful after Dr. Deming's introduction of quality into Japanese management in the 1950s. It revolutionized the Japanese industry. At the time, we in the U.S. did not listen, because we thought we knew what quality was. In the 1980s, quality was reintroduced to the U.S. We were much more open to Deming's thoughts in the 1980s because the American industry was now in trouble and rapidly losing market share to the Japanese.

Many other quality gurus emerged in the 1980s, such as Phil Crosby, who did a lot of work on the cost of poor quality. He claimed that 40% of the service industries' operating expenses are due to waste and re-work. If that could be eliminated, the impact on the bottom line would be signif-

Each company needs to take an approach that makes sense within its own organization and fits with the culture and goals it is trying to achieve.

icant. Tom Peters, author of *In Search of Excellence,* also preached that quality is the most important ingredient in selling products or services. He focused on customers and what they want.

Although each guru has his own message about quality, these messages are being interpreted by thousands of consultants and authors across the country, resulting in many differing definitions. It can be confusing to try to sort through the reams of available information and decide where to start and what to focus on first. That is the toughest, and most important, part. The answer lies in aligning the quality effort with the supercommunity bank concept and your own bank's culture. The meaning of quality for each individual institution can be very specific and customized. Each company needs to take an approach that makes sense within its own organization and fits with the culture and goals it is trying to achieve.

What do we mean by customer satisfaction or going the extra mile? Here is an example. Nancy, a personal banker, opened an account for a new customer. In error, the checks were delivered to the office instead of to the customer's home address. At the same time, the customer called to inquire about the check order, since he had not received them. During the conversation, Nancy learned that the customer had become disabled and was planning to send a taxi to pick up the checks. Nancy delivered the checks herself during her lunch hour. If a supercommunity bank has heroes like Nancy, integrating that service level into the culture, making that the norm, is a major differentiation factor and a competitive barrier that supercommunity banks can use in defending and expanding their customer relationships.

Another bank's customer who switched to a supercommunity bank wrote after opening an account that he was not pleased with the service he received at his previous bank. Because of too many service charges and a condescending attitude of the employees, he took his business to a supercommunity bank's personal banker. He said, "Your bank's smaller size is more than offset by the thoroughly friendly, warm, and open acceptance of me as a valued customer." This is the personification of the hypothesis we drew when we said that supercommunity banks can become superior competitors and outperform the local and the national banks.

Quality service is so important because 96% of dissatisfied customers do not complain; they just switch accounts.

Bank Marketing Association's Quality Focus Institute conducted a national consumer survey in 1992. It mailed a 72-question survey to 20,000 households and received 1,700 responses. The purpose of the survey was to help bankers identify what could be done to direct their service quality improvement initiatives. The benefit such redirection hopes to incur is to produce greater payback in overall customer satisfaction, retention, and cross-selling. The study resulted in a quality-focused service strategy map (Figure 9.1). It shows eight service quality dimensions in terms of customer satisfaction, improvement potential, and impact. There are four quadrants in the strategy map that help prioritize bank activities in terms of their potential impact and relative importance in customer satisfaction.

Quadrant I - Focus

This quadrant describes the service quality areas that should receive high priority:

FIGURE 9.1 Quality-Focused Service Strategy Map
Commercial Banks

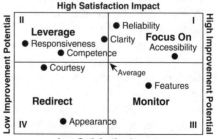

Data from BMA's consumer survey show the areas in which banks should be making more or less effort to satisfy customers.
Source: Bank Marketing Association

- *Reliability,* which implies consistent, accurate, and dependable delivery of products and services.
- *Accessibility,* which involves hours and locations available, approachability of employees, availability of senior management, accessibility of the CEO and the chairman, and the navigability of the layout, or the ease with which you can move through the branch or the bank facility.

These elements have a significant impact on the customer's perception of overall satisfaction and appear to offer a considerable potential for improvement.

Quadrant II - Leverage

This quadrant represents the financial institution's service quality strengths that can be further leveraged. They include:

- *Clarity.* How clearly do you communicate your policies and procedures as well as loan and CD terms? Clarity of communication is relevant also in communicating the bank's desired strategic position, commitment to the community, service level commitment, and other corporate-wide objectives and visions.
- *Responsiveness.* The willingness to serve, and the ability to quickly and correctly answer questions and respond to the customer's needs.
- *Competence.* Employee's skill, knowledge, professionalism, and helpfulness.

These are all behavioral aspects that can be specifically and precisely addressed through scripts, corporate incentives, and other programs within the bank that can enhance the bank's ranking in those elements. Banks should leverage these items because they have an impact on the overall satisfaction of consumers. Although the BMA survey states that potential for improvement in these areas is low, I believe banks should continue current service efforts in these areas because they appear to be right on target. Further, they can be improved with relative ease because mode of communication, telephone scripts, and other measurements of clarity, responsiveness, and competence can be accomplished relatively easily and at a low cost. The surveys presented later in this chapter provide one tool and example for accomplishing some of these values.

Quadrant III - Monitor

These are areas the survey deems to be of lower priority. They involve elements such as products and services, prices, and fees. Although these did not rate high in terms of satisfaction impact, they do offer considerable improvement potential. Banks should monitor these areas and continuously reassess their product features and pricing after taking care of high-ranking priorities. Experience indicates that most consumers do not respond to price cuts or fee increases if they do not involve a reduction in service levels. In other words, as shown in the *American Banker's Consumer Survey,* January 1992, customers do not defect for a 25-basis-point price differential on a CD. (**Note:** It appears that the switching margin has narrowed since rates declined below 6%, and 0.25% means a lot more when one's income is 3% than when it is 10%.

Product features do have an impact on customer satisfaction, but pricing, although relevant, is not a key variable. Supercommunity banks certainly found that long-term relationships can outweigh price sensitivity and that customer erosion does not occur when slight pricing adjustments take place. This intuitive and anecdotal experience certainly confirms the BMA survey results.)

Quadrant IV - Redirect

This should be the financial institution's lowest priority, according to the survey. Elements in Quadrant IV include:

- *Courtesy.* Characteristics such as friendliness, being considerate, and being respectful.
- *Appearance.* That refers to both the bank and its employees. Both elements do not appear to offer either much improvement potential or a significant satisfaction impact. Customers do not appear to pay a premium for bank facilities or employee appearance. In fact, one supercommunity bank, Collective Federal in New Jersey, opted for very austere facilities for both corporate management and for branches, yet their customer retention and satisfaction levels are exceedingly high. There does not appear to be a direct relationship between appearance and general courtesy (as opposed to responsiveness, professionalism, etc.) and customer satisfaction. Therefore, bank management may wish to review these items and consider redirecting the resources to other areas.

One word of caution as one draws conclusions based on this national survey. Your customers may be different. Your job is to meet their expectations, which may vary from the national benchmarks described above.

The Marquette Story

Marquette Bank Minneapolis has improved its income over 30% a year since 1989. While this earning improvement results from many factors, quality management had a lot to do with it, both nontangibly in ways that cannot be traced into a specific bottom-line improvement, and

> *"Inherent in the vision is for the Marquette Banks to be responsible, supportive, and responsive to the needs of the communities. Each Marquette employee plays a critical role in, and has a responsibility for making this vision a reality."*

quite tangibly in cost-savings and revenue enhancements that have been tracked and measured by Marquette. Quality initiative at Marquette started from the very top with a clear vision statement: "The vision of the Marquette Banks is to be the premiere, high-quality, community banking group within the markets we serve. High quality will translate to consistent high performance measured by profitability, growth, and asset solidness. Inherent in the vision is for the Marquette Banks to be responsible, supportive, and responsive to the needs of the communities. Each Marquette employee plays a critical role in and has a responsibility for making this vision a reality."

The senior management at Marquette also put together a position statement that further emphasized the importance of responsiveness and quality service. Among the vision statement components were:

- To be proactive in the development, maintenance, and enhancement of long-term customer relationships.
- To be perceived as a unique and leading provider of financial products in Minnesota, *primarily through outstanding customer service.*

Marquette's guiding principles include people, customers, products, and service. "*People* are the source of our strength and key to our success. Accordingly, they will be empowered to act. To prepare them for this responsibility, we will emphasize employee education and development, provide opportunity, and be responsive to their professional needs. Satisfied *customers* are essential to increasing customer satisfaction and achieving the goals of becoming a supercommunity bank. Part of *employee satisfaction* is that employees need to have the necessary knowledge to make decisions and share the vision of what the company is all about."

Marquette started the program with an advertisement that said, "If you had a nickel for every time a bank promised you unequalled service, well, you'd probably own a few banks by now, wouldn't you? The words, *unequalled service* have been dangled in front of you so many times they have probably lost most of their meaning by now. But it's our goal to change that with a truly unequalled service called The Marquette Visit. It's a way to get answers either by phone or in person to those nagging financial questions. . . . you will be pleasantly surprised to find out that there is, there really is, such a thing as unequalled service, and it won't cost you an extra nickel to get there."

Figure 9.2 (The Doberman Ad) is another example of Marquette's commitment to quality as it was communicated externally. Marquette and other banks like it took the time to communicate that commitment both externally and internally. For example, senior management said, "Our products should provide the highest value and be delivered with the highest degree of service to provide our customers with satisfaction *beyond their expectations.*" Marquette did not just want to meet customer expectations. It was committed to exceeding those expectations. That's where the value comes in, and that's where quality comes in. Quality has served at Marquette as well as in other companies as a rallying point.

As the banking industry restructures, a major segment of the business plans to use customer relationships as the anchor to its franchise value and profitability enhancement. For those banks, service is a "non-negotiable." Quality programs will allow these companies to translate their commitment to service into total customer satisfaction (if done right, of course.) Further, senior management can use the total quality management discipline to enhance products and service levels while, at the same time, reducing the cost of producing these

FIGURE 9.2 Marquette Bank's Commitment to Quality

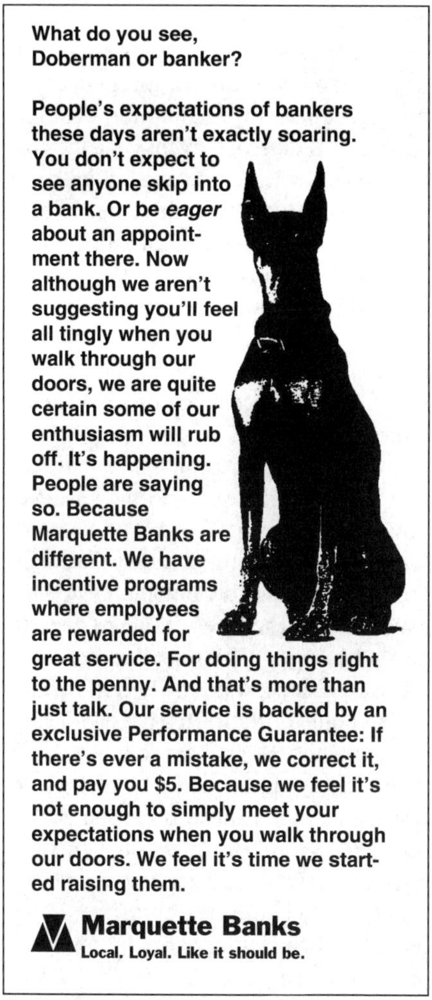

What do you see, Doberman or banker?

People's expectations of bankers these days aren't exactly soaring. You don't expect to see anyone skip into a bank. Or be *eager* about an appointment there. Now although we aren't suggesting you'll feel all tingly when you walk through our doors, we are quite certain some of our enthusiasm will rub off. It's happening. People are saying so. Because Marquette Banks are different. We have incentive programs where employees are rewarded for great service. For doing things right to the penny. And that's more than just talk. Our service is backed by an exclusive Performance Guarantee: If there's ever a mistake, we correct it, and pay you $5. Because we feel it's not enough to simply meet your expectations when you walk through our doors. We feel it's time we started raising them.

Marquette Banks
Local. Loyal. Like it should be.

Source: Marquette Banks.

products and services. At Marquette, both customer satisfaction improvement and profit enhancement are expected from any changes to products or processes. If both criteria are not satisfied, the change is not going to take place. As other banks consider quality programs, they may elect to use these criteria in their implementation of the program.

Quantification of profit improvement and customer satisfaction are necessary to implement quality improvement programs and to measure whether those criteria are being met. At Marquette, profitability increased by more than $2 million a year in a period of under two years due directly to the quality initiative. This amounts to 10% of the bank's total bottom line, a material contribution. Others, such as Banc One, attribute over 20% of total net income to their quality management efforts.

Definition of Quality

Most definitions of quality include three basic elements:

1. *Re-engineering work processes*— Figuring out how to do what you do better and more efficiently. Looking at the end result and rearranging the work to achieve that end result most effectively.
2. *Satisfying employees*—As Federal Express says: "Satisfied employees make satisfied customers."
3. *Meeting and exceeding customers' expectations*—Quality should be customer defined and driven. The commitment to quality must be clearly identified from the top. Many banks (and other companies) pay lip service to quality, but they cannot effectively implement it without a clear and unwavering commitment. Quality is best

integrated into a bank where the quality process is being used as a management tool for changing the corporate culture to one that is more customer focused and that provides high-quality service.

As a part of the process of defining what the bank wants to become and facilitating the change in the culture, vision and position statements need to be developed as well as guiding principles that serve as the credo of the organization. Typically, off-site sessions with a senior management team are conducted to generate a vision statement that reflects the opinion and brain power of the entire management team. The information then is taken back to the employees for their thoughts and feedback. The board is also often involved in the process through an off-site board retreat to gain board insights into the integration of quality into the company's identity.

As we have seen before, Marquette Banks integrated the concept of quality and defined it in their vision statement. "The vision of the Marquette banks is to be the premiere high quality community banking group within the markets we serve. High quality will translate to consistent high performance measured by profitability, growth and asset quality. Inherent in this vision is for the Marquette banks to be responsible, supportive, and responsive to the needs of the community we serve. Each Marquette employee plays a critical role and has a responsibility for making this vision a reality." Although the vision does not include specific definitions of high performance and its measurement in terms of customer satisfaction and employ-

ee fulfillment, these elements were defined in the position statement and guiding principles. The position statement describes Marquette as striving to be perceived as a unique and leading financial service provider through outstanding customer service. It is designed to cultivate the ability of each office to respond quickly and independently to the unique needs of its neighborhoods. The customer therefore is expected to consider quality service a major differentiation factor and an identity provider. To achieve that, Marquette must be proactive in the development, maintenance, and enhancement of long-term customer relationships.

Marquette advertising campaigns were designed to demonstrate to the customers how they were different. The company was not simply going to satisfy customers; they were going to raise the customers' expectations. They were going to go a step beyond superior quality service. For example, during a snowstorm on Halloween, a major hotel in their city needed a large change order. Bank staff was not able to come during the morning to pick up the change, and the bank was closing at noon due to the storm. Brinks was not operating either. Driving was near impossible, but Todd, a teller in a nearby office, volunteered to bring the change order to the hotel after the bank closed. This is what excellence is all about.

With advertising that pledges quality, the challenge of living up to the campaign claims was not easy. Constant attention to improving service levels is required to achieve this objective: it involves self-examination and continuous questioning of how things can be improved. An attitude change is needed when problems occur as well. Everyone needs to focus on uniting to resolve problems rather than placing blame.

The role of employees is critical to the success of a quality program. Satisfied employees are important to enhanced customer satisfaction. Part of the employee satisfaction is meeting their own needs to have the necessary knowledge to make decisions and share the company's vision of what the business is all about. Marquette's organizational structure and move toward empowerment changed the role of managers and employees alike. Employees now have more authority and responsibility for executing the decisions they make. Managers serve as a resource to the employees and participate in teams to solve problems and provide training.

Employee fulfillment became one of the measures of success of the Marquette quality program. Managers and their staff are measured in terms of employee satisfaction. One company, Old National Bank of Indiana, went so far as to require managers to give all their subordinates feedback on their work on a monthly basis. The results were astounding. Employee motivation and productivity increased many times. They did not feel "watched over" and monitored, as some had feared. Instead, employees felt nurtured and appreciated. They valued their managers' feedback more than financial incentives for ongoing performance. However, the ultimate measure is customer satisfaction. The goal is to provide customers with satisfaction beyond their expectations, a difficult and most ambitious goal to meet. An important aspect of this goal is that exist-

ing customers should be treated with the same degree of attention and diligence as new or prospective customers. We tend to focus our efforts in acquiring new customers, and thereby neglect and lose too many of our existing customers. This is a tremendous waste of resources, given that it costs seven times more to attract a new customer than to cross-sell an existing one.

Establishing the Quality Improvement Process

The following steps can be used to institute a quality improvement process in your bank:

- *Senior management commitment*—In order to have an effective quality program, the company must establish as a goal the implementation of a meaningful quality improvement process. The initiative for that process needs to be driven from the top, including a commitment from the chief executive.
- *Measurement of success*—Quality itself needs to be defined in a measurable way. It affects both revenue enhancement and cost reduction. Re-engineering work flows and finding ways to do things better at less cost without negatively affecting customer satisfaction is a quality initiative. The quality banner should be used to guide actions and support changes that are needed throughout the organization, ranging from business plans and incentive compensations to marketing and communications (Figure 9.3).
- *Chief quality officer*—Many companies appoint a chief quality officer as the

first step in signifying their commitment to quality. This initiative is then communicated to all officers and supervisors, while clearly setting expectations. The chief quality officer is the cheerleader for quality in the organization. He or she needs to work with both management and the employees to help embrace, endorse, and actually live the notion of quality improvement.

- *Training*—Training is an essential component of the concept. Professional development and education for all managers and employees is integral to the concept and is an easy way to begin. First and foremost, your chief quality officer should visit other companies that have successfully implemented quality improvement programs, both within and outside the financial services industry. In some companies even the directors get involved in the process, and one of their retreats is dedicated to the subject of quality. Should you elect to get the directors involved, have industry experts with a success story share their experiences with the board so they will understand better what the concept is all about. Overall, a training curriculum needs to be developed to arm the employees with the knowledge they need to bring about quality improvements across the company.

- *The structure of the process and quality councils*—In addition to identifying individual responsibility for the quality initiative and to providing training across the board, a quality council is often established as a vehicle to plan, monitor, and support the activities nec-

essary for effective implementation and continuity of a quality improvement process. At Marquette, the mission of the quality council was "to support and promote behaviors and attitudes among all employees that emphasize quality service and customer focus. This requires fostering a leadership style that empowers employees to provide high-quality service and continuously look for ways to further improve. Success will be measured by increases in customer satisfaction levels. Accomplishing this will result in enhanced financial performance with competitive advantage for the organization and improved quality of work life for our employees."

FIGURE 9.3 Marquette Bank's Quality Management 1992 Objectives

1. Complete the following quality improvement activities:

   - 70% of staff receive quality awareness training

   - 100% of new and updated position descriptions include quality criteria

   - 30% of employees participate on Quality Improvement Teams

2. Identify and develop Quality Leaders for all key business units and banks

3. Develop Quality Council as facilitating body for Quality Improvement Teams

4. Establish meaningful quality measures in all areas of the company

5. Translate quality improvement efforts into revenue enhancements and efficiency gains of $2,000,000

The mission defined what Marquette wanted to become and how they would know if they were successful. Banks that embark on a quality improvement program must define clearly and with measurable objectives where they want to go quantitatively and qualitatively. Without such clear definition you will not know whether you are making progress, and the subject of quality will remain amorphous.

The quality council is often responsible for spreading a common vision and an understanding of the quality concept across the organization (Figure 9.4). That is achieved, in part, by defining the appropriate standards that are important to customer satisfaction and by measuring performance along these standards. The council can also be used to ensure that appropriate progress is being made in implementing

FIGURE 9.4 Marquette Bank's Quality Council Goals

- Spread a common vision and understanding of quality across the organization

- Ensure standards exist in areas deemed important to customer satisfaction

- Ensure appropriate progress is being made in implementing the quality improvement process

- Establish company-wide initiatives to improve service quality

- Provide recognition systems that acknowledge quality improvements and reinforce behaviors consistent with delivering quality service

- Allocate resources and eliminate obstacles to ensure success of process

- Expand employees knowledge and understanding of the importance of consistently delivering high-quality service

the quality improvement process by monitoring customer surveys, establishing satisfaction measures, overseeing the quality training performed, and by monitoring the progress of quality teams. Company-wide initiatives should be established to improve service quality, as teams are set up to resolve cross-departmental and organizational issues. In addition, organization-wide surveys need to be done to measure overall customer and employee satisfaction on a periodic basis. Such measurement is essential to the success of the program because it identifies the desired result and puts a tangible aspect into quality. Further, recognition systems need to be provided that acknowledge quality improvements and reinforce behaviors consistent with delivering quality service. These can range from simple recognition systems, such as company-wide contests, plaques, and banners, to overall compensation systems.

Part of implementation also involves resource allocation and the elimination of obstacles to ensure the success of the process, such as limitation of financial resources, time, prioritization, and walls between divisions and companies. Again, senior management commitment can ensure that these obstacles are eliminated and that the proper resources are allocated to the quality initiative.

Quality leaders need to be appointed in each major business unit. They should spend about 25% of their time on the issue of quality and should be the cheerleader for their units. They typically provide support and resources to their management in getting quality integrated into the day-to-day activities.

FIGURE 9.5 Marquette Bank's Check Reorder Error Rates

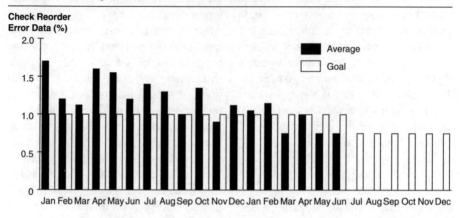

Check Reorder Error Data (%)

■ Average
□ Goal

Jan Feb Mar Apr May Jun Jul Aug Sep Oct Nov Dec Jan Feb Mar Apr May Jun Jul Aug Sep Oct Nov Dec

Results

Examples are helpful in illustrating the implementation of quality programs. At Marquette, for example, the check vendor and reorder program benefited substantially from their quality improvement initiative (Figures 9.5 and 9.6). The bank's check vendor project team approached the purchasing program as a quality initiative, looking to drive down errors, drive up turnaround time, and reduce overall expense. In evaluating different vendors, the team was able to negotiate and include specific quality standards in the new contract and consequently saved $550,000. And the vendor agreed to include quality standards in the contract and provide a monthly report of errors by office. This was a hard decision since the bank has always been with one vendor whose headquarters were in the same town as the bank itself. Despite the hard transition, the results were stunning. When error reports started, the average error rate was 1.65%.

At that rate, 3,000 customers received check orders with errors. The industry average was 1%, and that's what was established as the goal. Monthly reports continued to be provided to the offices, along with copies of all errors. A cross-departmental team was established to review the process and implement the changes. The team also reviewed results of customer satisfaction surveys with the vendor's staff and discussed strategies to increase customer satisfaction ratings. Within a year, customer errors dropped 56%. By the beginning of the next year, the goal was achieved and has consistently been exceeded since then. The best offices received recognition in the form of pizza parties and certificates of achievement. The reduction in errors meant that the vendors saved about $15,000 a year in reprinting costs. The efforts led the bank to be able to renegotiate a very favorable contract with the vendor again.

This example demonstrates how quality can be applied not only externally toward

FIGURE 9.6 Quality Improvement Teams

Issues	Identified Impact
Zero Balance Account Charges	$10,200
Loan Operations Quality Goals	
Proof New Employee Orientation	
Phone System Upgrade	
LifeSpan Account Conversion	69,200
Vault Job Responsibility Re-evaluation	
Data Entry Security Access	
ATM Card Ordering Procedures	
Automated Adjustment Log	7,000
Overdraft Fed Regulations Compliance	
Chek Systems Billings	15,000
Savings Ticket Filing Elimination	
Revise Unposted Procedures	1,000
Automate Control Disbursement Processing	2,756
Outgoing Mail Sort Analysis	
Cannon Falls Handling Code	
Address Changes	
Microfilm Research	3,000
Retail Overdrafts	25,000
Analysis of Overnite Couriers	6,000
Profitability Statement Paper Conversion	1,300
ATM Card Notice	
Apple Valley Quality Tracking	
Knollwood Teamwork and Product Knowledge	
CD Clean-up	500,000
Customer Loans Selling Video	
Customer Credit Training	$14,000
Total	**$654,456**

enhanced service levels and, therefore, enhanced revenues, but also internally to improve cost performance. Although many look at such improvement as cost-reduction initiatives, we consider them quality-driven programs, and the results—significant dollar savings—are generated through every examination of the way things are done in an effort to improve the quality of the product and to reduce errors (the zero

defect program). At the same time, quality affects service levels and customer satisfaction significantly.

Here is another example of how quality initiatives and employee participation can save money. Ken, a bookkeeper at Marquette, identified a problem with fee income in the area of returns, overdrafts, and chargebacks. Many customers were not being charged the "special instruction fee" of $25 per account. Ken decided to look into this and ordered a printout of all the customers who made that request. Then he researched each account and determined whether the special fee was appropriately charged. Ken made corrections to coding on corporate accounts and started monitoring on a monthly basis the small business accounts and charges that needed to be assessed. In addition, he established procedures to ensure that charges are passed to the accounts on an ongoing basis. This resulted in an $85,500 annual fee income increase, the work of one committed employee. Quality savings and revenue enhancements such as this are an integral component of supercommunity banking. With all employees on board, quality initiatives result in both revenue enhancement and cost containment without penalizing service levels, thereby allowing supercommunity banks to be cost-effective while offering superior service.

Marquette has used the quality management process as a marketing strategy through branded offerings such as the bank's Performance Guarantee. This program was introduced in 1988, and it communicates to the customer Marquette's quality orientation by thanking the customer for bringing calling errors to the

FIGURE 9.7

Quick: Which bank is sorrier?

**The Other
  Bank**

Dear Customer,

We are very sorry.

                    Sincerely,

                    [signature]

                    President
                    The Other Bank

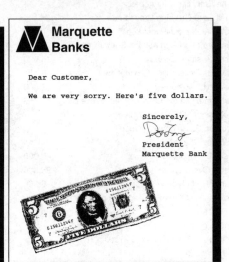

**Marquette
  Banks**

Dear Customer,

We are very sorry. Here's five dollars.

                    Sincerely,

                    [signature]

                    President
                    Marquette Bank

Let's say that both of these fine banks made a mistake on your checking account. Both would offer sincere apologies. But only one puts its money where its mouth is.

At Marquette Bank, your checking account is covered by our Performance Guarantee. If we make a mistake handling your account, we'll pay you $5 for the inconvenience. And that's a guarantee we put on every Performance Checking Account.

Our most basic account offers free checking. We have another that's geared for young active families. Still another that pays interest. One that meets the needs of senior citizens and one that's made for people who've already made it. Now quick

Which is the bank to have your checking account with?

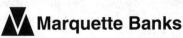

Marquette Banks

The Best News in Banking

Source: Marquette Banks

TABLE 9.1 Performance Guarantee Tracking—Marquette Banks

Errors	1992	1991	1990
Marquette Card or PIN not ordered as requested	28	71	51
Check order completed in unsatisfactory or incorrect manner	57	133	72
Customer charged in error for check printing	61	221	98
Account maintenance not done or done incorrectly	141	153	100
Accounts service charge charged in error	41	151	43
Check encoded for incorrect amount	190	364	237
Deposit or withdrawal encoded for incorrect amount	128	189	111
Other transaction errors	136	342	322
Statements received with missing or incorrect items	54	104	226

Note: Year-to-date June 30 totals. 1991 totals reflect acquisition of Midwest Federal, which increased volumes approximately 60%.

bank's attention and paying them $5 as a reward (Figure 9.7). Marquette kept track of the Performance Guarantee payments and the reason for payment (Table 9.1). By so doing, they have developed an excellent tool to measure quality improvement while prioritizing systemic problems for solution. Over the last three years, the Bank's payout is down by 33%. It totals only $12,000 annually. The goodwill generated and the money saved through lower account attrition and quicker problem resolution is significant. One should note that the payments for failures in the Performance Guarantee program are borne by the office responsible for the guarantee. This, in turn, enhances teamwork across offices in working to solve shared problems.

Working with vendors is another example of how financial institutions can make quality management pay. Data processing costs are often a bank's second largest expense category after personnel costs. Data processing lends itself well to classic quality management concepts such as emphasis on front-end definition and design along with strong project management, error reduction, and cost reduction over the life of a given set of software. Marquette used its multiyear relationship

> *One should note that the payments for failures in the Performance Guarantee program are borne by the office responsible for the guarantee. This, in turn, enhances teamwork across offices in working to solve shared problems.*

with their third-party facilities manager to implement quality initiatives in partnership with the vendor. Their new five-year data processing contract has language in the agreement itself that guides both parties in their efforts to drive down the per account costs while improving overall customer satisfaction. The contract has a full section devoted to quality standards and objec-

FIGURE 9.8 Vendor A Customer Satisfaction Survey

- Our reputation in the financial industry
- How well we understand your business
- Fulfillment of contractual and verbal promises
- How in touch we are with your industry's needs and today's industry issues
- The overall quality of our service
- Your confidence in our systems and services
- The overall range of our services
- How well we are performing to your expectations
- Our ability to bring solutions to your problems

tives. Included in the section are specific discussions of the quality partnership the vendor and Marquette are forging, with details on performance standards and proper resolution procedures (Figure 9.8 and 9.9). Guiding this partnership is the notion that standardization of software, elimination of custom programming, and heavy emphasis on customer training and service will translate to an improved bottom line. The contract requires that satisfaction surveys be taken for all system users and that improvements be obtained. Data processing costs were meaningfully reduced as a per account cost over the life of the contract as a result of this approach.

Investing in Quality

Marquette committed significant resources to its quality program. In the first six months of 1992, however, quantitative benefits associated with quality improvement exceeded the investment in the pro-

gram five times, with implied returns of 500% on the initiative. Overall company performance improved 30% as well, resulting in a return on assets of 1%.

Quality improvement pays in many institutions. One example is the $40 billion bank's effort depicted in Table 9.2, Figure 9.10, and Figure 9.11. As you can see, a major investment was made in the quality program. The bank instituted up to ninety-one quality councils and involved over twenty-three employees and over 101,000 customers in the process in 1990. This is a corporate-wide, in-depth commitment to the concept and implementation of quality. The results? Close to $12 million worth of savings. The savings grow exponentially as you follow the relationship between savings and investments in quality improvements from 1986 to 1990. Although this bank is especially successful in its quality improvement program, probably the result of its unwavering commitment to

FIGURE 9.9 Vendor A Performance Goals

- 98.5% monthly average requirement to deliver printed reports on time
- 98.5% monthly average on-line up-time
- 3.5 seconds average monthly response time for remote terminals; maximum response time not to exceed ten seconds for one inquiry and host turn around time not to exceed one second
- Phone calls returned same business day
- 80% of reported problems resolved within 3 days of receipt
- Status of DPR's communicated within three days of receipt
- Application releases implemented within six months of agreement to implement

TABLE 9.2 Quality Improvement Results at a $40 Billion Supercommunity Bank

	1986	1987	1988	1989	1990
Quality Councils	23	33	72	63	91
Quality Training	980	1,784	934	1,906	2,272
Quality Standards	269	789	1,370	1,354	975
Customers Surveyed	156,000	206,861	194,214	88,692	101,605
Employees Surveyed	4,500	6,432	11,877	12,137	23,114
Improvement Teams	96	277	488	871	1,306
Projects Completed	50	201	182	574	417
Savings/Revenue Enhancement	$774,000	$3,129,000	$4,101,000	$8,556,000	$11,961,826
Quality Awards	272	1,429	3,119	7,027	15,394

it, others are equally successful. Banc One, Marquette, and others like them have come to realize that although quality initiatives require significant investment, the benefits reaped from them by far outweigh the investment within twelve months of program commencement. These benefits are only the quantitative benefits that can be directly attributed to quality enhancement, such as consolidation of processes, product simplification, and simplification of processes to make them more efficient, to name only a few. There are many other qualitative benefits not incorporated into this figure. They involve customer satisfaction, employee satisfaction, and the ultimate enhancement of the franchise value.

The moral of this story is quality pays—in tangible dollars, in tangible benefits, and all around.

There are many do's and don'ts for implementing a quality initiative:

- Develop an infrastructure for the quality process.

FIGURE 9.10 TQM Savings Results at a $3 Billion Supercommunity Bank— Year One

CD's through proof	13,800
Postage paid envelopes	18,100
Travelers check consolidation	158,200
Cash in and out tickets	16,000
Eliminate social security advices	40,000
Service contract for ISC/bunker equipment	31,600
Drive in envelope group order	37,100
Teller receipt group order	11,700
Platform automation for mail tellers	2,500
Central proof	75,000
Eliminate free plus transactions on savings products	10,000
Single check vendor	550,000
Consolidated depository services	57,000
Stop mailing terms & conditions with ATM card	12,800
Elimination of paid parking	40,000
DDA product simplification	300,000
Central purchasing	140,000
One day availability on ATM deposits (MBM)	13,000
Total Savings in 1990	**$1,526,800**

FIGURE 9.11 TQM Savings Results at a $3 Billion Supercommunity Bank—Year Two

Eliminate sending receipts to correspondents	3,200
Consolidation of mortgage loan processing	52,000
Elimination of signature card capture	96,000
Single loan coupon vendor	5,000
Hold late mail overnight	20,000
Official check vendor	174,600
Vault services/couriers	22,000
Zip + 4 and bar coding	36,800
Group purchase of promotional items	15,000
Consolidation of savings product line	168,000
Standard Chex Systems contract	16,000
Total Savings in 1991	**$608,600**
GRAND TOTAL	**$2,135,400**

- Set realistic expectations. The process takes eighteen months to integrate into the company.
- It will take more time up-front than you anticipate. Plan well in advance for launching this comprehensive process.
- Recap your position periodically; you will realize that you have accomplished much more than you originally thought.
- Attempt to build quality as a way of life into the culture of the organization.
- A side benefit is enhanced communications and working relationships between departments, including those that had previously been strained.
- Avoid the perception that quality is just another program and a management fad that will go away.
- Spend considerable time educating and getting all senior management on board.
- Revise executive compensation to a reward system based on profitability

along with customer and employee satisfaction. This will move your quality process along faster.

- Do not kick off the process until your planning is completed and you are ready to involve the employees.

Quality as a Competitive Advantage

Supercommunity banks use quality programs as a differentiation factor and a competitive advantage to create barriers to entry by other companies. An example is the Performance Guarantee developed by Marquette and discussed earlier in this chapter. It was designed to differentiate the company in the marketplace as a banking organization committed to offering customers excellent service. The program focused on resolving customer complaints due to specific errors related to retail checking, savings, and time deposit accounts. It committed to paying the customer five dollars for bringing to the bank's attention an error resulting from a teller transaction, account transaction, or account opening or maintenance activities. The commitment to that program brought startling results. Despite a 60% increase in transaction volume (the result of an acquisition), the actual number of errors showed improvement in many areas. Overall, the program costs ranged from $12,000 to $21,000 over a three-year period. The company feels that for such a small expense it has been successful at differentiating itself in the marketplace. No other institution in town has begun to offer that guarantee.

The problem with a program like this is delivery. The banks across the supercommunity bank system must be able to administer the program consistently. In this situation, management found that some banks paid only when the customer asked for the money. Some paid anytime a problem was discovered, whether or not the customer brought it to their attention. Some also paid for service-related problems, although the program was not structured to include these elements. Therefore, administration of the program is important to its success. Another key is continuous feedback. Copies of the errors should be passed back to the departments where the error originated, so they can analyze for trends and determine what changes are required to eliminate the cause of the problem in the first place.

Total Quality Management— Implementation Tips

Knowing how the customers feel and what is important to them is essential to knowing how you are doing in your service efforts. Only the customers can tell you whether your commitment to quality is effective. Further, you want to put your buck where you get the most bang for it, and only the customers can tell you what is really important to them. Therefore, surveying your customer is of paramount importance and the best source for obtaining information on their needs.

Below are several examples of customer surveys you can readily implement in your bank.

Customer Satisfaction Survey

Figure 9.12 is an example of a very simple *customer satisfaction survey*. It communicates a clear and simple message to the customer. We, your bank, are committed to providing you with quality service and products. We want to meet your needs. Please take a few minutes to tell us how well we're doing. It is a postcard that is easy to fill but generates a lot of useful information for the bank.

Telephone Banking Survey

Figure 9.13 is a *telephone banking survey* that measures customer satisfaction on a specific product offering. It asks a handful of questions that allow the banker to understand where the pitfalls are and what matters most to the customer. The results exceeded expectations. The survey sensitized the staff to the importance of customer contact. A customer telephoned Banking Services and wanted to speak with the supervisor about why she had suddenly received service charges on her relationship account. The customer, who'd had her account with the bank since 1968, had never received a service charge previously. The supervisor discovered the customer had closed a $10,000 certificate. By closing the certificate, the customer brought her combined balance below minimum, which was the reason for the service charge. The supervisor explained all this to the customer and suggested she open another $10,000 certificate to bring her balance over the required minimum. Not

FIGURE 9.12 Customer Satisfaction Survey

ABC Bank
Member FDIC

CUSTOMER SATISFACTION SURVEY

At ABC Bank we are committed to providing quality service and products to meet our customers' needs. We appreciate your taking a few minutes to tell us how well we are living up to our commitment.

1. Reason for your visit today ❐ Deposit ❐ Cash Check ❐ Savings Withdrawal ❐ Open Account
   ❐ Information ❐ Close Account ❐ Problem Resolution ❐ Other_____
2. Were you assisted by ❐ Teller ❐ Banker ❐ Safe Deposit Personnel ❐ Lender ❐ Other_____
3. Were you greeted promptly ❐ Yes ❐ No
4. Quality of the service you received today

	Above Satisfactory	Satisfactory	Below Satisfactory
Friendly:	❐	❐	❐
Efficient:	❐	❐	❐

5. Does our service meet your expectations? ❐ Yes ❐ No - If no, how can we meet your expectations?
   _____
   _____
6. How does our service compare with other financial institutions you use?
   ❐ Better ❐ As Good ❐ Not as Good ❐ Do not use any other financial institution
7. Other comments you would like to share with us:
   _____
   _____
   _____
   _____

NO POSTAGE
NECESSARY
IF MAILED
IN THE
UNITED STATES

BUSINESS REPLY MAIL
FIRST CLASS   PERMIT NO.   CITY, ST

POSTAGE WILL BE PAID BY ADDRESSEE

ABC Bank
Joe Doe
1 First Avenue
Midwest, USA

FIGURE 9.13 Telephone Banking Survey

Thank you for the opportunity to be of assistance with your banking needs. In the ABC Bank tradition of providing the very best service possible, we need your input to monitor our performance. Your reply will be greatly appreciated.

Was our telephone banker courteous?
Yes_____ No_____

Was the telephone banker knowledgeable of the product you discussed?
Yes_____ No_____

Did the telephone banker provide clear answers to your questions?
Yes_____ No_____

Was the information you requested mailed promptly?
Yes_____ No_____

Did the telephone banker provide you with the service you requested?
Yes_____ No_____

How would you rate the service provided? Circle the number that reflects your opinion.

Excellent	Very Good	Satisfactory	Poor
10-9	8-7	6-5-4	3-2-1

Comments_____

---

only did the customer bring back the original $10,000, but she also brought additional deposits of $40,000.

Closed Accounts Survey

Similarly, Figure 9.14 and 9.15 relate to *closed accounts*. This chapter started with the story of the customer who closed the account and never heard from the bank. It is better to understand why each account is closed, so you can prevent future closings. The survey enclosed is designed to achieve that objective. It communicates a simple message. We're sorry you are closing your account with us. We would like to improve our performance, our service, and our

products to better meet your needs. Please let us know how we can do that. What the questionnaire says, in other words, is: "We are sorry we disappointed you. We would like to do better for you and for the rest of our customers. Please help us do that." This is a very subtle way to try to retain the account. But more importantly, it is also a useful tool to prevent other accounts from leaving. A typical survey administration procedure is to have the personal bankers hand it out and ask customers to complete it while they are taking care of the paperwork to close the account. The customer then leaves the survey with the receptionist. In business and trust accounts, the account officer can complete the survey. Weekly surveys should be compiled and results reviewed by the customer retention team to determine if the bank should reevaluate the policies or pricing. This is all consistent with the great emphasis on customer retention—a key to profitability.

Recently, a personal banker had a customer come to close a $25,000 CD. The customer did not intend to renew or open another CD because of low rates. The personal banker informed the customer of attractive rates on a seven-month special CD. She was able to persuade the customer to deposit $20,000 of the original $25,000 in the seven-month CD and sold the customer a money-market savings product where she deposited the remaining $5,000. Supercommunity banks should have very few accounts closed because of service issues since service and quality are a differentiation factor. In cases where the customer does indicate they left because of poor service, office branch managers

FIGURE 9.14 Closed Account Survey

We are sorry that you are closing your account(s) with us. We would appreciate your help in improving our service and products. To help us gather that information, please give us your comments on this short survey.

Thank you for your help.

1. The accounts closed:

   ❑ Checking _____
   ❑ Savings _____
   ❑ CD _____
   ❑ Loan _____
   ❑ Safe Deposit _____
   ❑ Trust _____
   ❑ Investment Services _____
   ❑ Other (please specify) _____

2. I closed my account(s) for the following reason(s):

   ❑ Moved, but still live in the same area
   ❑ Moved out of the area
   ❑ Lost or stolen account book
   ❑ Personal reasons (death, divorce, or marriage)
   ❑ Temporary account (escrow, trust, etc.)
   ❑ Consolidated my accounts at this bank
   ❑ Consolidated my account at
   _____
   ❑ Better services elsewhere (please explain)
   _____
   _____
   ❑ Better rate or price elsewhere (please explain)
   _____
   ❑ Inconvenient location
   ❑ Inconvenient banking hours
   ❑ Bank errors in account (please explain)
   _____
   _____
   ❑ Didn't get loan
   ❑ Discourteous personnel at
   _____
   ❑ Slow service at
   _____
   ❑ Dissatisfied with service charges (pls. explain)
   _____
   ❑ Other_____
   _____
   _____

3. I have had my account(s) here for:

   ❑ Less than one year
   ❑ 1 - 3 years
   ❑ 3 - 6 years
   ❑ 7 - 10 years
   ❑ More than 10 years

4. I currently use the services of another financial institution:

   ❑ Yes   ❑ No

   If yes, where_____
   and which services?

   ❑ Checking   ❑ Loan
   ❑ Savings   ❑ Safe Deposit
   ❑ CD   ❑ Trust
   ❑ Investment Services ❑ Other (specify)
   _____

5. I am aware of the recent plans to merge this bank with ABC Bank:

   ❑ Yes   ❑ No

6. These merger plans affected my decision to close my account(s) here:

   ❑ Yes (please explain)   ❑ No
   _____
   _____

7. Name_____

   Daytime Phone_____

8. Additional comments and suggestions:
   _____
   _____
   _____
   _____
   _____

Please fold and hand to receptionist

FIGURE 9.15 Closed Account Survey—Weeks of July 20 Through August 24, 1992

BRANCH	Total	%	1	2	3	4	5	6	7	8	9	10	11	12	13	14	15	16	17	18	19	20	21	22	23
Closed Account Surveys:	1508		16	33	109	47	25	89	36	42	26	136	26	21	71	75	87	261	33	7	5	30	221	83	29
Checking	689	46%	11	7	74	23	14	28	19	36	18	55	13	12	48	23	25	79	22	5	1	13	95	60	8
Savings	468	31%	5	16	21	17	11	37	13	6	7	50	10	8	14	28	31	58	8	1	3	6	92	21	7
CD	276	18%		10	5	6		21	4		1	29	3	1	5	22	27	82	3	1	3	9	31	2	13
Safe Deposit	60	4%			9			3				2			4	2	4	40				2	3		
Trust	0	0%																							
Investment Services	0	0%																							
IRA	12	1%													1			2							
Credit Line	3	0%													3								1		
Reason(s) for closing:	1826		17	41	137	60	33	108	43	46	30	173	35	28	102	87	102	306	46	7	6	42	245	93	39
Temporary account	30	2%		3	3		2	4			2		1	1			1					1	1	1	1
Consolidated accts at own bank	76	4%	1		5	5	2	6	1		2	5	2	1	4	3	8	7		2	2	2	20		1
Consolidated accts elsewhere	151	8%	1	3	5	5	2	4		1	2	23		3	12	9	4	36	2	2		3	28	3	3
Brokerage	0	0%																							
Bank 1	5	3%				2												3							
Bank 2	43	28%		1		2	1	1		1	1	8	3	3	3	1	1	6	2			1	11		
Bank 3	9	6%			1			1				3						1				1	1	1	
Bank 4	14	9%									1	3						1					1	2	
Credit Union	20	13%			2			1			1	4			3	1		1		2			9		
Bank 5	4	3%										2				1									
Bank 6	5	3%		2																					
Out of town	2	1%															1	1				1	1		
Other metro banks	24	16%		1	1	1	1	1				2	1			1	1	3	1		1	1	1		
No Response	25	17%	1	1	1			1				1			6	4	1	12		6			4		3
Better service elsewhere	85	5%	1	2	8	3	4	4	4		3	11	3	1	8	2	3	4	4			4	10	4	2
Better Rate/Price Elsewhere:	149	8%	1	9	11	7	2	11	5	1	3	24	2	2	7	11	3	23	4	0	1	4	10	1	7
Checking	36	24%	1		5		1		1	1	1	5	1	1	4	3	1	3	2			1	3		1
Savings	32	21%		3	1	1	1	1	1		1	5	1	1		2	1	6	1		1	1	5		1
CD's	72	48%		6	4	4	1	10	3			12			1	5	1	14	1	2	1	2	5	5	5
Other	9	6%			1	2			1		1	2		1	2	1			1			2	2	1	
Inconvenient location	123	7%	3	2	9	6	1	8	4	3	6	7	3	3	4	5	5	44	3	1		5	3	5	4
Inconvenient banking hours	12	1%			1			1			1	1	1	1	1	2	2	17			1	1		2	1
Bank errors in account	22	1%		2	2	2	2	1	2				1		1	2	2	3	1				4	1	
Didn't get loan	23	1%	1		2	4	1	4			2			5	5	2		5	3	2		1	6		1
Discourteous personnel	10	1%		3	2	2	1	2				5			3	2	2	6		2	2		6	5	
Slow service	2	0%										2					1	2				1		1	
Dissatisfied with service charges	56	3%	3	3	9	1	1	1	1		6	9	3	2	2	2	4	3	3		1	1	3	4	1
Moved out of the area	502	27%	8	5	48	9	10	18	17	33	10	37	9	25	25	18	25	60	17	2	8	8	65	60	6
Moved but in same area	37	2%	1	1	2	2	2	1	2	3		3	1	3	3	2	2	5	1			4	3	2	1
Personal reasons	302	17%	4	4	10	10	6	29	1	3	31	31	5		10	19	38	56	2	2	2	5	53	5	9
Dislikes FBS	32	2%	1	1	3	1		2	1		2	2	2	2	6	2	5	5	2	2	2	5	6	1	
Other/No response	214	12%	1	9	16	8	3	14	6	2	1	16	6	12	12	12	6	53	3	2	1	5	32	3	3

should call the customers to follow up if for no other reason than to apologize.

The results of the closed account survey for this particular bank (Exhibit 9.15) are interesting. It helped the bank identify two competitors that were capturing a lot of the business. Service accounted for only 5% of the defections. The reason quoted by the largest percent of closed-account customers (27%) was their moving out of the area. This not only helps the bank understand the competitive profile and potential defections but is also a good self-examination to know where improvements can be made. Quality is an ongoing feedback process, and this survey is an excellent example of a tool to achieve continuous feedback.

Customer Satisfaction Survey

The objective of the customer satisfaction survey (Figure 9.16) is to provide management with a clear picture of the strengths and weaknesses from the customer's perspective. It is designed to generate a sound basis for strategizing future enhancements in the quality process. The areas covered are presented below:

- Satisfaction with different services
- Satisfaction with interaction with staff
- Relative importance of various services and product features
- The bank's competitive strengths and weaknesses
- The bank's image among different groups

The survey methodology is simple. A letter announcing the survey from the bank president is mailed first. Surveys are mailed within a week of that letter. Each survey has approximately 80 questions. Individual bank results are compared with the average for all the affiliate banks participating, as well as Bank Administration Institute norms. Such surveys, combined with mystery shopper programs, can be used very effectively to improve employee performance and determine better ways to meet customer needs. Some supercommunity banks conduct customer satisfaction surveys by telephone. They use those to establish customer satisfaction goals for each office, and monthly calls are made to a sample of customers to assess the bank's performance.

The enclosed survey attempts to *quantify service levels* along twelve variables. It further attempts to uncover the customer's perception of quality in service, which is a tough proposition. Quality service is a fuzzy concept and is not perceived equally by all customers. Many surveys indicate high customer satisfaction in service, but that does not seem to reflect reality. In order to better understand that elusive concept, a simple survey like the one-pager in Figure 9.16 can help.

Lockbox Call Program

Quarterly calls are made to sample customers to determine how satisfied they are with their current level of service (Figure 9.17). Calls were found to be a more effective means of surveying customers than other available survey media. The response rate is higher, and more detailed information can be obtained about how well the bank is meeting customers' expectations.

FIGURE 9.16 Customer Satisfaction Survey

	Very Satisfied	Somewhat Satisfied	Somewhat Dissatisfied	Very Dissatisfied	N/A
I. How satisfied are you with the quality of service received at ABC Bank?					
1. Easy to read bank statements	1	2	3	4	N/A
2. Error-free bank statements	1	2	3	4	N/A
3. Timely arrival of bank statements	1	2	3	4	N/A
4. Telephone answered within 3 rings	1	2	3	4	N/A
5. Ease of obtaining information by phone	1	2	3	4	N/A
6. Prompt follow-up to questions and problems	1	2	3	4	N/A
7. Errors corrected promptly	1	2	3	4	N/A
8. Timely arrival of check orders	1	2	3	4	N/A
9. Quality of checks	1	2	3	4	N/A
10. Timely arrival of ATM card	1	2	3	4	N/A
11. Banking hours	1	2	3	4	N/A
12. Usual length of wait to be served	1	2	3	4	N/A
II. How satisfied are you with the bank staff?					
1. Greeting you with a smile	1	2	3	4	N/A
2. Concerned and caring	1	2	3	4	N/A
3. Helpfulness	1	2	3	4	N/A
4. Friendliness	1	2	3	4	N/A
5. Using your name	1	2	3	4	N/A
6. Handling phone transactions efficiently	1	2	3	4	N/A
7. Answering questions and resolving problems	1	2	3	4	N/A
8. Processing transactions without error	1	2	3	4	N/A
9. Knowledge of bank products and services	1	2	3	4	N/A
10. Thanking you for your business	1	2	3	4	N/A
11. Helpful in identifying your financial needs and solutions	1	2	3	4	N/A
12. Ability to help plan, find alternatives, and solve financial problems	1	2	3	4	N/A

Further, such calls can be used to develop the relationship with the customer, which, in turn, increases customer retention. Last, a phone call provides the caller with the ability to follow up and respond immediately if the customer is not satisfied. This can turn a dissatisfied customer into a more loyal customer. It was found that customers who have had a complaint but had it successfully resolved are more loyal than customers who did not have a complaint in the first place.

Similarly, the questionnaire (Figure 9.18) is a more detailed, two-page survey designed to disclose the customer's complete loan experience. Questions such as "what did that person do that was helpful or unhelpful" help the bank to understand why your customer approached you, how

FIGURE 9.17 Lockbox Call Program

Lockbox Customer Name:
Lockbox Contact: Phone#:
Mail Teller:
Date of Call:

Are all procedures being followed?

Is the backup work received neat, legible, and accurate?

If you have a question about the lockbox service, is your question responded to in a reasonable length of time and to your satisfaction?

Is the daily notification timely, complete, and accurate?

Any suggestion on ways we could better serve you?

Overall, how satisfied are you with the lockbox service we provide?

Other comments?

well the bank did, and explain more clearly the intangibles and the touchy-feely elements of the service component.

Consumer Loan Survey

It is helpful to implement the loan survey in conjunction with a loan campaign so that the two are linked in the customer's mind. The survey should be sent out after the loan transaction is completed, with the following objectives in mind:

* To find out how you're doing
* To communicate with the customers and involve them
* To find ways to improve service

The survey enclosed stresses personal attributes needed to deliver outstanding

service, the kind of service supercommunity banks want to be noted for, such as:

* Listening to customers
* Empathizing with their concerns
* Developing a sense of trust
* Answering objections
* Reflecting a sense of urgency
* Going the extra mile

The following story exemplifies the importance of these attributes as reflected in quality service: The customer phoned Dave, a consumer lender, at 8 a.m. He needed $5,000 by 10 a.m. to buy a car he had seen the night before. The owner of the car had another buyer and indicated he would sell it to the customer only if he could get the money to him before noon. The borrower lived thirty miles from the bank and could have had a choice of many closer banks, but he called Dave because he had worked with him before and knew he could count on him to come through. Dave faxed a blank copy of the application to the customer, which the customer completed and faxed back. Less than an hour from the time the customer's initial call took place, Dave approved the loan and called the customer back to come in and sign the papers as soon as he could get there. The customer had his loan by noon.

The surveys are not only tremendously informative and essential to the quality improvement program, they are also a highly effective marketing tool because they continue to communicate to the customer that the bank cares and that it continuously strives to fully meet their needs better and more efficiently every day.

FIGURE 9.18 Loan Questionnaire

Dear ABC Customer:
   Thank you for coming to ABC Bank for your loan. We hope you were pleased with the service you received.
   Would you take a few minutes to answer the questions below and let us know how we did? After you've answered the questions, simply use the enclosed stamped, addressed envelope and drop this in the mail.
   Thank you very much for helping. We value your business and your opinions.

1. Why did you choose ABC? Please check as many as apply.
__ Heard a radio advertisement
__ Read a newspaper advertisement
__ Received a postcard
__ Other_____

2. Who did you talk with first? Please check the best response.
__ Telephone banking representative
   (if you called 555-1234, this is who you talked to)
__ Receptionist/Operator - Which office?_____
__ Personal Banker or Lender - Which office?_____
__ Other_____

3. How helpful was the first person you talked with, either over the phone or in person? Please check one response.
__ Exceeded my expectations
__ About what I expected
__ Worse than I expected

4. How pleased were you with the lender you worked with? Please check one response.
__ Exceeded my expectations
__ About what I expected
__ Worse than I expected

5. How many hours did the process take, from your first phone call or visit until you received the funds? Please check one response.
__ Fewer than 8 hours
__ 8 to 24 hours
__ 24 to 48 hours
__ More than 48 hours

6. How pleased were you with the time the entire process took? Please check one response.
__ Faster than I expected
__ About what I expected (but could have been better)
__ Slower than I expected

7. How many hours should the process have taken?
   _____

8. Overall, how pleased were you with the experience of getting a loan at ABC Bank? Please check one.
__ Very pleased
__ Somewhat pleased
__ Somewhat disappointed
__ Very disappointed

9. Would you recommend ABC to a friend who needs a loan?
__ Yes
__ No
If no, why not?_____

If you would like to mention any ABC employee who was extremely helpful or needs some improvement, please write the name of that person here:
_____

What did that person do that was helpful or unhelpful?
_____
_____
_____

Please give us suggestions about how we could improve our lending services.
_____
_____
_____

If you would like to discuss our service further, please write your name and phone number below. We will call you.
Name_____
Best time to call_____Phone (___)_____

Thanks again for taking the time to help and for banking at ABC.

FIGURE 9-19 Deposit Operations Service-Level Agreement

Service	Standard
Stop Payments	Confirmation form mailed no later than day following receipt of stop request.
ATM Card Issuance	Cards issued within 3 business days of receipt of request.
New Account Set-ups (CIF) Account Maintenance CD/Monetary Transactions	All CIF material and information to CIF will be entered: • 1 day for critical items • 5 days for non-critical items
Pay-By-Phone	Transactions received by 3:00 pm are processed same day.
PIN Issuance	PINs produced and mailed twice weekly. Card and PIN issued within 1 week of card application receipt in Bookkeeping.
Retail DDA Checking Account and Savings Account Statements	Statements mailed on 3rd business day; error statements mailed by 5th business day.
Adjustments	Research completed and entries made within 2 to 5 business days after receipt of form. Rush requests processed as asked.
Courier Deadlines	Courier deadlines are met 100% of the time (exception CPU failure).
Encoding Errors	Encoding errors currently occur at the rate of 1/25,000.
Microfilm Research	All copies supplied within 2 to 5 business days excluding reconstruction and subpoenas. Rush requests processed as asked.
Bank-wide Outgoing Mail Processing	Outgoing mail is processed daily at pre-sort rate if received by 3:00 pm; First Class will be processed same day if received by 5:00 pm; Express and other mail is processed same day if received by 2:00 pm.

The Benefits of In-House Service-Level Agreements

Customer surveys are a highly useful and inexpensive tool used to generate information on external quality perceptions—a critical component of quality service. At the same time, internal surveys, in paying attention to employees and internal operations, are equally important. Quality is a battle on two grounds—the outside world with its perceptions and unquantifiable feelings, and the inside world with highly quantifiable performance measurement criteria. Staff areas have customers as well—internal bank people—and they should treat their customers with the same discipline, courtesy, and efficiency as personnel is expected to treat outside customers.

Examples of an internal quality enhancement and measurement programs follow.

Deposit Operations Survey

Deposit Operations signed a service-level agreement with senior management. The agreement satisfied standards for services such as stop payments, timeliness of ATM card issuance, and timeliness of new accounts set-up. The standards involved elements such as percent of time deadlines met, number of errors per 1,000 items, response time for specific tasks, both external and internal, and other quantitative criteria that helped to clarify and measure quality performance (Figure 9.19).

Operation surveys internally support the notion that quality is a real priority. Start the quality focus by educating the employees on how to play a role in making the bank a successful company and how to be a successful contributor. As part of this effort, each department needs to identify their key activities and set up systems to measure their work. Employees should begin tracking quality (errors) and productivity (volume) statistics and posting results on all charts installed in each department. Errors are then detected through sample tests from customer complaints.

In one successful case, employees began working together in teams to evaluate work processes and implement changes to improve operations. Pay incentives were developed to incorporate accuracy criteria and provide additional incentives for quality improvement. As goals were achieved, new, higher goals were established. Examples of the results of this successful program included the following:

- Productivity increased by 47%, bookkeeping by 61%, and statement processing by 23%.
- Errors in certain departments, such as adjustments and microfilm research, were reduced to single digits on transaction volumes in excess of $50,000.
- Corporate statements were mailed out in three days compared to six days previously.

- Retail statements were delivered on time—99.5% of the time versus 68% of the time prior to the quality initiative.
- Statement processing errors were reduced to 1.6/10,000 statements, compared to an industry standard of 168/10,000 statements.

In addition to departmental initiatives, teamwork is important to achieve success. For example, have operations and retail personnel begin working together to establish service-level agreements (goals). Customer service personnel can better meet the expectations of the customer with the help of the operations staff. Where special improvements are needed, cross-departmental teams of retail and operations staff need to be established to review the process and implement changes. For example, in the microfilm research department, requests were not properly completed. Copies were received much too late and procedures and forms were most inefficient. As a result of working together with retail staff, incorrect requests were reduced by 30%, and phone calls were also reduced by 30%. Over 56% of the requests were filled the same day, compared to 25% previously.

Another good example is address changes. These are difficult to implement and track in many companies, but they can be extremely annoying to the customer. In one supercommunity bank, address changes were not completed for all of the customers' accounts, and many changes were not processed on a timely basis. Jane, an account officer, met a communications manager at a seminar. He banked at the supercommunity bank she worked for and indicated he had been trying to get his address changed for nine months without success. His wife had made two different attempts at branch offices and recently had called telephone banking. No luck. Now, said the dissatisfied customer, his ATM card would not work, so he had requested a new one.

Although the request for a new card was processed, it was mailed to the old address. Frustrated, he did not know what to do. He called Jane. Jane contacted the operations area, and ensured the man that a new address had been entered. She also requested a new ATM card be mailed that day. The customer did receive the new ATM card the next day, but this is not helpful to the other customers who have to wait in line and who are frustrated when their needs are not being met. A change in the procedures was needed. As a result, the bank designed a new form that could be completed by the customer (the previous form was completed by the banker) and asked the customer to identify all types of accounts for which the address needed to be changed. Further, procedures were revised to include routing of the forms to the departments that had notoriously neglected making timely address changes.

Loan Operations

Loan operations also signed a service-level agreement (Figure 9.20). Again, timeliness and error frequency are the two key measures. What they translate into is higher service levels in elements such as new loan setups, payment processing, and other transaction processing, as well as file maintenance.

Quality goals should be established for all departments, including loan operations. One way to do that is to identify loan input

FIGURE 9.20 Loan Operations Service-Level Agreement

Service	Standard
New Loan Set Up Installment Credit	New loans received by 1:00 pm will be set up on the Installment Credit (IC) System same day.

New Loan Set Up
  Commercial
  Creditline, Worry Free
  Equityline
	New loans received by 3:00 pm (month-end 2:00 pm) will be set up on the appropriate system same day.

Equityline and Commercial Payment and Advance Processing	Payments and advances received by 3:00 pm (month-end) will be keyed same day.
Installment Credit Transaction Processing	Transactions received by 4:00 pm (month-end 3:00 pm) will be keyed same day.

Account File Maintenance
  Installment Credit
  Commercial
  Creditline, Worry Free
  Equityline
  Real Estate
	Critical maintenance done same day if received prior to 3:00 pm (month-end 2:00 pm); non-critical maintenance done within 3 business days.
	*Mass File Maintenance (50+ items) handled as special project

General Ledger Account Reconcilements	All account exceptions must be resolved within 7 days.

error targets. The way to go about it is to ask each individual to identify the most important function of his or her job, the perceived components of quality service, and to determine a way to measure these elements. The individuals should be responsible for tracking the results and establishing new goals when the original ones are reached. Graphs should be prepared monthly and used to monitor patterns being established. Identify areas requiring improvement and new staffing needs. There are many benefits of this monitoring, ranging from improved service in creating a team spirit to early detection of problems, providing greater attention to detail, and creating better measures for individual performance. The following story illustrates these points.

Due to a tremendous amount of business conducted daily in the installment loan department of a supercommunity bank, the online system needed to be "up" at all times. However, during one week the system was down a significant amount of the time during regular business hours. John of Loan Operations fielded phone calls from all six staff in the Installment Loan department of the bank, often many times during the day, in an effort to provide information needed to serve the customers. He was always there and willing to provide the information, although this was beyond his normal responsibilities. Essentially, John saved the day on numerous occasions. It was his professionalism that enabled the Installment Loan department to work through a difficult week without missing a beat.

The Loan Operations should have a service-level agreement similar to the deposit operations service-level agreement, working with retail and commercial staff to develop programs that ensure these departments receive information in a timely manner to adequately serve their customers.

Telephone Guidelines

The objective of the telephone guidelines is to improve service to customers whose contact with the bank is over the phone. One bank experienced many problems. The phone rang twenty times before it was answered. The voice mail messages were poor and unfriendly, and phone answering was all but rude. An interdepartmental quality team was established to improve service levels. They established and published telephone guidelines to create consistency and courtesy all across the board. To promote the guidelines, a telephone sleuth randomly called employees. Based on the sleuth's finding, Golden Phone trophies were awarded each month at the officers and supervisors meeting to the department with the best quality phone answering. The results of the measurement, as depicted in Figure 9.21, display key measures of performance of employees relative to standards on loan input errors. Each employee's performance is measured against the goal, and quality performance is rewarded.

Again, Figures 9.22 and 9.23 show service-level agreements for other departments. The purchasing department, for example, has turnaround time requirements as well as stocking/inventory management standards. The office services department has standards on mail delivery;

FIGURE 9.21 Loan Operations New Loan Input Errors

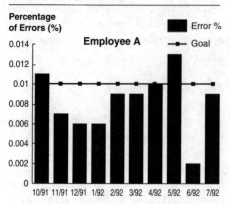

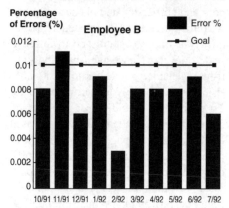

Figure 9.21 shows the percent of time when their standards were met.

Another interesting contract is the telephone guideline statement, which identifies standards and procedures to answering the phone so that all bank employees will respond uniformly and pleasantly to internal and external customers. All too often, we neglect that element of the business because it is not as clearly quantified and because it requires a widespread management program. Figure 9.24 shows that it could be very simple. Telephone manner management can be an important quality enhancement feature. So many people touch our bank by phone through secretaries and other clerical staff. A standard response creates essential familiarity, consistency, comfort, and similarity across branches and individuals, which is especially important to supercommunity banks with banks in many locations. Consistency of customer handling not only ensures adherence to certain quality standards, but also facilitates enhancing overall company-wide performance by creating similar procedures and atmospheres in all affiliate

FIGURE 9.22 Purchasing Department Service-Level Agreement

Service		Standard
Copy Center Requisitions	95.0%	0 - 1,000 = 1 day; 1,000 - 10,000 = 2 days; Special = 5 days
Office Supply Requisitions	95.0%	2 days
Stockroom Requisitions	90.0%	48 hours + delivery
Authorization For Expenditure Requisitions	95.0%	Order placed within one day
Stamp Requisitions	95.0%	Stamps = 5 days; Other items = 12 days
Graphics Requisitions	95.0%	5 days = 1 & 2 pages; 10 days = forms; 14 days/ date requested = long documents & manuals
Stockroom Back-Orders	97.5%	97.5% of stock items in inventory
MRP Stockroom Orders	95.0%	3 days plus delivery time
Stockroom/Office Supply Chargebacks	95.0%	By the 1st of the following month

FIGURE 9.23 Office Services Service-Level Agreement

Service		Standard
Mail Deliveries	98%	4 daily mail runs; 45 minute completion time
Report, Memo, etc. Distribution	96%	Project completed by 4:30 pm daily
Folding/Inserting Projects	98%	1 - 3,500 = 1 day; 3,500 - 10,000 = 2 days; 10,000 - more = 3 days
Special Messenger Deliveries	91%	Deliveries completed within 60 minutes
Statement Preparation	93%	Statements completed by 2:30 pm
Equipment Delivery	98%	Delivered 30 minutes before meeting
Air Express Delivery	96%	Express by noon; Same-Day-Service by 3:00 pm
Stockroom & Other Supply Deliveries	96%	Delivered by 3:00 pm

banks. This, in turn, eases transferring of employees across banks and branches as well as maximizes staff utilization across the whole company.

Teller Standardization Initiative

Teller standardization in supercommunity banks is a sensitive subject. All standardization is sensitive, but standardization of teller operations across banks is particularly sensitive. One supercommunity bank

FIGURE 9.24 Telephone Guidelines

When you answer the phone:

- Give your full name and department
- Answer the phone before it rings three times
- Transfer your calls to a secretary or voice mail when you are in a meeting
- When you transfer a caller, announce the call before you hang up

For voice mail users:

- Use the personal greeting option
- Always give the option of speaking with an individual

tried it. They established a teller standardization committee to evaluate the teller functions and identify areas where standardization could enhance customer service. One of the reasons this initiative was undertaken is that the president's wife tried to cash a check at an affiliate bank that was not the bank where the primary account was held. She was refused. That provided additional impetus to the teller standardization initiative. The flexibility of more effectively using teller staff by having tellers from different offices provide coverage when one office is short-staffed is another benefit sought by the program.

In one instance, a teller supervisor and another teller gave their notices within two weeks of each other. During the hiring process, the branch manager called the teller supervisor at another office and asked if she would help. She did indeed. She sent two tellers to the short-staffed office so that it would be adequately staffed. In addition, the supervisor herself volunteered to come to their office on Saturday and help train the new teller/supervisor. The result? Making the whole greater than the sum of the parts and making a seamless transition during the hiring process that was transparent to the customer.

The Retail Product Simplification Success Story

Marquette's goal was to significantly reduce consumer deposit types by developing a consistent product line and merging old products into new product lines without negatively affecting the customer or the organization. Before the program started, the bank had 1,043 different product types all across the board, 310 checking accounts, and 733 savings and CD products. After the retail product simplification program was implemented, only twenty-five different product types were available: six consumer checking accounts, four consumer savings accounts, eight CDs, and seven business accounts (Figure 9.25).

Cost savings of $468,000 resulted: $300,000 in the demand deposit area, and $168,000 in the savings department. The product simplification effort went beyond the checking and savings accounts. A decision was made that before any new product or account is created, customer preferences must be found out. The company moved into a market-driven mode. Several research methods were used in order to assess customer wants and needs, including focus groups, surveys, and secondary research done by other institutions and organizations. The customers were segmented into five different groups: income, credit needs, savings commitments, and other lifestyle characteristics. Accounts and product group bundles were designed

to meet the needs of those five customer segments. There were many benefits to this approach in addition to the cost savings, including the following:

• Improved service quality, because the customer service representatives had fewer products to learn, thereby reducing errors.
• Advertising dollars were more efficiently used since all the banks in the supercommunity bank system could benefit from promoting the same accounts.
• Organization flexibility was increased.

FIGURE 9.25 Retail Product Simplification

Before:	1,043	Different Product Types
	310	Consumer and Commercial Checking Accounts
	733	Consumer and Commercial Savings and Time Deposit Accounts
After:	25	Different Product Types
	6	Consumer Checking Accounts
	4	Consumer Savings Accounts
	8	Consumer Time Deposit Accounts
	7	Business Accounts
Savings:	$468,000	
	$300,000	DDA Product Simplification
	$168,000	Savings Product Simplification

FIGURE 9.26 The TQM Business Management Approach

TQM is a business management approach that has:	Key elements:
Focus on customer requirements to achieve financial results	Customer focus
Rigorous use of facts and analyses in every day decisions	Facts and analyses
Benchmarking against world-class performance	Benchmarking
Effective teamwork across the organization	Team work
Recognition for outstanding financial and customer satisfaction performance	Recognition
Information that helps people and systems continuously improve	Information and measurement
An atmosphere that fosters continuous improvement	Continuous improvement
Focus on effective recovery correction and prevention efforts and prevention	Recovery, correction,

As a simple example, it would have cost $4.7 million and eighteen months worth of process to change data processing vendors had the bank changed its name with a thousand product types.

Summary

Quality initiative can be viewed as a strategic weapon. It helps supercommunity banks become more competitive. The toughest part in implementing such programs is developing the mindset and getting employees committed to the program. The program takes time and can be frustrating when quick results are not easily identified; however, once the staff gets going on quality projects and sees the benefits, it creates tremendous motivation to continue. Do not expect uniform results. You may be very successful in some areas and not be able to get off the ground in others. Overall, implementation of quality initiatives is a tough process, but there are big paybacks. One must be prepared for a new way of management:

- Be willing to let decisions be made at lower levels because the employees who are closest to the customer are better equipped to make decisions.
- Such programs constitute a significant cultural shift for many bankers, but don't give up. Continue wrestling with them. The results will soon show up.
- Accept that quality programs do pay.

CHAPTER TEN

Total Quality Management—
How to Implement It

We all agree that quality management is a wonderful thing, but implementation can be elusive. The definition and measurement of quality are the difficult parts.

What is quality? Quality is the ability to conform to established requirements. It is the never-ending quest to improve a product and a service. Dr. Deming's philosophy, as presented in Figure 10.1, summarizes the definition of quality from the man who coined the term total quality management. Deming's approach focuses on the use of statistics to improve quality and productivity (Figure 10.2). "As quality improves," says Deming, "rework time, loss, and scrap decrease, thereby improving production. Improved production decreases other costs such as manufacturing costs, sales, liability costs, and others which, in turn, increases market share and helps the company stay in business, grow in size, and become more

profitable." In order to achieve these, Deming envisions a multidisciplinary project team that brings all the players involved in the production of a product or a service together to ensure consistent quality across the board (Figure 10.3).

Key to the implementation of quality is its measurement. Quality standards, as depicted in Figure 10.4, vary across the board. The major difference, however, is between manufacturing and service industries. This difference is depicted clearly between the standards developed by General Motors and the standards developed by the Malcolm Baldridge Award.

What Is Quality—The Malcolm Baldridge Definition

If cost was "king" in the late eighties, quality seems to be the buzzword for the nineties in the financial institution indus-

FIGURE 10.1 Dr. Deming's Philosophy

---

1. Create constancy of purpose toward improvement of product and service, with the aim of becoming competitive and to stay in business, and to provide jobs.

2. Adopt the new philosophy. We are in a new economic age. We can no longer live with commonly accepted levels of delays, mistakes, defective materials, and defective workmanship.

3. Cease dependence on inspection to achieve quality. Instead, require statistical evidence that quality is built into the product in the first place.

4. End the practice of awarding business on the basis of price tag. Eliminate suppliers that cannot qualify with statistical evidence of quality. Purchasing must be combined with design of product, manufacturing, and sales, to work with chosen suppliers to minimize total cost, not merely initial cost.

5. Improve constantly and forever every activity in the company, to improve quality and productivity and thus constantly decrease costs. It is management's job to continually work on the system.

6. Institute training and education on the job, including management.

7. Institute supervision. The aim of supervision should be to help people and machines to do a better job.

8. Drive out fear, so that everyone may work effectively for the company.

9. Break down barriers between departments. People in research, design, sales, and production must work as a team to tackle usage and production problems that may be encountered with the product or service.

10. Eliminate slogans and targets asking for zero defects and new levels of productivity, without providing methods. The bulk of the causes of low quality and low productivity belong to the system and thus lie beyond the power of the work force.

11. Eliminate work standards that prescribe numerical quotas. Improvement of quality will automatically improve productivity.

12. Remove the barriers that rob people of their right to pride of workmanship. The responsibility of supervisors must be changed from sheet numbers to quality.

13. Institute a vigorous program of education and retraining. New skills are required for changes in techniques, materials, and service.

14. Put everybody in the company to work in teams to accomplish the transformation. Create a structure in top management to push every day on the preceding points.

---

try. Everyone seeks to institute superior quality service as their way of differentiating and protecting the customer relationship. Quality, however, is an elusive concept. It can be subjective, and its definition and measurement are, at best, unclear. Quality, therefore, stands the risk of being relegated to the status of other overused buzzwords, such as synergy and empower-

ment, which everyone declares are good ideas, but no one quite understands them.

The Malcolm Baldridge National Quality Award Program attempted to define quality more precisely. It is interesting to review the award criteria. They serve as a useful framework to evaluate the definition of quality as it is used universally and as it applies to your institution. Each

FIGURE 10.2 The Deming Approach
The use of statistics improves quality and productivity.

of the criteria—values and concepts—used by the award committee to assess quality programs are briefly described in the sections that follow.

Customer-Driven Quality

Since quality is judged by the customer, products and service attributes should contribute to value to the customer and lead to customer satisfaction. Customer preferences and needs should be addressed using quality systems.

The concept of quality includes not only the product and service attributes that meet basic requirements, but also includes those attributes that enhance their services and differentiate them from the competition. Such enhancement and differentiation may include new offerings as well as unique product/product, service/service, or product/service combinations pertaining to the total experience of bank service.

Customer-driven quality is a strategic commitment. It is designed to increase market share and customer retention. It demands constant sensitivity to emerging customer and market requirements and the ongoing measurement of factors that determine customer satisfaction. It also demands awareness of developments in technology and time capability to rapid and

FIGURE 10.3 Multidiscipline Project Teams

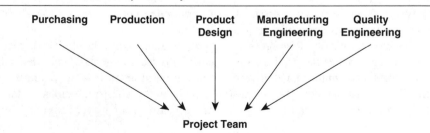

FIGURE 10.4 Quality Standards

	Targets for Excellence
General Motors	• Quality • Cost • Delivery • Management • Technology
Ford	Similar but more emphasis on statistical evidence on long-term relationships
Malcolm Baldridge	• Leadership • Information and analysis • Strategic quality planning • Human resource utilization • Quality assurance of products and services • Quality results • Customer satisfaction
ISO 9000	European standards focus on quality systems, procedures, and documentation

flexible response to customer and market requirements that extend well beyond zero defect and error reduction, beyond merely meeting customer needs or reducing complaints. A bank's approach to recovering from defects and errors is crucial to its improving service quality and customer relationships. To reiterate, experience indicates that a well-handled problem results in a customer who is more loyal than one who did not have the problem at all.

Leadership

A bank's mission, vision, and corporate culture must include clear and visible quality values and expectations. Reinforcement of those values implies the need for substantial personal commitment and involvement. The bank's managing team must take part in the development of strategies, systems, and methods for achieving excellence. The quality message needs to guide all activities and decisions of the bank and encourage participation and creativity by all employees.

Senior management should serve as role models, reinforcing the values and encouraging leadership in all levels of management. Leadership by example can be exercised through all stages of management, including planning, review, quality performance management, and employee recognition for quality achievement.

Continuous Improvement

Achieving the highest level of quality and competitiveness requires a well- defined, implementable approach to ongoing improvement. Improvement may take place in different ways, ranging from enhancement of the value to the customer to error reduction, responsiveness, and overall improvement of productivity and effectiveness. Improvement is driven not only by the objective to provide better quality but also by the need to be responsive and efficient. Seeking continuous improvement is a cultural characteristic and needs to be incorporated in the corporate value system. This addition to the overall, corporate-wide commitment to

---

Excellent design quality typically leads to major reductions in upstream problem handling, and therefore a reduction in aggravation, waste problems, and associated costs.

---

seek continuous improvement also requires the ability to assess progress and to develop information for future performance. Performance measurement is an integral part of the concept.

Participation

Achieving quality requires a fully committed, well-trained, and involved work force. A reward and recognition system should be designed to reinforce full participation in company quality objectives. Employees need education and training in quality skills related to performing their work and for understanding and solving quality-related problems. Training should then be reinforced through on-the-job applications and employee empowerment.

Fast Response

The ability to respond quickly to changes in the competitive marketplace and in customers' needs is a critical success factor in achieving quality. Fast response itself is often a major quality attribute. Response time improvement and quick turnaround should be included as a major focus within all quality improvement processes. This, again, requires the ability to measure response time and organizational flexibility. Improvements in response time may require the simplification of work processes. The result is often simultaneous improvements in quality and productivity.

Design Quality and Prevention

Quality systems place strong emphasis on design quality. Problem prevention is achieved through building quality into products and services as well as into the processes through which they are produced: getting it right the first time. Excellent design quality typically leads to major reductions in upstream problem handling, and therefore a reduction in aggravation, waste problems, and associated costs.

A major design issue is the design-to-introduction time. This product introduction time needs to be shortened, and defects need to be reduced prior to product introduction in order to meet the demands of the rapidly changing market. Consistent with the theme of continuous improvement and collective action, collaboration and partnership with vendors at the earliest stages of the process are important in enduring product quality and preventing defects prior to product introduction. This approach yields the maximum overall benefits of improvements and corrections, taking into account the vendors that service the bank as an integral part of the design, quality, and defect prevention program.

Long-Range Outlook

Achieving quality and market leadership requires a future orientation and long-term commitment to customers, employees, shareholders, and vendors. The strategic plan and resource allocation need to reflect these commitments and address training, employee development, supplier development, and other factors that affect quality. A key part of the long-term commitment is periodic review and assessment of the progress toward the long-term plans as well as the commitment to a clear strategic focus. Focusing on the profitability hurdles for the next quarter cannot be the only perspective to making resource allocation decisions.

Management by Fact

Meeting quality and performance goals requires that process management be based on reliable information. Facts needed for quality assessment and improvement are of many types. They may relate to customer satisfaction, products and services, operations, markets, competitive comparison, vendors, and employee-related cost and financial information. Such data need to be analyzed to support evaluation and decision making at various levels within the company regarding progress in quality achievement. Facts, data, and analysis support other corporate-wide purposes such as planning, performance review, operation improvement, and competitive comparisons.

Performance indicators are helpful in evaluating and improving competitive performance. Performance indicators are measurable characteristics of product, service, process, and operations. The company uses them to evaluate performance and to track progress. Indicators should be selected to best represent the factors that determine customer satisfaction and operational performance. A system of indicators tied to customer and company performance requirements represent a clear and objective basis for aligning all activities of the company toward common goals. Through the analysis of data obtained in the tracking processes, the indicators themselves may be evaluated and changed. For example, indicators selected to measure product and service quality may be judged by how well they jibe with customer satisfaction.

Partnership Development

The company should seek to build external and internal partnerships serving mutual and larger community interests. Partnerships may include employee relationships, cooperation with suppliers and vendors, customer relationships, and linkages with the community. When seeking partnerships, consider long-term objectives as well as short-term needs, thereby creating a basis for mutual investments and benefit.

Public Responsibility

A company's customer requirements and quality system objectives also need to address areas of corporate citizenship and responsibility such as business ethics, equal opportunity lending, community reimbursement, environment, and sharing of quality-related information in the company's communities.

Inclusion of public responsibility areas within a quality system means not only meeting the local, state, and federal regulatory requirements, but also treating them as areas for continuous improvement.

The Malcolm Baldridge Award groups the measurement parameters of quality into seven categories:

* Leadership
* Information and analysis
* Strategic quality planning
* Human resource development and management
* Management of process quality
* Quality and operational results
* Customer service and satisfaction

Why Integrate Total Quality Management into your Bank?

Even if this award program's definition of quality does not meet your own, it can serve as a useful framework to develop your bank's own definition of quality and the performance indicators by which your company should be measured. It is important to integrate this concept into the day-to-day life of management and employees alike, particularly in those banks where quality serves as a major differentiation factor in competitive advantage. As super-community banks rely on quality, service levels, and customer retention as a cornerstone to their strategic position, they can use the quality concepts described above and integrate them into day-to-day management to enhance corporate culture, employee satisfaction, and, most important, customer relationships and, therefore, the bottom line.

Total quality management is a full circle of integrated activities and continuous feedback. It includes elements such as:

* A clear organizational focus on activities
* An environment that enhances and nurtures quality improvement
* Processes that are structured and defined to seek and implement quality improvement
* Performance indicators to identify success
* Data-base decisions that support quality improvement
* Projects designed to improve quality as measured by the indicators identified earlier
* Feedback from the process to see whether success was achieved
* Implementation of the feedback to achieve continuous improvement

The benefits of the process are numerous, and some are listed below:

* Realistic specifications
* Proper standards
* Accurate predictions for forecasts and estimates
* Reliable measure of personnel and machine capabilities
* Producing quality product/service consistently
* Elimination of design problems

FIGURE 10.5 Summary of GAO Report

Performance Indicators	Increased	Decreased	Same
Better Employee Relations	75%	17%	8%
Improved Operating Procedures	91%	3%	6%
Greater Customer Satisfaction	70%	10%	20%
Increased Financial Performance	85%	15%	0

Source: R. Israel.

- Solutions to complex process problems
- Reductions of scrap and/or rework
- Time savings
- Lower administrative and/or production costs
- Accurate planning
- Less inspection
- Increased productivity
- Increased profits

The government accounting office further studied the return on quality efforts. The results are presented in Figure 10.5. The GAO found, much like supercommunity banks did, that quality management pays. It pays all across the board, but most importantly, it increases bottom-line performance.

Total Quality Management Implementation Process

The way to implement quality improvement is through the eight-step process illustrated in Figure 10.6, and described in detail below.

Step 1 - Organizational Focus

This is where the organization creates a market-driven, top-down approach. Through strategic planning, management develops a mission statement, a clear set of policies envisioned by corporate values, and an organizational structure that is committed to quality improvement. The bank should use customer surveys to obtain market feedback to measure performance and to identify the weak spots.

Step 2 - Positive Environment

Quality improvement is not easy and requires a nurturing environment. Remove barriers to it, as people will not perceive it initially to be a worthwhile or profit-generating activity. Create accountability among individuals and teams in a positive way

FIGURE 10.6 Total Quality Management

8. Continuous Improvement
1. Organizational Focus
2. Positive Environment
3. Define Processes
4. Identify Performance Indicators
5. Data-based Decisions
6. Improvement Projects
7. Assessment of Success

FIGURE 10.7 Flowcharting

Flowcharting the process you are trying to improve is the first step and may be the most significant and effective action toward improvement.

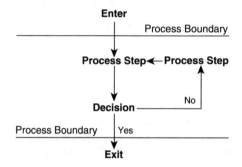

define the processes already in place to enhance quality. Flowcharts are useful in defining such processes. Standardize the process all across the affiliates and the nonbank affiliates of the holding company. Make the process consistent with the corporate culture and with what works best in your company. In some companies, very clear processes and monetary rewards are the best combination. In others, result-orientation and the definition of success are more important than a structured process definition. What works for you may vary from what works for others.

through reward systems. Ensure that incentives are in place to reward successful quality initiatives. Recognize that quality programs can enhance job satisfaction and pass that recognition along to the employees. Successful quality programs result in reduced turnover, improved attendance, reduced health costs, and enhanced job satisfaction. This, in turn, will create additional enhancements and incentives to your employees and to management in forging ahead with the quality program.

Step 3 - Define Processes

Total quality management is a process, not a procedure. That means that it is an ongoing, self-feedback, thought-intensive process as opposed to a mechanical implementation of a set of procedures. In order to achieve that environment, one needs to

FIGURE 10.8 Processing an Expense Report by Employee/Staff

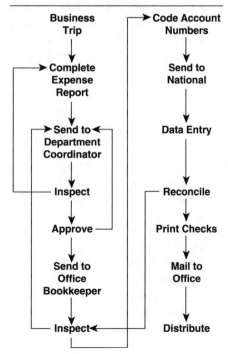

FIGURE 10.9 What is Statistical Quality Control?

Statistical	Through the use of numbers and data.
Quality	We study the characteristics of our process.
Control	In order to make it behave the way we want it to behave.

Source: R. Israel.

Flowcharting the process you are trying to improve is the first step toward improvement and may be the most significant and effective action you can take. Figure 10.7 is an example of a flowchart of the process in conceptual terms. Figure 10.8 is an actual example of a simple process—an expense report processed by the employee and the staff. Even such a simple action requires a complex process, several entry points, and two inspection points. Other processes may be much more complex.

Step 4 - Identify Performance Indicators

Quality focuses on output, not on input. What we are interested in is a result, or a successful conclusion to a process. Therefore, what goes in and the way procedures have been designed in the past is less relevant than what comes out, which is the result we are seeking. That result should be measured and translated into performance indicators. Examples of performance indicators in administrative processes would be time, cost, number of errors per 1,000 items, or specific measures of customer sat-

isfaction. The examples provided earlier in Chapter 9 of the service contracts between vendors and a bank and between internal departments and bank management provide numerous instances of effective performance indicators.

Step 5 - Data-based Decisions

Quality, although a fuzzy concept, is a data-based activity and can be quite precise. The decision on how to structure a process and what to look for can be made using a scientific method. Process control can be accomplished through statistical methods to achieve statistical quality control. Figure 10.9 defines statistical quality control. The methods typically used in quantifying quality management include, for example:

- *Pareto chart,* an example of which is presented in Figure 10.10, depicts delays in processing expense reports and the most frequent causes for those delays.

FIGURE 10.10 Pareto Chart
Delays In Processing Expense Reports

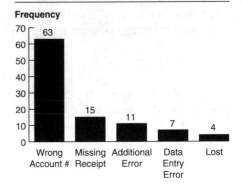

FIGURE 10.11 Distributions Can Differ in Any Combination of Location, Spread and Shape

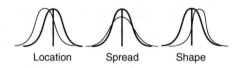

Location   Spread   Shape

- *Variation.* Uniformity of output is an important requirement for the improvement of quality. Consistency and standardization help reduce the process and product variation. However, all processes exhibit some measure of variation. Data collected from a process over time will form a pattern or a distribution that identifies the variation more clearly, then can be used to reduce it. Distributions can figure in location, spread, shape, or any combination of the above (Figure 10.11). Deming suggests to identify the source of variation and use that to break down departmental barriers. Specifically, management should work on the overall system and the source of the variations within.
- *Process capability* is another scientific method by which to manage quality. It implies the assessment of the degree to which the process performs up to management requirements. Every requisite to process capability is a process that is in statistical control over time. Figure 10.12 depicts four types of processes. Process A is out of control. There is no consistency across the board. Process B is in control, showing great consistency. Process C is in control but not capable. It does not produce the results we are

looking for. Process D is both in control and capable, showing consistency and yielding the output we are seeking.

Step 6 - Improvement Projects

Once the deficiencies in the processes are identified, improvement projects need to be assigned to continue the quality improvement process. First, the projects themselves need to be selected. What are we going to focus on? Good inputs to the selection of quality improvement projects are:

- Customer surveys
- Quality councils
- Employee suggestions
- Costs
- Management ideas

Most projects cross functional lines. That is significant because the project team

FIGURE 10.12 Process Control

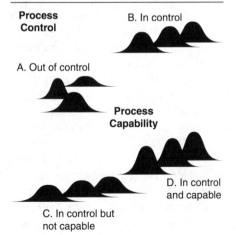

FIGURE 10.13 Rules for Brainstorming

- Do not criticize (by word or gesture) anyone's ideas.
- Do not discuss or evaluate any ideas, except possibly for reasons of clarification.
- Do not hesitate to suggest an idea because you think it sounds "dumb." Many times these ideas are the ones that lead to solutions.
- Only one idea at a time should be suggested by each team member.
- Do not allow negativism.
- Do not allow domination by one or two individuals. Everyone must get involved for maximum effectiveness.
- Do not have a gripe session.

that is selected needs to reflect the disciplines that are affected by the process. A cross-functional team is selected, and a leader is chosen. In addition, a facilitator to the process needs to be chosen who will function as manager of the team and ensure that the input is solicited from all parties. At that point, the project can begin. The team has several tools available to it as it embarks on the project. These tools range from facilitators and members with group dynamic skills to brainstorming and other more quantitative, project-oriented tools including cause-and-effect diagrams.

Brainstorming is one of the more effective tools of the project team. It is an idea-generating technique that uses the thinking capacity of the group as a whole. It encourages creative thinking applying the principle, "The whole is greater than the sum of its parts," which is an underlying principle in the supercommunity banking concept and should be easily transferable to the brainstorming process of the project team. Brainstorming is of special relevance

because it is a creative process, and quality improvement, although a data-based activity, requires creativity. Figure 10.13 lists a few rules for brainstorming that can be used by the project team to channel the energy into productive and constructive discussions versus a gripe session.

Cause-and-effect diagrams (Ishakawa Diagram) are another tool available to the project team that provide more discipline and data-base information to the group. It is a visual tool used to organize the teams' ideas into categories. The categories could be people, methods, services, environment, and others. The important part of the diagram is the clusters it generates, which help the group prioritize its activities and investigate the more important elements and ideas identified through the process. The way to develop a cause-and-effect diagram is as follows:

- The facilitator asks all group members to come up with ideas for project enhancement or quality improvement.
- The facilitator lists all ideas.
- The facilitator asks the group to identify the top three ideas on the board.
- The facilitator marks the top three ideas from each member of the team.
- Clusters are identified and individual responsibility for investigation allocated.

Step 7 - Assessment of Success

Once the projects are completed and the project teams make their presentations, success needs to be assessed. A candid look at the project's result is essential. Benefits such as enhanced employee satisfaction, reduced cycle time, improved market share, improved customer satisfaction, and increased profitability should be tracked based on the performance indicators identified earlier. Negatives, such as the cost of

> *Total quality management
> . . . is an ongoing process that
> needs to be institutionalized
> and integrated into day-to-day
> management and into
> employee activities.*

nonconformance, also need to be identified. Last, successful efforts should be rewarded through quality awards, incentive programs, and other vehicles.

Step 8 - Continuous Improvement

Project completion is not the end of quality management. Total quality management, like strategic planning, is an ongoing process that needs to be institutionalized and integrated into day-to-day management and into employee activities. Further, customer awareness needs to be ongoing through surveys, focus groups, and satisfaction analyses. Heightened customer awareness results in heightened quality awareness, which, in turn, keeps the process alive. The payoffs, as discussed earlier, are significant.

Summary

Total quality management is a clear but imprecise process. The tools presented here are a point of departure for supercom-

munity bank management to integrate total quality management into their daily routines. It is your management's commitment to and continuous employee awareness of the process and its importance that will make a difference in your company. Quality is essential to the supercommunity bank strategy. There are many ways to achieve TQM, but none will be successful without that commitment and ongoing reinforcement.

Measuring Quality in the Service Business—Learning From the Best

Achieving quality in service businesses is a difficult proposition. Quantification and flow documentation are much more difficult to accomplish than in service businesses. The production unit—the employee—is fungible and utilized to generate many products—checking, savings, loans, investments, and so on. Measurement and benchmarking therefore becomes a daunting task. Two service companies, The Ritz-Carlton Hotels and AT&T's Universal Credit Card, won the Malcolm Baldridge Quality Award this year. Their experiences and methodologies are instructive in developing quality programs and accurate measurement systems in supercommunity banks.

The Ritz-Carlton Hotel Company's Quality Initiative

Introduction

The Ritz-Carlton hotel company is structured like a supercommunity bank. Strategic decisions, corporate values and culture, and other themes are originated at the "holding company" level and monitored by its senior management. At the same time, the company recognizes the unique characteristic of each hotel (bank) and empowers local management to run that hotel within the corporate guidelines. As a service business similarly structured to supercommunity banks, the Ritz-Carlton's experience with the quality initiatives bears a lot of relevant and directly implementable lessons to supercommunity banks.

History

In 1983, W.B. Johnson Properties set out to create a first—an American hotel group with products and services designed to appeal to and suit the demands of both the prestigious travel consumer and the corporate travel and meeting planner worldwide.

Until that time, the U.S. luxury hotel industry was extremely fragmented and mostly limited to independently operated hotels. Independent business center hotels provided personalized service in small facilities that were not responsive to corporate and association meetings or multiple location requirements. Several independent resort hotels represented the geographic, climatic, historical, cultural, and artistic variations of their regions successfully, but were limited by their single location. Hotel groups had previously provided products and services that responded to corporate travel and meeting requirements. However, the highest standards of the travel industry were not continuously applied.

Furthermore, *because hotel service delivery (like banking) depends on an indi-*

vidual's ability to properly execute various tasks, wide service variability existed.

Because customers perceived uncertainty in selecting intangible hotel products and services and needed a reliable single supplier, W.B. Johnson Properties made a clear commitment to quality.

The company's "born at birth" approach to quality began by focusing on the principal concerns of its customers. By comparing the research of the travel industry against the company's own findings, they identified the most important, yet least consistent, quality within hotels— *highly personalized, genuinely caring service delivery.* (Bank customers appear to have similar preferences.)

The company then proceeded to build a reliable, customer-driven, service-delivery system, based largely on a commitment to a set of principles and designed to provide premium service.

This new system would eventually understand the individual expectations of more than 240,000 customers while also preventing difficulties from ever reaching them. (At Ritz-Carltons there are as many as one million employee/guest interfaces each day.) The entire system is also expected to instantly pacify a dissatisfied customer and correct their problem immediately. Further down the quality road, the company learned how to identify pattern problems and how to resolve these opportunities permanently.

Today, Ritz-Carlton customers are placing greater emphasis on reliability, timely delivery, and price value. Again, bank customers are not much different. The key is for every community bank to identify *its* customer's price value equation.

Leadership

At The Ritz-Carlton, *the senior leadership group (the executive committee) doubles as the senior quality committee.* This indicates a clear commitment to the process from the top. The senior leaders personally devised the following two original quality strategies to broaden the quality leadership of the Ritz-Carlton:

New hotel start-up assurance. Since 1984, the senior leadership has personally assured that each new hotel product and service provides the characteristics expected by its main customers. An important

---

They key is, for every community bank, to identify its customer's price value equation.

---

aspect of this quality practice takes place during the concentrated and intense "seven-day countdown," when the company's senior leaders work side by side with new employees. During these formative sessions, which all new employees must attend, the president communicates the company's principles. He personally creates the employee/guest interface image and facilitates each work area's first vision statement. Throughout the entire process, the senior leaders monitor work areas for "start-up," instill the corporate values, model the ideal relationship management, insist upon 100% compliance to customer's requirements, and recognize outstanding achievement.

The establishment of a set of corporate values, or "Gold Standards." The Gold Standards represent an easy-to-understand definition of service quality and are aggressively communicated and internalized at all levels of the organization. The constant and *continuous reinforcement* techniques of the corporate values, led by *senior leaders,* include training, daily line-up meetings, pocket cards outlining the principles, bulletin board postings, and other methods unique to each hotel. As a result, Ritz-Carlton employees have an exceptional understanding and devotion to the company's vision, values, quality goals, and methods. Successful supercommunity banks strive to articulate their corporate values clearly, as well, and communicate them on an ongoing basis to *all* employees (see Chapter 8).

Beyond the values, The Ritz-Carlton has other quality-related statements:

- *The Credo* serves as a guide for all employees. It makes known that highly personalized customer satisfaction is the highest priority and is everyone's job. It goes on to define the critical features of every product and service provided.
- *The Three Steps of Service* define the activities and decisions of customer interface (a most useful tool for bank customer interface personnel, especially tellers and CSRs).
- *The Ritz-Carlton Basics* describe the guest problem-solving process as well as grooming, housekeeping, safety, and efficiency standards. The lateral service principle makes known the value of internal customer satisfaction. Staff

functions within the hotel—and within banks—also have customers, albeit internal bank customers. Market discipline and service level expectations should be imposed on internal functions as well as the line, i.e., customer handling functions.

- *The Motto (Ladies and Gentlemen Serving Ladies and Gentlemen)* is more than a phrase. It is a culture, effectively created by senior leaders and experienced by customers and employees.

Company-wide, employees are devoted to the organization's principles. A full 96% of employees said "excellence in guest services" is a top priority, even though the company has added 3,000 new employees over the past three years.

Lessons learned: When senior leaders personally instill a strong vision and a set of principles in their employees and then give them the confidence, freedom, and authority to act, people take responsibility for their jobs and do whatever is necessary to satisfy their customers.

Information and Analysis

Quantification of quality benchmarking and continuous measurement for continuous improvement are integral to quality management. The Ritz-Carlton uses a real-time and proactive approach to capturing and using customer satisfaction and quality-related data. Systems for the collection and utilization of customer reaction and satisfaction are widely deployed and extensively used throughout the organization. Information efforts are centered on various customer segments and product lines. The approach allows every employee to collect and utilize quality-related data on a daily basis. These systems provide critical, responsive data which include:

- On-line guest preference information
- Quantity of error-free products and services
- Opportunities for quality improvement

For example, the automated property management systems enable the *on-line access and utilization of guest preference information* at the individual customer level. All employees collect and input this data and use it as part of their service delivery with individual guests. A platform automation system is the closest banks have come to this technological innovation.

The *quality production reporting system* is a method of aggregating hotel-level data from nearly two dozen sources into a summary format. It serves as an early warning system and facilitates analysis. The processes employees use to identify quality opportunities for improvement are standardized in a textbook and are available throughout the organization. Some team improvement methods are functional (within a work area), while others are cross-functional (within a hotel). And some opportunities receive the attention of national cross-functional teams (across hotels).

Systems for the collection and utilization of *employee performance data* are used exclusively to assess the capabilities of a prospective employee to meet specific job requirements. (Characteristic behaviors displayed by successful employees form the basis of a structured, empirical interview-and-selection process.) Hiring the right people up front reduces turnover and enhances service quality.

The "born at birth" *benchmarking approach* focuses entirely on hotel industry best practices and performances. Currently, the company studies the best in any industry through the use of industry watchers and consultants.

Today, the goal of The Ritz-Carlton's business management systems (the data component of its quality effort) is to become more integrated, more proactive, and more preventive. Efforts are underway to continuously check the work to determine whether employees are providing what the customer wants most. These test measures are then statistically charted to help teams determine when and where to act. The quality, marketing, and financial results of each hotel are aggregated and integrated to determine what quality factors are driving the financial outcome. These systems, combined with benchmarking, enable leaders and teams to better determine goals and justify expenditures.

Lesson Learned: Responses from listening posts, combined with systems accessible to all, are needed just to keep pace with everchanging individual customer demands.

Strategic Quality Planning

The Ritz-Carlton's primary objective, during its early years, was opening new hotels that met the highest travel industry quality ratings on opening day. This required detailed planning and was achieved through a detailed pre-opening control plan. A specially selected staff from other hotels throughout the company ensured all work areas, processes, and equipment were ready.

Today, the quality plan continues to be the business plan. The primary objectives are to improve the quality of the products and services, reduce cycle-time, and improve price value and customer retention. Through benchmarking studies within and outside the hotel, The Ritz-Carlton has developed a disciplined, integrated planning system.

At each level of the company—from corporate leaders to managers and employees in the 720 individual work areas of the company—teams are charged with setting objectives and devising action plans, which are reviewed by the corporate steering committee. These teams enhance the quality and productivity of the Ritz-Carlton by: (1) aligning all levels around the common vision and objectives; (2) encouraging all employees to think beyond the demands of day-to-day activities; (3) increasing communication among the diverse functions that make up the Ritz-Carlton; (4) simultaneous, integrated problem solving. In addition, each hotel has a quality leader who serves as a resource and adviser to teams and workers, developing and implementing their quality plans. Action plans proceed through a screening process that ensures the plans have been adequately researched, and they also are not undertaken unless they are adequately resourced.

Future plans are based on clear quality and customer satisfaction priorities. Priorities include becoming virtually defect-free by 1996 and plans to be the first hospitality company with 100% customer retention. In addition, focus on cycle time reduction and streamlining to provide continuous price/value improvement for the customers will also receive more attention. All plans center on directing the resources of the Ritz-Carlton—time, money, and people—to the wishes and needs of guests and travel planners, as well as employees.

Lesson Learned: Action plans developed by each level of the organization must be screened to ensure that they: (1) have been adequately researched: (2) have been adequately resourced; (3) contain no complexity before they are undertaken.

Human Resources Utilization

A most important resource in any organization is the people. This is especially true in a service company and a growing, quality organization. Accordingly, the human resources function works in a closely coordinated effort with each function of the operations to enhance the work force's ability to effectively satisfy customer expectations.

All hotels have a director of human resources and a training manager on their staff. Both are assisted with their planning efforts by the hotel's quality leader. Each work area has a departmental trainer on staff who is charged with the training and certification of new employees in that unit.

The Ritz-Carlton's commitment to planning and to realizing the full potential of its people begins with the hiring process. They use a highly predictive instrument to determine the capability of a candidate to meet the requirements of each

of their 120 job positions. This technology, known as "character trait recruiting," reduces service variability, acts as an aid to productivity, and has enabled us the company to reduce turnover by nearly 50% in the past three years.

Once a hotel is open, the training manager and the senior hotel executives work as an orientation team, over a period of two days, to personally demonstrate the Gold Standards and to instill these values

---

> *"character trait recruiting,"*
> *. . . has enabled the*
> *company to reduce turnover*
> *by nearly 50% in the*
> *past three years."*

---

in all new employees. This orientation unit reconvenes three weeks later for a follow-up session to monitor the effectiveness of the instruction and to make necessary changes. At this stage the employee is considered a Lady or Gentleman of the Ritz-Carlton.

The next review is done by the work area leader and their departmental trainer. The new employees undergo a comprehensive training period to master the procedures of their respective position. At the end of the training period the employee must pass written and skill demonstration tests to become certified. Work area teams are responsible for setting the quality certification performance standards of each position.

Every day, in every work area, during every shift, a quality line-up meeting of employees occurs for a briefing session. During these sessions, employees receive instructions on becoming a certified quality engineer. Each employee becomes capable of identifying the wasteful complexity within their work. They are given examples of mistakes, rework, breakdowns, delays, inconsistencies, and variations. Although this may be overzealous, the company's impressive results indicate otherwise.

Through these and other mechanisms, *employees receive over 100 hours of quality education* to foster premium service commitment, solve problems, set strategic quality plans, and generate new ideas. Training is a critical element to quality service in hotels as well as banks.

Effective involvement and *empowerment* grow, in part, from effective quality training. Each individual employee can:

- Move heaven and earth to satisfy a customer.
- Contact appropriate employees to help resolve a problem swiftly (lateral service concept).
- Spend up to $2,000 in order to satisfy a guest.
- Decide the acceptability of products and services.
- Decide the business terms of a sale (sales and marketing).
- Become involved in setting the plans of their work area.
- Speak with anyone regarding any problem.

Although banks should not go as far as the Ritz-Carlton's $2,000 empowerment limit, many supercommunity banks have found that empowering a teller to resolve customer problems up to $50 is an inexpensive and effective way to improve service levels.

There are many opportunities for *employee recognition.* A total of 39 awards are given to employees for excellence in a wide variety of areas. Performance appraisals are based on the expectations explained during the orientation, training, and certification processes.

Individuals who consistently apply the performance standards receive verbal and written praise. Top performers receive the coveted new hotel start-up team assignment. Team-oriented awards include bonus pools when solutions they recommend to problems are successfully implemented and effective. In addition, employees of the Ritz-Carlton share in achievement through the gratuity system (money from customers for tasks performed), an immediate quality and productivity incentive program. The system of sharing gratuities is thoughtfully and purposefully integrated with customer service goals in a manner that enhances an employee's performance against these goals.

Personal security is also addressed at the Ritz-Carlton through preventative health plans, cross training, and retirement. The leadership principle is genuine care and concern for each employee.

Employees are surveyed annually to ascertain their levels of satisfaction and understanding of the company's quality standards. Workers are keenly aware that excellence is a top hotel and personal priority. Also, a 1% increase in employee satisfaction results in a 22% *decrease* in customer dissatisfaction.

Lesson Learned: A collective quality commitment must be gained from the entire work force. There is no substitute for selecting employees who believe in the organization's values.

Management of Quality Process

Since the Ritz-Carlton is primarily a professional hotel management company, quality assurance most often begins with a private developer interested in creating a high-quality hotel project in appealing, diverse travel destinations. The process for assuring the quality of the new hotel products and services has evolved over eight years of benchmarking, development, and improvement.

The product management process has three integral parts: interactive team pyramid, basic product management process, and regional product management process. The entire process and its goals are supported by the senior leaders of the company who work as a binding agent with professional development planning experts, from several fields, to prevent and resolve new hotel developmental issues.

Several critical aspects contribute to the effectiveness of the Ritz-Carlton's product management process:

- Standard design team (tantamount to a standardized acquisition process in supercommunity banks).
- Forced interface of all design, marketing, operations, and legal functions throughout each project to anticipate requirements and evaluate progress.
- Concentrated focus on basic, regional, and individual customer requirements.

- Synchronized start-up control plan that tests and evaluates the performance of facility construction, furnishings, equipment, systems, staffing, suppliers, food preparation, service delivery, and guest interface.
- Continuous emphasis on corporate values and prevention of problems.
- Final assessment of products and services by senior leaders before opening day.

Problems are expected to be resolved prior to initial customer occupancy, while teams from operating hotels improve the entire process.

Customized hotel products and services, such as meetings and banquet events, receive the full attention of local hotel cross-functional teams. These teams are effective due to several aspects of their product management process:

- All internal and external suppliers become involved as early as possible in the design of the event. (Vendor partnerships are a powerful concept for supercommunity banks and can be used to leverage the bank's distribution network and customer base without sacrificing quality service.)
- Production and delivery capabilities are verified prior to each event.
- Samples are prepared, then critiqued by event planners.
- "After-event" assessments are conducted for continuous improvement.
- *All suppliers who come in contact with the customers must apply the Ritz-Carlton values.* Supercommunity banks set similar standards for vendors who

interface with customers, from check order vendors to credit card processors. These standards ensure that the customer is served in a consistently high and seamless style by partner vendors as well as by the bank.

An important part of delivering quality in hotels after their initial launch is using systematic controls. There are three types of controls:

- *Self control* of the individual employee based upon their spontaneous and learned behavior, managed through selection and development processes.
- *Basic control mechanism,* which is carried out by every member of the work force. The first person who detects a problem is empowered to break away from routine duties, investigate and correct the problem immediately, document the incident, and then return to their routine. These incidents are aggregated on a daily quality production report and pattern problems are investigated and corrected permanently.
- *Critical success factor control,* which is underway for critical processes. Process teams are using customer and organizational requirement measurements to determine quality, speed, and cost performance. These measurements are compared against benchmarks and customer satisfaction data to determine corrective actions and resource allocation.

To make sure they deliver quality products and services, the Ritz-Carlton continually conducts both self audits and outside audits. *Self audits* are carried out internally at all levels, from one individual or function to an entire hotel. Process walk-throughs occur daily in hotels while senior leaders assess field operations during formal reviews at various intervals. Through a cooperative effort with external suppliers, their capabilities are audited. *Outside audits* of processes, products, and services are performed by independent travel and hospitality rating organizations, such as the American Automobile Association and the Mobil Travel Guide. These organizations decide if the hotels are providing the products and services required by the customers at a higher level than the competition.

The means used to improve audit findings revolve around four points:

1. All audits must be documented by the person performing the audit.
2. Any documented audit finding must be submitted to the senior leaders of the unit being audited.
3. Senior leaders of the unit are responsible for taking action.
4. Implementation and effectiveness of recommended corrective actions are assessed from the previous audit, using the same data.

Lesson Learned: New products and services that get off to a good start are most reliable and efficient. The major thrust of the quality effort is to prevent difficulties from ever reaching a customer.

Quality and Operational Results

In addition to product and service quality improvements, the quality-conscious culture of the Ritz-Carlton has led to significant improvement in process measurement. Some examples are given below:

* No two guest needs are identical. The hotel's objective is to predetermine the needs and expectation of each guest. Within the past three years the hotel's work-force systems have detected and recorded the preferences of 120,000 individual customers, a *100% improvement.*
* The upfront teamwork and cross-functional cooperation achieved through the synchronized start-up control plan has contributed to 100% delivery of new ready-to-rent guest rooms on time since 1989, and a *12% reduction in the number of employees per guest room* needed during these pre-opening activities. This same start-up teamwork effort with external suppliers has simplified the start-up process. The average number of days to ship a ready product, for five critical supplies, has been reduced from twenty to just one.
* The efforts of the Ritz-Carlton to reduce turnover have been centered on the use of predictive interview instruments. Since 1989, *turnover has improved nearly 47%,* which is 16% better than "industry best." A leading British firm, with turnover nearly identical to the Ritz-Carlton's, applied these same techniques. They registered nearly the same improvement performance over the same time period.
* In hotels, productivity is measured by the number of hours worked per available guest room. Within a three-year period, The Ritz-Carlton has *reduced the number of hours worked per guest room by 8%.* This improvement occurred during a period when 22% of the workload involved the efficiency barriers of new hotel products.
* The Ritz-Carlton's management information systems division is concerned with the reliability of *six critical automated systems.* Through varied and repeated testing and team problem solving, the systems' performance at new hotels has increased by nearly 100% over the past three years.
* As a result of the Ritz-Carlton's lateral service principles and team-based improvement mechanisms, *cooperation ratings between departments have improved from 78% in 1989 to 86% in 1991.*
* *The company is a leader*—generating revenue per available guest room. Department profits, per available guest room, are at nearly five times the industry average.

Lesson Learned: Never underestimate the value of even one idea or quality improvement effort.

Customer Satisfaction

Customer satisfaction is a deeply held value at the Ritz-Carlton and begins with an understanding of the needs and expectations of their customers. Customer information is gathered in a number of ways:

* From the extensive research by the travel industry
* From focus groups of different market segments

- From preferences detected by all employees who come in contact with customers daily
- From customers who have just used the hotels
- Through guest and travel planner satisfaction system
- From information collected at various points in new hotel development

There are five major means by which the Ritz-Carlton *integrates customer satisfaction* and other quality-related data into its business management system. All apply directly to supercommunity banks:

1. By installing corporate values.
2. By creating a cross-functional senior leadership group that addresses relationship management and business simplification to make it easy for a customer to do business with the Ritz-Carlton. (Customer relationship management is the central theme around which every employee activity is organized).
3. By selecting quality leaders at the corporate office and in the field to work with supplier partners to aggregate, integrate, and analyze quality data.
4. By fully utilizing the potential and expertise of the entire work force through various mechanisms of involvement and empowerment.
5. By employing customer-driven marketing and sales efforts that determine the needs of various market segments and communicate company capabilities to these customers.

Customer contact employees (the hotel's teller and CSR equivalent) are afforded excellent career opportunities. Former receptionists and servers can be found on the Executive Committee of almost any Ritz-Carlton Hotel.

It is simple for customers to voice their needs and expectations to the Ritz-Carlton. Public spaces and employee work stations are designed to facilitate employee-customer interface. Is that a consideration in your branch design?

Customer service managers are available in each hotel twenty-four hours a day. Guest comment cards, addressed to the president, are available in every guest room. Employees are supported by technology, including automated systems, to provide on-line access to guest preference information for personalized service delivery. The repeat guest system, for example, recognizes customers on the basis of their expectation that they will receive special personal recognition for their loyal patronage. A platform system can be used in the same manner.

When customer standards need to be reset, problem-solving teams or process improvement teams are frequently used. Standards for customer interface are set nationally to ensure uniformity of what customers want most. Each hotel then develops customized tasks and performance standards with employee teams to address their own unique situation (much like a supercommunity bank). The guest and travel planner measurement system verifies how well performance standards are met (much like the BancOne financial reporting system). The standards are reset whenever customer needs and expectations change.

When customers do have complaints, the company uses a customer management system that is largely driven by employees, not managers. Customer complaint management has been elevated to high levels at The Ritz-Carlton. Every customer complaint is considered important. The person who first becomes aware of a problem is the owner of that problem and is responsible for resolving it quickly and completely. The goal is 100% complaint resolution prior to guest departure. Within the past three years, complaints per 100 comments have dropped 27%. These are effective benchmarks for supercommunity banks as well.

One major method for assessing customer satisfaction has been a guest and travel planner satisfaction system (much like the BancOne financial reporting system). Quarterly surveys are conducted asking guests and planners to rate their rational and emotional reactions to various aspects of product and service delivery. The timely delivery of important attributes is not sufficient for most demanding travel consumers; they seek a memorable experience, a feeling that cannot be captured by normal customer satisfaction survey systems and scales. There is no substitute for customer feedback. It is the most effective way to learn how well you're doing and where improvement can still be made.

The resulting customer satisfaction data is separated into major customer segments and product lines, then given comprehensive analysis. The individual hotels are responsible for their units' performance, while the senior leaders concentrate on the problems of the entire system (a structure identical to the supercommunity bank with a holding company and individual bank

subsidiaries). Direction for change is set on both the local and national levels. Annually, this data passes through a strategic planning process to establish objectives and action plans.

The result? Customer satisfaction continues to achieve high levels. A full 97% of prestigious travel consumers had their expectations met and had a memorable experience. The satisfaction levels of customers who plan meetings were 97% on staff members, 97% with sales personnel, 95% with facilities, and 94% with procedures for two consecutive years. The Gallup Survey has found the Ritz-Carlton Hotel Company to be the first choice of customers, with a 94% satisfaction rating compared to the closest competitor, with a 57% satisfaction rating for the past two years. A nationwide study of frequent business travelers found they are the clear choice of customers who use their competitors—they outperformed their best competitor an average of 15 points on nine attributes.

While customer satisfaction has been increasing, adverse indicators of customer dissatisfaction, such as rebates and complaints, have declined. Perhaps the best indicator of customer satisfaction is customer retention. Over the past three years, key national account retention has improved 20% toward the goal of 100% retention. Over the past three years, the company's business center hotels have retained 97.1% of their key local corporate accounts.

The Ritz-Carlton places a great deal of importance on its local market relationship. In 1991, all Ritz-Carlton Hotels held a premium share of their local market area (again, a clear parallel to supercommunity banking).

Finally, the Ritz-Carlton also measures its gains and losses in market yield (revenue per available room versus competitors). Over a three-year period they were the market leader over the best competitors of all markets combined. In other words, the numbers beat out the theory that quality leads to retention, and retention leads to share.

Total quality management is an important differentiation tool for supercommunity banks. Its measurement, monitoring, and reward are prerequisites to an effective quality improvement program which is well integrated into day to day bank management.

CHAPTER ELEVEN

The Board of Directors

The Role of Your Board—
Setting up the Expectations

Supercommunity banks have placed special emphasis on and excelled in several critical success factors, including the utilization of the board of directors.

Many bankers view their board as an unnecessary burden. Supercommunity banks see them as a source of invaluable business advice, guidance, and a business development tool. Supercommunity banks have been able to take full advantage of boards by assigning different roles to various levels of directors. Many institutions have more than just one board. There typically is the holding company board, which oversees the entire enterprise and puts a focus on all the subsidiary activities, bank and nonbank alike. Each subsidiary bank

board, in turn, gets more involved in setting the strategic direction for its bank as well as assuring compliance with regulations. These directors also bring business development potential and provide the necessary link to the community. Many supercommunity banks also have been especially adept at making use of advisory boards. Advisory boards may seem neither fish nor fowl, not fully empowered to either make policy or take responsibility for it. Just because they do not have the legal authority and liability does not mean their usefulness is limited. The supercommunity phenomenon has turned that lack of authority and liability into an important advantage.

While advisory boards do not have to worry about the potential liabilities troubling so many board members these days, they do have a status in their ability to participate in the "old boy network." Advisory boards thus become highly effective in developing business relationships, particularly for larger, fast-growing banks concerned about losing touch with their local markets. Some institutions have more than 700 people sitting on various advisory boards. The attendance fees for such board members are low, often not more than $100 per meeting, and their returns in terms of community goodwill and specific business opportunities are high.

The board of directors at supercommunity banks can be an important contributor to the bank's success beyond the typical role that boards usually play. Due to the community orientation of SCBs, the boards constitute an important link between the bank and the community.

Holding Company Boards

The role of the holding company board of the supercommunity bank is different from the role of each individual subsidiary's board. The holding company has a broader strategic guidance role and considers the total company when making decisions and recommendations.

Supercommunity banks typically keep the holding company board involved in strategic issues corporate-wide and the subsidiary boards involved in reviewing individual loans, watching over the individual banks, and performing business development. Many supercommunity banks provide for holding company representation on the subsidiary boards; some do not. Such representation facilitates the communication process between the holding company and the subsidiaries, ensuring

that corporate-wide considerations are included in decision making at the subsidiary level, something that is not always easy to accomplish. At the same time, this communication can become technically cumbersome when the number of subsidiaries is large. In situations where there is no holding company representation on the subsidiary boards, special attention should be given to communicating holding company strategy, concerns, and progress to the individual boards to ensure that a proper balance is kept between individual bank considerations and holding company considerations.

Many supercommunity banks strive to induce the public to view board membership at the banks as the most prestigious in the state. Those that have done so successfully, such as BB&T and U.S. Bank Corp., end up with stellar boards and with little difficulty attracting additional board members. Some believe that only line management people should become board members; that is, no doctors, lawyers, or other professionals. Others look for board members who are community leaders and can help in the business development arena. At Norwest, for example, the advisory board structure is used to attract public officials who cannot serve on legal boards, such as the local superintendent of schools as well as community leaders, including civic-minded housewives and minorities.

Advisory Boards

With bankers finding it increasingly difficult to recruit and keep prominent local business people on the boards, advisory boards are an excellent vehicle that can serve several important and complementary purposes, such as public relations and business development, without incurring the legal liability. Further, as mergers give banks the opportunity to consolidate charters and reduce their numbers of directors, acquired bank boards can be recast as advisory boards.

While advisory boards do not fit in with reducing overhead and taking a more centralized approach, they clearly fit into the supercommunity bank culture. They give the bank the needed ties to the business community, give the directors visibility in the community, and, at the same time, have no legal liability. You can have the best and brightest local people serve on an advisory board and fill key roles in business development and community ties. The cost associated with such board membership is often more effective than advertising. "Administering one of the most extensive networks of advisory directors, Branch Banking & Trust Company of North Carolina spends a good deal of money," said Kelly S. King, president and CEO, "but the amount, including monthly fees, is less than what would be spent on the same number of conventional boards. It is some of the best money we spend."

Principal subsidiary of the $7 billion asset company, BB&T has only one formal bank board, but there are advisory panels in fifty North Carolina cities, each with ten to twelve members. Each board reports to one of the ten regional presidents in the state. While they may not have all the power and liabilities of the central board, BB&T keeps them closely involved in bank affairs with discussions of profitability and regulatory issues as well as community affairs. "They meet monthly," said Mr. King. "We feel that is the best way to keep in touch. There are also annual meetings bringing together the directors of each region." He called the advisory directors "very active, not figureheads," playing roles that are in keeping with "our whole thrust to be independent and be decentralized at the local level." The advisory boards "are our eyes and ears in the community," said Mr. King.

BB&T, a successful supercommunity bank, uses the advisory boards and regional presidents to break itself down into locally rooted community banks although they do not have separate charters. This $7 billion company has only one charter but, in effect, runs itself as ten separate banks that make decisions locally and have local boards much like any other supercommunity bank with separate charters.

Norwest, a $40 billion supercommunity bank, has done a particularly effective job in utilizing advisory boards as the link into the community. "Together we're number one, second to none," says Richard N. Kovacevich, president and CEO of Norwest, in his statement, *Shared Visions: Community Banking Board Member Handbook:*

"Service is our primary product. We differentiate ourselves by delivering a superior level of service and by being innovative and responsible both to customer and to community needs. We seek local advice and counsel to help us meet the financial and human needs of each community. Our vision is viable only if we can identify and act upon real concerns in real communities. Community board members are critical to the success of this approach. They share that responsibility. Only by working together as a cohesive team will we be able to reach our goal. We expect to attract people who are real pros at what they do and who share the vision of being the best. Community board members are community leaders, talented professionals, and motivators of others. They lend their unique perspectives to other board members and to the management of the bank. Community board members share the vision of being the best."

Mr. Kovacevich expressed a very strong sentiment above regarding the importance of community banking to Norwest. And he is right. Norwest is a large supercommunity bank with over $40 billion in assets. The company could find it hard to stay close to its local community roots. This is where the community board members come in. As Kovacevich stated, he looks at his community members as the pipeline into the community, the communication channel that facilitates understanding community needs and meeting them for this banking giant. Community board members are critical for supercommunity banks of every size, and especially at Norwest's size. The company's management recognizes it, hence its special attention to the advisory board members and its attempt to select the best and create an elite of board members for its community banks. The company attempts to make this a coveted position where only the best can succeed, and given Norwest's financial results, they certainly have come a long way toward achieving their vision, "Together we're number one, second to none."

As Ken Murray, the head of community banking for Norwest, says, "Community banking is more than just a name, it's the way we do business. The name 'community banking group' states very simply why we serve our customers as we do. Above all, we are here to serve our local customers locally. 'Community' means local. It implies a down-the-street presence, a personal touch, exceptional service, commitment, confidence, and being a good neighbor in every way. The word 'group' was chosen because success depends on acting as a team rather than operating independently. In fact, it was through discussions with all our employees that the name 'community banking group' was formulated. When Dick Kovacevich came to Norwest he asked what he needed to change so that we could successfully ask for and get all other customer business and thus meet our goals. One of the most commonly repeated needs was preservation and preferably an increase in community presence and commitment. The rationale was that we serve these people every day. They need to know that we are here for them in this community, not just in a faraway headquarters."

Norwest reorganized to reflect what Kovacevich was told. Norwest Community Banking Group has a structure that allows each bank to meet its community goals while serving the customer in the best possible way. The community banking board is an integral part of that structure. The board members take an active role in assuring that each bank knows the needs of the community and that it acts accordingly.

"Our mission is to provide the personal service of a community bank with the extensive product and service resources of

Norwest Corporation—the best of both worlds," says Murray.

Consistent with this shared vision approach, Norwest defines the mission and role of the community board members. Members are selected based on their expertise in business and community service, their reputation as community leaders, their talent as professionals and motivators of

---

"Community board members are expected to take an active interest in the performance of the community bank on whose board they serve, and to take the responsibility in seeking out information that is necessary to fulfill this role."

---

others, and their ability to lend their unique perspective to other board members and the management of the bank. Their role is to provide the president with an outside objective source of expertise. They should counsel and support the bank in achieving business and community goals.

The board member handbook states, "Community board members are expected to take an active interest in the performance of the community bank on whose board they serve, and to take the responsibility in seeking out information that is necessary to fulfill this role. This would include advising the president on the bank's public image, observing the competition, stressing operational improvements, and identifying new business and community opportunities." Each Norwest presi-

dent is responsible for selecting the community board members within their marketplace, and they serve as the chairperson of the community board. Each president is responsible for keeping the board members informed about significant policy changes, management decisions, local market, and new business development strategies. The bank presidents and regional managers report to a regional president who is responsible and has assigned territory for all community banking group activities.

Norwest clearly spells out the responsibility of its community board members who, importantly, are all advisory board members. Their responsibilities include:

1. Familiarity with those policy statements of Norwest Bank that define the bank's mission and describe in general terms how the bank staff is charged to carry out its work. Along with the president, the community board members are expected to contribute to the bank's community marketing initiatives to assure that Norwest is meeting the banking needs of its entire community. The board will review annually its Community Reinvestment Act statement, including its community relations. {Author's note: by defining one of the board members primary responsibilities to identify community needs and assure the bank's responsiveness to those needs, Norwest positions the board member not merely as a simple business developer, but as an important communication channel between the bank and the community, a vehicle to transmit the community's needs to the bank and a powerful tool in meeting those needs.}

2. Board members and the president are expected to maintain the confidentiality of all discussions and agenda items at board meetings to maintain the confidence of the customers and the community. They are subject to a code of ethics to affirm their beliefs in the standard and desire to maintain the reputation of the bank. It is requested that all community board members enter into the spirit of that code.

3. Community members review the statement of condition, income statement, and other financial performance reports of the bank on a periodic basis. They also may review the plans and provide dimension and guidance for their bank's lending practices. They are expected to know the bank's business plan and be willing to help execute the plan through participation and development and retention activities.

4. As community representatives, board members are expected to monitor the marketplace as to the competitiveness and effectiveness of the Norwest product and service delivery practices. They should advise and counsel the president about matters concerning the effectiveness of the operation in the local marketplace.

5. Board members are responsible for attending board meetings.

6. Community board members are expected to provide the president with their perceptions of customer attitudes, community affairs, and business conditions.

7. Community board members assist the bank's business development activity by identifying new customers and services, and by suggesting changes in existing services that would enhance the bank's market position.

8. Board members are encouraged to exercise the responsibility faithfully through regular meeting attendance and scrupulous protection of customer confidentiality.

By offering this set of responsibilities, Norwest puts meat on the bones of the advisory board membership and makes it a true contributor to bank management and local rooting, even without the legal ties of full board membership. Like BB&T, Norwest successfully motivates hundreds of community board members to fulfill an effective role in community relations and customer development by making them an integral part of the management team. It is that commitment that makes the difference, not the legal liability. The responsibilities' structure makes the advisory status transparent, almost an advantage. Norwest successfully created advisory boards that provide all the upside of a board membership without the downside of legal liability.

To support the advisory board member structure, Norwest provides board member guidelines, suggestions on size of community board depending on the amount of deposit and its location, and a suggested agenda for board meetings that specifies, much like full board members, frequency of meetings, terms of office, stock ownership, business commitment, and an annual performance review as well as a retirement policy and a conflict of interest policy.

Other supercommunity banks stick to a more traditional board format. Each of the twelve banks of Marquette Banks in Minnesota, for example, has a fully empowered board, and the reasoning behind it is much like BB&T's. "It's the only way we know how to maintain that critical link to the communities we serve," said Albert J. Colianni, Jr., executive vice president and chief operating officer of Marquette. One member of each board is designated by Minneapolis headquarters, and the rest are active in the bank's local area. "They work hard providing feedback and giving banks an outreach into their communities," Colianni said.

"Our management style is very decentralized under regional presidents. The boards are important communication vehicles.

Other supercommunity banks rely heavily on advisory boards. "Our advisory directors serve on these boards because they get a kick out of being on a board of directors. It makes them feel important to be a bank director. Also, they are curious to see what other companies we may be doing business with are up to. They want to look behind the curtain to see if Joe's chain of stores is really doing as well as it appears from the front Joe puts up in the country club.

The boards serve us in a number of ways. They help with credit decisions, they provide us with market knowledge, but, most especially, they serve as a business development network. These people are proud to be on the board of directors, and they really get into the role. They want us to do well and are not shy about referring business our way.

I'm really happy with our advisory board of directors. They developed out of the original boards, which were in place when the smaller banks were acquired and merged into our bank. The boards helped the presidents by providing them with some insights on how the bank is perceived in the market. They provide knowledge about some of our credit customers, such as payment history, reliability, that sort of thing."

Board Responsibilities

Supercommunity bank management should provide guidance to the board as to their duties and responsibilities.

Holding company boards should:

1. Comply with all applicable rules and regulations related to corporate covenants as well as traditional corporate fiduciary responsibilities.
2. Guide the overall strategic direction of the company, including principal business focus and merger and acquisition activities.
3. Approve and monitor performance expectations and results by regularly reviewing appropriate financial reports.
4. Oversee compliance with all regulatory and supervisory requirements, including but not limited to the Securities and Exchange Commission and the Federal Reserve System.
5. Select, evaluate, and retain competent executive management. The evaluation should ensure an adequate oversight program that covers motivation, reward, and discipline, if necessary.
6. Improve and monitor the capital management policies and practices of the institution to include capital adequacy, dividend levels, and shareholder relations.

7. Approve and monitor compliance with safety and solidness policies and standards. This specifically should include corporate asset quality levels and the consolidated loan review position, as well as the corporation's system of internal controls.

8. Approve and monitor compliance with companies' policies and procedures. This should include the areas of lending, asset liability management, Community Reinvestment Act, investments, audit, human resources, and trust operations.

9. Oversee and assess the various boards, including the selection, evaluation, and discipline, if necessary, of holding company and bank board members, and the establishment and monitoring of the appropriate structure, composition, and activities of the holding company and subsidiary bank boards.

Similarly, subsidiary bank boards have the responsibility to:

1. In cooperation with and in support of the holding company board, guide and monitor the strategic direction of local banks.

2. Monitor the performance of the banks by regularly reviewing appropriate financial reports.

3. Assist and monitor local community involvement and contact by being engaged, preferably, in a leadership role in community activities. Wherever possible, bank board members also should assist management in their efforts to achieve local leadership roles in these activities. Also included in this is the responsibility under the Community Reinvestment Act for assessing the needs of the local community as well as guiding and assisting management of the institution in meeting those needs.

4. Encourage, oversee, and participate in the business development efforts of the local bank by participating in business development programs, being involved as an active solicitor of new business, and serving as a source of referrals for management follow-up. All bank directors should commit to maintain good principle, personal, and business banking relationships with the institution. If a loan of a board member becomes delinquent and gets classified, the board member must resign.

5. In cooperation with and in support of the holding company board, approve policies and monitor compliance with safety and solidness standards. This specifically would include bank asset quality levels, the bank loan review position, and compliance with all policies and procedures, as well as the bank's system of internal controls.

6. Oversee compliance with all regulatory and supervisory requirements, including those of the Comptroller of the Currency, Federal Deposit Insurance Corporation, State Department of Banking, and the Federal Reserve System.

7. Provide oversight responsibility for the lending activities of the subsidiary bank by approving loans in excess of authority delegated to officers and committees. Ensure compliance with approved poli-

cies and procedures in providing input to local market economic and value conditions.

8. Approve and monitor compliance with all bank policies and procedures, including assurance that such policies and procedures are consistent with the overall corporate strategic direction.

9. In cooperation with and in support of the strategic direction established by the holding company, provide oversight responsibility for product-related activities of the subsidiary banks that are managed centrally, such as trust operations, and ensure compliance with approved policies and procedures in performance of the necessary fiduciary duties. Input to local customer needs and participation in and support for local marketing efforts also should be provided.

Board Members Selection Criteria

Figure 11.1 outlines a possible bank board committee structure. This is a typical committee structure that includes audit, business development, executive, lending, and trust committees. Special emphasis is given on business development for the bank board committees, a reflection of the reliance on the local subsidiary board to provide linkage and business development support through the community. Figure 11.2 outlines the typical committees of a holding company of a supercommunity bank.

A planning committee is an important committee, which is not present typically at the bank level. Its role is to oversee the strategic direction of the company and to

provide guidance to the holding company and, through it, to the individual subsidiaries for the company's overall strategy. Figure 11.3 lists board membership criteria

---

. . . active members in their principal occupation can contribute a lot more than inactive members who are fully retired. Strict enforcement of that rule may eliminate some attractive board members, but will certainly create a more lively board discussion.

---

for both holding company and subsidiary boards. Although these are but guidelines and suggested structures much like the committee structure, the reasoning behind them is solid. For example, mandatory retirement at age 70 can be used to ensure that fresh blood is being injected into the board on a regular basis. Similarly, active members in their principal occupation can contribute a lot more than inactive members who are fully retired. Strict enforcement of that rule may eliminate some attractive board members, but will certainly create a more lively board discussion. Requiring board members to be local residents can help as an anti-takeover measure.

Figures 11.5 and 11.6 are examples of abbreviated board evaluation tools which correspond to the criteria identified above. Ongoing board evaluation is important, and more detailed forms for such evaluation are provided in Figures 11.5 and 11.6. The purpose of the evaluation is to ensure

FIGURE 11.1 Bank Board Committee Structure

Committee Name	Meeting Schedule	Primary Responsibility
Audit	Quarterly	1. Review compliance with internal control policies and procedures. 2. Work with corporate audit committee to monitor the safety and soundness of the bank.
Business Development	Quarterly	1. Provide guidance and support to management relative to acquisition of new business and maintenance of existing customers. 2. Encourage and evaluate the business development activities of the bank board members and community board members.
Executive	As Needed	1. Act for the board between meetings if necessary 2. Serve as a source of advice and counsel to the CEO. 3. Evaluate the performance of bank board members and recommend their election or removal to the corporate executive committee. ("Nominating Committee.")
Lending	As Needed	1. In support of corporate credit policy, approve credit policies for the banks. 2. Approve credits under policies and limits delegated by the board. 3. Review and approve recommended individual or joint officer lending limits. 4. Monitor bank asset quality characteristics.
Trust	Monthly	1. Review the activities of the trust function for compliance with approved policies, procedures, and fiduciary responsibility. 2. Insure compliance with all regulatory requirements for trust oversight and control. 3. Monitor local customer needs and satisfaction and assist in trust business development activities.

FIGURE 11.2 Holding Company Board Committee Structure

Committee Name	Meeting Schedule	Primary Responsibility
Audit	Quarterly	1. Approve the corporate audit plan, policies, and procedures. 2. Monitor the activities of the audit function. 3. Review the reports of the company's independent CPA firms. 4. Recommend the selection of the independent CPA firm. 5. Advise the board of any serious, uncorrected violations of generally accepted control procedures.
Executive	As Needed	1. Act for the board between meetings. 2. Serve as the nominating committee. 3. Provide advice and counsel to the CEO.
Human Resources	As Needed	1. Review and recommend corporate compensation policy. 2. Provide oversight of the pension and 401(K) plan. 3. Grant equity-based management incentive awards. 4. Review and recommend action on all management employment contracts. 5. Evaluate the CEO and recommend appropriate compensation and benefits.
Planning	As Needed	1. Oversee planning the strategic direction of the company. 2. Review and recommend the company's strategic plan. 3. Provide guidance for the annual strategic retreat.

that all board members are working toward the same objective and that, indeed, they are active participants.

Summary

Board membership in a supercommunity bank can be an especially rewarding experience for civic leaders who wish to make a contribution to their community. At the same time, it is a demanding position, which entails the board members' commitment to the bank. The special role of the supercommunity bank board member as providing linkage between the bank and the community it serves implies significant responsibilities that should not be taken lightly by either the board member or bank management.

FIGURE 11.3 Board Membership Criteria

Holding Company Board:

1. *Age.* Members must retire at the next annual meeting after reaching age 70. Enforced strongly.
2. *Occupation.* Members must be engaged in their usual and customary principal occupation and must be at least 50 percent actively involved in that pursuit. Alternative: may stay until one year after you retire from _____ business.
3. *Residence.* Members (except "at large" members) must reside in the trade area, which is defined as a county or contiguous county where a banking subsidiary has an office. Anti-takeover measure.
4. *Attendance.* Absent "extreme, mitigating circumstances," any member who attends less than 75 percent of board and committee meetings for two consecutive calendar years is not eligible to serve past the next annual meeting.
5. *Investment.* All members are "encouraged" to own at least $50,000 market value of holding company stock within three years of initial service.
6. *Financial Responsibility.* Members are expected to adhere to the "highest financial standards" in their dealings with member banks.
7. *Evaluation.* Each member is to do an annual self-evaluation of their contribution prior to each annual meeting. The Executive Committee also does a formal evaluation as part of its nominating procedure and appoints emeritus directors (over 70), who are not paid to attend meetings and are limited to two years.

Subsidiary Bank Boards:

All of the above criteria also apply to bank board members with the adjustment that the stock ownership request is reduced to $25,000. In addition, in an effort to reflect the business development and community focus of the banks, the following also apply:

1. Preference for members with a sales, marketing, and distribution orientation is shown.
2. Commitment to business development and willingness to be evaluated by participation in it.
3. Involvement in the community in a leadership role.

FIGURE 11.4 Responsibilities and Rewards of Serving on Boards

What supercommunity bank executives expect of local bank directors. (1 is the highest priority, 5 is lowest.)

How subsidiaries' directors are compensated. (Some banks use multiple methods.)

		Percentage of banks	Average pay
Improve community relations	2.01		
Attract new business	2.30	Per meeting fee — 82%	$368
Make policy decisions	2.47	Annual fee — 53%	$4,678
Make strategic decisions	3.13		
Give advice only	4.14	Stock, options — 7%	N/A

FIGURE 11.5 Executive Committee Evaluation of a Board Member

Age
Has the incumbent reached retirement age?

Attendance
Has the director attended at least 75 percent of board meetings and assigned committee meetings for the past year? If not, were there circumstances that prevented attendance?

Occupation
Is the director at least 51 percent actively engaged in his/her principal business or profession and is it his or her usual and customary occupation?

Residence
Does the director have his/her primary legal residence within the Bank's trade area, which is defined to mean a county or contiguous county where one of the Bank's offices serves that market?

Investment
Does the director have at least $25,000 in market value of the stock within three years of his/her initial selection?

Community Involvement
Has the incumbent demonstrated leadership through active involvement in agencies or organizations that support the continued enhancement of the markets we serve?

Business Development
Has the incumbent regularly participated in the referral of business to the bank?

FIGURE 11.6 Board Member Self-Evaluation

---

1. Have I regularly referred business opportunities to the bank? Approximately how many new clients have I referred in the previous twelve months?

2. Have I participated publicly in marketing the bank (ambassador at bank sponsored/supported functions—public support through appropriate centers of influence, i.e., Chamber, Rotary, etc.)?

3. Have I fulfilled my duties to monitor the safety and soundness of the bank by active participation during board meetings?

4. Have I provided visible leadership to my community through civic, economic development, and other channels? Have I participated in CRA activities?

5. Have I attended at least 75 percent of all board meetings?

6. Have I made a personal financial contribution to the organization (do I maintain a financial relationship with the Bank)?

CHAPTER TWELVE

Centralization vs. Decentralization*

Bankers constantly wrestle with the question of centralization versus decentralization. The issue is especially critical for the growing number of multibank holding companies avowing a commitment to supercommunity banking. By definition, such organizations seek to combine two often conflicting goals: community orientation and cost efficiency. Decentralization and empowerment of local personnel are essential ingredients in community orientation. Centralization and standardization are critical components for achieving operating efficiencies. The nagging questions are: How far do you go? What functions can be centralized without compromising service? How should you go about centralizing? What are the pitfalls?

Typical Supercommunity Bank Practices

The functions or departments that are typically centralized within a supercommunity banking environment vary from bank to bank. The general rule is this: Staff functions are best centralized, while line functions are best decentralized (Figure 12.1).

A recent survey of chief executives of supercommunity banks gives some indication of the direction being taken. The survey indicated that a basic tenet of the supercommunity banking strategy is that cost efficiency is driving the centralization and downsizing of many customer-transparent functions. Respondents to the survey reported that these areas typically

* The author wishes to thank Richard Israel for his valuable contribution to this chapter.

FIGURE 12.1 The Mixed Blessings of Centralization

Supercommunity executives see improvements in these areas . . .

Sources: American Banker, BDO Seidman.

. . . but some report deterioration in these functions.

Data processing	28%
Operations	26%
Product diversification	21%
Accounting	16%
Lending	16%

Customer service	13%
Response times	6%
Communication	4%
Operations	3%

included the following:

- Data processing
- Back office operations
- Product development
- Accounting
- Purchasing and accounts payable
- Human resources
- Audit
- Regulatory compliance
- Marketing
- Quality control
- Loan processing
- Loan workout

Not all institutions reported having centralized all of these functions. Some, like data processing and proof-in-transit, for example, were uniformly consolidated under a single area. Others, such as quality control, were handled in a variety of ways at different institutions.

The survey further reported which areas CEOs think should *not* be centralized:

- Loan underwriting
- Pricing
- Customer service
- Branch operations
- Sales

The surveyed supercommunity banks reported that the important benefits of letting certain key areas remain decentralized included the following:

- Local community orientation
- Autonomous decisions
- Meeting individual needs
- Fostering entrepreneurial spirit
- Quick decision making
- Maintaining loan quality
- Improved responsiveness

Most supercommunity banks stressed the local community focus as the greatest benefit of not consolidating certain functions. Financial analysis of supercommunity bank performance indicated that, in addition to the community orientation, asset quality dramatically benefits from the centralization of credit underwriting. Supercommunity banks' nonperforming loans are roughly a third of the industry average.

Benefits of Centralization

Supercommunity banks centralize certain functions for the following reasons:

Cost Reduction

The number one reason supercommunity banks centralize functions is to reduce costs. Generally speaking, cost reduction opportunities stem primarily from economies of scale.

Prior to merger, as individually operating, independent banks, the decomposed community institutions that make up a supercommunity bank each maintained all the necessary functions to operate. Each institution had, by definition, some excess capacity. Through the process of merger, consolidation, and centralization, supercommunity banks take advantage of the opportunity to reduce duplication, increase standardization, and reduce excess capacity, thereby managing more effectively on the margin. Further, combined functions that are technology-dependent, such as check processing, can invest in larger, more efficient technology, thereby achieving economies of scale. The larger combined function can exercise greater bargaining power in negotiations with vendors, as well. Several institutions have negotiated favorable outsourcing agreements or bulk purchase agreements such as check orders, for example, using their ability to address the market as a single entity.

Streamlining Opportunity

Shifting to a centralized structure for customer-transparent functions presents an opportunity to improve work flows, redesign processing strategies, and improve management reporting. Many supercommunity banks take advantage of this opportunity to implement new ways of doing things and to retrain employees in new standardized methods and procedures. This re-engineering opportunity can take many forms. At First Security of Utah, for example, re-engineering the indirect lending process allowed the loan approval process to be reduced to a thirty-minute turnaround time, which gave each subsidiary a significant new advantage in this highly competitive product area. At Mid-Am, centralization provided an opportunity to institute new asset/liability management reports, which significantly improved the holding company's ability to manage interest rate risk and liquidity for the combined company.

Better Control

Most supercommunity bankers believe that control can be improved through a centralized approach. There is little doubt that it is easier to impose change and maintain control if processes and decisions are made in one place, as opposed to many. As a result, there is a managerial impetus to centralize functions as much as possible. The danger in centralizing for control purposes is that, if carried too far, control can dampen entrepreneurial spirit.

At one New Jersey supercommunity bank, for example, efforts to centralize the treasury function were not received well by the president of one of the subsidiaries. He felt that the holding company's approach to asset/liability management was too risk-averse and that his approach had consistently proven to be more profitable. He received the news that the function would be consolidated at the holding company level and that he should reduce his staff in that area. The subsidiary president felt that this was just one more example of holding company interference in the way he did business. Despite his objections, however, the function was successfully and profitably consolidated at the holding company.

Centralization can improve control in a very positive way. Loan workout was consolidated in a centralized area at BMJ, with win/win benefits being perceived by all parties. As a result of centralization, overall workout costs were more easily tracked and controlled as a result of centralization. Subsidiary presidents were happy to get rid of the headache of the problem loans in the workout areas. Bottom line (and recoveries) was improved without hurting morale.

At Summit Bancorp, the centralization of purchasing allowed better control of forms inventories. Through a structured program of re-order point monitoring, it was possible to work more closely with the printers and thereby reduce inventory levels by a significant percentage, which, in turn, reduced overall costs.

Accountability and Responsibility

The CEO of a $5 billion supercommunity bank in Ohio related a story of how his bank's holding company had made a decision eight months earlier to introduce an annuity product throughout its subsidiaries. After the initial communication from the corporate office about this new program, the implementation and product introduction was left to each subsidiary. Eight months later, the holding company CEO received a memo from the board of one of the subsidiaries indicating that the

bank had never introduced the product because management had decided it was inappropriate for that market. In this case, while the president of the subsidiary in question was accountable for having decided not to make the product introduction, no one at the holding company level had been tracking the product introduction at each subsidiary or measuring its success. As a result, the holding company CEO learned about the subsidiary's decision far too late to address the issue.

Some supercommunity banks establish clear responsibility for products, functions, new initiatives, and the like at a centralized location. This ensures accountability and that one manager has responsibility to monitor and report progress on a period basis. It also facilitates leverage. In many supercommunity banks, individual subsidiaries develop technical expertise that can be leveraged throughout the system while housed in one bank. Centralization does not necessarily imply ownership by the holding company, but rather ownership at a single location—bank or holding company—for efficiency, control, and expertise development, with distribution systemwide.

We have seen this monitoring or reporting responsibility assigned in a variety of locations within the organization. It could be assigned to a centralized resource at the holding company, but this is not necessarily the case. Often, new product champions are located within one of the subsidiaries. It is not necessary to build the overhead of large centralized holding company staff to achieve the goals of leverage, accountability, and responsibility. Also, product management and matrix organizations do not often work at supercommunity banks, but product ownership does.

Improved Communications

Through centralization of certain functions, supercommunity banks enhance communications. By establishing a centralized point of control, supercommunity banks can ensure that data is disseminated and aggregated completely and efficiently. In the case of the bank that chose not to introduce annuities, it obviously had not been made clear that the annuity program was not optional. The holding company had also not been informed in a timely manner. Communications had broken down. If there had been a single point of contact and communication, the problem could have been avoided.

This is not to say that product introduction necessarily has to be made systemwide. Most supercommunity banks have a consistent shelf of products from which each subsidiary selects appropriate services, albeit standardized. At LaSalle, for example, one subsidiary is located in an upscale market, while another is in a blue-collar environment. Their product needs are different and should be reflected in different product offerings, yet each product's features can be consistent throughout the system. Systemwide product introduction does have its benefits, especially when fee income, critical mass, intensive products are involved. In these cases, the subsidiaries should undertake product distribution to the benefit of the holding company even if local demand is not robust.

Resource Allocation

All banks face the problem of applying resources effectively. Supercommunity banks have certain special problems and opportunities in this regard as a result of their unique structure and strategy. Most supercommunity banks have grown through the merger of several smaller community banks. Often these small community banks have developed specialty areas or business niches over the years. For example, First Virginia has among its subsidiaries an institution that has developed a strong indirect auto lending program; LaSalle has merged into its structure a thrift with a strong mortgage servicing capability; Keystone has identified subsidiaries with a valuable franchise in the area of trust services. Community First has acquired an insurance agency with one of its bank acquisitions.

Each of these supercommunity banks had both a problem and an opportunity with respect to these subsidiaries with product specialty. The problem was that the subsidiaries tended to specialize and may have been missing the revenues associated with a broader product line. The opportunity was that all the other subsidiaries could benefit from the presence of the specialist subsidiary within the supercommunity bank system if they could each learn from the specialist and expand their own product lines to include that of the specialist.

Both the solution to the problem and the opportunity for these supercommunity banks was centralization. In each case, the supercommunity bank centralized origination, processing, and managerial control for the function or product involved. Typically, the control was centralized not at the holding company but at the specialist subsidiary where the expertise was already resident. Other subsidiaries within the company learned to use the strength of the specialist in developing their own distribution of the product or service. In some sense, this constitutes a wholesale distribution approach to resource allocation through centralization within the super-

---

It is almost uniformly the case that the underwriting decisions are made locally for most supercommunity banks. Many, however, handle the related documentation control, file maintenance, statement spreading and the like in a centralized fashion.

---

community banks. In this regard, the expert within the institution becomes "vendor" or "distributor" of the product or service with the institution. This centralized approach to internal corporate networking allows the right resources to be applied in meeting the overall strategic goals of the supercommunity bank.

Streamlined Decision Making

Some might argue that centralization of customer-transparent functions and processes might impose additional layers of management and systems that could

hamper efficient decision making. This is not so. For one thing, if properly implemented, supercommunity banks find it possible to empower local decision makers through improved support and service levels from centralized service facilities. In situations where centralization impedes decisions, supercommunity banks have abandoned that strategy in a flexible response to what doesn't seem to work.

Some areas work better in a decentralized mode. It is almost uniformly the case that the underwriting decisions are made locally for most supercommunity banks. Many, however, handle the related documentation control, file maintenance, statement spreading, and the like in a centralized fashion. The local decision makers report that it is possible to decompose the underwriting process into functions that can be efficiently centralized, resulting in improved support and faster decisions. At the same time, an attempt at full centralization of the commercial loan guarantee's function proved unsuccessful at a $3 billion supercommunity bank in Michigan. Credit files had to stay close to the loan officer, and their centralization was a mistake. In another example, management of a $12 billion supercommunity bank initially sought to centralize the controllership and accounting function of the subsidiaries at the holding company. Over time they found that many of the subsidiaries eventually developed duplicate financial staffs to meet the information and "number crunching needs" of local management in making financial decisions. Rather than forcing the subsidiaries to give up their financial personnel, holding company management elected to give control over the numbers (except for key consolidation activities) to the local banks. This retrenchment to the old policy of decentralized accounting was the right thing to do for this institution. It resulted ultimately in less staff, in the elimination of "policing" activities by the holding company to ensure that accounting staff populations were not growing and in more efficient and effective financial decision-making at the subsidiary level.

Similarly, a centralized customer service function at a $10 billion supercommunity bank created such havoc through poor service that the individual subsidiaries had to build their own customer service units to untangle the mess produced by the central unit. Decentralization in this case resulted in 100% increase in staff, rather than in savings. The lesson: centralization is a valid concept only when well-executed. When poorly carried out it can be a costly approach. That is why it is important to impose service standards and market discipline or centralized service functions.

Ultimately, whether or not a given function can be centralized without inhibiting fast and effective decision making will be determined by how the centralization effort is implemented. Attention must be paid to the maintenance of good communications between the back office and the line personnel. Furthermore, the centralized support functions must operate within a service culture that dictates high levels of performance and responsiveness.

Staff Career Development

Developing centralized processing environments provides supercommunity banks more than an opportunity to reduce staff and thereby achieve cost reductions. Very often the centralized environments are larger and more technologically sophisticated than the environments found in smaller independent community banks. These environments provide qualified staff new opportunities for learning and advancement. The possibility of moving from the acquired subsidiary to the holding company, for example, is often regarded as a significant career development opportunity by the staff. As a result, centralization can provide management a better environment for grooming future management and for attracting and retaining the highly qualified personnel that, individually, the smaller community banks could not. This can result not only in upgrading of staff but improvement in overall morale and reduced turnover.

Benefits of Decentralization

While centralization works well in some areas, decentralization is the best choice for others.

Supercommunity banks take advantage of their organizational structure by keeping line functions decentralized at the local level. This allows them to maintain their position in their communities as a "hometown" community bank but still reap the benefits of operational economies that come from centralization. Some of the specific benefits of decentralizing are discussed below.

Maintain Local Franchise

Supercommunity banks try to foster the look and feel of a community bank at the local level. Service levels are high. Bank employees know their customers well and understand their needs. Employees are empowered to make decisions. At Georgia Federal, tellers can make decisions about account errors and are authorized to make corrections on their own, even if it results in a loss to the bank of up to $50. The high levels of personalized service create real loyalty among the customer base toward the bank and its employees. Research has shown that this customer loyalty translates into a strong local franchise that delivers competitive advantages to the bank. One benefit of the strong franchise that super-community banks can capitalize on is the

> *The high levels of personalized service create real loyalty among the customer base toward the bank and its employees.*

consistently higher net interest margins they command; others, including customer retention and superior asset quality, also accrue.

Loan Quality

In most supercommunity banks, loan underwriting is performed by locally based account officers. They know their borrowers as more than a statistical profile because they establish relationships that are broader and deeper than the customer relationships in larger, centralized banks. As a result, loan underwriting is handled

more effectively in supercommunity banks. Troubled loans are identified earlier, and workouts tend to be resolved more effectively in supercommunity banks than in other centralized institutions. The asset quality statistics of supercommunity banks from December 31, 1992, summarized below, tell the story:

Asset Quality Indicator	Non-SCB Average %	SCB Average %	Top 20 SCBs %
Nonaccrual loans/Total Loans	3.16	1.62	.88
ORE/Total Assets	.99	.55	.32
Provision for loan losses/ Total Loans	1.22	.97	.99
Chargeoffs/Total Loans	1.35	1.00	.91

Management Motivation

After being acquired by a supercommunity bank, local subsidiary management typically remains in place, and is often given considerable autonomy in key business decisions for its bank. The opportunity to continue to function as entrepreneurs and to have a say in how things are done is an attractive component of the merger from the point of view of local management before and after the merger. Management tends to be motivated and successfully retained for a longer time. This motivational aspect of the supercommunity bank structure is sometimes destroyed when the centralized controls constrain management's entrepreneurial spirit. The super-community bank structure implies the dynamic tension between centralized control and local decision making. If properly handled, the freedom to respond to customer needs gives subsidiary managers motivation and the sense of ownership unique to committed management.

Faster Decisions

A centralized back office can result in better service levels to line personnel, which can speed routine operations and reduce bottlenecks in decision making. The other side of faster decisions is the local decision-making power of subsidiary management. Supercommunity banks typically empower local personnel to make loan decisions. Often there is no imposition of a centralized credit committee or other decision-making body to slow the process. This gives supercommunity banks a competitive edge compared to larger or centralized institutions.

Quality Control

Many supercommunity banks control quality at both the holding company level and at the subsidiary level. At the local subsidiary, the line personnel can monitor quality directly. They are closer to the customer and are therefore better able to keep in touch. It is also easier, less costly, and more effective to correct any problems that may develop.

On the loan side, in the decentralized setting of the typical supercommunity bank, each subsidiary has considerable control over sales, marketing, and underwriting decisions. Sometimes this can lead to a problem of too much independence, which might result in compromises in credit quality. One proven way to maximize local effectiveness without penalizing

asset quality is the establishment of a holding company loan review group. Such a group typically audits portfolios, provides guidance on improving lending practices, fosters credit discipline, and "reigns-in the mavericks."

How Do Supercommunity Banks Do It?

How do supercommunity banks go about choosing areas to centralize? Each institution has its own methods, but the one that seems to work best is outlined below:

Target Candidates for Centralization

Take an inventory of functions and look at each one as if you were building it from scratch. Ask critical questions such as:

- Is it functioning correctly?
- How do internal constituencies feel about quality?
- How much does the function cost?
- Is it on target to budget?
- Does it "touch" the customer?

Develop Screening Criteria

Generally speaking, functions that have a *high fixed cost* are targets for centralization and re-engineering. The high fixed cost probably presents an opportunity to reap the benefit of economies of scale.

Functions and activities that are *transparent to the customer* can generally be targeted for centralization. This will allow for greater productivity without compromising the line functions that directly affect the customer.

Figure 12.2 Loan Product Activity Grid

Business Units	Sales	Client Acquisition	Transaction Execution	After Market Management
Audit/Review			Ongoing Security	
Human Resources Management			Training	Incentive Programs
Bank Office			Loan Banking Ongoing Verification	Funding Disbursing Servicing
Marketing	Identify Customer Product Design			
Lending	Contact Customer Pricing	Credit Underwriting Approval Verification		Cross-Sell Collection Retention

Product Life Cycle →

☐ = Targets for Centralization

Control and support functions, too, can often be centralized. Control functions might typically include accounting, human resources, audit, loan review, purchasing, and the like.

In addition to looking at each function as a whole, supercommunity banks sometimes evaluate the activity components of a function and find creative ways to centralize pieces of the operation. An activity grid like the sample Loan Product Activity Grid in Figure 12.2 can be used to decompose key functions and identify targets for centralization. Using the sample grid, it was determined that most of the transaction execution and after-market management functions could be handled effectively in a centralized mode. By decomposing the functions into component parts, it became possible to look at narrower, more feasible opportunities for centralization.

Centralize But Also Re-engineer

Most supercommunity banks undertake substantial efforts at redesigning the way they do work. This means doing things differently in areas that are centralized and in areas that are not. To accomplish this, one of the hallmarks of the strategy is the introduction of re-engineering techniques:

Question old rules. Many supercommunity banks set up cross-functional quality teams to design new ways of doing things. The team leader then champions the idea in his or her subsidiary as a prototype to be rolled out across the others.

Organize around outcomes not tasks. In loan processing operations, for example, supercommunity banks put decision points at the local subsidiary, but they build controls where processing work is performed (in centralized loan operations areas).

Treat geographically dispersed resources as a single resource. As described in the centralization section above, many supercommunity banks centralize where the expertise is and make the expert serve all the subsidiaries. Centralization does not necessarily mean growing a huge holding company.

Ongoing Performance Measurement

Most supercommunity banks establish performance standards that reflect their structures. Specific performance standards must be set for the centralized service or back-office function as well as for the line areas of the subsidiaries. Centralized service facilities should establish contracts with their internal customers that quantify standards for timeliness and accuracy. The service standards are most often established through a benchmarking process that incorporates the service level available in the market. For example, a data processing service facility can contract with its users to provide a specific level of service. Performance is monitored by users whose satisfaction is taken into account in evaluating the performance of centralized service facilities.

Measuring the performance of subsidiaries in a decentralized supercommunity bank presents special challenges. Performance measures for centralized banks or bank holding companies are often linked most strongly to the performance of the company as a whole, using indicators such as return on equity. In supercommunity banks, incentives must be structured in such a way that employees are motivated and encouraged to excel but not to the

detriment of others in the company in other areas or to the detriment of the company as a whole. Subsidiary presidents, for example, are often given performance targets that include not only their own subsidiary's ROA but also the ROE of the holding company.

Another example involves nontraditional investment services (mutual funds, brokerage), which are centralized sometimes at one of the subsidiaries. To get individual employees to refer business to the nonbank subsidiary, supercommunity banks develop compensation systems for referrals. To get subsidiaries to pull together, revenue credits are recorded in a dual fashion that allows each involved subsidiary to receive credit for its part in generating new business. For example, a branch accrues referral points for itself, whether traditional deposits or nontraditional investments are involved. Similarly, the individual referral source accrues points. Compensation is then related to the team performance (the branch) as well as the individual.

Cost Allocation of Centralized Facilities

Centralized service providers charge local subsidiaries for work performed and services rendered. Allocation methodologies used to accomplish vary among institutions (see Appendix 5). The organizational structure of supercommunity banks, as both centralized and decentralized, implies that cost allocation is an issue with a significant role in performance measurement, motivation, and the overall profitability of individual organizational units. In many subsidiaries of supercommunity banks, for example, the local management complains that the charges they receive for centralized services are too high (or that quality of service is too low given the charge). Frequently, they contend that the allocation methodology is inaccurate or unfairly calculated. As a result, the manager may believe that the "unfair" allocation is responsible for lack of profitability.

The allocation methodology must be handled in a way that reflects the multiple constituencies that typically result from the centralized/decentralized structure of supercommunity banks. This means that holding company management must take steps to properly negotiate costs and allocations among the parties to manage the sometimes conflicting motivations of each constituency.

One successful strategy fosters a spirit of cooperation and teamwork through the introduction of a corporate culture communications program. The service culture in the program instills a market mentality that encourages centralized service facilities to cost out their services at rates that would be charged by external markets. Similarly, user constituencies (the line units and subsidiaries) are encouraged to negotiate with the service provider for quality and service performance standards that both parties could live with. The result is a market-driven structure to the allocations and sounder measures of performance overall.

Summary

Supercommunity banks exhibit a wide variety of organizational structures, combining differing levels of centralization and decentralization. Each institution comes to grips in its own way with the need to reconcile individual group, subsidiary, and corporate goals in ways that clearly differ from more purely centralized institutions.

How far to go in centralization versus decentralization often varies among companies based on marketplace, strengths, opportunities, and strategic goals. But these are the three guiding principles for striking your own balance:

- Do not centralize to the detriment of customer service.
- Do not centralize to the detriment of asset quality.
- Centralize areas that are volume-sensitive and that lend themselves to economies of scale.

In short, centralize staff functions; decentralize the line. Finding creative ways to sustain the local franchise provided by a community banking strategy while benefiting from a centralized back office is a core strength that supercommunity banks learn to exploit. It is also the foundation of a story of dynamic tension between the desire to appear small, personal, and service-oriented to the customer and the need to process work in the most efficient and effective fashion. That is why supercommunity banks walk the line between the two structures and successfully operate in centralized and decentralized ways at the same time.

CHAPTER THIRTEEN

Incentive Compensation

Incentive compensation has been under debate in supercommunity banks for years. On the one hand, we all believe in rewarding for performance and in providing people with incentives to do the things we would like them to do. On the other hand, incentive compensation is associated with a broker mentality, a transaction orientation, and acting in the best interest of the incentive program rather than in the best interest of the customer. Given that conflict, many banks are uncertain whether incentive compensation is an appropriate tool for managing relationships in the context of supercommunity banking. Successful supercommunity banks appear to use sales incentives and other incentive compensation methods that increase the cross-sell ratios to new and existing customers, reduce employee turnover, and better communicate corporate goals to employees.

Significant by their absence are rewards for customer retention. Only 4% of 100 banks surveyed by Leeds & Associates reported using incentives for account retention among branch managers. The majority of rewards are issued for cross-selling of products and services. Banks are just beginning to understand the impact of account retention and have not linked it yet to incentive compensation of the retail staff. Similarly, only 13% of the banks rewarded branch managers for customer satisfaction. As mentioned elsewhere in the book, rewarding for customer satisfaction is important because if customers can be satisfied, they can be retained.

Incentive compensation is an important management tool to direct employees toward corporate-wide objectives and reward them for performance. The example below illustrates how incentive compensation was used at all levels of one organization, from senior management to tellers, to consistently pull every employee in the same direction.

Structuring A Relationship-Oriented Incentive Compensation Program

This is how one supercommunity bank's "pay for profitability" sales performance incentive compensation program starts.

- You know you are important—you ARE the bank to our clients.
- You know you are good—you effectively identify prospects, make client calls, profile, probe for needs, know your products, make professional proposals, and ask for the business.
- You prove it—use The Book of Business Incentive Compensation Program to prove how effective you are.

The bank's compensation program begins by explaining that the policy of "pay for performance" has been refined into a policy of "pay for profitability." "And that's great news for you," says the booklet. "You will be rewarded for concentrating your sales efforts on making total client relationships profitable, not for the sheer number of transactions you process or the number of accounts you open. The Book of Business Incentive Compensation Program treats you like the professional you are. It leaves the responsibility of identifying and making choices about how to increase the total profitability of your personal book of business in your hands. You can watch your incentive totals climb along with the profitability of your client relationships.

"The Book of Business Incentive Compensation Program is a very effective tool in helping you achieve your professional goals. It provides you with reports showing the total dollar amount of profit or loss for each of your assigned clients' accounts. You target both the most profitable clients to assure that they are satisfied and to court them for additional business, and the least profitable clients whose banking relationships you analyze to identify any problems and to propose more appropriate services for account types. As you watch the total profitability of your book grow, you reap a percentage of that growth as your reward.

"Not only that, but your branch core deposit totals and profitability figures grow. You share in the branch's profit incentive compensation pool. The bank's quarterly goals are divided into regional goals, regional goals are subdivided into branch goals, and branch goals are reapportioned into individual goals—everyone counts. When you and your fellow branch employees are demonstrating peak performance in achieving your personal goals, you earn your quarterly personal incentive plus a share of the branch's profit incentive. For that reason, you are not left on your own. Teamwork counts! Share your successes and your problems at sales and staff meetings. Get help from your branch sales manager or regional market manager if you need it. Ask for clarification of the program when necessary. And then do your best. When everyone is doing their best, our bank-wide goals can be met. You know you've got what it takes. Use the Book of Business Incentive Compensation Program to prove it."

The reason this program is so effective is because it has many of the key elements of a successful incentive compensation program:

- *Bank-wide objectives impact individual rewards.* The program ensures that corporate-wide performance will affect the individual bonus levels of every participant in the program, including tellers. Everyone has a vested interest in the success of the company as a whole.
- *Branch performance affects individual rewards.* Although corporate-wide performance is important in anchoring every employee to the company and providing a sense of ownership, most employees are anchored to a smaller unit, such as the branch. Giving everyone a stake in the success of each branch is a tool to develop teams within the branch and to avoid unhealthy competition.
- *Individual goals are specified.* Everyone knows what their objectives and what is considered success. Goals are developed individually, one-on-one, between every employee and their supervisor to ensure buy-in of both sides to target performance levels. Incentives are provided only when these performance levels are achieved, and they are increased significantly as performance levels are exceeded.
- *The reward is for relationship management, not for number of transactions.* The program provides an incentive to individuals toward thinking of their customers as individuals with a set of needs. It is the banker's role to meet those needs; therefore, the incentives are not provided for a specific product push, but rather for meeting the overall needs of the customer base and for managing the relationships. This incentive program is especially geared toward customer retention and customer satisfaction as opposed to product line, management, and bank profitability. The underlying assumption is that by enhancing customer relationships, profitability will grow as well.

- *Positioning the banker as a problem solver.* The program is designed proactively to reward bankers for coming up with creative solutions to their customers' financial management issues.
- *Ownership over the customer base.* Individuals are assigned a "book of business," a number of customers for whom they are responsible. This is true for both corporate and individual customers. This allows each banker to have a sense of ownership over their customer base, to get to know them better, and to provide them with individualized service since every banker has a vested interest in the satisfaction of their "book of business" customers.

In summary, the program provides incentives that are linked to corporate-wide goals, branch goals, and individual goals, which are set by the supervisor together with the individual banker. The program is geared to serve relationships and enhance customer retention and to provide the banker with a sense of ownership over the customer base and a relationship orientation in handling the customers.

A Relationship-Oriented Incentive Corporate Program—An Example

The incentive plan is designed to reward all levels of organization for performance and profitability. The bank recognizes the contributions employees make that enable the bank to achieve and exceed its strategic and profit objectives. The incentive compensation program links the employees' incentives directly to the profit performance of the accounts assigned to them as well as to the overall profitability of the branch and the company. The plan is also designed to increase employee communication and understanding of the company objectives, and it provides added measurement methods for the employee valuation process. Three levels of employees are in the incentive programs: senior executives, branch and middle management, and branch operations personnel.

Senior Executives

The objectives for the senior executive compensation plan was twofold:

1. To build equity ownership; and
2. To link shareholder return to management compensation.

In order to accomplish these objectives, each senior officer had three components in their compensation: a base salary, a cash bonus that is granted annually, and long-term stock grants comprised of both non-qualified options and of restricted performance shares. Since the bank's philosophy was to achieve performance—to target

compensation levels through increasing incentives, not by increasing base salary—the philosophy has been that it is conceivable that a top executive may receive no increases in base compensation, depending on performance. The base compensation is important because it serves as the basis for calculating other incentives.

For example, cash bonus that is provided annually is defined as a percentage range measured on the base that grows over time and over performance. Senior management had incentive compensation in the form of annual cash bonuses ranging from 25% to 60% of their base. The annual cash bonus was paid based on the achievement of specific objectives—corporate-wide vision, departmental, and individual. If threshold objectives were not achieved, no incentive was paid. Only 75% percent of the incentive was paid when threshold performance levels were achieved. When the target was met, 100% of the annual cash bonus was to be paid, and outstanding performance was to be rewarded by 150% of the cash bonus. In general, the higher the position, the greater the weight on the corporate performance relative to other objectives. For example, the CEO's performance is determined by 75% corporate objectives and 25% individual objectives.

The incentive compensation to senior management was also accompanied by stock options. The non-qualifying stock options are another annual reward that is determined in a similar way to the cash bonus. The options vest one-third each year for three years, and the grant prize is established each year based on the stock's fair market value. Restricted performance stock (RPS) is available only to the very senior executives in the company and is based on the achievement of three-year corporate objectives. It is a special benefit designed to reward top management when the corporation's strategic performance achieves or exceeds expectations. If the objectives are not met, the grant is zero. These RPS grants are especially valuable in providing senior management a strategic vantage point on the business and mitigating the short-term horizon many senior managers are compelled to take based on their incentive compensation and the stock market yield of corporate performance.

This incentive compensation program is an effective way to reward senior management for performance or, alternatively, to withhold reward if performance does not meet the objectives. However, some companies encounter a situation where corporate performance exceeds expectations year after year, or reaches very high levels consistently each year. At that point, senior management and the board should recognize that increasing performance expectations may not be reasonable. For example, if a company produces 22% return on equity and 10% internal growth annually, management may be hard-pressed to improve performance. The board should recognize this as it sets the objectives and target performance levels for senior management, so that senior management is still rewarded handsomely if performance is sustained, even if it does not improve.

Branch and Middle Management

This segment of the plan is designed to provide incentives for sales organization

participants in a relationship-oriented environment. The plan has two objectives:

- To link compensation to profit performance of existing customers, and
- To link compensation to the overall performance of the branch.

Linking performance to the profitability and retention of customers, as well as to the overall branch profitability, provides the individual banker with incentives to be a team player, yet with enough control over his or her own book of business to make a significant difference in the customer satisfaction levels and in the overall profitability of the account. The participants in the mid-level management program include branch sales managers, customer service managers, and other platform people. Performance is measured based primarily on new business acquisition (loans and low-cost deposits) *and* customer retention. Much like the senior management program, incentives accrue using threshold target and outstanding achievement levels (20%, 40%, and 60%) over a preset base amount.

The allocation of incentive amounts is designed to enhance teamwork. The financial service officer (FSO) or branch service officer received 75% of the earned incentives each quarter, with a balance of 25% at year-end, to enhance employee retention. The branch manager receives an override of 50% of each FSO total if minimum threshold levels are met. The branch incentive portion of the program is allocated among the branch manager, customer service manager, and the initial sales officer in a 30%, 20%, and 50% split. And 50% of the FSO portion is reallocated to the FSOs based on the book of business incentive amount earned. This way, everyone benefits when the branch is doing well.

In order to administer the program, quarterly goals for each branch and each FSO are set by the branch manager and the regional marketing manager. Every individual in the program has specific goals, arrived at during discussion with that individual. In addition, the company put in place policies and procedures for the assignment of new and existing customers to bank officers, assignment of existing accounts to customers, resolution of disputes over customer account ownership, and treatment of unusual or nonrecurring adjustments. These are critical to the success of the program since customer ownership becomes the driving force behind the incentive.

Branch Operations Personnel

Branch operations also have an incentive compensation plan since every person at the bank has a customer, an internal or an external one. The objectives of the branch operations plan are:

- To maintain high levels of customer service, and
- To create awareness of and focus on bank objectives.

Objectives are provided for both customer referrals as well as attainment of operating performance standards that, much like sales goals, are set in a discussion between the banker and the supervisor. Tellers and assistant customer service managers participate in that program, thereby encompassing all levels of bank staff, including those people who touch the customer most—the

---

Every individual in the program has specific goals . . . In addition, the company put in place policies and procedures for the assignment of new and existing customers to bank officers, assignment of existing accounts to customers, resolution of disputes over customer account ownership, and treatment of unusual or nonrecurring adjustments.

---

tellers. Participants in this program receive a sales referral fee for each bank product booked based on the schedule of fees for each type of product. They could conceivably receive up to four times the number of average hours worked per week in dollars, and the assistant customer service managers receive overrides on the teller incentive payments earned depending on the level of operating performance and referrals achieved. In other words, managers get rewarded if they do a good job of managing the people who report to them to achieve their performance objectives and their sales contribution.

There is an ongoing debate, however about whether incentive compensation is effective at non-officer levels. Some are concerned that incentive compensation and bonuses may even hurt teamwork at the lower levels. At one bank, team spirit was built at the lower levels through the "above and beyond" program. In that program, spontaneous cash awards were given to selected individuals who had exceeded expectations, as reported by their peers. This peer support enabled individuals to accrue points toward bonuses.

At Old National, a recently installed program requires every unit manager to meet with each employee monthly to review performance against goals and provide ongoing feedback. Initial results were very positive and included team building, employee motivation, lots of communication, and reciprocal feedback. Although the program includes cash bonuses of 4% to 6% of base compensation, it appears that its success relates to the feedback feature of the bonus.

Most incentive programs that work make an effort to identify those participants who are not motivated toward selling and marketing by rewards and instead use those individuals more for transactional or processing tasks.

Teller Incentives

For many clients, tellers are the bank. From answering inquiries about opening accounts, to account servicing, to referral to other bank services, the teller is usually the client's primary resource in point of contact with the bank. Teller/client relationships are critical to the success of the supercommunity bank. For these reasons, tellers should be encouraged to build, and be rewarded for building, quality customer relationships. A compensation plan for

tellers can be constructed to be relationship oriented. The tellers' efforts in helping the bank achieve its goals will then determine what their level of income will be under the incentive portion of the plan.

Although not all tellers are full time or salaried, it is recommended that even hourly tellers participate in the incentive programs as well as the on-call tellers who are the least integrated into the bank's employee network. Even the on-call tellers should be eligible to participate in the referrals portion of the monthly individual incentive plan. Many banks have additional personnel who perform teller duties. People who spend at least 75% of their time performing teller-type duties should be eligible to earn incentive compensation under the teller incentive program.

An effective incentive compensation program for tellers compensates the teller for referrals as well as the attainment of performance standards (the latter should be open only to salaried and hourly tellers as well as eligible teller-like people, such as branch service officers).

Referrals

If a teller receives incentive dollars each time a client books a bank product, or a service the teller suggested, it pays for the teller to know the bank's product and to talk to the customers about them. Referral incentives should be tightly linked to the goals of the bank and should be clearly communicated to the tellers by their supervisors. Customer service staff, including tellers, should be familiar with the bank's relationship-orientation values, customer relationship targets, and referral incentive fee schedules so that they can direct their attention and efforts to the right place. Some banks provide an additional 20% referral bonus incentive when incentive rewards for referrals exceed a certain amount. It is a good idea to compensate high-referral tellers even beyond the straight referral rate.

Another special incentive override that is an effective tool to motivate tellers to think of the customer relationship in its entirety is to provide an additional referral bonus incentive if the number of referrals in one month is higher than the preceding twelve-month average. The signal these

---

It is a good idea to compensate high-referral tellers even beyond the straight referral rate.

---

incentives sends to the teller is to look at the customer as a relationship rather than a transaction (cashing a check, or making a payment or an inquiry).

Attainment of Performance Standards

As mentioned before, all employees should have clear performance standards that are communicated to them unequivocally by their managers. Teller performance standards revolve around attendance and accuracy of the work. It is recommended that a teller meet all the performance standards before they are eligible

for incentives for performance quality. The following are examples of such standards:

- Not more than one unlocated cash difference between $10 and $25.
- No operating losses.
- No more than three proof errors per month if you work between one and twenty hours per week, or five proof errors per month if you work twenty-one hours or more per week.

As in the referral incentives program, there should be a premium performance bonus for those tellers who do not only attain performance standards but go beyond those standards. The following are examples of standards to be included in the premium portion of the bonus:

- No absences from work.
- No unlocated cash differences over $10.
- No operating losses.
- No more than two proof errors per month if you work between one and twenty hours per week, or four proof errors per month if you work twenty hours or more per week.

It is appropriate to link the amount of money earned in incentives by achieving the performance standards to the average number of hours worked performing teller activities per week during each month. An example is presented in Table 13.1.

Incentive compensation can become a meaningful part of a teller's overall compensation. Under the program utilizing the principles described above, a teller working forty hours per week, making fifteen referrals, and achieving his or her performance standards will get a 15% incentive compensation for the month.

Teller coaches who use the opportunity to generate referral incentives while coaching new tellers in the branch should be compensated for the referral incentives for each two-week training period performed during the month so that their motivation for coaching tellers will not be diminished. Figure 13.1 is an example.

There is a recent ongoing debate whether incentive compensation is effective at non-officer levels. Some are concerned that incentive compensation and bonuses may hurt teamwork at the lower levels. At one bank, team spirit was built at the lower levels through the "above and beyond" program. In that program, spontaneous cash awards were given to selected individuals who had exceeded expecta-tions, as reported by their peers. This peer support enabled individuals to accrue points toward bonuses. At Old National, a recently installed program expects every unit manager to meet with each employee monthly to review performance against goals and to provide ongoing feedback. Initial results were very positive and included team building, employee motivation, lots of communication, and reciprocal feedback. Although the structuring included cash bonuses of 4% to 6% of base compensation, it appears that its success relates more to the feedback feature of the program.

Most incentive programs that work make an effort to identify those participants that are not motivated by rewards toward selling and marketing, and then use those individuals more for transactional or processing tasks.

TABLE 13.1 Teller Performance Standards and Incentives

Performance Standard			Performance Standard		
Avg Hours Worked*	Regular	Premium	Avg Hours Worked*	Regular	Premium
40	$80	$160	24	$48	$96
39	78	156	23	46	92
38	76	152	22	44	88
37	74	148	21	42	84
36	72	144	20	40	80
35	70	140	19	38	76
34	68	136	18	36	72
33	66	132	17	34	68
32	64	128	16	32	64
31	62	124	15	30	60
30	60	120	14	28	56
29	58	116	13	26	52
28	56	112	12	24	48
27	54	108	11	22	44
26	52	104	10 or less	20	40
25	50	100			

*Average hours actually worked per week.

FIGURE 13.1 TELLER COACHES COMPENSATORY REFERRAL INCENTIVE

A. Calculate the average monthly referral incentive earned by the coach for the most recent three months in which the did no training.

For example: Coach did not coach during the following months and earned these referral incentives:

August, 1992,	$100.00
September, 1992,	$50.00
November, 1992,	$75.00 $225.00 divided by 3 = $75.00
	monthly average referral incentive

Note: Using this example, assume the branch coach trains in October, does not train in November, and trains another teller in December. The compensatory referral incentive for December would be calculated on the average monthly referral for August, September, and November - the last three months in which no training occurred.

B. Divide the average monthly referral amount by two (weeks) to determine compensatory incentive for each coaching period and multiply by the number of coaching periods completed during the month.

For example: $75.00 divided by 2 = $37.50 times 1 coaching period in October = $37.50 for the two weeks compensatory referral incentive.

C. Add the compensatory referral incentive amount to any other referral incentive earned that month.

Example: October compensation for the following individual:

Coach is a Teller, Level III - working 40 hours.
Achieves regular performance standards.
Trained one new teller in October.
Had an average monthly referral of $75.00.
Makes five $2 referrals.

1) Base Salary, $1,415.00
2) Individual Incentive
Two Week's Compensatory Referral Incentive ($75.00 divided by 2 x 1) = $37.50
Regular Performance Incentive   80.00
Referrals (5 X $2 each)   10.00 $127.50

3) Total Compensation for October $1,542.50

Represents 9.0% incentive for the month.

CHAPTER FOURTEEN

Supercommunity Banks
Speak About SCB Banking*

In 1991 and 1992 BDO Seidman and American Banker conducted the first and second annual surveys of super-community banks. The results were used to confirm and expand the definition of this strategic position and its critical success factors. The strategies and tactics presented in this book were confirmed and enhanced by the surveys, as presented below.

Background—1991 Survey

In August 1991 a survey was sent to 450 supercommunity banks nationwide, to the chief executive officer of each bank holding company. Over 26% of the survey recipients responded to it. The responses, in the form of fill-out questionnaires, were received from 125 holding companies ranging in size from $33 billion down to $170 million. A detailed statistical profile of institutions participating in the survey as

well as a breakdown by size appears as questions 18-20 of this report.

Survey Results

Executive Summary

The supercommunity bank outperforms the industry. Although SCBs did not escape asset quality problems their profitability is still impressive. Quality service levels are perceived to be the greatest competitive advantage of the SCB. Accordingly, back-office and staff functions are the most likely to be consolidated while the loan decision itself and pricing matters are most frequently mentioned as decentralized activities. A strong community focus is a key to much of the SCB approach. Size is important too, however, with some support for the notion that middle to larger-sized institutions offer the greatest potential.

---

* This chapter is based on the survey conducted by American Banks and BDO Seidman in August, 1991. Reprinted with permission

1. How do you define your strategic niche?

Market	Percent including this as niche*
Community banking	31
Small business & middle market	30
Retail focus	22
Quality service	14
Relationship banking	10
Geographic focus	7

*Respondents may have indicated more than one; does not sum to 100.

Most respondents viewed their primary strategy as community banking with a focus on the retail market and smaller commercial customers. It is significant that relationship banking and quality service were also mentioned as focal points, while no one considered wholesale banking their primary focus.

2. Who are your primary competitors?

Competitor	Percent answering "yes" by asset size ($ billions)				
	Overall	>10	5-10	1-5	<1
Other local banks	61	56	43	59	66
Local community banks	46	67	14	48	46
Super-regional banks	66	100	100	68	56
Money-center banks	8	0	0	11	8

The majority of institutions view their chief competition as coming from the super-regional banks. The larger the institution, the more likely it is to hold that view. This is where the supercommunity banking philosophy provides the competitive advantage to billion-plus companies, who need to outlocal the nationals and outnational the locals.

	Percent answering "yes" by asset size ($ billions)				
	Overall	>10	5-10	1-5	<1
3. How many subsidiaries are in your holding company? (actual average number of subsidiaries)	6	15	3	7	3
4. Do you keep separate boards of directors in each of your subsidiaries?	85	88	10	91	79
5. Do you keep separate presidents in each of your subsidiaries?	90	100	100	93	85
6. Do you maintain separate charters for the subsidiaries?	88	100	85	96	81

Generally, the larger institutions have more subsidiaries. The majority of institutions over $1 billion maintain separate boards, presidents, and charters at the subsidiary level. Those are essential to maintaining the community identity of the company and its individual subsidiaries, and play an import role in the bank's linkage to the community and business development.

7. What are the three largest revenue generators in your banks today?

Product/Service	Percent placing this in top three*
Loans	46
Consumer/Installment	40
Commercial loans	33
Real estate/mortgage	27
Investments	17
Credit cards	7
Mortgage servicing	6
Correspondent banking	4
Securities/brokerage	4
Home equity loans	3
Capital markets	1
Annuities	1

*Percentages not intended to sum to 100.

Supercommunity banking thrives on the core of the banking business. Its core product line generates superior profits due to superior execution. As a result, product expansion is designed to meet emerging customer needs or to create a source of income to augment the net interest margin.

8. What will the three largest revenue generators in your banks be three years from now?

Product/Service	Percent placing this in top three*
Same as today	59
Loans	11
Insurance	10
Trust	7
Investments	4
Mortgage servicing	4
Mortgage origination	3
Cash management	3
Brokerage	1
Credit cards	1
Annuities	1
Other	4

*Percentages not intended to sum to 100.

The majority of respondents indicated that their top three revenue generators in three years will be the same as the top three today. Additionally, fee-based products such as insurance, trust, and cash management represent new products that will play a bigger role in the future.

9. How many people could you eliminate if you were not committed to community banking?

Size in billions ($)	Number eliminated
Overall	146
>10	925
5–10	203
1–5	161
<1	

The commitment to the supercommunity bank strategy is costly. Significant additional savings can be realized from full consolidation of the banks. However, the service levels, which are so important, will greatly suffer from such consolidation. Further, additional costs are more than compensated for by the revenues generated by the people who represent cost-cutting opportunities.

10. What do you view as the strongest competitive advantages of your strategic position?

Advantage	Percent listing item
Personalized quality service	44
Experienced staff	31
Location/convenience	21
Product diversification	19
Community involvement	16
Local autonomy	14
Independent/local	11
Prompt decisions	11
Reputation	11
Community knowledge	10
Performance	10
Sales culture	9
Asset quality	7
Market share	7
Capital	6
Flexibility	6
Efficiency	6
Responsiveness	4
Employee retention	4
Low-cost consciousness	4
Corporate culture	3
Strong local franchise	1

Service is one of the "nonnegotiables" of the supercommunity bank, and is also considered the single greatest competitive advantage of the SCB by both the respondents and the industry.

11. What are the greatest benefits of not consolidating and maintaining the separate nature of your holding company's subsidiaries?

Benefit	Percent listing items
Local orientation/autonomy	32
Community	27
Serving individual markets differently	9
Entrepreneurial spirit	9
Quick decisions	6
Quality loan portfolio	4
Referrals/board investment	4
Responsiveness	1

Most respondents recognized a local community focus as the greatest benefit of not consolidating. That focus enhances business development and community relations. In addition, it translates into superior asset quality, which is central to the performance of SCBs.

12. What areas of your institution are centralized?

	Percent answering "yes" by asset size ($ billions)				
Area	Overall	>10	5–10	1–5	<1
Loan operations	44	78	71	34	42
Bookkeeping	66	78	100	65	61
A/L management	74	78	71	72	75
Investments	88	100	100	93	81
Marketing	62	67	71	59	62
Purchasing	74	67	100	78	61
Data processing	93	100	100	96	88

Larger entities appear to be more likely to centralize key operations areas. In general, staff and back-office areas are the likely consolidation candidates. Line functions remain decentralized. Data processing is centralized in most companies (39%), followed by investments (88%) and asset liability (74%). All three functions offer significant leverage opportunities without penalizing service levels.

13. What areas must not be consolidated?

Area	Percent listing items
Loan underwriting	54
Pricing	17
Customer service	13
Marketing	11
Human resources	9
Branch operations	9
Board	1
Bookkeeping	1
Sales	1

The loan decision must remain close to the customer. The community knowledge is key to quality assets and is considered as one of the major advantages of nonconsolidation.

14. What are the most important areas for cost control in your institution?

Area	Percent listing area
Salaries	81
Interest	69
Loan losses	64
Overhead	40
Operations	23
Benefits	16
Headcount	4

15. What are the areas of your operations which you are most likely to automate?

Area	Percent listing area
Customer Information File (CIF)	100
Platform	77
Teller	46
Imaging	31
ATMs	29
Client sourcing	26
Centralized processing	13
Optical disk storage	4
Voice mail	3
Networking	3

The most commonly mentioned areas are customer focused rather than back-office focused. Banks with sophisticated customer information file capabilities typically move in the direction of relationship banking. Platform and teller automation directly affects the bank's ability to provide effective customer service and cross-sell. As acquiring a new customer is more costly than cross-selling an existing one, CIF and platform automation are important facilitators to enhance cross-selling.

16. What are the three performance measurements monitored at the holding company level?

Most institutions at the holding company level monitor return on equity most frequently, followed by return on assets and earnings per share.

17. What are the top three performance measurements monitored at the individual subsidiary level?

The majority of respondents indicated that return on assets was the most frequently monitored indicator for individual banks, followed by net interest margin and return on equity.

18. Average asset size and population

Asset size in $ billions	Average size in $ billions	Number of Institutions
>10	18	9
5–10	6	7
1–5	2	46
<1	.5	61
Overall	3	125

19 Average deposits

Asset size billions in $ billions	Average deposits in $ billions
>10	13.7
5–10	5.3
1–5	1.9
<1	0.4
Overall	2.2

20. Key Ratios

	Percent				
	Overall	**>10**	**5–10**	**1–5**	**<-1**
CDs/deposits	48	66	54	47	45
Nonperforming loans	2.7	2.4	2.0	1.7	2.6
Return on assets (1989)	.95	1.05	0.71	1.03	.90
Return on assets (1990)	.88	.69	.57	.91	.92
Return on equity (1989)	12.32	15.26	9.83	13.49	11.22
Return on equity (1990)	11.64	9.90	8.20	11.88	12.11
Assets per employee (millions)	1.92	1.77	1.78	2.15	1.78
Non-interest income/total income	13.91	28.7	16,63	13.50	11.38
Non-interest expense/assets	4.20	3.55	3.30	5.82	3.12
Salary/non-interest expense	47.57	51.08	49.80	49.96	44.72

The key ratio analysis suggests that the larger institutions are stronger on an overall basis. The $1-5 billion size category bears closer examination. This category is the only category in 1990 to have both higher than average ROE and higher than average ROA. It has a relatively low ratio of CD-type deposits and its proportion of nonperforming assets is categorically the lowest of the respondents. This size category has low non-interest income compared to the largest size category, and it has relatively high salary expense compared to the smallest group. This size category represents less than half of the institutions under $5 billion but controls 80% of the assets. Taken together this profile suggests that the $1-5 billion size group may have greater growth opportunity and greater strength in the near term compared to the smaller and largest supercommunity banks.

Background—The 1992 Survey

In September 1992, BDO Seidman and *American Banker* conducted a survey of 330 supercommunity banks nationwide. The survey was sent to the chief executive officer of each bank holding company. Over 33% of the survey recipients responded to it. The responses, in the form of filled-out questionnaires, were received from 116 holding companies ranging in size from $50 billion to $300 million. A detailed statistical profile of institutions participating in the survey, as well as a breakdown by size, appears in the last section of the report.

Executive Summary

One of the driving forces in the banking industry's move toward supercommunity banking has been the pursuit of operating efficiencies through centralization, but questions still persist about whether these efficiencies are actually being realized. An overwhelming percentage of the respondents indicated efficiencies have been realized at their institution as areas of service have improved with centralization. Only one respondent felt his institution had not experienced improved service levels through centralization.

An examination of the survey data shows there is a consensus among the respondents regarding the key current income-producing services, but considerably less agreement with respect to future income-producing services. Over 75% of the respondents consider transaction accounts, trust services, and loans to be key current income-producing services at their institutions. However, asked which fee income producing services offer the most potential in the next five years, their responses differed considerably. While transaction accounts, trust services, and loans were still listed as the top three services, trust was the only one identified by over 75% of the respondents. There was greater diversity among the respondents with nontraditional bank products such as annuities, brokerage, and insurance services receiving increased emphasis as future sources of income. There is a relationship between this expected diversity in future sources of income and the respondents' identification of the need for product profitability information as the highest among lacking and most needed information at their institution.

The respondents' comments were also in close agreement with respect to the impact of FDICIA on their institution. Almost all respondents indicated that this regulation has had a negative impact on their institution, such as increased expenses or the need to hire additional staff to cope with the act. Consistent with their attitude toward FDICIA, over 65% of the respondents indicated that a reduction in the regulatory burden is the top legislative priority in the next year or two, followed by an expansion in banking powers and interstate banking.

	Percent answering "yes" by asset size ($ billions)				
	Overall	**>10**	**5–10**	**1–5**	**<1**
1. How many subsidiaries are in your holding company?	7.5	20.3	9.8	8.7	4.3
2. Do you keep separate boards of directors in each of your subsidiaries?	95.5%	80.0%	100.0%	100.0%	94.9%
3. Do members of the holding company board sit on subsidiary boards?	84.3%	87.5%	44.4%	75.8%	94.8%
4. How many years do holding company board members serve?	2.07	3.00	3.00	2.06	1.74

Most respondents indicated holding company board members serve on separately maintained subsidiary boards. Generally, board members of institutions with assets greater than $5 billion serve longer terms than board members of institutions smaller than $5 billion.

5. How are holding company board members removed, if needed?

	Number	**Percent of total**
Not reelected	22	27.8%
Mandatory retirement	18	22.8%
Board committee vote	16	20.3%
Resignation requested	11	13.9%
Shareholder vote	7	8.9%
Fraud/delinquent loans	5	6.3%
Total respondents	79	

Quality board membership is even more important to supercommunity banks than to many companies, since their board constitutes a key link into the community and a powerful business development tool. As a result, having the right people on the board matters.

The majority of respondents indicated members of the board are removed either by not being reelected or through a mandatory retirement age. It appears that establishing policies regarding expected standards of performance and removal procedures for board members may be an area institutions need to address, especially if managing board membership is a concern.

6. How are board members compensated?

	Percent answering "yes" by asset size ($ billions)				
	Overall	>10	5–10	1–5	<1
Stock, options	6.9%	0.0%	22.2%	10.3%	3.6%
Per meeting fee	92.4%	100.0%	100.0%	93.5%	89.5%
Average value of per meeting fee	$368	$500	$700	$410	$314
Annual fee	52.5%	71.4%	88.9%	50.0%	45.3%
Average value of annual fee	$4,678	$0	$7,833	$4,962	$4,052

The majority of institutions larger than $1 billion compensate board members on a per meeting basis. Also, most offer an annual fee in addition to the per meeting fee. Conversely, few institutions use stocks or options to compensate board members. This is consistent with the impartial perspective board members are expected to maintain.

7. What is the role of the subsidiary board? (Rank in order of importance with "1" being the most important.)

	Asset size ($ billions)				
	Overall	>10	5–10	1–5	<1
Maintain good community relations	2.01	1.83	2.56	1.94	1.98
Bring in new business	2.38	2.00	2.67	2.33	2.40
Make policy and operations decisions	2.47	3.20	2.57	2.52	2.36
Make strategic decisions	3.13	4.00	2.43	3.08	3.17
Advisory only	4.14	3.20	4.60	4.25	4.25

The primary role of subsidiary boards involves maintaining good community relations and bringing in new business to the bank. This is consistent with the supercommunity banking concept of maintaining strong community relations at the subsidiary bank level. Advising the holding company on policies and business decision making was the least important role for the subsidiary boards according to the respondents.

8. How does your organization measure service quality? (Rank in order of importance with "1" being the most important.)

	Asset size ($ billions)				
	Overall	>10	5–10	1–5	<1
Customer surveys	1.52	1.67	1.45	1.66	1.45
Employee feedback	2.18	2.67	2.63	2.19	2.04
Error and rework tracking	2.86	2.75	2.70	2.86	2.91
Customer advisory groups	3.19	3.14	3.25	3.15	3.20
Other	3.33	1.00	0.00	4.00	3.75

Generally, institutions measure service quality through customer surveys and employee feedback. Quantitative error tracking and customer advisory groups were least important. Respondents did recognize the importance of quality as perceived by the customers to their success.

9. Is quality control handled at the subsidiary or holding company level?

	Percent answering "yes" by asset size ($ billions)				
	Overall	>10	5–10	1–5	<1
Holding company level	4.39%	0.00%	9.09%	9.38%	1.64%
Subsidiary company level	33.33%	10.00%	27.27%	53.13%	27.87%
Both	62.28%	90.00%	63.64%	37.50%	70.49%

Over 95% of institutions indicated that quality control is handled at the subsidiary company level or both the subsidiary and holding company level. Apparently, institutions are unwilling to risk a potential deterioration in quality control that could occur through centralization. When a supercommunity bank is evaluating possible areas to achieve cost savings, quality is considered an area that cannot be compromised. At the same time, consistency, standardization, and re-engineering can all be accomplished through centralized vehicles, thereby enhancing quality overall.

10. What areas of service have improved as a result of centralization?

	Number	Percent placing this in top three*
Data processing	33	28.4%
Operations	30	25.9%
Product diversification	24	20.7%
Accounting/AP department	19	16.4%
Lending	18	15.5%
Human resources/services	13	11.2%
Audit/loan review	12	10.3%
Marketing	11	9.5%
Investment management	11	9.5%
Compliance	10	8.6%
Retail branches	8	6.9%
Proof and transit	7	6.0%
A/L management	7	6.0%
None	1	0.9%

*Percentages not intended to sum to 100.

Data processing, operations, and product diversification are the areas respondents most frequently cited as having improved as a result of centralization. It appears that institutions are achieving the efficiencies expected through centralization. In addition, it also appears that supercommunity banks are providing a broader product line to their subsidiary banks through diversification programs at the holding company level, consistent with the strategic paradigm.

11. What areas of service have deteriorated as a result of centralization?

	Number	Percent placing this in top three*
Customer service	15	12.9%
None	14	12.1%
Response time	7	6.0%
Communication	5	4.3%
Operations	4	3.4%
Mortgage originations	3	2.6%
Product innovation	2	1.7%
Marketing	2	1.7%
Audit	1	0.9%

*Percentages not intended to sum to 100.

   Respondents indicated that if an area of service deteriorated as a result of centralization, generally it was related to customer service or response time. However, the small
percentage of respondents identifying these services (19%) is an indication that the supercommunity banking philosophy of decentralizing customer service responsibilities has
offset the potential degradation to customer service that could occur through centralizing
services at the holding company level.

12. How does your organization define quality service?

	Percent answering "yes" by asset size ($ billions)				
	Overall	>10	5–10	1–5	<1
Meeting customer needs when and where they want it	73.63%	75.00%	88.89%	67.86%	73.91%
Timely, accurate transaction processing	14.29%	12.50%	0.00%	14.29%	17.39%
Other	12.09%	12.50%	11.11%	17.86	8.70%

Generally, respondents defined quality service as meeting customer needs when and
where they want it.

13. At what profit center levels is your institution tracking profitability?

	Percent answering "yes" by asset size ($ billions)				
	Overall	>10	5–10	1–5	<1
Bank	95.7%	80.0%	100.0%	97.0%	96.8%
Department	65.5%	60.0%	81.8%	75.8%	58.1%
Branch	64.7%	60.0%	81.8%	75.8%	58.1%
Relationship	37.9%	50.0%	45.5%	30.3%	38.7%
Product	37.9%	80.0%	81.8%	24.2%	30.6%
Other	9.5%	40.0%	18.2%	6.1%	4.8%
Household	6.0%	0.0%	18.2%	3.0%	6.5%

Most institutions track profitability by bank, department, and branch. The majority of institutions larger than $5 billion track profitability by product.

14. What type of profitability information is lacking and most needed at your institution?

	Percent answering "yes" by asset size ($ billions)				
	Overall	>10	5–10	1–5	<1
Product	59.5%	30.0%	18.2%	75.8%	62.9%
Relationship	54.3%	70.0%	63.6%	75.8%	62.9%
Household	32.8%	30.0%	27.3%	39.4%	30.6%
Branch	16.4%	10.0%	9.1%	15.2%	19.4%
Department	13.8%	0.0%	9.1%	18.2%	14.5%
Other	5.2%	10.0%	18.2%	6.1%	1.6%
Bank	2.6%	10.0%	0.0%	6.1%	0.0%

Institutions with assets less than $5 billion indicated profitability reporting by product type is the information most needed at their institution. The move toward product profitability information can most probably be attributed to the expanding and diversified product line supercommunity banks are offering or plan to offer in the future.

15. Does your institution's profitability analysis fully allocate holding company costs to its subsidiaries?

	Percent answering "yes" by asset size ($ billions)				
	Overall	>10	5–10	1–5	<1
Allocate costs	53.4%	80.0%	54.5%	54.5%	48.4%

Respondents were fairly evenly divided in their response to whether they fully allocate holding company costs to subsidiaries. This may indicate that either a consensus regarding the benefits of allocating costs to subsidiaries has not developed, or a large number of institutions have not yet developed the capabilities to allocate costs. There is some evidence, however, that larger institutions are more focused on or capable of allocating costs.

16. What are the most important success measures you use for the holding company? (Rank in order of importance with "1" being the most important.)

	Asset size ($ billions)				
	Overall	**>10**	**5–10**	**1–5**	**<1**
Return on equity	1.64	1.56	1.27	1.56	1.74
Return on assets	1.97	2.22	1.82	2.20	1.86
Net interest margin	3.23	3.63	3.44	3.29	3.10
Capital ratios	3.25	2.88	3.00	3.33	3.33
Other	3.29	4.17	3.00	2.78	3.29

The majority of respondents identified return on equity as the most important measure of success for the holding company. Return on assets was rated the second most important measure. This is reasonable given investor expectations regarding the return on their investment.

17. What are the most important success measures you use for the subsidiary banks? (Rank in order of importance with "1" being the most important.)

	Asset size ($ billions)				
	Overall	**>10**	**5–10**	**1–5**	**<1**
Return on assets	1.71	1.89	1.70	1.93	1.58
Return on equity	2.22	2.38	1.75	2.35	2.19
Net interest margin	2.73	3.00	2.22	2.76	2.78
Other	3.00	4.17	3.00	2.10	3.13
Capital ratios	3.32	2.88	3.57	3.33	3.34

For the subsidiary banks, return on assets was identified as the most important measure of success. Return on equity was rated the second most important measure; however, its overall importance is significantly lower for the subsidiary banks than for the holding company. Consistent with responses for the holding company (question 16 above), net interest margin was rated the third most important measure, but it is given considerably more weight in the case of subsidiary bank success measures.

	Percent answering "yes" by asset size ($ billions)				
	Overall	>10	5–10	1–5	<1
18. Did your institution raise capital in the past year?	32.76%	80.00%	45.45%	27.27%	25.81%
19. Does your institution regularly declare dividends?	87.93%	100.00%	100.00%	87.88%	83.87%
20. Approximately what percent of your common stock is institutionally owned?	16.62%	4978%	30.82%	13.27%	9.58%

The majority of respondents regularly declare dividends. Generally, as institutions increase in asset size, there is a greater likelihood of having raised capital in the past year and a larger percentage of their stock being institutionally owned. This is to be expected given the easier access and economies of scale larger institutions possess in dealing with capital markets. Also, it is not unreasonable that institutional investors would have greater awareness and confidence to invest in larger supercommunity banks.

21. If your institution raised capital in the past, how?

	Number	Percent of total
Common stock	23	63.9%
Retained earnings	6	16.7%
Private placement	4	11.1%
Owner infusion	1	2.8%
Commercial paper	1	2.8%
Merger	1	2.8%
Total respondents	36	

The institutions responding indicated that common stock is the most likely method to be used when raising capital.

22. If your institution regularly declares dividends, what type?

	Number	Percent of total
Cash	77	76.2%
Cash and stock	20	19.8%
Stock	4	4.0%
Total respondents	101	

Most institutions issue cash dividends as opposed to stock.

23. How important is it for your institution to monitor P/E ratios?

	Percent answering "yes" by asset size ($ billions)				
	Overall	**>10**	**5–10**	**1–5**	**<1**
Very important	40.87%	80.00%	45.45%	36.36%	36.07%
Important	39.13%	10.00%	36.36%	45.45%	40.98%
Not important	2.00%	10.00%	18.18%	18.18%	22.95%

24. How important is it for your institution to monitor market vs. book price?

	Percent answering "yes" by asset size ($ billions)				
	Overall	**>10**	**5–10**	**1–5**	**<1**
Very important	40.00%	70.00%	45.45%	36.36%	36.07%
Important	42.61%	20.00%	36.36%	51.52%	42.62%
Not important	17.39%	10.00%	18.18%	12.12%	21.31%

The majority of institutions consider monitoring price to earnings ratios and market vs. book price to be either important or very important. However, institutions with assets greater than $5 billion placed significantly greater emphasis on these ratios.

25. What special programs does your institution engage in to increase its stock price?

	Number	Percent of total
None	26	26.8%
Meet with analysts	19	19.6%
Investor relations	18	18.6%
Earnings performance	12	12.4%
Dividend reinvestment	8	8.2%
401K stock option plan	8	8.2%
Consultants/investment bankers	6	6.2%
Total respondents	97	

The respondents indicated that, if their institutions engaged in a special program to enhance their stock price, either they would meet with analysts or maintain an investor relations department or program. However, a significant number of respondents indicated their institution did not engage in any special programs. It may be helpful for these institutions to consider developing a program to enhance their stock value.

26. What are the key income producing services at your institution in 1992?

	Percent answering "yes" by asset size ($ billions)				
	Overall	**>10**	**5–10**	**1–5**	**<1**
Transaction accounts	81.03%	70.00%	100.00%	81.82%	79.03%
Trust services	78.45%	100.00%	100.00%	87.88%	66.13%
Loans	77.59%	60.00%	72.73%	69.70%	85.48%
Brokerage	14.66%	20.00%	18.18%	12.12%	14.52%
Other	12.17	20.00%	18.18%	21.21%	4.92%
Insurance	12.07%	0.00%	18.18%	9.09%	14.52
ATM	12.07%	30.00%	9.09%	6.06%	12.90%
Annuities	8.62%	0.00%	9.09%	9.09%	9.68%

The majority of respondents indicated that transaction accounts, trust services, and loans are the key income producing services for their institutions. However, institutions with assets greater than $5 billion placed significantly greater emphasis on trust services. Institutions with assets less than $5 billion placed significantly greater emphasis on loans as an income producing source. Economies of scale and critical mass are brought to bear in trust services much more than in lending activities.

27. What are the three fee income producing services that will offer the most potential to your organization during the next five years?

	Percent answering "yes" by asset size ($ billions)				
	Overall	**>10**	**5–10**	**1–5**	**<1**
Trust	80.17%	80.00%	90.91%	90.91%	72.58%
Loans	53.45%	20.00%	45.45%	42.42%	66.13%
Transaction accounts	46.55%	30.00%	27.27%	54.55%	48.39%
Annuities	38.79%	30.00%	45.45%	42.42%	37.10%
Brokerage	28.45%	30.00%	27.27%	42.42%	20.97%
Insurance	24.14%	10.00%	27.27%	21.21%	27.42%
Other	12.93%^	60.00%	18.18%	9.09%	6.45%
ATM	10.34%	10.00%	9.09%	6.06%	12.90%

Respondents identified trust as the key income producing service in the future. However, institutions larger than $5 billion placed slightly less emphasis on it as a future versus current source of revenue. On the other hand, institutions smaller than $5 billion placed greater emphasis on it as a future versus current source of revenue. Generally, most institutions placed greater emphasis on brokerage services and annuities as future revenue sources. Institutions smaller than $5 billion emphasized loans and transaction accounts.

28. Do the individual subsidiaries offer different fee income producing services one from another?

	Percent answering "yes" by asset size ($ billions)				
	Overall	>10	5–10	1–5	<1
Do subsidiaries offer different fee income services?	56.03%	70.00%	18.18%	54.55%	61.29%

Generally, subsidiary banks offer different fee income services. Subsidiary banks of institutions larger than $10 billion are most likely to offer different fee income services. This is indicative of the decentralized philosophy of supercommunity banking, and the flexibility given to most subsidiary management teams. The holding company offers a standardized shelf of products, and each subsidiary picks those that best meet the need of its customers.

29. How does your institution typically develop new fee based service capabilities?

	Percent answering "yes" by asset size ($ billions)				
	Overall	>10	5–10	1–5	<1
Build own capabilities/systems	75.00%	80.00%	77.78%	83.87%	68.97%
Use outside vendor	25.00%	20.00%	22.22%	16.13%	31.03%

Typically, institutions develop new fee based service capabilities in-house. This may indicate that either the perceived industry trend toward outsourcing is not as pervasive as originally thought, or supercommunity banks prefer to maintain service capabilities in-house, possible to ensure high-quality customer service levels.

30. For the holding company, what level of employees receive incentive for good performance?

	Percent answering "yes" by asset size ($ billions)				
	Overall	>10	5–10	1–5	<1
President	87.07%	90.00%	100.00%	90.91%	82.26%
Senior executives	88.79%	100.00%	100.00%	93.94%	82.26%
Middle managers	45.69%	70.00%	45.45%	36.36%	46.77%

On what indicators are the incentives based?

Holding company performance	76.72%	90.00%	100.00%	81.82%	67.74%
Subsidiary performance	51.72	40.00%	54.55%	45.45%	56.45%
Other	21.55%	50.00%	18.18%	30.30%	12.90%

The majority of respondents indicated that the president and senior executives of the holding company receive incentives for good performance. Typically, these incentives are based on a combination of the holding company and subsidiary bank's performance. However, institutions larger than $5 billion placed greater emphasis on the holding company's performance.

31. For the subsidiaries, what level of employees receives incentive for good performance?

	Percent answering "yes" by asset size ($ billions)				
	Overall	**>10**	**5–10**	**1–5**	**<1**
President	88.79%	100.00%	90.91%	87.88%	87.10%
Senior executive	81.90%	80.00%	90.91%	75.76%	83.87%
Middle managers	43.97%	30.00%	36.36%	36.36%	51.61%
On what indicators are the incentives based?					
Holding company performance	53.45%	90.00%	81.82%	57.58%	40.32%
Subsidiary performance	80.17%	60.00%	72.73%	78.79%	85.48%
Other	16.38%	30.00%	36.36%	18.18%	9.68%

The majority of respondents indicated that the president and senior executives of the subsidiary banks also receive incentives for good performance. These incentives are also usually based on a combination of the holding company's and subsidiary bank's performance. However, institutions smaller than $5 billion placed greater emphasis on the subsidiary bank's performance.

32. Are incentives provided to non-officer staff?

	Percent answering "yes" by asset size ($ billions)				
	Overall	**>10**	**5–10**	**1–5**	**<1**
Incentives to non-officer staff	66.38%	70.00%	81.82%	69.70%	61.29%

Most respondents indicated that non-officer staff are provided with incentives. However, non-officer staff in institutions larger than $5 billion are more likely to receive incentives.

33. What has been the impact of FDICIA on your institution?

	Number	**Percent of total**
Increase in expenses	49	47.6%
Additional work/staff	27	26.2%
Excessively burdensome	11	10.7%
No impact (yet)	8	7.8%
Divestiture of real estate activity	3	2.9%
Difficulty with interpretation	3	2.9%
Significant but not devastating	2	1.9%
Total respondents	103	

Almost all respondents indicated that FDICIA has had a negative impact on their institution. The most frequently cited responses were an increase in expenses and the need to hire additional staff to cope with the act. Apparently, the regulation has created some difficulties within the industry. Congress should consider reevaluating the original objective versus the consequences of the act.

34. Have you contacted your representative in Washington on legislative matters related to FDICIA during the last year?

	Percent answering "yes" by asset size ($ billions)				
	Overall	>10	5–10	1–5	<1
Contacted representative	75.86%	100.00%	81.82%	84.85%	66.13%

The majority of respondents indicated they had contacted their Washington representative with regard to FDICIA. It is a positive sign for the industry that most institutions have made an effort to communicate to Washington their opinion of the regulation. Generally, the larger an institution the more likely it was to have contacted a Washington representative. It is possible that these larger institutions have more contact with their representative because their larger size offers them greater access. It is important that these institutions recognize and use their ability to act as industry advocates in Washington.

35. What are the top three legislative priorities for the next year or two?

	Number	Percent placing this in top three
Reduce regulatory burden	78	67.2%
Expanded powers/products	38	32.8%
Interstate banking	35	30.2%
Repeal of FDICIA	16	13.8%
FDIC fees	16	13.8%
Regulation of nonbanks	11	9.5%
Tax reform	8	6.9%
Consolidate regulatory agencies	8	6.9%
Mark to market accounting	3	2.6%
Uniform limited liability	2	

*Percentages not intended to sum to 100.

The majority of respondents cited a reduction in the regulatory burden as the top legislative priority in the next year or two. An expansion in the products banks can offer and interstate banking were also listed as important legislative matters to be dealt with in the future.

36. Total asset size and population

Asset size ($ billions)	Average size in billions	Number of institutions
>10	24,588,958	10
5–10	7,853,945	11
1–5	2,297,170	33
<1	3,908,556	116

37. Total deposits

Asset size ($ billions)	Total deposits in billions
>10	19,452,276
5–10	6,278,099
1–5	1,931,127
<1	499,755
Overall	3,129,611

38. Key Ratios

	Percent answering "yes" by asset size ($ billions)				
	Overall	>10	5–10	1–5	<1
Non-CD deposits as a percent of total loans	49.3%	72.60%	51.88%	47.85%	46.70%
Nonperforming loans as a percent of total loans	1.78%	1.99%	1.68%	1.90%	1.69%
Return on assets–1990	0.88%	0.79%	0.88%	0.90%	0.89%
Return on assets–1991	0.95%	1.01%	0.95%	0.91%	0.96%
Return on equity–1990	11.84%	12.09%	11.85%	11.89%	11.77%
Return on equity–1991	12.44%	14.39%	12.49%	12.29%	12.22%
Net interest margin–1990	4.32%	4.17%	4.19%	4.32%	4,36%
Net interest margin–1991	4.43%	4.53%	4.38%	4.37%	4.45%
Assets per employee–1990	1,823,933	1,819,657	2,079,456	1,863,297	1,762,064
Assets per employee–1991	1,904,886	1,857,246	2,163,322	1,937,945	1,854,784
Non-interest income as a percent of total income–1990	12.20%	23.14%	18.18%	10.97%	9.96%
Non-interest income as a percent of total income–1991	13.61%	25.17%	19.18%	12.24%	11.41%
Non-interest expense as a percent of total expense–1990	35.14%	38.73%	35.98%	34.08%	35.02%
Non-interest expense as a percent of total expense–1991	38.84%	44.96%	41.79%	37.50%	38.03%
Price to earnings ratio–1990	7.83	8.10	7.62	8.48	7.42
Price to earnings ratio–1991	10.46	10.38	10.83	11.53	9.74
Market vs. book price–1990	0.92	0.98	0.88	0.93	0.90
Market vs. book price–1991	1.10	1.32	1.35	1.15	0.97
Stock trading volume–1990	5,490,096	24,363,520	6,232,164	1,936,084	417,383
Stock trading volume–1991	6,336,587	29,424,184	7,109,544	2,388,037	1,072,692

CHAPTER FIFTEEN

Maintaining Independence

Remaining independent is an issue on every CEO's mind. It is especially vivid for the management and boards of supercommunity banks since these banks have very strong franchises and outperform the industry. They have many suitors and present attractive acquisition candidates. If the charter of the CEO and the board is to do what is in the best interest of the shareholders, the question becomes, is selling the bank for a hefty premium the right thing to do? Many supercommunity banks do not share that feeling. They believe it is in the best interest of the shareholder to stay independent as a supercommunity bank and create a strong income stream that is supported by an enhancement for the long-term franchise value. If maintaining corporate independence is a goal for the supercommunity bank, is that a feasible alternative? And if

so, how can supercommunity banks enhance their chances to stay independent?

The depository institution industry is shrinking. As evidenced in Figures 15.1 and 15.2, the number of financial institutions is continuing to decline. The number of thrifts has been cut in half, and the number of commercial banks has been cut by 25%. Overcapacity in the business, as mentioned in Chapter 1, is taking its toll. In addition, low-cost producers and megabanks are looking for economies of scale through size advantages.

And advantages which the industry could rely on in the past, such as product monopoly created by regulation, chief deposits, and protected franchises, were ended by technology and de facto deregulation. The asset side and the liability side of depository institutions has been deregulated. The checking account, once the pri-

**FIGURE 15.1 Number of Thrift
Institutions**

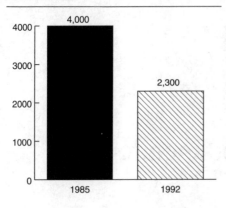

vate domain of commercial banks, and the mortgage, once the private domain of thrifts, are now subject to national competition, interstate volatility, yankee ingenuity, deregulation, and technology, contributed to the national market on both the asset side and the liability side of the balance sheet. Commercial banks, mortgage companies, finance companies, Freddie Mac and Ginny Mae, credit card companies, conduits, and investment banks, as well as nonfinancial companies, all compete on the asset side for all kinds of loans and investments. Similarly, the liability side of the balance sheet has become a national market through national deposit gathering, mutual funds, CMA accounts, and investment banker intervention.

At the same time, the deregulation of the early 1980s with 1980 DIDMCA and the 1981 Garn-St. Germaine Bill was foiled by re-regulation with the 1989 FIR-REA and 1991 FDICIA. The results? Numerous failures, inappropriate regulatory response, questions as to the overall via-

bility of the industry, the entry of nontraditional competitors, and industry consolidation. As a member of the deposit-poor institution segment of the financial services industry, you must ask yourself: Should I sell out? Is there a future as an independent? Is critical mass the only answer? If so, what is critical mass? $50 billion? $100 billion? $200 billion?

This book is predicated on the assumption that supercommunity banks can successfully compete in their restructuring of the financial services industry. Even if they do so, can they stay independent and avoid being gobbled up by megabanks and other franchised builders?

Staying independent is a feasible alternative, but not an easy one. One needs to combine an effective strategy yielding high stock prices with short-term protection in the structure of the corporation and its stock ownership. Supercommunity banking is an effective strategy to yield high profits and enhance shareholder value over the long-term. It has been a successful strategy even in a world where traditional

**FIGURE 15.2 Number of Commercial
Banks**

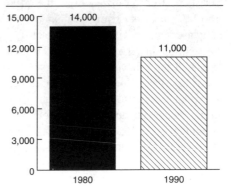

charter-focused strategies are no longer valid and where competition is business-focused, not charter-focused. As super-community banks build their strategy, they build on strengths such as product knowledge, distribution network, customer relationships, or dominant market position. They compete against a variety of institutions, recognizing that competition varies by business. As competitors align by a product line, supercommunity banks have to sharpen their strategic position by leveraging the community-oriented distribution system and the customer relationship with the efficiencies of centralized, customer-transparent functions. Examples of product-specific competition are presented in Table 15.1.

If supercommunity banks compete along these business lines and others, they can still retain the competitive advantage described throughout this book. The key is

TABLE 15.1 Product-Specific Competition

Real Estate Finance

Strategic Position	Critical Success Factors	Competition
• Leverage branch and origination infrastructures	• Origination network	• Depository institutions
• High-Quality underwriting	• Turnaround time	• Finance companies
• Funding expertise	• Service	• Mortgage banks
	• Asset quality underwriting	• Mortgage brokers
	• Funding rate	• Government agencies
	• Servicing quality	

Consumer Finance

Strategic Position	Critical Success Factors	Competition
• Leveraging retail Franchise to originate Consumer loans	• Technical knowledge	• Depository institutions
• Low-cost local funding	• Underwriting	• Finance companies
• Funding expertise	• Interstate/pricing	• Nonbank banks
	• Target marketing	• Credit card companies
	• Fee Income opportunities	
	• Distribution system	
	• Flexible products	

Community Banking

Strategic Position	Critical Success Factors	Competition
• Leveraging customer Loyalty	• Service, service,service!	• Depository institutions
• Focus on small and Middle market business	• Commitment to the Community	• Mutual funds
• Community roots and Customer service	• Convenience	• Finance companies
	• Experience economies of scale	

to translate this competitive advantage into superior stock prices so that being acquired will become an expensive proposition for a potential acquiror. As they often say, "There is no unfriendly offer, just an unfriendly price."

Although short-term protection such as poison pills, staggered board elections, leveraged ESOPs, and limited shareholder flexibility can be incorporated into the corporate charter and ownership structure and, in many cases, should appropriately be incorporated, the best defense in maintaining independence is an offense. Superior performance and making the company as expensive as possible to acquire is indeed the best defense. Following your own path through clear strategic focus, which is implied by supercommunity banking as a strategic position, is another necessary ingredient to marshall resources and focus activities on return to the shareholders. Staying close to the customer also helps enhance the franchise value since the customer represents an income stream that ultimately gets translated into stock price. The following are among the important principles to maintaining independence:

- The best defense is an offense.
- Follow your own path.
- Stay close to the customer.
- Differentiate, uncommoditize.
- Be flexible.

Bank consolidation has been underway for several years. The pace of mergers has quickened recently as the prices of publicly traded banks soared, thereby creating more valuable currency, which allowed banks to purchase others at substantial pre-miums to book value without unacceptable dilution (Figure 15.3, 15.4). Since 1990, when lower stock prices inhibited the consolidation phase, there has been a dramatic increase in the number of mergers and acquisitions (Figure 15.5). Growing pressure for cost reductions, more demanding shareholders, technological advances, broader markets, and increasing sophisticated customers have created an atmosphere enabling and encouraging mergers and acquisitions among financial institutions. The number and size of bank mergers has thus increased dramatically. In 1991 alone, more than 500 banks announced plans to merge. The total value of transactions completed in 1991 exceeded $20 billion, five times the $4.1 billion 1990 total. This trend is expected to continue, driven by earnings pressure and the need to improve shareholder value.

It is interesting to note that most studies have shown that few mergers truly increase shareholder value when designed to bring about cost efficiencies. Federal Reserve Board economists in a study of 134 mergers concluded that, "No more than one merged bank out of ten" became more profitable than banks that remained independent. Even more surprisingly, the study indicated the same statistics remain true for in-market mergers. Further, a Harvard Business School study of New England bank mergers reflects the lack of success in most bank mergers. It found similar failures in profitability in at least half of the cases studied.

These studies demonstrate how difficult it is to bring about a successful merger. Even successful acquisitions were not achieved fully and easily. For example, in

FIGURE 15.3 Commercial Banking Companies
Summary of Public Equity Offerings, 1987-1992

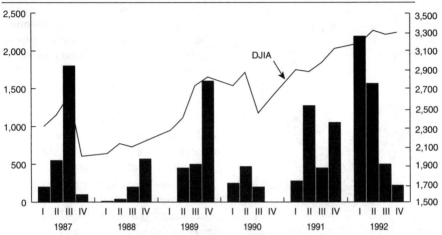

the 1985 merger between Wells Fargo and Crocker National Bank, a model for successful acquisition, management was unable to generate cost savings for the first six quarters, although the FRB study concedes that after that time sizable benefits were produced. It therefore appears that even with extremely favorable market conditions and top quality management, material cost savings and/or revenue enhancements are far from certain. Although this evaluation may be unfair, since most large bank mergers and acquisitions were aimed at entering new geographic markets rather than bringing about cost savings or profitability enhancement, all bank valuation experts agree that post-merger integration is the most crucial factor to a merger's success.

When banks evaluate their strategic future, they often wish to commit to long-term independence. In order to do so, they should use supercommunity banking as a part of the long-term ongoing philosophy designed to enhance value. Long-term, value-building strategies and tactics are often straightforward. Improving the fundamentals of the institution's balance sheet and income statement will obviously improve the basis for any potential merger or sale. In addition, non-financial aspects such as management depth, information systems, and a strategic position are helpful to enhancing short-term and long-term franchise value.

It is expected that during the 1990s many banks, particularly supercommunity banks, will continue to seek in-market mergers as a way to build market share and, through it, enhanced profitability as well as community presence. The opportunities are significant since many large

**FIGURE 15.4 Commercial Banking
Sector—Equity Capital Raised by
Issuer's Region**

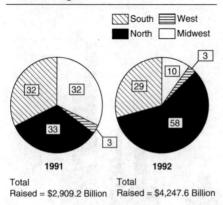

1991   1992
Total   Total
Raised = $2,909.2 Billion   Raised = $4,247.6 Billion

regional companies have shown a declining interest for owning more community
banks, particularly rural banks. Consequently, a strategy many supercommunity banks may follow in the 1990s involves
mergers of one or more institutions to
increase size and stock liquidity while
building a stronger banking company cov-
ering larger geographic areas.

This is important to maintaining independence since many shareholders want to
liquefy their investments. The large majority of financial institutions in the United
States have extremely limited trading in
their stock. This is especially true when a
fairly large block of stock is placed on the
market. In the past, shareholders received
dividends usually equal to other alternative
investments, had great stability in their
investment with little or no risk of failure,
received prestige by being a director and a
large shareholder, received favorable treatment as customers of the institution, and
indirectly benefited from the success of a

strong independent institution in the resulting beneficial impact to the community,
since most large shareholders tend to be
business people whose primary businesses
depended on their local economies.
Virtually all these factors have changed in
today's environment. Financial institution
dividends have not kept up with other
investment alternatives. The banking and
thrift industries are considered very
volatile, with record numbers of failures
each year. Many individuals view being a
director as an excessive risk rather than a
prestigious position. And new laws and
regulations have eliminated an insider's
ability to obtain favorable treatment; therefore, creating shareholder liquidity is
important to maintaining independence.
Maintaining a large base of shareholders is
another. In an industry where industry or
price differentiation is insufficient to create

**FIGURE 15.5 Bank & Thrift Merger
and Acquisition Transactions
1988-1992**

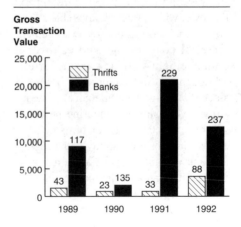

Gross
Transaction
Value

a competitive advantage, one method to obtain customer loyalty is to have the customer actually own part of the institution. Supercommunity banks are well-known in their breadth of customer ownership, which enhances customer retention and loyalty as well as the leeway management has in running the institution barring major institutional investors.

Stock repurchases and ownership restructuring plans have significant advantages in maintaining independence. Although virtually all banks and thrifts are prohibited from purchasing their own stock, a bank or thrift holding company may repurchase its stock, and supercommunity banks are mostly bank holding companies. Further, an employee stock ownership plan (ESOP) used separately or with the holding company may also purchase an institution's stock. The ability to buy its stock is a major advantage to an institution and its shareholders, especially where limited trading of stock is available, or where stock is held primarily in large blocks. Repurchasing your own stock is an alternative that can significantly improve earnings per share and return on equity. Since the October 1987 stock market crisis, over ninety of the 150 largest U.S. bank holding companies have implemented stock repurchasing programs.

Figure 15.6 provides an analysis of the impact of a stock repurchase plan on a hypothetical $100 million holding company that has no assets other than its ownership of its wholly owned financial institution subsidiary. The holding company is considering a repurchase of up to 10% of its outstanding shares. The institution has arranged a credit facility with an upstream correspondent bank to finance the program. The effect of the stock repurchase program on the value of the institution's stock can be illustrated as follows:

The market price is $80 per share before the transaction, and with the repurchase at 100% of book value, pro forma

> *Repurchasing your own stock is an alternative that can significantly improve earnings per share and return on equity.*

earnings rise 5.2%. From the perspective of return on equity, the buy-back program will be successful so long as the after-tax cost of debt incurred to buy the stock is less than the rate of return on the core earnings of the institution. From the perspective of earnings per share, there does come a point at which the absolute cost of interest exceeds the relative benefit of lower number of shares (which did not happen in the pricing range example shown in Figure 15.6).

Some of the reasons for recent stock repurchase programs include the following:

- Earnings per share, return on equity, and book value per share may be immediately increased after many stock repurchases and/or ownership restructurings.
- Current tax laws favor debt over equity because of the deductibility of interest as opposed to non-deductibility of dividends.

FIGURE 15.6 Example of a Stock Repurchase Plan

EXAMPLE OF STOCK REPURCHASE PLAN

Assumptions

Assets	$100,000,000	Current "market price" per share	$80.00
Equity/asset ratio	8.00%	Equity	$8,000,000
Earnings	$1,000,000	Number of shares	100,000
Return on equity (ROE)	12.50%	Tax Rate (state and Federal)	34.00%
Book value per share	$80.00	Earnings per share (EPS)	$10.00
Interest rate	10.00%	Shares repurchased (10% of outstanding stock)	10,000

Offering Price		Pro Forma Values						
Price/Book %	Share Price	Debt Assumed	Earnings	EPS	Book Value	Book/Value Per Share	ROE (%)	Equity/ TA (%)
50%	$40.00	$400,000	$973,600	$10.82	$7,600,000	$84.44	12.81%	7.60%
60%	$48.00	$480,000	$968,320	$10.76	$7,520,000	$83.56	12.88%	7.52%
70%	$56.00	$560,000	$963,040	$10.70	$7,440,000	$82.67	12.94%	7.44%
80%	$64.00	$640,000	$957,760	$10.64	$7,360,000	$81.78	13.01%	7.36%
90%	$72.00	$720,000	$952,480	$10.58	$7,280,000	$80.89	13.08%	7.28%
100%	$80.00	$800,000	$947,200	$10.52	$7,200,000	$80.00	13.16%	7.20%
110%	$88.00	$880,000	$941,920	$10.47	$7,120,000	$79.11	13.23%	7.12%
120%	$96.00	$960,000	$936,640	$10.41	$7,040,000	$78.22	13.30%	7.04%
130%	$104.00	$1,040,000	$931,360	$10.35	$6,960,000	$77.33	13.38%	6.96%
140%	$112.00	$1,120,000	$926,080	$10.29	$6,880,000	$76.44	13.46%	6.88%
150%	$120.00	$1,200,000	$920,800	$10.23	$6,800,000	$75.56	13.54%	6.88%

NOTES:

1. Pro forma earnings per share increase across the entire range of potential repurchase prices (from 50% to 150% of book value). For example, if the repurchase occurred at book value, or $80 per share, earnings per share would increase 5.2%, from $10.00 to $10.52 per share.

2. Pro forma book value in dollar terms decreases by the amount of debt assumed. Generally Accepted Accounting Principals require that treasury transactions be recorded as reductions of equity.

3. Pro forma book value per share increases if the repurchase price is below book value, whereby the transaction is anti-dilutive with respect to book value per share. Book value per share decreases if the repurchase price is above book value, so in those instances, the transaction would be dilutive with respect to book value per share.

4. Pro forma return on equity rises following the share repurchase program in all cases shown.

5. Management, directors and other long term "core" investors have increased their ownership percentages without any personal cash expenditures. If these individuals had attempted to increase their ownership percentages through the purchase of newly issued or already outstanding stock, any payments would be in after-tax (or doubly-taxed) dollars. Also, such individuals may be limited in deducting interest on any debt incurred to buy such stock because of the portfolio investment interest rules. By using a bank holding company, the stock repurchase is paid for by before tax dollars and the holding company may deduct all interest incurred on the repurchase loan.

- Current tax laws do not favor reinvesting cash into fixed assets.
- The cost of incurring debt to retire equity is relatively low when the interest rate is low.
- Repurchase plans communicate to the market that management is optimistic about the company's future and feels the stock is undervalued.
- Stock repurchases support stock prices by stabilizing the market and providing a floor or a minimum price for the stock.
- Stock repurchases may be more financially attractive and flexible than dividend increases.
- Unfriendly takeover attempts have caused greenmail stock repurchases.

Stock repurchase or other ownership restructuring plans are often directly related to an unwanted or unsolicited attempt to change control. Institutions with depressed stock prices in relation to their true value may be the subject of unsolicited and unwanted tender offers for third parties or companies with no previous relationship with the institution. The trend toward such unfriendly takeovers for large institutions and supercommunity banks could accelerate once all legal barriers are eliminated through cross-country acquisitions. Many supercommunity banks find unwanted changes in control initiated by insiders as well. These insiders may be current major shareholders seeking more control, shareholders who wish to purchase additional stock at low prices to sell out to a larger institution at a quick profit, or local wealthy investors.

Remaining independent may imply adopting a comprehensive anti-takeover plan. The primary benefits are:

- It deters unwanted investors.
- It is a valuable negotiation tool when the board is approached by an unwanted investor.
- It provides specific defenses useful as a tender offer once other similar maneuvers commence.

Companies amending their charters and bylaws to include such protective provisions as part of advance planning have generally had their anti-takeover defenses upheld in court. In many cases, firms with strategies implemented in response to a specific bid have had such provisions invalidated on the basis that they were put in place only to protect existing management and were not in the best interest of the shareholders. Last-minute reactionary strategies are usually ineffective. Certain types of structural anti-takeover techniques used with bank holding companies include the following:

- Insert in the charter's bylaws, supermajority provisions requiring a higher percentage of stock to be voted in favor of an unfriendly offer.
- Stagger and limit the method of electing directors to make obtaining control more difficult.
- Provide in the charter various factors the board may consider in evaluating an unfriendly offer other than price (impact on employees, the community, its customers, etc.).

FIGURE 15.7 The Decision Makers: The Role of the Institutional Investor and the Bank Stock Analyst

- Institutional investors represent the largest source of capital in the United States .
- They own approximately $115 billion in bank equities and $10 billion in thrift equities.
- Bank stock analysts provide a conduit between the company and portfolio manager through their investment analyses.
- Their investment perspective may be from the buy side or the sell side.
- A favorable rating by a well-known market figure like Warren Buffett may have a trigger effect on a stock.
- Bank stock analysts provide coverage on anywhere from 10 to 50 companies, and they will only recommend a relatively small percentage of stocks at any one time.

- Delete mandatory preemptive rights.
- Eliminate cumulative voting rights.
- Insert a fair price section in the bank holding company's charter.
- Consider the use of poison pills.
- Authorize additional stock available for issuance to a white knight or other friendly investors.
- Insert special provisions providing for advantageous methods of calling or not calling directors' and shareholders' meetings.
- Structure all defenses as optional with the board rather than automatically activated.

Employment contracts containing golden parachute provisions may also be entered into by key officers at the holding company level. They serve as a deterrent to raiders because of the cost they add to an acquisition. If properly structured, the contracts can help guarantee objective advice by management during a takeover attempt. Without such arrangements, management's objectivity may be influenced by negotiating with a raider who could be their future boss.

To take full advantage of the alternatives of ownership restructurings and stock repurchase plans, one may opt for obtaining the line of credit in advance of actually needing the funds. Having the liquidity ready and available increases the company's flexibility to take action when needed.

In summary, remaining independent as a strategic objective needs to be assessed by management and incorporated into the strategic plan to ensure maximizing the likelihood of staying independent so long as it is in the best interest of all stockholders. Ultimately, however, the best defense is an offense; namely, improving performance and making the stock price as high as possible is in the best interest of a super-community bank's constituencies, whether the objective is to remain independent or to maximize the sales price.

Stock Price Management

Managing your bank's stock price is an important component in taking an offensive posture about maintaining independence. Generally, bank stock prices are driven by three variables: the economy,

TABLE 15.2 Top Bank Institutional Investors
Ranked by Market Value of Bank Holdings as of September 30, 1992

Rank	Investor	September 30 Shares Owned	%Chng Shares Owned[1]	September 30 Mkt. Value ($M)	% Chng Market Value[1]
1	Wells Fargo Inst Tr NA	109,474,915	2.60	3,479.91	-0.04
2	Fidelity Mgmt & Res Corp	125,013,162	-22.03	3,388.36	-29.95
3	Capital Research & Mgmt	69,155,664	-1.28	3,079.65	0.01
4	Bankers Trust N Y Corp	86,622,254	-3.05	2,987.40	-5.31
5	Wellington Management	69,356,694	5.45	2,372.27	-0.37
6	Mellon Bank Corporation	59,361,246	6.28	2,035.73	3.11
7	Bernstein Sanford C & Co	64,317,998	-7.71	1,825.07	-16.91
8	College Retire Equities	49,083,242	3.66	1,744.86	0.85
9	Delaware Management Co	41,136,300	1.77	1,722.65	2.61
10	Alliance Capital Mgmt	43,343,435	17.56	1,571.01	11.21
11	Janus Capital Corp	38,347,418	12.96	1,504.57	12.69
12	Barrow Hanley Mewhinney	36,897,000	2.36	1,314.85	-4.51
13	Morgan J P & Co Inc	38,717,944	-0.21	1,177.22	-4.18
14	New York St Common Ret	31,415,822	0.10	1,176.24	-2.60
15	State Farm Mut Auto Ins	29,372,680	10.60	1,155.94	5.49
16	NationsBank Corporation	28,553,647	5.72	1,153.26	3.87
17	State Street Boston Corp	32,396,329	13.66	1,111.26	10.48
18	Boston Company Inc	29,795,413	27.03	1,080.16	26.57
19	Calif Public Emp. Ret	30,365,850	2.00	1,032.44	0.03
20	Calif State Teachers Ret	29,414,573	2.22	990.78	0.48
21	Banc One Corporation	22,325,698	11.21	959.51	9.17
22	Capital Growth Mgmt	25,758,000	-21.53	879.21	-8.69
23	Michigan State Treasurer	29,853,982	2.35	876.63	-6.23
24	Capital Guardian Trust	21,037,336	2.94	868.84	-2.64
25	Prudential Ins Co/Amer	24,353,975	11.58	841.85	9.04
26	New York St Teachers Ret	22,718,847	0.06	813.72	-4.22
27	Society Corporation	17,775,233	NA	794.96	NA
28	Lazard Freres & Co	21,968,321	5.66	791.64	2.02
29	Northern Trust Corp	20,661,902	-1.74	784.90	-1.49
30	PNC Financial Corp	24,431,209	0.66	757.91	-1.49
	Total For all Publicly Traded Banks:	**3,259,069,492**	**3.17**	**113,892**	**1.02**

[1] Percent change from June 20.

Sources: CDA Investment Technologies, Rockville, Maryland, and SNL Securities, L.P., Charlottesville, Virginia.

fundamentals of the company, and the value of the company as a takeover target. For example, banks with the highest multiples are typically located in the highest growth parts of the country, thereby reflecting the market perception that a healthy economy will translate into a healthy bank. Fundamentals of the company have a lot to do with stock pricing as well; hence, the importance of solid performance by supercommunity banks. Supercommunity banks have a special advantage in that regard because their performance is not only excellent relative to the industry but also more stable. Investors pay premium dollars for stability of performance and a predictable income stream, and supercommunity banks have the leg up in that department.

Finally, the effect of takeover activity on a bank stock cannot be underestimated. Neighboring transactions have been known to move a bank's stock price by 15% to 45% in anticipation of additional transactions in the same market. After the stock market crash of 1987 and industry difficulties of the late 1980s and early 1990s, stock premiums are a given to banks with a good liquidity position and excellent capitalization. Supercommunity banks, by and large, perform exceptionally well in both these categories.

Supercommunity banks can actively manage their stock ownership as well as stock price. Institutional bank stock investors are helpful in enhancing the liquidity and ultimately the price of the company's stock (Figure 15.7). Institutional investors include pension funds, insurance companies, and index funds (Table 15.2).

Banknorth, the largest supercommunity

bank in Vermont, increased its institutional shareholder base up to 25% with a coordinated program toward that end. The bank established a detailed and user-friendly quarterly report that was distributed to brokers and institutional investors beyond the shareholder base. It embarked on a program to actively bring itself to the institutional investor's attention, developed an analyst's presentation, and started courting local brokers. Local brokers can have an important role in attaining major institutional investors and in bringing your bank to their attention. However, since it costs roughly $10,000 to add a bank to an investment bank's research universe, brokers are reluctant to expand coverage.

One should note that institutional investors are not all good or all bad. Although they can exert significant pressure on a bank, much more so than the fragmented ownership, there is an advantage to dealing with a sophisticated investor over a less sophisticated major shareholder or local investor who decides he wants to run the bank or oust management. That is why, while Mid-A of Ohio tried to minimize the number of institutions holding their stock, Bank North sought to increase theirs and raised institutional holdings from 6% to 20%.

A high stock price is beneficial not only as an independence-maintaining tool but also as a facilitator to making acquisitions and pooling transactions without undue dilution. A good stock price also creates opportunities to raise new equity through additional offerings. One should not issue too much equity at once. A good benchmark is not to exceed 15% to 20% of total equity in any one issue.

FIGURE 15.8 Taking Advantage of a High Stock Price

Capital Raising

- Generally, issue stock when prices are high and repurchase when they are low
- Stronger capital ratios provide greater flexibility
- Windows open and close—perfect timing is hard to achieve
- Don't sell too much

Mergers and Acquisitions

- Industry is consolidating
- Increase in market share is difficult to achieve
- Common stock is the preferred currency from an accounting and regulatory perspective
- Don't dilute yourself unless it can be over come within a relatively short period of time

Investor communications require having a cohesive and understandable story, highlighting what makes your company different or special. A clear strategic focus is an important first step to a good story. If the story is too different or difficult to understand, some may not like it. For example, although the use of minority interests in subsidiary banks is very important to maximizing community roots, many investors do not understand it and require further explanation. Some investors do not perceive the earnings dilution justified by the strategic and performance benefits. Using the supercommunity bank strategy as a point of departure has been an effective tool for stock price management for many supercommunity banks. It is considered a good story and is reflected by the higher premiums commanded by

supercommunity bank stocks when fully understood by the investment community (Figure 15.8).

In general, recommendations for enhancement of stock price through investor relations include the following (Figure 15.9):

- *Avoid surprises* by keeping the investment community abreast of developments of the company. This includes gaining credibility during tough times by informing investors of development of anticipated difficulties as they occur, as well as letting the community know when things are going well.
- Deal with investors and prospective investors in a *straightforward* and honest manner. Avoid puffery and unwarranted hype that will be disproved when the next numbers are released. Predictability is the key to success.
- Increase liquidity by *broadening investor interest,* which can be accomplished through visiting major investors, investment houses, and analysts on a regular basis as well as devel-

FIGURE 15.9 Enhancing Stock Price

- Ongoing process
- Cultivate local brokers and large institutional investors
- Encourage visits by analysts, salesmen, and investors
- Use of public relations firms (pros and cons)
- Quality of information
- Honesty in dealing with investors—no surprises
- Building confidence within the marketplace

oping communication vehicles to heighten corporate exposure.

- *Tell a story* in your communications that sets forth a clear strategic focus. Also, show your track record in implementing your plans in order to gain credibility for the future.
- If you must use a *public relations* firm to get the word out, make sure you use one with experience in the field. It is better to have a public relations firm than to not have anyone doing that part of the investor relations job. If you cannot designate an internal person, outsource.
- Designate someone within the company as being responsible for the *investor relations function.* This person should take a proactive role that may include contacting investment houses and institutional investors as well as developing interest among local brokers. It could be that person's job to manage the stock price in conjunction with senior management and to be alert to opportunities for enhancement.

Although there are no guarantees for maintaining independence at any price, the higher the stock price the greater the likelihood of fending off unwanted suitors as well as the likelihood of maximizing shareholder value if a transaction does occur. What you would do for everyday bank management is the same thing you should do for maintaining independence. However, combining that with a proactive management of the stock price and a relationship with the investment community will enhance the likelihood of staying independent toward the long-term maximization of shareholder value.

CHAPTER SIXTEEN

Conclusion: Where Do Supercommunity Banks Excel?

Supercommunity banks have achieved a sustainable competitive advantage and a prosperous strategic niche by outperforming their competitors in several key areas. These areas are integral to the supercommunity bank's strategy and are based on the three-pronged position on which the strategy is predicated:

- Community banking orientation to the customer
- Cost efficiencies that are transparent to the customer
- A broader product line that captures the full customer relationship

In the course of successfully implementing this strategic position, supercommunity banks were committed to placing special emphasis on several critical areas:

board utilization, quality service, stock ownership, and people management. Consequently, they have excelled in those areas.

Board Utilization

Many banks look at their board as a necessary burden. Others look at it as a source of invaluable business advice and guidance, as well as an important business development tool. Supercommunity banks have excelled in their ability to fully utilize the board concept and designate different roles for various board levels. Many have more than just one board. They typically have a holding company board that provides a strategic umbrella to the company and brings focus to all the subsidiary activities, banks and nonbanks alike. The individual bank boards, in turn, are more involved in setting the strategic direction for the bank as well as ensuring compliance at the bank level. They also offer potential in developing business and linking the bank into the community.

Supercommunity banks have also been noted for their superior use of the advisory board concept. Advisory boards are often seen as lame ducks, since they do not have the legal liability and the legal authority of formal boards. Supercommunity banks, on the other hand, turned the lack of legal liability to an important advantage. Their advisory board members do not have to worry about the potential liability that is so troublesome to many board members nowadays. At the same time, they have the status of board membership and the ability to participate in the community network, which is very rewarding to many. Supercommunity banks have been effective in creating an aura of status around their advisory board, thereby making membership a sought-after position.

In addition, the advisory board members at the supercommunity bank function as an important business development tool that connects the bank to its community at the most local level and highlights the community orientation of the company. These advisory boards have therefore become a highly effective business development tool and community linkage mechanism for many supercommunity banks, particularly for larger supercommunity banks concerned about being removed from their local markets. Some have over 700 advisory board members.

The attendance fees for such board members are low and often do not exceed $100 per meeting. But the returns to the bank in terms of community goodwill and specific business development opportunities are very high.

Quality Service

The word *quality* is overused in today's banking environment. In fact, it is often misused by many who pay lip service to it but are incapable or unwilling to make the

---

Most successful super-community banks . . . are committed to providing those service levels both on the front line, in customer contact through tellers and floor people, and in the back office, in customer service management, error reduction, and other programs designed to convert quality into a true competitive advantage.

---

necessary commitment to developing it. Most successful supercommunity banks have learned the secret of quality service as the customer defines it. They are committed to providing those service levels both on the front line, in customer contact through tellers and floor people, and in the back office, in customer service management, error reduction, and other programs designed to convert quality into a true competitive advantage. Higher-quality service creates higher customer satisfaction. This, in turn, enhances customer retention.

Despite the debates on the subject, customer retention intuitively is linked to enhanced profitability. There are some facts to support this notion when customer retention is translated into additional referrals, larger balances, more accounts, other relationships with the bank, and greater price elasticity.

All the above imply that customer retention enhances profitability. Supercommunity banks are believers in that concept. They, therefore, are truly committed to providing quality service. Banks ranging in size from $70 billion to $250 million are trying to integrate quality into their service delivery systems. A new differentiation factor is that quality is measured by the customer's needs and perceptions, not by the bankers. U.S. Bancorp, for example, provides quality by offering different mechanisms of varying degrees of personal service intensity to meet the wide range of customer preferences for personal contact. Those of us who do not want to face the teller have an 800-number twenty-four hours a day, seven days a week, which we can call to transact our business. The capabilities of this telephone delivery system are wide and extend beyond the typical complaint handling or direct marketing roles often associated with telephone banking. The telephone is used as a true convenience mechanism to bring banking to the customer where she wants it, when she wants it. By the same token, the branch network and other more personal delivery mechanisms are used to meet the needs of customers who prefer greater contact. For them, US Bancorp has options ranging from a personal banker, to the teller, to the ATM.

Both large and small supercommunity banks have been very successful in implementing specific quality enhancement programs and demonstrating the profits accrued to them as a result of these initiatives. These profit enhancements range in the millions of dollars for a $3 billion company and in the tens of millions for a $50 billion bank. Quality in these institutions has a major role in creating a competitive advantage and a barrier to entry for other players as well as realizing profit opportunities in enhanced revenues and cost efficiencies.

Stock Ownership

Supercommunity banks are typically widely owned by thousands of community members. Although they welcome institutional involvement and have witnessed greater institutional investment in recent years as the strategy has proven itself, supercommunity banks continue to be widely invested within their communities. Their customers and prospects own a piece of the company. This phenomenon has many benefits: Customer/owners build their own investment every time they do business with the bank. That sense of ownership is irreplaceable and directly contributes to price elasticity. Further, stock ownership is an excellent marketing mechanism used by the bank to market services to its owners as well as to create further goodwill and positive public relations among the communities it serves.

Also, the wide distribution of stock ownership in many supercommunity banks permits them greater flexibility in longer-term strategic management versus short-term, quarter-by-quarter profit management. Such ownership is more patient than some institutional investors and is often looking for longer-term results rather than short-term performance. That is not to imply that all individual investors tolerate inadequate bank performance, whether the bank is a supercommunity bank or not. It does mean, however, that supercommunity banks often have a friendlier owner base, which permits them to take a longer-term perspective of their business, thereby optimizing it more than if they were compelled to manage performance to quarterly targets.

People Management

People are the greatest asset of supercommunity banks next to the customer and the franchise. Without the people there can be no customer satisfaction. Supercommunity banks are very aware of that fact. Accordingly, they invest in their people. They are much more friendly institutions to work for than many other, more centralized companies that are more cost driven. Supercommunity banks stand by their employees more and expect the same loyalty in return.

As a result, an informal survey indicated that they have many more longer-term employees than other banking companies. There appears to be a direct relationship between the length of employment of bank personnel and customer retention. Customers develop loyalties to individual bank staff; the greater the continuity of personnel, the stronger the loyalty.

Consolidation brought with it tremendous dislocation of customer relationships as long-term relationships with banking

officers were severed due to major layoffs. Supercommunity banks typically avoid such layoffs. Consolidation efficiencies occur almost exclusively in the back office, which is transparent to the customer. Customer-handling people are generally retained. Employment policies and general attitudes within the corporation are friendly and allow for greater decision making and, therefore, job satisfaction at the bank and local level. (This empowerment works so long as performance meets expectations and does not decline below acceptable levels.)

This working environment contributes to the quality service discussed earlier. The supercommunity bank often treats its people the way they want their people to treat the customers. This creates a chain reaction that enhances service levels as well as employee satisfaction.

Summary

Supercommunity banks often excel in the four areas described above. They make better use of their boards and their employees and link into their communities not only as customers but also as investors. Quality service is the other major component to the strategy's success since it constitutes as a strong competitive advantage that is not easily displaced. As these banks continue to prosper, they will find other unique areas in which to excel beyond those mentioned here. They also continue to successfully manage the basics and do not forget the fundamentals of the business. They have strong core earnings and better asset quality than in the industry as a whole (due to their conservative lending policies and closeness to the customer). The areas where they excel generate the additional profits that are the icing on the cake beyond the core earnings, while enhancing their franchise value by building a competitive advantage using elements unique to their strategy: their board members, their investor base, their employees, and their attitude to the customer. Who says Yankee ingenuity is dead? These supercommunity banks have created a unique and profitable business in an industry where many experts predicted it could not be done.

The competitive success of supercommunity banks in the future hinges not only on the implementation of the strategy prescriptions as described in this book, but a few additional elements, which are critical success factors for future prosperity.

1. *Strategic Focus.* In face of intensifying competition, finite resources, and the need to differentiate, strategic focus is a critical success factor to every bank, including supercommunity banks. Knowing who you are and communicating it effectively to all members of the team is essential to the delivery of services the supercommunity bank way. Marshalling all the resources to work together toward that end is essential to success.

2. *Leverage.* Supercommunity banks have many leverage points, including a loyal customer base, an effective distribution network, areas of expertise and knowledge, and strategic differentiation. You should build on these leverage points and other strengths to expand and fully implement supercommunity banking

and reach further to capture customer business and exceed customer needs.

3. *Quality.* Quality is becoming a competitive advantage and a sustainable barrier. Supercommunity banks are well positioned to implement quality throughout the system and use it as a competitive barrier. Not paying attention to quality and not integrating it into the company could be a costly mistake. Quality service can generate customer retention which, in turn, generates market share which, in turn, generates profits. Low quality causes defection, customer attrition, and employee dissatisfaction.

4. *Corporate culture and values.* These are important in every company, but especially so in supercommunity banks where every person can make a difference in the implementation of the strategy. The dependence on quality and service levels as a differentiation factor in retention enhancement makes the employee understanding of the type of company you want to be imperative. Those companies that successfully articulated their corporate culture and values and integrated them into their management are more profitable and more successful than those who did not.

Supercommunity banking is a strategic framework. All supercommunity banks share the three themes in common: community banking service, customer-invisible cost savings, and a broad product line. However, they each chart their own course to get there. Although the themes repeat themselves, some would do so with a greater emphasis on cost management and others would reach the same place with a greater emphasis on quality service and customer retention. The product lines of supercommunity banks, although similar, are not identical. What all supercommunity banks share, in addition to the three-pronged strategy, is the commitment to be customer-driven in structuring their business, delivery systems, and product lines. As you contemplate becoming a super-community bank or improving your position as a supercommunity bank, I recommend the following:

- Follow your own path—Define your unique composition of supercommunity banking within the strategic prescription.
- Stay close to the customer—Being customer driven is one of the nonnegotiables of supercommunity banking.
- Differentiate, uncommoditize—Compete on elements other than service.
- Be flexible—The world is changing, and you must change with it.

Adopting a clear strategic framework such as supercommunity banking will give you the context within which to make the decisions. Day-to-day decisions, however, need to remain flexible and responsive to the changing world and the changing customer needs and expectations.

Supercommunity banking is a strategy for success and prosperity for banks in the 1990s. The strategic fundamentals are offered in this book. However, implementation of the strategy for your institution requires careful analysis and planning, and a clear understanding of the implementation of the strategic prescriptions in your institution. You cannot become a super-community bank simply by calling yourself one. It is the thoughtful strategic planning process and detailed implementation of the strategy with the unwavering commitment of senior management that will make you a successful supercommunity bank.

EPILOGUE

"I find the great thing in this world is not so much where we stand as in what direction we are moving: to reach the port . . . we must sail sometimes with the wind and sometimes against it—but we must sail, and not drift, nor lie at anchor."

—Oliver Wendell Holmes

The rules of the game:

1. Face reality as it is, not as it was or as you wish it to be.
2. Be candid with everyone.
3. Don't manage, lead.
4. Change before you have to.
5. If you don't have a competitive advantage, don't compete.
6. Control your destiny or someone else will.
7. If you don't know where you're going, no road will take you there.

Board of Directors Guidelines and Evaluation Form

General Guidelines for Directors

I. Responsibilities of Individual Directors

a) The individual director must be diligent in performing the job by:

1) attending all board and assigned committee meetings regularly;

2) requesting and reviewing closely all meeting materials, auditor's findings, and supervisory communications;

3) asking questions and requesting explanations;

4) being familiar with general industry trends and regulatory developments pertinent to the institution; and

5) attending other functions sponsored by the bank to which board members are invited.

b) The individual director must gain a basic understanding of banking as a business, banking as an industry and the bank laws and regulations;

c) The individual director must exercise independent judgment and must be loyal to the bank's interest.

d) The individual director must commit adequate time in order to be informed as a participant in the affairs of the institution.

e) The individual director should bring insight, interest and involvement to the board to strengthen the bank.

f) The individual director should be familiar with the recent history of the bank and have an understanding of what makes it unique among its competitors.

g) The individual director should endeavor to establish a general atmosphere of trust, confidence, enthusiasm,, and understanding commensurate with the bank's image of providing security to the public.

II. Responsibilities of Directors (Generally)

a) Directors should first establish and maintain the board's independence and to ensure the following:

  1) that the quality of the bank's management is competent and well qualified;

  2) that management refrains from insider abuse and continues to act competently and honestly;

  3) that the institution has internal controls and plans for the future;

  4) that it monitors the institution's business performance; and

  5) that it controls the bank's direction and determines how the bank will conduct it's business.

b) Directors must be knowledgeable and active to meet the duties of the institution, its stockholders, its depositors and the public.

c) Directors should be independent and actively involved in the bank's affairs, even if it means conflict with management.

d) Directors should work with management to develop programs to keep members informed with periodic briefings.

e) Directors should establish with management the operating policies under which it will operate and the institution's long and short business objectives.

f) Directors remain accountable for monitoring operations to ensure that they are carried out in compliance with the law and regulations and that these operations are consistent with safe and sound banking practices.

g) Directors should ensure that the bank has plans and policies appropriate to its market situation.

h) Directors should establish what the bank is and what it wants to become. Only then can it know whether it has the sources and capabilities to reach its goals.

i) Directors are responsible for defining for the bank what banking practices and levels of risk, are acceptable.

j) Directors should ensure that all major activities are covered by clearly communicated written policies which should be reviewed annually. The policies should include:

  1) loan portfolio management;

  2) loans and loan review;

  3) funds/asset liability management;

  4) management information systems;

  5) contingency funding

  6) investment; and

  7) trust activities

There should also be codes of ethics and policies on conflicts of interest.

k) Directors should monitor all policies to ensure that they conform with changes in laws and regulations, economic conditions and the institution's circumstances.

l) Directors are responsible for ensuring that bank management has incorporated a sound system of internal controls into the bank's day-to-day operations procedures.

m) Directors must be able to verify the accuracy and the reliability of the day-to-day operations reports which it receives through management.

n) Directors should be able to evaluate performance against the bank's own targets and against the performance of its peers.

o) Directors should identify what information they would like to see, and how frequently and request that management provide those reports to them.

p) Directors should provide for independent third party reviews and testing of compliance with board policies and procedures, applicable laws, and accuracy of the information provided by management.

q) Directors should personally review any reports of examination or other supervisory activity and any other correspondence from the bank's supervisors and discuss issues of concern with examiners.

r) Directors should avoid all preferential transactions involving insiders or their related interests. This may expose the institution to a greater than ordinary risk of loss.

s) Directors should be familiar with and actively encourage the bank's management to monitor and consistently improve employee productivity.

t) Directors should be involved in ensuring that the bank's services and priorities are regularly brought to the attention of the community.

Criteria for Maintenance of Outside Directorship

1. All outside directors must regularly attend schedules Board meetings. Regular attendance requires the outside director to attend all Board meetings, with the understanding that 2 unexcused absences require resignation or removal. The chairman of the Board of Directors will determine, under the circumstances, whether such absence is excused. It is the burden of the director to convince the Chairman in that regard.

2. All directors must spend a reasonable amount of time with bank management in understanding the operating policies under which the institution operates as well as its long and short term business objectives.

3. All directors must participate in the formation of the mission statement of the Bank and any changes in that mission statement.

4. All directors are responsible for personally reviewing all reports of examination or other supervisory activity and to discuss issues of concern with Bank examiners if called upon to do so.

5. All directors must be familiar with the policies of the Bank with respect to loan portfolio management, loans and loan review, funds/asset liability management, management information systems, contingency funding, investment policies, and trust activities.

6. All board members are required to read all materials provided to them prior to each board meeting and to suggest agenda items where appropriate. Any failure to do so will result in an adverse recommendation by the evaluation committee as to the individual directors retention.

7. All directors are expected to actively participate in committee assignments. Active participation will be determined by the chairman of each committee of the board. The chairman of each committee will be required to recommend retention of each individual director who is a member of his or her committee. Such recommendations will be made to the evaluation committee.

8. All directors of the Bank must utilize the services of the Bank in some meaningful way.

9. An evaluation committee will be appointed by the chairman. Its task will be to annually evaluate all members of the board, whether or not such members terms are expiring, and to recommend to the chairman the retention and/or renomination of board members.

10. All board members will be required to acknowledge in writing their understanding as to the general guidelines for directors of _____ and as to the specific criteria required for retention and/or renomination of the board.

11. An outside director will be required to encourage others to do business with the Bank and will be judged, in part, upon his or her success in achieving this goal.

Bank Board Assessment Questionnaire

Directions:

- This questionnaire is composed of eight sections. Each section has a different focus. Please read the section headings carefully.

- The majority of the questions use the format of answering yes, no or sometimes as follows:

  ___yes   ___no   ___sometimes

- Whenever a different question format is used, specific directions are provided. Please read each question carefully.

- The information you are providing on this questionnaire is greatly appreciated.

Section I—Board Membership

1. Do you feel that you have adequate opportunity to understand and discuss your responsibilities and opportunities for growth as a Board member?

   ___yes   ___no   ___sometimes

2. Do you understand your responsibilities as a Board member?

   ___yes   ___no   ___sometimes

3. Are you satisfied with your attendance at Board meetings?

   ___yes   ___no   ___somewhat satisfied

4. Are you satisfied with the attendance of other Board members at the Board meetings?

   ___yes   ___no   ___somewhat satisfied

337

5. Are you satisfied with your attendance at Committee meetings?

    ___yes   ___no   ___somewhat satisfied

6. Are you satisfied with the attendance of other Board members at Committee meetings?

    ___yes   ___no   ___somewhat satisfied

7. Do you prepare for Board meetings by reading the materials provided to you prior to the meetings?

    ___yes   ___no   ___sometimes

8. Do you feel the materials provided to you prior to the meetings are adequate and meet your needs rather than the needs of management?

    ___yes   ___no   ___somewhat satisfied

9. Are you satisfied with other Board members' preparation for the meetings?

    ___yes   ___no   ___somewhat satisfied

10. Do you suggest agenda items when appropriate?

    ___yes   ___no   ___sometimes

11. Do you participate actively at board meetings on a regular basis?

    ___yes   ___no   ___sometimes

12. Are you satisfied with the participation of other Board members at meetings?

    ___yes   ___no   ___somewhat satisfied

13. Do you attempt to keep abreast of important issues that were discussed at meetings you missed?

    ___yes   ___no   ___sometimes

14. Do you actively participate in committee assignments?

    ___yes   ___no   ___sometimes

15. Are you satisfied with the participation of other Board members in committee assignments?

    ___yes   ___no   ___somewhat satisfied

16. Do you regularly attend other functions sponsored by the Bank to which Board members are invited?

    ___yes   ___no   ___sometimes

17. Are you satisfied with other Board members' attendance at other functions sponsored by the Bank?

    ___yes   ___no   ___somewhat satisfied

18. Are you satisfied that no conflict of interest exists in your relationship to the Bank as a Board member?

    ___yes   ___no   ___somewhat satisfied

19. Are you satisfied that no conflicts of interest exist with any other Board members in their relationship to the Bank?

    ___yes   ___no   ___somewhat satisfied

20. Do you understand the requests made of you as a Board member and stockholder according to the Bylaws of the Bank?

    ___yes   ___no   ___sometimes

21. Do you like the sequence and conduct of matters discussed at Board meetings?

    ___yes   ___no   ___sometimes

22. Do you feel committed and challenged by your membership on the Board?

    ___yes   ___no   ___sometimes

23. Do you feel the Board has a wide enough scope of experience and perspective due to the composition of its membership?

    ___yes   ___no   ___sometimes

24. Are recommendations presented in such a way that Board members are able to understand any statements made by Officers and all supporting documentation?

    ___yes   ___no   ___sometimes

25. Are you satisfied with the length of the meetings? If no, please explain (too long, too short, etc.).

    ___yes   ___no   ___somewhat satisfied

    Explain:

26. Are you satisfied that the items on the agenda are adequately covered in the time provided? If no, please explain.

    ___yes   ___no   ___somewhat satisfied

    Explain:

Additional comments you would like to make regarding this section:

Section II—Mission of the Bank

1. Do you have input into the Bank's written statement which defines its purpose as a company?

    ___yes   ___no   ___sometimes

2. Do you, as a Board member, periodically review the Bank's written mission statement (creed)?

___yes   ___no   ___sometimes

3. Are you familiar with the recent history of the Bank with an understanding of what makes it unique among its competitors?

___yes   ___no   ___some knowledge in this area

4. To what degree is the Board of Directors involved in a periodic review of the bank's goals and timetables?

Please circle appropriate number.

    1   2   3   4   5

    Not Involved   Very Actively Involved

Additional comments regarding this section that you would like to make?

Section III—Planning

1. Do you have input into the formulation of the goals and objectives of the Bank?

___yes   ___no   ___sometimes

2. Do you have input regarding the evaluation and revision of the goals and objectives?

___yes   ___no   ___sometimes

If yes, how often?

3. Do you have input into the formulation of goals specifically related to profitability?

___yes   ___no   ___sometimes

4. Do you have input into the formulation of goals specifically related to capital adequacy?

___yes   ___no   ___sometimes

5. Do you provide input concerning the Bank's ability to meet changing customer needs?

___yes   ___no   ___sometimes

6. Do you provide input concerning the operational considerations that are a part of the Bank's goals and objectives?

___yes   ___no   ___sometimes

7. Do you provide input when you learn of new products and/or services offered by the Bank's competitors?

___yes   ___no   ___sometimes

8. Do you provide input concerning the Bank's planning process as a whole?

___yes   ___no   ___sometimes

9. How well does the Board of Directors provide leadership in the implementation of the Bank's planning process?   Please circle appropriate number

    1   2   3   4   5

    Not Well   Very Well

10. To what extent do you refer to the Bank's plan when making decisions throughout the year?

Please circle the appropriate number

1	2	3	4	5
Not Well			Very Well	

Additional comments regarding this section you would like to make:

Section IV—External Relationships of the Board and the Bank

1. Do you provide feedback for measuring the public's perception of the Bank?

___yes   ___no   ___sometimes

2. Are you involved in ensuring that the Bank's services and priorities are regularly brought to the attention of the community?

___yes   ___no   ___sometimes

3. Do you express your opinions concerning existing services?

___yes   ___no   ___sometimes

4. Do you express your opinions concerning those services the Bank should offer in the future?

___yes   ___no   ___sometimes

5. Should you be asked to serve as a representative or spokesperson for the Bank?

___yes   ___no

6. As a Board member, do you endeavor to establish a general atmosphere of trust, confidence, enthusiasm, and understanding commensurate with the Bank's image of providing security to the public?

___yes   ___no   ___some of the times

7. Should you make on-sight calls to customers?

___yes   ___no   ___sometimes

8. Can you build business for the Bank more effectively by means other than outside calls to customers?

___yes   ___no

Additional comments regarding this section that you would like to make:

Section V—Financial Management

1. Are you satisfied with your input when loans are presented for approval to the Board or a committee of the Board?

    ___yes   ___no   ___somewhat satisfied

2. Do you fully understand your regulatory limits as a Board member when making loan decisions?

    ___yes   ___no   ___sometimes

3. Are you familiar with how the Bank manages industry concentration in lending (for example small business, agriculture, real estate)?

    ___yes   ___no   ___some knowledge in this area

4. Are you familiar with the Bank's program for review and the rating of loans?

    ___yes   ___no   ___some knowledge in this area

5. Do you understand the role of the Officers' loan committee in the approval process for loans?

    ___yes   ___no   ___some knowledge in this area

6. Are you familiar with the Bank's allowance for loan loss and how it changes based on regulatory examination or external audit?

    ___yes   ___no   ___some knowledge in this area

7. Are you aware of how the Bank's loan loss allowance compares with those of its peer group?

    ___yes   ___no   ___some knowledge in this area

8. Are you familiar with the Bank's investment portfolio?

    ___yes   ___no   ___some knowledge in this area

9. Do you understand the average maturities and yields of state and local government investments reported to the Board?

    ___yes   ___no   ___some knowledge in this area

10. Are you familiar with the regulations applying to real estate owned by the Bank?

    ___yes   ___no   ___some knowledge in this area

11. Do you understand the Bank's Asset Liability management responsibilities?

    ___yes   ___no   ___some knowledge in this area

12. Are you familiar with the accounting policies and practices utilized by the Bank and how they work?

    ___yes   ___no   ___some knowledge in this area

13. Do you understand the changes made in accounting practices or policies that are reported to the Board?

    ___yes   ___no   ___some knowledge in this area

14. Do you understand what is meant by non-accrual?

    ___yes   ___no   ___some knowledge in this area

15. Concerning financial statements, do you ask questions regarding the major fluctuations between current year and previous year information that is reported to the Board?

___yes   ___no   ___sometimes

16. Do you ask questions concerning unusual or nonrecurring amounts in income or expense, which affect the Bank's financial statements?

___yes   ___no   ___sometimes

17. Do you feel you are provided adequate information to judge and/or approve the borrowings of other Board members?

___yes   ___no   ___sometimes

18. Do you understand the following terms which describe key measures relating to financial performances?

Return on Average Assets

___yes   ___no   ___some knowledge in this area

Return on Equity

___yes   ___no   ___some knowledge in this area

Net Interest Margin

___yes   ___no   ___some knowledge in this area

Primary Capital to Average Assets

___yes   ___no   ___some knowledge in this area

Non-performing Loans to Total Loans

___yes   ___no   ___some knowledge in this area

Net Losses to Average Total Loans

___yes   ___no   ___some knowledge in this area

Additional comments regarding this section that you would like to make:

Section VI—Board/Officer Relationships

1. Do you understand the differences between the roles and responsibilities of the Board and the Officers of the Bank, with respect to functions and expectations?

___yes   ___no   ___some knowledge in this area

2. Are you satisfied that a supportive environment of mutual trust and respect exists between the Board and the Officers of the Bank? Please circle the appropriate number

  1   2   3   4   5

Not Satisfied   Very Satisfied

3. Are you satisfied with your support of the Officers of the Bank in the implementation of Board policy?

Please circle the appropriate number

    1   2   3   4   5

Not Satisfied   Very Satisfied

4. Do you feel there should be a regular evaluation of the relationship between members of the Board and the Bank's Officers?

    ___yes   ___no

5. As you are now appraising yourself as a Board member, do you feel the Board should regularly appraise the performance of the Chief Executive Officer?

    ___yes   ___no

If yes, how do you feel this would be best accomplished?

6. Are you comfortable with the bank's plan for management succession?

    ___yes   ___no

Additional comments regarding this section that you would like to make:

Section VII—Board/Employee Relationships

1. Are you satisfied with the Board's involvement in setting employee salaries (too much, too little involvement)?

    ___yes   ___no   ___some knowledge in this area

2. Do you have involvement in the approval of employee benefits?

    ___yes   ___no   ___some knowledge in this area

3. Do you understand the policies pertinent to employment with the Bank?

    ___yes   ___no   ___some knowledge in this area

4. How satisfied are you that the Board actively encourages the Bank's management to monitor and consistently improve employee productivity? Please circle the appropriate number

    1   2   3   4   5

Not Satisfied   Very Satisfied

5. Are you familiar with how the Bank provides employees with incentives that recognize exceptional performance? Please circle the appropriate number

    1   2   3   4   5

Not Satisfied   Very Satisfied

6. Are you familiar with the training programs the Bank provides to support needed skill levels of employees?

    ___yes   ___no   ___some knowledge in this area

7. Are you familiar with the training programs the Bank provides to ensure employees are updated regarding current developments in the financial services industry?

    ___yes   ___no   ___some knowledge in this area

8. Are you actively involved in the referral of applicants for potential employment with the Bank?

    ___yes   ___no   ___somewhat involved

Additional comments regarding this section that you would like to make:

Section VIII—General Assessment

1. Do you feel we should have a formal training program for Board members?

    ___yes   ___no

2. Please indicate your strongest areas of expertise, based on either your personal experience or your background.

___Real Estate Lending   ___Marketing

___Commercial Lending   ___Public Relations

___Consumer Lending   ___Government Relations

___Investments   ___Corporate Business

___Finance/Budget   ___Management

___Legal Affairs   ___Employee Relations

___Trusts   ___Benefit Packages

___Agribusiness   ___Small Business

___Planning   ___Other - Please specify_____

3. Please indicate any areas from the list above in which you would like to become more knowledgeable:

4. How would you rate yourself in the following areas as they relate to your membership on the Board of Directors? (A rating of "1" being poor, a rating of "3" being within the realm of my ability and expertise, and a rating of "5" being outstanding.)

	Poor			Outstanding	
Stock Ownership	1	2	3	4	5
Quality of input to management, officers and the Board	1	2	3	4	5
Value of your business both loan and deposit	1	2	3	4	5
Amount of business you influence to the Bank	1	2	3	4	5
Prospects you provide	1	2	3	4	5
Business you save	1	2	3	4	5

Your committee service   1   2   3   4   5

Your leadership value
   as Chairman, Committee
   Chairman, or head of
   task forces.   1   2   3   4   5

Your overall rating as
   a Board member   1   2   3   4   5

5. What issues have most occupied the Board's attention during the last year?

6. What issues during the last year, should have been given the Board's attention, but were not covered?

7. What issues covered during the last year were not appropriate and should not have been discussed?

8. What goals did the Board accomplish during the last year?

9. What problems did the Board encounter in its performance during the last year?

10. Have you any goals to set for yourself for the coming year to strengthen your performance as a Board member?

Additional comments regarding this section that you would like to make:

Any other comments you would like to make regarding the Board, your membership, the Bank, its Officers, management, or the employees.

Appendix Three

Executive Compensation Policies and Procedures

Assigning Application Accounts to Customers

To facilitate the Book of Business concept each application account (e.g., DDA, Savings, CD, Commercial Loan, etc.) may be assigned to one and only one customer. This prevents counting application account balances and income more than once. If multiple customers share a single application account, such as when more than one borrower co-signs a note, a determination must be made as to which customer will receive credit for the account. This information must be communicated to loan operations so that the loan is properly boarded on the CIF (Customer Information File) system. Disputes between officers as to which customer is to receive credit must be resolved according to the Dispute Resolution Procedures. Once account assignments are designated, they cannot be changed without written authorization from the officer's Regional Administrator (RA).

To maintain CIF integrity, each new customer established on the CIF system *must* have a valid Social Security Number or Tax Identification Number. To encourage this, officers will *not be credited* with opening new accounts *unless a valid SSN or TIN is obtained.*

To receive proper credit for opening a new account, the responsible officer must indicate his or her *officer number and branch* on the signature card (for deposit accounts) or boarding document (for loan accounts). The account will be established on the CIF system as a "Book of Business" customer; personal accounts will be programmed with a customer type 21, commercial accounts will be programmed with a customer type 02 on the IF1A screen.

Assigning Customers to the Branch

New customers will be assigned to the branch that opens the account. Once a customer has been assigned to a branch, it cannot be changed without written authorization from the RA. If there is a dispute about which branch a customer is assigned to for the purposes of Book of Business, it must be resolved according to the Dispute Resolution Procedures.

Assigning New Customers to Officers Within a Branch

New customers will be assigned to the officer responsible for opening the account. To receive proper credit for the customer's account, the officer must clearly designate his or her officer number in the OFFICER CODE column of the signature card for deposit accounts, or in the space designated for officer number on the loan boarding documents. Once a customer has been assigned to an officer, the assignment cannot be changed without written authorization from the RA. Disputes about which officer is to be assigned to which customer must be resolved according to the Dispute Resolution Procedures.

Assigning Existing Customers to Officers Within a Branch

Substantial solicitation of new business from an existing customer must be evident to add an existing account relationship to an officer's Book of Business. Solicitation of the new business must be documented with call reports, pipeline reports, and profiling form, etc. Existing clients may only be added to an individual officer's Book of Business *with the Branch Sales Manager's and Regional Administrator's approval **provided** that the officer has the appropriate documentation of proactively soliciting new business from the client.*

Assigning "Walk-in" Customers to Officers Within a Branch

Non-solicited walk-in business contributes to the branch's overall profit performance and all participants in the branch portion of the incentive compensation plan benefit from these account relationships. Therefore, walk-in clients may only be added to an individual officer's Book of Business *with the Branch Sales Manager's and Regional Administrator's approval **provided** that the officer has the appropriate documentation (call/pipeline reports, profiling form, etc.) of proactively soliciting the client's business.*

Officer Resignations or Reassignments

In the event that an officer transfers to another branch or resigns from the bank, the officer's Book of Business will be reassigned as follows. The appropriate RA must give written authorization whenever an account is changed from one officer to another or from one branch to another.

1. If the officer leaves the bank and is replaced by a new officer, every effort should be made to allow the new officer to assume the resigning officer's entire Book of Business. The new officer's number will be assigned to the accounts in the Book. A photocopy of the resigning officer's Book of Business should be sent to the appropriate RA for approval and then forwarded to the Customer Profitability Department who will input the necessary changes to each customer's CIF.

2. If it is necessary to reassign accounts from the resigning officer's Book of Business to another account officer(s), the new officer(s)' number must be assigned to the accounts assumed by that officer. A photocopy of the resigning officer's Book of Business should be sent to the appropriate RA for approval and then forwarded to the Customer Profitability Department who will

input the necessary changes to each customer's CIF. The officer(s)' Threshold and Base performance levels may be adjusted to reflect the addition of the new accounts to the officer(s)' Book.

3. If an officer transfers to another branch, the officer may transfer selected accounts to his or her new Book of Business. The officer must send a maintenance request approved by his or her RA to the Customer Profitability Department to have the branch number changed on the customer's CIF. However, every effort should be made to leave the accounts in the originating branch.

Dispute Resolution Procedures

Any disputes involving the assignment of customer's accounts to a particular officer's Book of Business will be resolved as follows:

- If the dispute is between officers within the same branch, the dispute will be resolved by the branch's Sales Manager. Once the customer has been assigned to an officer, the assignment cannot be changed without written authorization from the appropriate RA.
- If the dispute is between officers of different branches within the same region, the dispute will be resolved by the RA.
- If the dispute is between officers or branches of different regions, the dispute will be resolved by the Manager of the Banking Division.

Loan Fees

Currently, the bank does not record loan fees collected from the customer on its loan application systems; instead, loan fees are posted directly to the general ledger by the loan operations and branch personnel. Since loan fees are not accounted for in the loan application systems, the Profitability System does not have an automated method of reflecting the collection of these fees for each account on the Profitability System. Therefore, customers are not credited with these amounts in the profitability calculation for their accounts.

To correctly account for these fees in the profitability calculation, each branch officer or loan operations person who processes loan fees must *record the customer's CIF account number on the general ledger ticket*. The GL tickets will be retrieved from the Controller's Department each month and the loan fees will be manually credited to the customer's profitability account. If the customer's CIF number is not recorded on the GL ticket, the officer's Book of Business will not reflect credit for the fees.

This policy applies to the following fee accounts:

- Portfolio Real Estate Fees
- Loan Origination Fees - Construction
- Loan Extension Fees - Construction
- Commitment Fees - Construction
- Loan Origination Fees - Commercial
- Other Income - Commercial Loans
- Commercial Loan Leasing Fee Income
- Loan Origination Fees - Installment
- PCL Reserve Line Fees

Other fees, such as document fees or appraisal fees, will not be credited to the officer's Book of Business at this time.

Loan fees under $500.00 will be credited in full to the officer's Book for the month in which they are earned. Loan fees over $500.00 will be amortized over the life of the loan according to the bank's policy for the accounting of loan fees and will be credited monthly to the officer's Book.

Financial Sales Officer Incentives Program

Participants

Sales Managers, Financial Sales Officers and Branch Service Officers (if applicable) are eligible to participate in the Book of Business (Book) Incentive Compensation Program.

Note: Hereafter, all references to the "FSO" is defined to include eligible FSOs and BSOs.

Incentive Compensation

The Book Incentive Compensation program is based on the amount by which the FSO's Approved Book Profit exceeds the FSO's Approved Base Profit.

Establishing Threshold, Target, and Outstanding Performance Level Amounts for the Book of Business

The Bank will assign quarterly Threshold, Target and Outstanding performance level amounts to each FSO's Book based on the officer's position level (e.g. FSO I, II, or III), the market area in which the FSO works, and the goals established for the FSO's branch which are based on the Bank's annual objectives.

Achievement of the Threshold, Target and Outstanding performance level amounts determines the rate at which the FSO accrues his or her profit incentive.

Book of Business Incentive Payment Accruals

An FSO will earn Book Incentive Compensation according to the following schedule. If an FSO does not achieve the THRESHOLD performance level amount established for his or her Book, then no performance incentive is earned.

1. Achievement of THRESHOLD Amount: 20% times the amount by which the Approved Book Profit amount exceeds the Approved Base Profit amount.

2. Achievement of TARGET Amount: 40% times the amount by which the Approved Book Profit amount exceeds the Approved Base Profit amount.

3. Achievement of OUTSTANDING Amount: 60% times the amount by which the Approved Book Profit amount exceeds the Approved Base Profit amount.

If the branch achieves a minimum Threshold performance level, the Sales Manager will earn an incentive override of 50% of the total Book Incentive Compensation amount paid to the FSOs assigned to his or her branch. However, *if no funds are accrued in the Branch Incentive Compensation pool,* and the branch achieves a minimum Threshold performance level, the 50% incentive override will be shared between the Sales Manager (30%) and the CSM (20%).

Timing and Retension of Incentive Compensation

At the end of each quarter, the performance incentive compensation amount for each Book of Business will be calculated. Employees will receive 75% of their Book performance incentive no later than the third pay period following quarter-end. If the remaining 25% of the Book Incentive is less than $100, the employee will receive the full incentive earned for that quarter.

If the remaining 25% of the Book performance incentive amount is $100 or more, it will be retained for the participant until the end of the year. The accumulated amount retained each quarter will be paid to that participant if the participant achieves his or her Threshold performance level amount (or better) at the end of the fourth quarter. Incentive compensation amounts that are retained throughout the year will be paid no later than the third pay period following year-end.

Branch Incentive Compensation Program

Participants

Sales Managers, Customer Service Managers, Financial Sales Officers, and Branch Service Officers (if applicable) are eligible to participate in the Branch Incentive Compensation Program.

Incentive Compensation

The Branch Incentive Compensation Program is based on the amount by which the Branch's Approved Profit amount exceeds the Branch's Approved Base Profit amount.

Establishing Threshold, Target, and Outstanding Performance Level Amounts for the Branch

The Bank will assign quarterly Threshold, Target, and Outstanding performance level amounts for each Branch based on the Bank's annual objectives.

Achievement of the Threshold, Target, and Outstanding performance level amounts determines the rate at which the Branch accrues a profit incentive compensation pool.

Branch Incentive Payment Accruals

The Branch will accrue a profit incentive compensation pool according to the following schedule. If the Branch does not achieve the THRESHOLD amount established for the Branch, then no profit incentive dollars are accrued for the Branch's performance incentive compensation pool.

1. Achievement of THRESHOLD Amount: 20% times the amount by which the Branch's Approved Profit amount exceeds the Branch's Approved Base Profit amount.

2. Achievement of TARGET Amount: 40% times the amount by which the Branch's Approved Profit amount exceeds the Branch's Approved Base Profit amount.

3. Achievement of OUTSTANDING Amount: 60% times the amount by which the Branch's Approved Profit amount exceeds the Branch's Approved Base Profit amount.

Timing and Retention of Incentive Compensation

At the end of each quarter, the performance incentive compensation amount for each Branch will be calculated. Branch participants will receive 75% of the branch's performance incentive no later than the third pay period following quarter-end. If the remaining 25% of the branch performance incentive is less than $100, the participants will receive the full incentive earned for that quarter.

If the remaining 25% of the branch performance incentive compensation amount is $100 or more, it will be retained for the branch until the end of the year. The accumulated amount retained each quarter will be paid to the Branch participants after the fourth quarter if the Branch achieves their Threshold performance level amount (or better) at the end of the fourth quarter. Incentive compensation amounts that are retained throughout the year will be paid no later than the third pay period following year-end.

Distribution of the Performance Incentive Pool

The amount accrued in the Branch Performance Incentive Compensation Pool will be distributed as follows, unless otherwise specified by the Banking Division Manager and/or the Incentive Compensation Review Committee.

30%   Sales Manager

20%   Customer Service Manager

50%   Financial Sales Officers

The FSO's portion of the Branch pool is divided among the FSOs in direct proportion to the Book Incentive amount earned by each FSO.

For example: Total Branch Incentive Compensation = $4,000

Total FSO portion of the Branch Pool = (50%)

FSO	Book Incentive Earned	% of Total Earned	FSO Portion of Branch Pool	Branch Iincentive Earned
FSO A	$ 400	40%	40% × $2,000	$800
FSO B	$ 500	50%	50% × $2,000	$1,000
FSO C	$ 100	10%	10% × $2,000	$200
TOTAL:	$1,000	100%		$2,000

Assistant Customer Service Manager Incentive Program

As an Assistant Customer Service Manager you are responsible for ensuring quality service through a well trained and developed operations staff. Your pay package — base salary plus incentives — is designed to reward you for accomplishing your objectives.

This brochure describes the key components of your pay package plus performance standards used as promotional guidelines.

Please review the information carefully. Your Customer Service Manager will be happy to clarify or answer any questions you may have.

Components

The Assistant Customer Service Manager (ACSM) pay package is made up of two components: base pay and monthly incentive pay.

I. Base Pay

Base pay is the salary you earn based on your assigned grade and performance level. As the name implies, base pay is what the Bank pays you for expected performance.

Since your job is incented, base pay is limited to a "target salary" specific to your grade level. These target salaries for 1993 are listed below:

Job Title	Salary Grade	Target Salary*
ACSM I	20	$/month
ACSM II	21	$/month
ACSM IIB	21	$/month

* Amounts based on a 40-hour work week; prorated for fewer hours

II. Incentive Pay

There are two ways you can receive monthly incentives: individually through referrals and through an override on incentives earned by the eligible tellers and Branch Service Officers assigned to the branch.

1. Referral Incentives:

   You receive monthly incentive dollars when a client books a bank product or service you suggested. These referral incentives are tightly linked to the goals of the Bank; you will receive updates on the referral product/incentive fee schedule as changes occur.

2. Override Incentives:

10% Referral Override Incentive:

   You will receive 10% of the total incentive dollars paid for the month to eligible tellers and BSOs assigned to the branch, if the branch meets its Referrals Per FTE goal for the month but the minimum number of eligible tellers/BSOs do not achieve regular or premium performance and minimum monthly referral requirements.

- OR -

15% Performance Override Incentive:

You will receive 15% of the total incentive dollars paid for the month to eligible tellers and BSOs assigned to the branch, if the specified number of tellers/BSOs outlined in the chart on the following page receive regular or premium performance incentive AND meet or exceed their minimum monthly referral requirement.

Note: The tellers/BSOs who receive performance incentive DO NOT have to be the same tellers who meet referral requirements.

- OR -

20% Override Incentive:

You will receive 20% of the total incentive dollars paid for the month to eligible tellers and BSOs assigned to the branch, if ALL receive their regular or premium performance incentive AND meet their minimum monthly referral requirement.

How the ACSM's Override Incentive is Calculated

The ACSM's Override is calculated based on the information supplied to the Controllers Department on the Teller Incentive Report.

The number of eligible tellers and BSOs who have individually received referral and/or performance incentive is determined. If the branch meets its Referrals per FTE goal for the month, the 10% override is calculated. If the minimum number of eligible tellers/BSOs as specified in the chart on the previous page, or if all eligible tellers/BSOs meet the required criteria, the appropriate (15% or 20%) override is calculated as follows:

1. The referral incentive amount(s) paid to the ACSM, are subtracted from the total incentive amount paid for the month.

2. The result from Step 1 is multiplied by the applicable override percentage (10%, 15% or 20%).

For example:

$ 451.00	Total Incentive Amount earned at branch
− 24.00	ACSM's Referral incentive
$427.00	Amount on which the ACSM's override is calculated

$427.00 × 10% = $42.70 (if branch meets its Referrals Per FTE goal), OR,

$427.00 × 15% = $64.05 (if specified number of eligible tellers meet performance and incentive criteria) OR,

$427.00 × 20% = $85.40 (if all eligible tellers and BSOs meet performance and incentive criteria)

ACSM's Total Compensation for the month based on the example with all eligible tellers meeting performance and incentive criteria:

$1,710.00	Target Base Salary - ACSM I
24.00	ACSM's Referral Incentive
85.40	ACSM's Incentive Override
$1,819.40	Total Compensation for the Month

Represents a 6.4% incentive compensation for the month.

Note : Monthly incentive payments are included in the second paycheck following the month in which they are earned.

Eligibility For Incentive Payout

Employees are eligible to receive incentive payments only if they are active employees at the time of disbursement. Employees who either voluntarily or involuntarily terminate employment after the measurement period but before disbursement of incentives are not eligible to receive incentive payments.

Terminated employees on salary continuation programs and employees on personal leaves of absence at the time of disbursement are considered to be inactive employees for incentive payout purposes, and are therefore not eligible to receive incentive payments.

Employees on other types of leave (including disability, maternity, family care or military leaves) are considered active and eligible to receive incentive payments.

Leave Commencement or Return

An employee eligible to participate in an incentive plan who commences a disability, maternity, family care or military leave after the middle of the incentive measurement period or returns from a disability, maternity, family care or military leave before the middle of the incentive measurement period will participate in the Plan for that period on a prorated basis.

Teller Incentive Program

Tellers Account For 95% of All Customer Contact

For many clients, tellers ARE the Bank. From answering inquiries about opening accounts, through account servicing, to referrals for other bank services, the teller is usually the client's primary resource and point of contact with the Bank. Quality teller - client relationships are critical to our success as a supercommunity bank.

For these reasons, we encourage and reward tellers for building quality client relationships. This is the basis for our teller compensation plan which has two components:

1. Base Salary

2. Monthly Individual Incentives

As a teller, your efforts in helping the Bank achieve its goals will largely determine what your income will be under the incentive portion of the plan.

This document contains an explanation of our two part Teller Salary and Incentive Program plus an outline of promotional criteria. Please take time to review this material. If you have any questions about the program, please contact your Assistant Customer Service Manager or Customer Service Manager.

I. BASE SALARY

Your base salary is determined by your level of experience and your employment status.

A. Salaried Teller

You are considered a "salaried teller" if you are regularly scheduled to work twenty-one (21) hours or more per week. As a salaried teller you can receive employee benefits and are eligible to participate in the Monthly Individual Incentive Program. Your base salary is as follows:

Teller I $/month*

Teller II $/month*

Teller III $/month*

*(Based on 40 hours worked per week; prorated for fewer hours.)

B. Hourly Teller

When you work twenty (20) hours or less per week, you are considered an "hourly teller". Like the salaried teller, you are eligible to participate in the Monthly Individual Incentive Program, but are not eligible to receive employee benefits except vacation. As an hourly teller, your base salary is as follows:

Teller I $/hour

Teller II $/hour

Teller III $/hour

C. On-Call Teller

Depending on the volume of business, the Bank employs "on-call" tellers. In this category you are eligible to participate in the Referrals portion of the Monthly Individual Incentive Plan, but are not eligible to receive employee benefits. In addition, you will receive a $1.00 premium over the established hourly rate for your teller classification level. Base salaries are as follows:

    Teller I $/hour

    Teller II $/hour

    Teller III $/hour

D. Branch Services Officer

A Branch Services Officer (BSO) who spends at least 75% of their time performing teller-type duties are eligible to earn incentive compensation under the Teller Incentive Program. BSO eligibility to participate in the Teller Incentive Program will be agreed upon by the Customer Service Manager and Regional Administrator when the BSO is assigned to the branch. Target salaries are as follows:

Salaried BSO $/month

Hourly BSO $/hour

II. Monthly Individual Incentives

There are two ways tellers and BSOs receive monthly individual incentives: through referrals (open to all tellers and BSOs) and attainment of performance standards (open to salaried and hourly tellers and eligible BSOs).

A Referrals (All Tellers and BSOs)

You receive incentive dollars each time a client books a Bank product or service you suggested. So, it pays for you to know the Bank's products and to talk to your customers about them!

Referral incentives are tightly linked to the goals of the Bank. Please see your Assistant Customer Service or Customer Service Manager for the latest referral incentive fee schedule.

The monies you earn through referrals can continue to grow. When you exceed $35 in referral awards in one month, you earn an additional 20% referral bonus incentive. Or, if the number of referrals is higher than the preceding twelve months' average, you'll earn an additional 10% referral bonus incentive.

B. Attainment of Performance Standards (Salaried and Hourly Tellers and eligible BSOs)

Tellers and BSOs who meet the standards established for attendance and accuracy of their work earn monthly performance incentives. Specifically, to qualify for a **regular** performance bonus you'll need to meet **all of the following standards:**

_   Not more than one unlocated cash difference between $10 and $25

_   No unlocated cash differences over $25

_   No operating losses

_   No more than three proof errors per month if you work between 1-20 hours per week or five proof errors per month if you work 21 hours or more per week.

To qualify for a **premium** performance bonus, you'll need to meet **all of these standards:**

_   No absences from work

_   No unlocated cash differences over $10

_ No operating losses

_ No more than two proof errors per month if you work between 1 and 20 hours per week or four proof errors per month if you work 21 hours or more per week.

The amount of money you'll earn by achieving these performance standards is based on the average number of hours **worked** performing teller activities per week during each month:

Performance Standard			**Performance Standard**		
Avg Hours Worked*	**Regular**	**Premium**	**Avg Hours Worked**	**Regular**	**Premium**
40	$80	$160	24	$48	$96
39	78	156	23	46	92
38	76	152	22	44	88
37	74	148	21	42	84
36	72	144	20	40	80
35	70	140	19	38	76
34	68	136	18	36	72
33	66	132	17	34	68
32	64	128	16	32	64
31	62	124	15	30	60
30	60	120	14	28	56
29	58	116	13	26	52
28	56	112	12	24	48
27	54	108	11	22	44
26	52	104	10 or less	20	40
25	50	100			

* Average hours actually worked per week.

Summary

We've outlined how the Bank pays its tellers:

1. Base Salary

2. Monthly Individual Incentives

Let's look at an EXAMPLE of how this translates into dollars. Suppose we have a teller who -

_ Is a Teller, Level II - working 40 hours

_ Makes 15 - $2 referrals

_ Achieves premium performance standards

Salary and incentives for this teller would be as follows:

1)   Base Salar $1,275
2)   Individual Incentives
     • Referral (15 × $2 ea) $30
     • Premium Performance Standard   160
                                               ─────
                                                               $190
3)   Total Compensation for the Month $1,465

Represents 14.9% incentive compensation for the month.

Note: **Monthly** incentive payments are included in the second paycheck following the month
             in which they are earned.

Teller Coaches Compensatory Referral Incentive

Teller coaches will be reimbursed for lost referral incentive opportunity while coaching new tellers
in the branch. Coaches will receive a compensatory referral incentive for each two week training
period performed during the month according to the following formula.

A. Calculate the average monthly referral incentive earned by the coach for the most recent three
   months in which they did no training.

For example: Coach did not coach during the following months and earned these referral
                    incentives:

August, 1992 $100.00

September, 1992 $ 50.00

November, 1992 $ 75.00 $225.00 divided by 3 = $75.00 monthly average referral
                                    incentive.

Note: Using this example, assume the branch coach trains in October, does not train in
             November, and trains another teller in December. The compensatory referral incentive
             for December would be calculated on the average monthly referral for August,
             September, and November - the last three months in which no training occurred.

B. Divide the average monthly referral amount by two (weeks) to determine compensatory incentive for each coaching period and multiply by the number of coaching periods completed during
   the month.

For example: $75.00 divided by 2 = $37.50 times 1 coaching period in October = $37.50 for the
                    two weeks compensatory referral incentive.

C. Add the compensatory referral incentive amount to any other referral incentive earned that
   month.

Example: October compensation for the following individual:

_ Coach is a Teller, Level III - working 40 hours.

_ Achieves regular performance standards.

_ Trained one new teller in October.

_ Had an average monthly referral of $75.00.

_ Makes five $2 referrals.

1) Base Salary			$1,000.00
2) Individual Incentive			
• Two Week's Compensatory Referral			
Incentive ($75.00 divided by 2 × 1) =		$37.50	
• Regular Performance Incentive		80.00	
• Referrals (5 × $2 each)		10.00	$127.50
3) Total Compensation for October			$1,127.50

Represents 9.0% incentive compensation for the month.

Eligibility For Incentive Payout

Employees are eligible to receive incentive payments only if they are active employees at the time of disbursement. Employees who either voluntarily or involuntarily terminate employment after the measurement period but before disbursement of incentives are not eligible to receive incentive payments.

Terminated employees on salary continuation programs and employees on personal leaves of absence at the time of disbursement are considered to be inactive employees for incentive payout purposes, and are therefore not eligible to receive incentive payments.

Employees on other types of leave (including disability, maternity, family care or military leaves) are considered active and eligible to receive incentive payments.

Leave Commencement or Return

An employee eligible to participate in an incentive plan who commences a disability, maternity, family care or military leave after the middle of the incentive measurement period or returns from a disability, maternity, family care or military leave before the middle of the incentive measurement period will participate in the Plan for that period on a prorated basis.

Bank Incentive Compensation Plans
Case Study Examples
Outline

I. Objectives

  A. Reward all Levels of Organization for Performance and Profitability

    1. Senior Executives

      a. Group I - Top Executives.

      b. Group II - Senior Management.

    2. Branch (Middle) Management

      a. Sales organization participants.

      b. "Book of Business".

    3. Branch Operations Personnel

      a. Assistant Customer Service Managers.

      b. Tellers.

  B. Link Compensation to Operating Unit Performance.

  C. Increase Employee Communication and Understanding of Company Objectives.

  D. Provide Added Measurement Methods in Employee Evaluation Process.

II. Senior Executive Compensation Plan - Groups I and II

  A. Objectives

    1. Build equity ownership.

    2. Link shareholder return to management compensation.

    3. Create an ownership mentality in senior management.

  B. Three Components

    1. Base salary.

    2. Annual cash bonus.

    3. Long-term stock grants.

      a. Non-qualified options (NQSO).

      b. Restricted Performance Shares (RPS).

  C. Base Salary

    1. Limited to mid-point of range for specific position.

    2. Top executives may receive no increase in base.

    3. Goal is to achieve target compensation levels through increasing incentives - not by increasing base salary.

    4. Provides "base" for computing all other incentives.

D. Annual Cash Bonus

1. Percentage Ranges measured on Base - Rises over Time.

    a. Group I - 25% to 60%.

    b. Group II - 15% to 20%.

2. Paid based on achievement of objectives - corporate, division department, individual.

3. Levels of achievement determine percentage paid.

    a. Below "Threshold" - 0%.

    b. Threshold - 75%.

    c. Target - 100%.

    d. Outstanding - 150%.

4. Weighting of objectives varies by position - in general, the higher the position, the greater weight on corporate performance (Example: CEO = 75% corporate; 25% individual).

E. NQSO Grants

1. Annual award using measurement methods similar to cash bonus.

2. Vest _ each year for 3 years.

3. Grant price established each year based on stock's fair market value.

F. RPS Grants

1. Only Group I executives participate.

2. Based on achievement of 3-year corporate objectives.

3. If objectives are not met - grant is zero

4. New 3-year plan is established each year (roll forward, "evergreen" concept).

G. Administration

1. Board establishes annual and 3-year corporate objectives each year.

2. Bonuses and stock grants are awarded in first quarter of year following performance measurement year.

3. Employee Benefits Committee of Board makes final decisions on all awards/grants.

4. Failure to meet significant individual goals may result in no incentive awards.

III. **Branch Management Plan**

A. Objectives

1. Link compensation to profit performance of inventory of customer accounts.

2. Link compensation to overall performance of branch.

B. Two Components

1. "Book of Business" profitability.

2. Branch profitability.

C. Participants

1. Branch Sales Managers, Customer Service Managers (CSM's), Financial Sales Officers (FSO's) and Branch Service Officers (BSO's).

2. CSM's participate in Branch profitability incentives only.

D. Methods of Measurement

1. Achievement of performance levels exceeding preset base profit amounts.

2. Based primarily on new business acquisition (loans and low-cost deposits) and customer retention.

3. Accrual made using Threshold, Target and Outstanding achievement levels (20%-40%-60%) over preset base amounts.

E. Allocation and Payment of Incentive Amounts

1. Book of Business portion

a. FSO/BSO receives 75% of earned incentive each quarter; balance of 25% after year-end.

b. Branch Manager receives override of 50% of FSO totals if minimum threshold levels are met.

2. Branch Incentive portion

a. Payments structure same as Book of Business (see E.1. a. above).

b. Allocation of incentive pool to Branch Manager, CSM and FSO's is 30%-20%-50%.

c. 50% FSO portion reallocated to FSO's based on Book of Business incentive amount earned.

F. Administration

1. Quarterly goals for each branch and FSO are set by Branch Manager and Regional Marketing Manager.

2. Policies and Procedures are in place for:

a. Assignment of new and existing customers to bank officers.

b. Assignment of accounts to customers.

c. Resolution of Disputes.

d. Treatment of unusual or nonrecurring adjustments.

IV. Branch Operations Plan

A. Objectives

1. Maintain high levels of customer service.

2. Create awareness of and focus on bank objectives.

B. Two Components

1. Customer referrals.

2. Attainment of operating performance standards.

C. Participants
   1. Tellers.
   2. Assistant Customer Service Managers (ACSM's).
D. Methods of Measurement
   1. Referral fee per bank product booked based on schedule of fees for each type of product.
   2. Can receive up to 4 times number of average hours worked per week (in dollars).
   3. ACSM's receive 10%-20% overrides on teller incentive payments earned depending on level of operating performance and referrals achieved.
E. Payment of awards are made monthly in cash.
F. Administration
   1. Tied to guidelines for promotion eligibility.
   2. Plan managed by Banking Division and Controller's Division.

APPENDIX FOUR

Due Diligence Work Program*

Bank		Date	

Section of Work Financial Statement Review and General Diligence (Project 1)

Due Diligence Scope and Procedures Revised February 1, 1991	Work Paper Ref.	Prepared By	Reviewed By
Scope			
Review and analysis of historical financial data.			
Procedures			
1. Review consolidated and consolidating historical financial data for the last two fiscal years ended _____ and the most recent _____ months ended_____. Profile significant balances and analyze variances, isolate unusual and nonrecurring items, etc., and summarize. Such information should include audited financial statements, FRY-6, FRY-9, etc.			

* Courtesy of Marquette Bancshares

Bank   Date

Section of Work Financial Statement Review and General Diligence (Project 1)

Due Diligence Scope and Procedures Revised February 1, 1991	Work Paper Ref.	Prepared By	Reviewed By
2. Review all significant accounting policies, procedures and practices with the chief financial officer and controller. Document variances from those disclosed in the annual report and summarize significant undisclosed policies. Obtain a copy of any published policies and procedures.			
3. Contact the public accounting firm representatives for the bank and review workpapers and make inquiries related to the above periods.			
4. Review management letters for the prior three years.			
5. Obtain copies of minutes of all board and committee meetings; review and summarize.			
6. Obtain full audit committee packages (all exhibits and handouts) for the past three years, review and summarize.			
7. Obtain a copy of the bank's business plan or its equivalent; review and summarize.			
8. Obtain a copy of the short term and long range forecasts; review and summarize.			
9. Obtain a comprehensive list of all nonloan contracts. Discuss these contracts with the in-house counsel and the chief financial or executive officer and identify all key contracts. Note that certain contracts may be reviewed in other project areas such as leases for facilities, insurance, etc. Summarize these discussions and distribute copies of significant contracts to other project leaders.			
10. Review and inquire concerning all related party relationships, transactions, violations of laws, sensitive payments, etc.; review and summarize.			
11. Inquire and establish an understanding of deposits, loans, arrangements, relationships, etc., regarding non-U.S. parties; review and summarize.			
12. Establish an understanding of all interbank activities and transactions. Review, summarize and pursue, as required.			

Bank   Date

Section of Work   Credit Quality (Project 2)

Due Diligence Scope and Procedures Revised February 1, 1991	Work Paper Ref.	Prepared By	Reviewed By
Scope			
To identify and quantify: additions to or downgrades of criticized loans; additional reserves needed for criticized assets; loans which should be placed on nonaccrual; potential nonperforming loans; and on a macro basis, the estimated present value of future cash flows cash flows from collection of loans and REO.			
Procedures			
1. Summarize loan portfolios by type, both dollar amounts and percentages of the total loan portfolio.			
2. Obtain and review past due, nonaccrual, overdraft and loan watch lists. In addition, obtain and review special watch lists developed for Board of Directors meetings and loans recently reviewed by examiners.			
3. Obtain and review loan or lending policies.			
4. Perform a specific review of loans included on the reports mentioned in 2 above.			
a. Obtain the appropriate loan file with appropriate bank personnel. Review and discuss the loan with applicable person.			
b. Review loan file documentation standards.			
c. Review lending practices performed on this loan to the loan or lending policies for conformity.			
d. Determine the need for a specific loan loss reserve on this loan. Determine a "best/worst" case estimate.			
5. For loans not specifically reviewed, determined a general reserve balance using UCC Loan Administration guidelines.			
6. Summarize best and worst case totals, compare to the reserve for loan loss balance per books for reasonableness. Make recommendations regarding specific loans or the adequacy of the loan loss reserve.			

Bank		Date	

Section of Work   Credit Quality (Project 2)

Due Diligence Scope and Procedures **Revised February 1, 1991**	**Work** **Paper Ref.**	**Prepared** **By**	**Reviewed** **By**
7. Determine existence of large, old overdrafts and the daily monitoring of overdrafts.			
8. Determine existence of overlines purchased or sold.			
9. Review list of Other Real Estate Owned (OREO) and perform the following:			
a. Review accounting and mark-to-market procedures used by bank personnel.			
b. Perform specific review procedures to assess market value of the OREO compared to current book value, to determine any potential liability arising from environmental factors related to OREO, and to determine the extent of other claims on the OREO.			
c. Summarize OREO properties and observations.			

Bank	Date

Section of Work   Investments (Project 3)

Due Diligence Scope and Procedures Revised February 1, 1991	Work Paper Ref.	Prepared By	Reviewed By
Scope			
Address the required "mark-to-market" adjustments for the investment portfolio and summarize the nature of all "nontraditional" investments.			
Procedures			
1. Obtain investment policy approved by Board of Directors.			
2. Obtain and review a detailed profile of the investment portfolios specifying cost, market par values and maturity of all investments.			
3. Determine the location of and the necessity to verify the existence/ownership of major investments.			
4. Inquire and investigate as to the status of account reconciliations in this area and isolate unreconciled balances.			
5. Establish an understanding of the bank's valuation, amortization and accrual policies. Evaluate the propriety of these policies and review specific accounts.			
6. Determine market value adjustments by portfolio.			
7. Determine significance of any possible near/intermediate term disposition plans.			
8. Determine the nature of and policies related to interest rate SWAPs, hedging of futures transactions and the status of any current open contracts.			
9. Determine the nature of and policies related to repurchase or reverse repurchase contracts.			
10. Determine the nature of and policies related to any trading accounts or other nontraditional investment activities.			
11. Summarize escrow/pledging agreements.			
12. Identify total nontaxable securities for use in income tax planning considerations.			

Bank			Date	

Section of Work   Funding and Liquidity (Project 4)

Due Diligence Scope and Procedures **Revised February 1, 1991**	**Work** **Paper Ref.**	**Prepared** **By**	**Reviewed** **By**

Scope
Review the funding and liquidity policies employed and address the current and projected funding liquidity position of the bank on a consolidated basis and by individual unit bank as required.
 	
Procedures
1. Review funding and liquidity position and policies with management of holding company or lead bank to determine status of:
 	
  - Excess liquidity
  - Summary deposit trend over last 12 months and projections for next 6 months
  - Amounts of cross-border deposits
  - Foreign currency exposure
  - Nature and extent of significant deposit marketing or growth efforts
  - Nature of the largest depositors and the significance of their deposits to the company's funding
  - Nature and extent of use of futures, hedges and resultant exposures
  - Asset/liability management process and current interest rate exposures
 	
2. Review status of Federal Reserve or other back-up funding arrangements:
 	
  - Nature and amount of borrowing available
  - Amount of potential borrowing available
  - Recent or anticipated borrowing needs
 	
3. Determine nature of parent company cash flow requirements over next 6 to 12 months and determine how these needs will be met.
 	
4. Summarize status of current parent company, subsidiary or intercompany borrowing arrangements.			

Bank	Date

Section of Work   Funding and Liquidity (Project 4)

Due Diligence Scope and Procedures Revised February 1, 1991	Work Paper Ref.	Prepared By	Reviewed By
5. Inquire and investigate as to the status of account reconciliations in this area and isolate unreconciled balances.			
6. Review methods and evaluate propriety of interest accruals.			

Bank   Date
_____

Section of Work   Other Assets (Project 5)

Due Diligence Scope and Procedures Revised February 1, 1991	Work Paper Ref.	Prepared By	Reviewed By
Scope Summarize the nature and balances of the components of other assets and assess current value and realizability. **Procedures** 1. Obtain a summary of the components of other assets. Explain significant variations in balances over the last two years. 2. Verify existence of significant balances, as appropriate. 3. Summarize realizability and support for conclusions of this project.			

Bank	Date

Section of Work   Liabilities and Debt (Project 6)

Due Diligence Scope and Procedures Revised February 1, 1991	Work Paper Ref.	Prepared By	Reviewed By
Scope Ensure all liabilities and obligations are properly recognized and recorded and that all outstanding debt obligations are properly recorded and covenants, restrictions, etc., are fully identified and properly disclosed. Commitments and contingencies, tax liabilities and compensation related obligations are addressed in separate project areas. **Procedures** 1. Perform a variation analysis of the accrued liability balances of the latest financial statements with the balances of the previous yearend. 2. Discuss accounting policies and procedures for liability recognition and address monthly cutoff procedures with the chief financial officer, controller(s) and/or internal auditor(s). 3. Ensure that normal, recurring accruals have been properly accounted for such as accrued vacation, salaries and wages, real estate and property taxes, operation expense accruals, etc. 4. Determine to what extent, if any, that subsequent payment or other verification procedures are appropriate. 5. Obtain copies and review all borrowing contracts. 6. Summarize all outstanding debt obligations and document significant terms, covenants and restrictions.			

Bank   Date
_____

Section of Work   Income Taxes (Project 7)

Due Diligence Scope and Procedures Revised February 1, 1991	Work Paper Ref.	Prepared By	Reviewed By
Scope Determine any material tax risks or exposure areas in federal income taxes, state income and franchise taxes, and information reporting, including the status of any current RARs. Determine the current tax position of the financial institution, including refund potential, loss and credit carry-forwards available and their expiration dates, any SRLY limitations, and refund claims pending. **Procedures** 1. Review federal income tax returns for all open years and summarize significant issues. 2. Review form 1139 carryback claims and form 1120X filings, State Franchise Tax return filings, federal RAR reports and any proposed assessments, pending adjustments, etc., for open RARs. 3. Discuss status of the last two years income tax returns. 4. Review projection data regarding the current year's tax position and develop strategy for summarizing utilization of net operating loss carryforwards, if they exist. 5. Discuss information reporting compliance procedures with tax director or appropriate bank personnel. 6. Discuss state income tax return filings and review returns, if material. 7. Discuss any state income, franchise, sales and use or property tax examinations in progress or unresolved issues. 8. Review analysis of "cushion" and discuss with tax director. 9. Review any FASB 96 calculations performed. Discuss status of implementations and any analysis of adoption methods performed.			

Bank   Date
_____

Section of Work   Commitments, Contingencies and Litigation (Project 8)

Due Diligence Scope and Procedures Revised February 1, 1991	Work Paper Ref.	Prepared By	Reviewed By
Scope			
Address all contingent commitments and potential liabilities that will not be addressed in connection with our diligence procedures on other project areas. Other work plans currently address the following:			
- Credit Quality - loan commitments, letters of credit, etc.			
- Funding and Liquidity - Interest rate swaps, caps and futures.			
- Income Taxes - All contingent tax matters and accruals.			
- Compensation - All benefit plan obligations.			
- Facilities Management - Lease commitments.			
- Data Processing - Service and maintenance contracts and commitments.			
- Compliance and Examination - Compliance with laws and regulations.			
However, this area will be responsible for summarizing commitments and contingencies across all project areas.			
Procedures			
1. Contract Review - Obtain, review and summarize all significant contractual obligations not addressed in other project areas. Such contracts may include advertising, maintenance services, consulting arrangements, sale and purchase obligations, and loan service commitments and arrangements.			
2. Inquiries - Inquire of the chief executive and financial officers, in-house legal counsel and other appropriate personnel and those individuals authorized to enter into contractual commitments, as well as the existence of commitments and contingencies not previously identified.			
3. Disbursements Review - Analyze appropriate expense accounts and major disbursements to ensure such payments relate to contractual commitments which have been identified and summarized.			

Bank   Date
_____

Section of Work   Commitments, Contingencies and Litigation (Project 8)

Due Diligence Scope and Procedures Revised February 1, 1991	Work Paper Ref.	Prepared By	Reviewed By
4. Litigation - Obtain a summary of all outstanding and potential legal claims not otherwise in the Credit Quality and Trust project areas. Upon discussion and analysis with internal and external counsel, summarize the nature of the claims, the potential range of exposure, including legal fees, management's and counsel's assessment of an unfavorable outcome (i.e., settlement or vigorous defense).			
5. Circulate legal counsel representing the banks and coordinate your review in this area with the MEI/BSI counsel.			
6. Prepare a concise summary of all commitments, contingencies and significant litigation.			

Bank			Date

Section of Work   Nonbanking Operational and Financial Review (Project 9)

Due Diligence Scope and Procedures Revised February 1, 1991	Work Paper Ref.	Prepared By	Reviewed By
Scope			
Summarize the principal nonbanking activities: assess the overall operational and control environment employed to manage these operations; address compliance with the applicable regulatory rules and regulations; and summarize the significant commitments and risks of such operations.			
Procedures			
1. Summarize the principal nonbanking operations activities. Obtain information concerning personnel requirements, organizational and reporting structure and the level of earnings/losses of such activities.			
2. In connection with the Internal Audit and the Compliance and Examination work plans, review the scope of internal audit's and external examiners' review over nonbanking operations and discuss the impact of their findings upon the scope of our work in this area.			
3. Brokerage - Document the scope of the brokerage operation in terms of securities held in inventory, customers and data processing systems to support brokerage activities.			
4. Insurance - Summarize the insurance products marketed and assess the risk, if any, which the operations undertake.			
5. Underwriting - Document the scope of the underwriting operation and the types of products underwritten. Assess the risk, if any, which the operations undertake.			

Bank		Date	

Section of Work   Budgetary Analysis and Prospective Financial Modeling (Project 10)

Due Diligence Scope and Procedures **Revised February 1, 1991**	**Work** **Paper Ref.**	**Prepared** **By**	**Reviewed** **By**
Scope In connection with this transaction, the conduct of a thorough budgetary analysis and the development of prospective financial models reflecting the transaction are effective due diligence activities and may be necessary for completion of the merger and assistance agreements and various regulatory filings. Our review will be focused on establishing a thorough understanding of the current planning and budgetary functions and the latest budgets and planning materials. **Procedures** 1. Obtain the bank's most recent consolidating budgetary package and review with the chief financial officer. 2. Establish an understanding as to how the budget is prepared and the key assumptions used. 3. Establish an understanding of the support for the key assumption. 4. Evaluate actual performance in comparison to budgeted results and isolate and understand key variances. 5. Obtain and review the bank's most recent business plan and forecast data and perform procedures similar to those outlined above. 6. Prepare combined prospective financial data and review with key MEI and BSI management. Such data should be constructed to focus on operating results and cash flow data.			

Bank			Date

Section of Work   Organization and Administration Review (Project 11)

Due Diligence Scope and Procedures Revised February 1, 1991	Work Paper Ref.	Prepared By	Reviewed By
Scope and Procedures:			

Scope and Procedures:

1. Establish a thorough understanding of the legal and operational organization of the financial institution(s).

2. Review each institution on a functional or activity basis and develop information along these lines for personnel, direct and indirect costs, revenues, profitability, etc.

3. Review the legal, operational and reporting relationship between the holding companies, lead banks, unit banks and branches.

4. Thoroughly review the entire organization chart starting at the director level.

5. Be sensitive to all relationship matters at all levels and among the associated banks, depositors and borrowers.

6. Develop an understanding of nonbank operations and coordinate with the separate review being performed in those areas.

7. Coordinate with participating counsel on such matters as:

   a. Stock certificate reviews

   b. Reviews of corporate articles and bylaws

   c. Review of charters, minutes, etc.

   d. Validity and clearance of titles, etc.

8. Summarize observations resulting from the above and coordinate follow-up activities as required in other affected project areas.

9. Develop issues and observations to be used in the merger management planning efforts.

Bank	Date

Section of Work   Compensation Profile and Analysis (Project 12)

Due Diligence Scope and Procedures Revised February 1, 1991	Work Paper Ref.	Prepared By	Reviewed By
Scope Summarize cash and noncash compensation paid to employees, officers and directors and address significant commitments related to providing employee benefits.			

Procedures

1. Summarize compensation programs for existing executive management.

2. Obtain a listing of the 100 highest compensated individuals in descending order.

3. Have the bank profile the remaining employees by category for current annual compensation, as follows:

$100,000 and above	_____
$75,000 to $100,000	_____
$50,000 to $75,000	_____
$25,000 to $50,000	_____
$25,000 or less	_____

4. Summarize all significant employee benefit plans and quantify future commitments and obligations.

5. Obtain copies of all significant employee retirement benefit plans, actuarial valuations and related documents.

6. Summarize obligations and funding status for all compensation programs.

7. Review actuarial assumptions as compared to actual experience and explain significant variances.

8. Identify, profile and obtain documentation addressing the following programs and all other employee benefit and compensation programs not specified:

   a. Vacation and holiday

   b. Severance

   c. Sick leave/pregnancy, etc.

   d. Insurance programs including workers' compensation, disability, medical and dental.

   e. Education assistance programs

Bank   Date

Section of Work   Compensation Profile and Analysis (Project 12)

Due Diligence Scope and Procedures Revised February 1, 1991	Work Paper Ref.	Prepared By	Reviewed By
9. Determine to what extent the institution offers post-retirement benefits and summarize.			
10. Summarize option programs and determine how they will be treated in the merger (cancelled, exchanged, cashed out, etc.).			
11. Summarize results in this program area and indicate issues for further consideration.			

Bank	Date

Section of Work Facilities Management (Project 13)

Due Diligence Scope and Procedures **Revised February 1, 1991**	**Work Paper Ref.**	**Prepared By**	**Reviewed By**
Scope Address commitments to existing and future facilities and provide a summary of the carrying value of bank premises by location and an assessment of current market value.			

Procedures

1. Obtain a summary listing and description of existing property and facilities by location including a general description of the condition of such facilities and whether they are owned or leased.

2. Obtain copies of all significant lease agreements and summarize in terms of facilities leased, term, rate and any unusual provisions such as purchase options, rent escalations, commitments to add additional space, etc.

3. For owned facilities, summarize commitments to major tenants in term of rate, term and any unusual terms.

4. Select key facilities to visit and inspect to evaluate condition and market value.

5. Inquire as to the existence of any violation of building codes or EPA requirements (e.g., asbestos).

6. Obtain an overall evaluation on the fair market value of existing facilities by location and revalue significant lease arrangement at current market rates.

7. Coordinate activities in this area with designed MEI/BSI consultants as needed. Summarize results for use in an overall merger/acquisition report.

Bank	Date

Section of Work   Trust Department Review (Project 14)

Due Diligence Scope and Procedures Revised February 1, 1991	**Work Paper Ref.**	**Prepared By**	**Reviewed By**
Scope			
Obtain an understanding of Trust Department operations and address compliance with regulatory/fiduciary requirements and summarize significant pending or threatened litigation related to the trust function.			
Procedures			
1. Obtain trust organization chart and review management reporting lines.			
2. Arrange to meet with individuals responsible for key areas (trust administration, operations, property management, employee benefits, systems support, securities processing, accounting, etc.).			
3. Inquire as to any significant non-traditional or special trust arrangements. Review related contracts and documents as appropriate.			
4. Through inquiry and discussions with trust officers, attempt to determine sensitivity and loyalty of trust client base.			
5. Obtain and review trust statement of operations (P&L) for the past two years and most recent interim period. Obtain and evaluate relevant operating statistics (recurring trust fees, fees for special services, personnel costs, general and administrative expenses, etc.).			
6. Obtain and review the most recent copies of the following reports (as applicable):			
a. Study and evaluation of internal accounting controls (SAS #44)			
b. NYSE transfer agent and registrar function			
c. Other customer or regulator-required (such as Options Clearing Corporation)			
d. Third-party servicer or servicing bureau reviews			

| Bank | Date |

Section of Work   Trust Department Review (Project 14)

Due Diligence Scope and Procedures Revised February 1, 1991	Work Paper Ref.	Prepared By	Reviewed By
With regard to internal audit reports, determine scope (comprehensive, limited, etc.) and review for unsatisfactory/inadequate internal control ratings. Review follow-up performed (if any), as well as current status. Review audit workpapers as appropriate.			
7. Determine management policies and procedures to ensure compliance with Officer of the Comptroller of the Currency (OCC) Regulation No. 9.			
8. Inquire as to any significant pending or threatening litigation arising out of trust operations.			
9. Regarding common trust/collective investment funds:			
a. Inquire as to existence and financial reporting requirements.			
b. Obtain and review most recent annual financial statements.			
10. Inquire as to handling of trust tax return responsibilities.			
11. Evaluate procedures for monitoring actual performance related to investment review and compliance with trust instrument provisions, court orders, etc.			
12. Determine the frequency and effectiveness of physical verification procedures.			
13. Determine and evaluate reconciliation procedures and review latest month-end reconciliation results.			
14. Determine if further verification procedures are warranted.			
15. Determine the nature and extent, if any, where trust services are provided for bond issues and the status thereof.			

Bank	Date

Section of Work   Insurance/Risk Management (Project 15)

Due Diligence Scope and Procedures Revised February 1, 1991	Work Paper Ref.	Prepared By	Reviewed By
Scope Address the adequacy of current insurance overages and summarize the significant claims outstanding as well as any contingent liabilities. **Procedures** 1. Obtain and review all insurance contracts and a summary of insurance coverages (health, accident, life, property, directors' and officers' liability, fiduciary bonding, etc.) including the carrier, amount of coverage, term, cost and policy restrictions. 2. Determine if confirmation with carriers is appropriate. 3. Discuss with appropriate bank personnel and insurance carrier contacts, the existence and status of outstanding and potential claims. 4. Document any areas in which the financial institutions are self-insured, subject to retroactive premium adjustment, or participate in any other risk retention programs. 5. Assess the policies and procedures regarding the obtaining and maintaining of insurance coverages (in terms of centralized versus decentralized, etc.). 6. Determine the extent and effectiveness of risk management initiative within the organization.			

Bank	Date

Section of Work

Due Diligence Scope and Procedures Revised February 1, 1991	Work Paper Ref.	Prepared By	Reviewed By
Scope Review and evaluate data processing systems employed in terms of effectiveness, organization, efficiency and cost and provide general observation in terms of the effect of the merger on the data processing environments of these institutions.			

Procedures

1. Obtain organization chart and summary of personnel involved by primary locations.

2. Review the data center operations (DCO) function budget compared to actual and analyze financial cost.

3. In connection with the above, review a profile of DCO personnel by function with associates' direct cost.

4. Discuss, observe and document the nature of the overall operating control and security environment.

5. Review overall operations environment and status of major controls and any major reconciliation problems.

6. Review company-prepared, top-level inventory summary of primary hardware and software owned and leased, and various operating center locations.

7. Obtain and review the related contracts and summarize terms.

8. Determine nature and amount of significant lease commitments and potential cancellation options and resultant costs.

9. Obtain contracts and summarize outside service bureau contracts and arrangements.

10. Review high-level inventory of current developments securities in-process and scheduled.

11. Perform high-level inventory obsolescence review.

Bank	Date

Section of Work

Due Diligence Scope and Procedures Revised February 1, 1991	Work Paper Ref.	Prepared By	Reviewed By
12. Review internal audit EDP reports and discuss scope, findings and general observations with audit representatives.			
14. Determine extent of branch bank operating conversions.			
15. Obtain status report on major conversions recently completed and those scheduled.			
16. Summarize our work in this area into observations related to:			
a. Commitments to be addressed in connection with purchase accounting considerations.			
b. Issues related to ongoing operations of the institutions.			
c. Issues and observations related to merging the data center operations for these institutions.			

Bank   Date
_____

Section of Work   Compliance and Examination (Project 17)

Due Diligence Scope and Procedures **Revised February 1, 1991**	**Work** **Paper Ref.**	**Prepared** **By**	**Reviewed** **By**

Scope
 	
Summarize the significance of matters disclosed in the recent regulatory examinations and relate these findings to the work performed in other work plan areas.
 	
Procedures
 	
1. Review results of recent regulatory examinations with holding company management.
 	
2. Perform high-level review of copies of recent examination results and related communications with regulators.
 	
3. Review any supervisory agreements, entered into with the regulatory authorities and the related response from management. Determine if the company/bank is operating in accordance with the agreement and management's plan for corrective action.
 	
4. Obtain approval from holding company management to communicate directly with primary regulatory authorities to obtain their direct input on:
 	
  a. Status of recent/pending examinations
 	
  b. Status of regulatory enforcement actions
 	
  c. Comments on overall company operations, asset quality, personnel, etc.			

Bank   Date
_____

Section of Work   High-Level Internal Control Review (Project 18)

Due Diligence Scope and Procedures Revised February 1, 1991	Work Paper Ref.	Prepared By	Reviewed By
Scope Obtain an understanding of the overall control environment and assess and evaluate the integrity of and reliability of the underlying financial and operating reporting systems.			
Work Plan			
1. Through review of policy and procedural materials and discussion with chief financial officers, controllers, the director of internal audit and\or individual department heads as required, gain an overall understanding of the internal control management environment.			
2. Discuss with appropriate personnel (chief financial officer, controller, director of internal audit, etc.) their evaluations of the internal control environment and structure and, specifically, areas of perceived weakness and breakdowns in internal control over the past 18 months.			
3. Coordinate this area with our discussion with the internal auditors and our review of their management reports.			
4. Review internal audit reports, regulatory agency examination reports and management reports from the institutions' independent public accountants and summarize the significant internal control weakness noted and relate to the above.			
5. Determine where and to what extent personnel cutbacks have weakened controls.			
6. Also, specifically review the overall status of reconciliation activities through the various bank operations functions focusing on reconciliation controls and the current status of unreconciled differences.			
7. Determine to what extent unit banks/branches are controlled through uniform policies, practices and reporting procedures.			

Bank	Date

Section of Work   High-Level Internal Control Review (Project 18)

Due Diligence Scope and Procedures Revised February 1, 1991	Work Paper Ref.	Prepared By	Reviewed By
8. Summarize our observations into a concise memorandum setting forth conclusions and areas of greatest risk.			
9. Discuss with any project team leaders the extent, if any, where due diligence project scopes should be revised.			

Bank			Date	

Section of Work   Internal Audit Review (Project 19)

Due Diligence Scope and Procedures Revised February 1, 1991	Work Paper Ref.	Prepared By	Reviewed By
Scope Obtain an understanding of the organization, effectiveness and quality of the internal audit function and correlate the significant internal audit recommendations with our due diligence scopes.			
Procedures			
1. Obtain Internal Audit (IA) organization chart. Note reporting lines to audit committee, board of directors, company/bank management, etc.			
2. Review organization structure (fully or partially centralized/decentralized), noting regional staff locations and responsibilities, if any.			
3. Determine extent to which annual IA plan is developed relating to banks/branches/areas to be examined, timing and extent of work to be performed (full audit, review only, other limited scope or agreed-upon procedures). Determine basis on which rotational schedule is followed (if applicable).			
4. Ascertain if policies and procedures are in place to ensure that IA plan is followed and completed on a timely basis. Understand how timing conflicts and staffing shortfalls are addressed and resolved.			
5. Select representative recently performed audits for overall review and perform the following steps:			
a. Obtain audit workpapers and reports issued.			
b. Review the audit programs.			
c. Discuss the criteria used to establish audit frequency, risk assessment and specific audit scopes.			
d. Review workpaper techniques (organization, documentation and conclusions).			
e. For the reports issued, review for completeness, consistency with audit working papers, timing of issuance and distribution (including and associated summaries).			

Bank   Date
_____

Section of Work   Internal Audit Review (Project 19)

Due Diligence Scope and Procedures **Revised February 1, 1991**	**Work Paper Ref.**	**Prepared By**	**Reviewed By**
f. Discuss followup procedures on deficiencies reported (including discussions with the audit committee and/or senior management).			
6. Determine the overall extent to which the IA working papers/reports can be relied on and/or should be further reviewed as part of the due diligence work for each bank.			
7. Request a summary of all internal audits performed and reports issued for each bank and the parent company for the last two years, noting the dates of the audits and areas covered:			
a. Identify all unsatisfactory/inadequate internal control ratings.			
b. Review followup performed (if any), as well as current status.			
8. Make inquiries of the director of internal auditing and review related working papers and reports (as applicable) with respect to:			
a. Special audits, reviews, or investigations conducted in the last two years at any of the banks or the parent company.			
b. The existence of (or potential for) material weaknesses in internal controls, irregularities, sensitive transactions, illegal acts or material errors.			
c. Current status of any such matters, including the identification of any loss exposure, contingencies or claims.			

APPENDIX FIVE

Cost Allocation—
Methodologies

Methodology for Calculation of Annual
Affiliate Billings from Holding Company

1. Determine annual budgeted costs for each division:

	Cost Allocation Basis
Systems Division:	
Data Processing	Transaction Volumes
Item Processing	Transaction Volumes
Central Operations	Staff Hours
ATM Services	Staff Hours
Administrative Services Division	Staff Hours
Personnel and Benefits Division	Staff Hours
Finance and Investment Division	Staff Hours
Audit Division	Staff Hours

Costs are estimated based on past year's actual results, review of current year user (affiliate banks) budgets, planned changes in products and/or services by affiliates and planned capital expenditures (e.g., system upgrades).

2. Prepare detail annual functional cost budgets.

3. Estimate projected transaction volumes and staff hours by user and by type of service rendered.

4. Identify and separate "core" services (monthly recurring services) from "project" services.

5. Compute reasonable profit margin ("add-on" to projected costs) for each Division (usually amounts to a 5-10% add-on).

6. Compute affiliate billing amounts for each user (cost + profit margin) using information obtained in steps 1–5 above.

7. Compare billing rates by division and by type of service (EDP,IP) to independent surveys and vendor quotes. (This is necessary to comply with FRB Rule 23B - Transactions with Affiliates. A file should be maintained and updated annually documenting comparisons of internally-generated rates to outside vendor rates. This file is essential for periodic regulatory examinations.)

8. Execute new service contracts with each user affiliate.

EXHIBIT A

MANAGEMENT FEE TIME ALLOCATION WORKSHEET

EMPLOYEE NAME:_____

PERIOD:_____

DATE	CLIENT	ALLOCATION CODE	SERVICE CODE	ALLOCATED HOURS	ACTIVITY DESCRIPTION

	NVB	Per Unit	Monthly Cost	Annual Cost
System processing CPUs	95,331	0.05500	$5,243.21	$62,918.46
Printer:pages printed	10,200	1.00000	10,200.00	122,400.00
Forms:				
DDA /Savings/CD	25,266	0.11000	2,779.26	33,351.12
CD Checks	381	0.11000	41.91	502.92
NSF Mailings	5,568	0.11000	612.48	7,349.76
Mailers	2,614	0.11000	287.54	3,450.48
Account Analysis	993	0.11000	109.23	1,310.76
ACT STatements	2,014	0.11000	221.54	2,658.48
Loan	1,025	0.11000	112.75	1,353.00
Fiche: Zytron	2,376	1.00000	2,376.00	28,512.00
Account Maintenance:				
DDA	30,435	0.17000	5,173.95	62,087.40
Savings	32,097	0.11000	3,530.67	42,368.04
Time	15,603	0.28500		0.00
Loan	10,018	0.57000	5,710.26	68,523.12
GL	7,178	0.28500		0.00
Data Lines	0	125.00000	0.00	0.00
DP services:				
Data operators (4 +1/2 sup)	90.00%	10,000.00	9,000.00	108,000.00
Programmers (@ 1/2 time)	90.00%	2,000.00	1,800.00	21,600.00
CBS Coordinator (@ 1/2 time)	90.00%	2,000.00	1,800.00	21,600.00
Communications (@ 1/2 time)	90.00%	2,000.00	1,800.00	21,600.00
PC Support	90.00%	2,000.00	1,800.00	21,600.00
Special Projects	90.00%	2,000.00	1,800.00	21,600.00
			$54,398.80	$652,785.54
			63.73%	

Data Processing
Based on 12/31/92 actual volumes

	NVB	SVB	BLC	SSVB	Total Volumes	Per Unit	Monthly Cost	Annual Cost
System: processing CPUs	95,331	9,438	16,614	21,587	142,970	0.05500	$7,863.35	$94,360.20
Printer: pages printed	10,200	900	2,250	1,650	15,000	1.00000	15,000.00	180,000.00
Forms:								
DDA/Savings/CD	25,266	2,626	4,424	5,278	37,594	0.11000	4,135.34	49,624.08
CD Checks	381	63	87	150	681	0.11000	74.91	898.92
NSF Mailings	5,568	928	1,896	1,576	9,968	0.11000	1,096.48	13,157.76
Mailers	2,614	91	283	205	3,193	0.11000	351.23	4,214.76
Account Analysis	993	83	40	0	1,116	0.11000	122.76	1,473.12
ACT STatements	2,014	252	278	407	2,951	0.11000	324.61	3,895.32
Loan	1,025	0	212	0	1,237	0.11000	136.07	1,632.84
Fiche: Zytron	2,376	394	654	658	4,082	1.00000	4,082.00	48,984.00
Account Maintenance:								
DDA	30,435	3,978	6,181	8,077	48,671	0.17000	8,274.07	99,288.84
Savings	32,097	2,179	3,961	4,949	43,186	0.11000	4,750.46	57,005.52
Time	15,603	1,362	2,676	4,280	23,921	0.28500	6,817.49	81,809.82
Loan	10,018	1,458	1,944	2,639	16,059	0.57000	9,153.63	109,843.56
GL	7,178	461	1,852	1,642	11,133	0.28500	3,172.91	38,074.86
Data Lines	0	0	0	0	0	125.00000	0.00	0.00
DP services:								
Data operators (4+ 1/2 sup)	90.00%	2.00%	4.00%	4.00%	100.00%	10,000.00	10,000.00	120,000.00
Programmers (@ 1/2 time)	90.00%	2.00%	4.00%	4.00%	100.00%	2,000.00	2,000.00	24,000.00
CBS Coordinator (@ 1/2 time)	90.00%	2.00%	4.00%	4.00%	100.00%	2,000.00	2,000.00	24,000.00
Communications (@ 1/2 time)	90.00%	2.00%	4.00%	4.00%	100.00%	2,000.00	2,000.00	24,000.00
PC Support	90.00%	2.00%	4.00%	4.00%	100.00%	2,000.00	2,000.00	24,000.00
Special Projects	90.00%	2.00%	4.00%	4.00%	100.00%	2,000.00	2,000.00	24,000.00
							$85,355.30	$1,024,263.60

	SVB	Per Unit	Monthly Cost	Annual Cost
System processing CPUs	9,438	0.05500	$519.09	$6,229.08
Printer:pages printed	900	1.00000	900.00	10,800.00
Forms:				
DDA /Savings/CD	2,626	0.11000	288.86	3,466.32
CD Checks	63	0.11000	6.93	83.16
NSF Mailings	928	0.11000	102.08	1,224.96
Mailers	91	0.11000	10.01	120.12
Account Analysis	83	0.11000	9.13	109.56
ACT STatements	252	0.11000	27.72	332.64
Loan	0	0.11000	0.00	0.00
Fiche: Zytron	394	1.00000	394.00	4,728.00
Account Maintenance:				
DDA	3,978	0.17000	676.26	8,115.12
Savings	2,179	0.11000	239.69	2,876.28
Time	1,362	0.28500		0.00
Loan	1,458	0.57000	831.06	9,972.72
GL	461	0.28500		0.00
Data Lines	0	125.00000	0.00	0.00
DP services:				
Data operators (4 +1/2 sup)	2.00%	10,000.00	200.00	2,400.00
Programmers (@ 1/2 time)	2.00%	2,000.00	40.00	480.00
CBS Coordinator (@ 1/2 time)	2.00%	2,000.00	40.00	480.00
Communications (@ 1/2 time)	2.00%	2,000.00	40.00	480.00
PC Support	2.00%	2,000.00	40.00	480.00
Special Projects	2.00%	2,000.00	40.00	480.00
			$4,404.83	$52,857.96
			=========:	=========:
			5.16%	

	BLC	Per Unit	Monthly Cost	Annual Cost
System processing CPUs	16,614	0.05500	$913.77	$10,965.24
Printer:pages printed	2,250	1.00000	2,250.00	27,000.00
Forms:				
DDA /Savings/CD	4,424	0.11000	486.64	5,839.68
CD Checks	87	0.11000	9.57	114.84
NSF Mailings	1,896	0.11000	208.56	2,502.72
Mailers	283	0.11000	31.13	373.56
Account Analysis	40	0.11000	4.40	52.80
ACT STatements	278	0.11000	30.58	366.96
Loan	212	0.11000	23.32	279.84
Fiche: Zytron	654	1.00000	654.00	7,848.00
Account Maintenance:				
DDA	6,181	0.17000	1,050.77	12,609.24
Savings	3,961	0.11000	435.71	5,228.52
Time	2,676	0.28500		0.00
Loan	1,944	0.57000	1,108.08	13,296.96
GL	1,852	0.28500		0.00
Data Lines	0	125.00000	0.00	0.00
DP services:				
Data operators (4 +1/2 sup)	4.00%	10,000.00	400.00	4,800.00
Programmers (@ 1/2 time)	4.00%	2,000.00	80.00	960.00
CBS Coordinator (@ 1/2 time)	4.00%	2,000.00	80.00	960.00
Communications (@ 1/2 time)	4.00%	2,000.00	80.00	960.00
PC Support	4.00%	2,000.00	80.00	960.00
Special Projects	4.00%	2,000.00	80.00	960.00
			$8,006.53	$96,078.36
			9.38%	

	SSVB	Per Unit	Monthly Cost	Annual Cost
System processing CPUs	21,587	0.05500	$1,187.29	$14,247.42
Printer:pages printed	1,650	1.00000	1,650.00	19,800.00
Forms:				
DDA /Savings/CD	5,278	0.11000	580.58	6,966.96
CD Checks	150	0.11000	16.50	198.00
NSF Mailings	1,576	0.11000	173.36	2,080.32
Mailers	205	0.11000	22.55	270.60
Account Analysis	0	0.11000	0.00	0.00
ACT STatements	407	0.11000	44.77	537.24
Loan	0	0.11000	0.00	0.00
Fiche: Zytron	658	1.00000	658.00	7,896.00
Account Maintenance:				
DDA	8,077	0.17000	1,373.09	16,477.08
Savings	4,949	0.11000	544.39	6,532.68
Time	4,280	0.28500		0.00
Loan	2,639	0.57000	1,504.23	18,050.76
GL	1,642	0.28500		0.00
Data Lines	0	125.00000	0.00	0.00
DP services:				
Data operators (4 +1/2 sup)	4.00%	10,000.00	400.00	4,800.00
Programmers (@ 1/2 time)	4.00%	2,000.00	80.00	960.00
CBS Coordinator (@ 1/2 time)	4.00%	2,000.00	80.00	960.00
Communications (@ 1/2 time)	4.00%	2,000.00	80.00	960.00
PC Support	4.00%	2,000.00	80.00	960.00
Special Projects	4.00%	2,000.00	80.00	960.00
			$8,554.76	$102,657.06
			10.02%	

Item Processing
Based on 12/31/92 actual volumes

	NVB	SVB	BLC	SSVB	Total Volume	Per Unit	Monthly Cost	Annual Cost
Cash letter preparation	330	50	69	75	524	0.05000	$26.20	$314.40
Proof of Deposit	1,414,887	197,363	370,091	314,363	2,296,704	0.02750	63,159.36	757,912.32
Exception Items	29,002	2,142	3,290	10,880	45,314	0.04000	1,812.56	21,750.72
Item processing rejects	13,830	1,563	2,715	3,297	21,405	0.02000	428.10	5,137.20
Fine sort tickets	115,591	115,591			115,591	0.02000	2,311.82	27,741.84
Statement rendering/notice preparation & mailing:								
DDA	27,056		6,989	5,514	39,559	0.50000	19,779.50	237,354.00
Specialine	568	0	0	0	568	0.25000	142.00	1,704.00
Savings	1,718	0	402	359	2,479	0.05000	123.95	1,487.40
ACT	943	0	0	0	943	0.25000	235.75	2,629.00
CD notice	0	0	0	360	360	0.05000	18.00	216.00
Commerical loan	868	0	0	0	868	0.25000	217.00	2,604.00
Account analysis	0	0	0	0	0	0.05000	0.00	0.00
Deposit correction notice	740	0	0	203	943	0.05000	47.15	565.80
Inactive account letters	128	0	0	0	128	0.05000	6.40	76.80
Statement stuffers	16,313	0	0	8,875	25,188	0.02000	503.76	6,045.12
Special mailings	0	0	0	0	0	0.05000	0.00	0.00
Issued Bulletins	2,000	0	0	0	2,000	0.05000	100.00	1,200.00
Dun & Bradstreet	0	0	0	1	1	40.00000	40.00	480.00
Other processing:								
Adjustments	81	0	25	27	133	3.50000	465.50	5,586.00
NSF processing	0	0	0	4,290	4,290	0.50000	2,145.00	25,740.00
Returned items	0	0	0	843	843	0.50000	421.50	5,058.00
Unqualified items	72	0	24	11	107	0.50000	53.50	642.00
Contract Collections	291	2	159	2	454	2.00000	908.00	10,896.00
Research/Photography/Telephone & special projects	133	1	10	27	171	10.00000	1,710.00	20,520.00
							$94,655.05	$1,135,860.60

	Productivity Percentage	SVB	BLC	SSVB	NVB	NVDC	NVBC	BSC	ADMIN	ANNUAL HOURS
PORTERFIELD	92.00%			1,803					157	1,960
ROBIN (20 HOURS)	92.00%				920				80	1,000
DUNHAM	92.00%				1,803				157	1,960
KIRKPATRICK	92.00%				1,840				160	2,000
RUPP	92.00%			336	1,200		267		157	1,960
SHIMEL	92.00%					200	700	903	157	1,960
TODD	93.40%						468		132	2,000
Call Reports (4)			96	96	128		96			
Quarterly Filings (4)		40					80			
Management Reports (12)				96			192			
Consolidation (12)							384			
GL Maintenance				48	48		96			
Analysis/projects							0			
NELSON	85.00%		0	0	1,660				300	1,960
Analysis/projects			0	0	0					
NEWCOMER	78.00%		0	0	200	0	720	240	434	1,960
Tax work		16	16	16	40	16	16			
Quarterly Fillings		80	2	2	2		160			
Analysis/projects			0	0	0		0	0		
ANNUAL HOURS		136	114	2,397	7,841	216	3,179	1,143	1,733	16,759
Staff support @ $18.00/hr		$720	$1,728	$42,822	$106,902	$3,600	$41,094	$16,254	$17,986	$231,106
Admin @ $46.00/hr		4,416	828	828	87,492	736	41,216	11,040	33,773	180,329
		$5,136	$2,556	$43,650	$194,394	$4,336	$82,310	$27,294	$51,759	$411,435
Staff support @ $20/hr		$800	$1,920	$47,580	$118,780	$4,000	$45,660	$18,060	$0	$236,800
Administration @ $50/hr		4,800	900	900	95,100	800	44,800	12,000	0	$159,300
Tax – AA		1,960	1,960	1,960	4,200	1,960	1,960			$14,000
		$7,560	$4,780	$50,440	$218,080	$6,760	$92,420	$30,060	$0	$410,100
Monthly Finance Support		$0	$0	$3,805	$17,435	$333	$6,512	$2,505	$0	$30,590 x12
Quarterly Finance Support		1,200	505	505	665	0	2,880	0	0	5,755 x4
Analysis/project Support		0	0	0	0	0	0	0	0	0 x12
Tax Support (annualized)		67	67	67	167	67	67	0	0	500 x12
TOTAL		1,960	1,960	1,960	4,200	1,960	1,960			$14,000 x1
		$3,227	$2,532	$6,337	$22,467	$2,360	$11,418	$2,505	$0	$50,845

	NVB	Per Unit	Monthly Cost	Annual Cost
Cash letter preparation	330	0.05000	$16.50	$198.00
Proof of Deposit	1,414,887	0.02750	38,909.39	466,912.71
Exception items	29,002	0.04000	1,160.08	13,920.96
Item processing rejects	13,830	0.02000	276.60	3,319.20
Fine sort tickets		0.02000	0.00	0.00
Statement rendering/notice preparation & mailing:				
DDA	27,056	0.50000	13,528.00	162,336.00
Specialine	568	0.25000	142.00	1,704.00
Savings	1,718	0.05000	85.90	1,030.80
ACT	943	0.25000	235.75	2,829.00
CD notice	0	0.05000	0.00	0.00
Commerical loan	868	0.25000	217.00	2,604.00
Account analysis	0	0.05000	0.00	0.00
Deposit correction notice	740	0.05000	37.00	444.00
Inactive account letters	128	0.05000	6.40	76.80
Statement stuffers	16,313	0.02000	326.26	3,915.12
Special mailings	0	0.05000	0.00	0.00
Issued Bulletins	2,000	0.05000	100.00	1,200.00
Dun & Bradstreet	0	40.00000	0.00	0.00
Other processing:				
Adjustments	81	3.50000	283.50	3,402.00
NSF processing	0	0.50000	0.00	0.00
Returned Items	0	0.50000	0.00	0.00
Unqualified items	72	0.50000	36.00	432.00
Contract Collections	291	2.00000	582.00	6,984.00
Research/phototcopy/telephone & special projects	133	10.00000	1,330.00	15,960.00
			$57,272.38	$687,268.59
			60.5%	

	SVB	Per Unit	Monthly Cost	Annual Cost
Cash letter preparation	50	0.05000	$2.50	$30.00
Proof of Deposit	197,363	0.02750	5,427.48	65,129.79
Exception Items	2,142	0.04000	85.68	1,028.16
Item processing rejects	1,563	0.02000	31.26	375.12
Fine sort tickets	115,591	0.02000	2,311.82	27,741.84
Statement rendering/notice preparation & mailing:				
DDA	0	0.50000	0.00	0.00
Specialine	0	0.25000	0.00	0.00
Savings	0	0.05000	0.00	0.00
ACT	0	0.25000	0.00	0.00
CD notice	0	0.05000	0.00	0.00
Commerical loan	0	0.25000	0.00	0.00
Account analysis	0	0.05000	0.00	0.00
Deposit correction notice	0	0.05000	0.00	0.00
Inactive account letters	0	0.05000	0.00	0.00
Statement stuffers	0	0.02000	0.00	0.00
Special mailings	0	0.05000	0.00	0.00
Issued Bulletins	0	0.05000	0.00	0.00
Dun & Bradstreet	0	40.00000	0.00	0.00
Other processing:				
Adjustments	0	3.50000	0.00	0.00
NSF processing	0	0.50000	0.00	0.00
Returned Items	0	0.50000	0.00	0.00
Unqualified items	0	0.50000	0.00	0.00
Contract Collections	2	2.00000	4.00	48.00
Research/phototcopy/telephone & special projects	1	10.00000	10.00	120.00
			$7,872.74	$94,472.91

	BLC	Per Unit	Monthly Cost	Annual Cost
Cash letter preparation	69	0.05000	$3.45	$41.40
Proof of Deposit	370,091	0.02750	10,177.50	122,130.03
Exception Items	3,290	0.04000	131.60	1,579.20
Item processing rejects	2,715	0.02000	54.30	651.60
Fine sort tickets		0.02000	0.00	0.00
Statement rendering/notice preparation & mailing:				
DDA	6,989	0.50000	3,494.50	41,934.00
Specialine	0	0.25000	0.00	0.00
Savings	402	0.05000	20.10	241.20
ACT	0	0.25000	0.00	0.00
CD notice	0	0.05000	0.00	0.00
Commerical loan	0	0.25000	0.00	0.00
Account analysis	0	0.05000	0.00	0.00
Deposit correction notice	0	0.05000	0.00	0.00
Inactive account letters	0	0.05000	0.00	0.00
Statement stuffers	0	0.02000	0.00	0.00
Special mailings	0	0.05000	0.00	0.00
Issued Bulletins	0	0.05000	0.00	0.00
Dun & Bradstreet	0	40.00000	0.00	0.00
Other processing:				
Adjustments	25	3.50000	87.50	1,050.00
NSF processing	0	0.50000	0.00	0.00
Returned items	0	0.50000	0.00	0.00
Unqualified items	24	0.50000	12.00	144.00
Contract Collections	159	2.00000	318.00	3,816.00
Research/phototcopy/telephone & special projects	10	10.00000	100.00	1,200.00
			$14,398.95	$172,787.43

	SSVB	Per Unit	Monthly Cost	Annual Cost
Cash letter preparation	75	0.05000	$3.75	$45.00
Proof of Deposit	314,363	0.02750	8,644.98	103,739.79
Exception Items	10,880	0.04000	435.20	5,222.40
Item processing rejects	3,297	0.02000	65.94	791.28
Fine sort tickets		0.02000	0.00	0.00
Statement rendering/notice preparation & mailing:				
DDA	5,514	0.50000	2,757.00	33,084.00
Specialine	0	0.25000	0.00	0.00
Savings	359	0.05000	17.95	215.40
ACT	0	0.25000	0.00	0.00
CD notice	360	0.05000	18.00	216.00
Commerical loan	0	0.25000	0.00	0.00
Account analysis	0	0.05000	0.00	0.00
Deposit correction notice	203	0.05000	10.15	121.80
Inactive account letters	0	0.05000	0.00	0.00
Statement stuffers	8,875	0.02000	177.50	2,130.00
Special mailings	0	0.05000	0.00	0.00
Issued Bulletins	0	0.05000	0.00	0.00
Dun & Bradstreet	1	40.00000	40.00	480.00
Other processing:				
Adjustments	27	3.50000	94.50	1,134.00
NSF processing	4,290	0.50000	2,145.00	25,740.00
Returned items	843	0.50000	421.50	5,058.00
Unqualified items	11	0.50000	5.50	66.00
Contract Collections	2	2.00000	4.00	48.00
Research/phototcopy/telephone & special projects	27	10.00000	270.00	3,240.00
			$15,110.97	$181,331.67

	1993 Budget	1993 Budget		
Version #1–CO Services				
Direct Costs:				
Salaries & Benefits	$402,404.00	$402,404.00	Average working days	
Less:	0.00	0.00	in a month	21.00
	0.00	0.00	Working hours per day	8.00
Total Direct Costs	402,404.00	402,404.00	Average hours in month	168.00
Overhead	58,564.00	0.00	Number of employees	10.50
Overhead rate		1.145		
Chargeable Costs	460,968.00	460,752.58	Total hours available	1,764.00
Profit Margin	1.00	1.00	Number of months	10.73
Costs + Margin	$460,968.00	$460,752.58	Chargeable Hours	18,927.72
Per Unit Cost	$24.35	$24.34		
Version #2–CO Services				
Direct Costs:				
Salaries & Benefits	$402,404.00		Average working days	
Labor	0.00		in a month	21.00
(with 25% benefits)	0.00		Working hours per day	8.00
Total Direct Costs	402,404.00		Average hours in month	168.00
Overhead Rate	1.145		Number of employees	10.50
Chargeable Costs	460,752.58		Total hours available	1,764.00
Profit Margin	1.083		Number of months	10.73
Costs + Profit	$498,902.89		Chargeable Hours	18,927.72
Per Unit Cost	$26.36			

	Productivity Percentage	SVB	BLC	SSVB	NVB	ADMIN	ANNUAL HOURS		
COCKE	95.00%	0	0	0	1,862	98	1,960		
BROWN (30 hrs)	95.00%	0	800	0	606	74	1,480		
GREEN	95.00%	0	0	0	1,900	100	2,000		
ENGLEMAN	95.00%	0	0	0	1,900	100	2,000		
HARVEY	95.00%	0	0	0	1,900	100	2,000		
FAYE	95.00%	0	0	100	1,800	100	2,000		
HOFFMAN (30 hrs)	95.00%	0	0	0	1,406	74	1,480		
DONNA SNOWDEN	95.00%	0	0	0	1,900	100	2,000		
LONG (Supervisor)	95.00%	0	0	0	1,900	100	2,000		
JAEGER/ADMIN ASST	50.00%	0	0	0	1,000	1,000	2,000		
ANNUAL HOURS		0	800	100	16,174	1,846	18,920		
Staff support @ $26.37/hr		$0	$21,096	$2,637	$350,035	$19,672	$393,440		
Administration @ $26.37/hr		0	0	0	76,473	29,007	$105,480		
ANNUAL AMOUNTS		$0	$21,096	$2,637	$426,508	$48,679	$498,920		W ADMIN
Staff support @ $22.00/hr		$0	$17,600	$2,200	$333,828	$0	$353,628		
Administration @ $50.00/hr		0	0	0	145,000	0	$145,000		
ANNUAL AMOUNTS W/O ADMIN		$0	$17,600	$2,200	$478,828	$0	$498,628		W/O ADMIN
Monthly Central Ops Support		$0	$1,467	$183	$27,819	$0	$29,469	x12	$353,628
Administrative Support		0	0	0	12,083	0	$12,083	x12	$145,000
		$0	$1,467	$183	$39,902	$0	$41,552		$498,628

	1993 Budget	1993 Budget		

Version #1–ATM Services
Direct Costs:

	1993 Budget	1993 Budget		
Salaries & Benefits	$101,233.00	$101,233.00	Average working days	
Less:	0.00	0.00	in a month	21.00
	0.00	0.00	Working hours per day	8.00
Total Direct Costs	101,233.00	101,233.00	Average hours in month	168.00
Overhead	83,608.00	0.00	Number of employees	4.00
Overhead rate		1.826		
Chargeable Costs	184,841.00	184,851.46	Total hours available	672.00
Profit Margin	1.00	1.00	Number of months	11.91
Costs + Margin	$184,841.00	$184,851.46	Chargeable Hours	8,000.16
Per Unit Cost	$23.10	$23.10		

Version #2–ATM Services
Direct Costs:

	1993 Budget		
Salaries & Benefits	$101,233.00	Average working days	
Labor	0.00	in a month	21.00
(with 25% benefits)	0.00	Working hours per day	8.00
Total Direct Costs	101,233.00	Average hours in month	168.00
Overhead Rate	1.826	Number of employees	4.00
Chargeable Costs	184,851.46	Total hours available	672.00
Profit Margin	1.040	Number of months	11.91
Costs + Profit	$192,245.52	Chargeable Hours	8,000.16
Per Unit Cost	$24.00		

	Productivity Percentage	SVB	BLC	SSVB	NVB	ADMIN	ANNUAL HOURS		
Eldridge	98.00%	84	211	550	1,115	40	2,000		
Jovel	98.00%	0	0	374	1,586	40	2,000		
Reisinger	98.00%	84	211	550	1,115	40	2,000		
Tosteneon	98.00%	0	0	374	1,586	40	2,000		
ANNUAL HOURS		168	422	1,848	5,402	160	8,000		
Staff support @ $24.00/hr		$4,032	$10,128	$44,352	$129,648	$3,840	$192,000		
		0	0	0	0		$0		
ANNUAL AMOUNTS		$4,032	$10,128	$44,352	$129,648	$3,840	$192,000		W ADMIN
Staff support @ $23.00/hr		$3,864	$9,706	$42,504	$124,246	$0	$180,320		
Net expense of network chgs.		8,400	(600)	(5,040)	9,240		$12,000		
ANNUAL AMOUNTS W/O ADMIN		$12,264	$9,106	$37,464	$133,486	$0	$192,320		W/O ADMIN
Monthly Personnel Support		$322	$809	$3,542	$10,354	$0	$15,027	x12	$180,320
		$700	($50)	($420)	$770		$1,000	x12	$12,000
		$1,022	$759	$3,122	$11,124	$0	$16,027		$192,320
		14hr	35hr	154hr	450hr				

	1993 Budget	1993 Budget
Version #1–Administrative Services		
Direct Costs:		
Salaries & Benefits	$166,856.00	$166,856.00
Less:	0.00	0.00
	0.00	0.00
Total Direct Costs	166,856.00	166,856.00
Overhead	52,142.00	0.00
Overhead rate		1.312
Chargeable Costs	218,998.00	218,915.07
Profit Margin	1.00	1.00
Costs + Margin	$218,998.00	$218,915.07
Per Unit Cost	$22.30	$22.20

Average working days in a month	21.00
Working hours per day	8.00
Average hours in month	168.00
Number of employees	5.00
Total hours available	840.00
Number of months	11.715
Chargeable Hours	9,840.60

	1993 Budget	1993 Budget
Version #2–Administrative Services		
Direct Costs:		
Salaries & Benefits	$62,500.00	$104,356.00
Labor	0.00	0.00
(with 25% benefits)	0.00	0.00
Total Direct Costs	62,500.00	104,356.00
Overhead Rate	1.312	1.312
Chargeable Costs	82,000.00	136,915.07
Profit Margin	1.00	1.00
Costs + Profit	$82,000.00	$136,915.07
Per Unit Cost	$41.80	$17.40

Average working days in a month	21.00	21.00
Working hours per day	8.00	8.00
Average hours in month	168.00	168.00
Number of employees	1.00	4.00
Total hours available	168.00	672.00
Number of months	11.667	11.727
Chargeable Hours	1,960.06	7,880.54

	Productivity Percentage	SVB	BLC	SSVB	NVB	NVDC	NVBC	BSC	ADMIN	ANNUAL HOURS			
ROBERTS (Maint)	95.00%	0	0	0	1,622	0	0	240	98	1,960			
EDWARDS(Supply)	95.00%	12	12	124	1,306	24	104	280	98	1,960			
DEVORE (Supply)	95.00%	12	12	124	1,344	24	104	280	100	2,000			
LUNDEEN	90.00%				1,284	0	0	480	196	1,960			
GOODSELL	80.00%								392	1,960			
Facility management		8	8	24	1,104	24	24	240					
Insurance		8	8	8	24	8	8	8					
Vendor managment		0	0	0	24	0	0	40					
Special projects		0	0	0	0	0	0	0					
ANNUAL HOURS		40	40	280	6,708	80	240	1,568	884	9,840			
Staff support @ $17.40/hr		$418	$418	$4,315	$96,674	$835	$3,619	$22,272	$8,561	$137,112			
Administration @ $41.80/hr		$669	$669	$1,338	$48,154	$1,338	$1,338	$12,038	$16,386	$81,928			
		$1,086	$1,086	$5,653	$144,828	$2,173	$4,957	$34,310	$24,946	$219,040			W ADMIN
Staff support @ $19.50/hr		$468	$468	$4,836	$108,342	$936	$4,056	$24,960	$0	$144,066			
Administration @ $47.50/hr		$760	$760	$1,520	$54,720	$1,520	$1,520	$13,680	$0	$74,480			
										$0			
		$1,228	$1,228	$6,356	$163,062	$2,456	$5,576	$38,640	$0	$218,546			W/O ADM
Monthly Personnel Support		$102	$102	$530	$13,589	$205	$465	$3,220	$0	$18,212	x12	$218,5-
Analysis/project Support		$0	$0	$0	$0	$0	$0	$0	0	0	x12	
										0	x1	
		$102	$102	$530	$13,589	$205	$465	$3,220	$0	$18,212		$218,5-

	1993 Budget	1993 Budget			

Version #1—Personnel Services
Direct Costs:

	1993 Budget	1993 Budget			
Salaries & Benefits	$241,768.00	$241,768.00	Average working days		21.00
Less:	0.00	0.00	in a month		
	0.00	0.00	Working hours per day		8.00
Total Direct Costs	241,768.00	241,768.00	Average hours in month		168.00
Overhead	32,502.00	0.00	Number of employees		5.75
Overhead rate		1.134			
Chargeable Costs	274,270.00	274,164.91	Total hours available		966.00
Profit Margin	1.00	1.00	Number of months		11.76
Costs + Margin	$274,270.00	$274,164.91	Chargeable Hours		11,360.16
Per Unit Cost	$24.10	$24.10			

Version #2—Personnel Services
Direct Costs:

	1993 Budget	1993 Budget			
Salaries & Benefits	$83,750.00	$158,018.00	Average working days		
Labor	0.00	0.00	in a month	21.00	21.00
(with 25% benefits)	0.00	0.00	Working hours per day	8.00	8.00
Total Direct Costs	83,750.00	158,018.00	Average hours in month	168.00	168.00
Overhead Rate	1.134	1.134	Number of employees	1.75	4.00
Chargeable Costs	94,972.50	179,192.41	Total hours available	294.00	672.00
Profit Margin	1.00	1.00	Number of months	11.565	11.846
Costs + Profit	$94,972.50	$179,192.41	Chargeable Hours	3,400.11	7,960.51
Per Unit Cost	$27.90	$22.50			

Version #3—Personnel Services
Direct Costs:

	1993 Budget	1993 Budget			
Salaries & Benefits	$83,750.00	$158,018.00	Average working days		
Less:	0.00	0.00	in a month	21.00	21.00
(with 25% benefits)	0.00	0.00	Working hours per day	8.00	8.00
Total Direct Costs	83,750.00	158,018.00	Average hours in month	168.00	168.00
Overhead Rate	1.134	1.134	Number of employees	1.75	4.00
Chargeable Costs	94,972.50	179,192.41	Total hours available	294.00	672.00
Profit Margin	1.05	1.05	Number of months	11.565	11.846
Costs + Profit	$99,721.13	$188,152.03	Chargeable Hours	3,400.11	7,000.51
Per Unit Cost	$29.30	$23.60			

	Productivity Percentage	SVB	BLC	SSVB	NVB	NVDC	NVBC	BSC	ADMIN	ANNUAL HOURS
BRADLEY	95.00%	88	0	180	1,122	12	100	360	98	1,960
THOMAS	95.00%	88	0	180	1,160	12	100	360	100	2,000
WHITNEY	95.00%	0	0	0	1,900	0	0	0	100	2,000
CHOW	90.00%								200	2,000
Benefits admin		80	24	180	1,052	24	80	360		
Special projects		0	0	0	0	0	0	0		
BAILEY	77.00%								451	1,960
Policy admin		0	0	100	1,149	12	48	200	0	
Benefits admin		0	0	0	0	0	0	0	0	
Retirement plans		0	0	0	0	0	0	0	0	
Special projects		0	0	0	0	0	0	0	0	
WAGNER–3/4 time	80.00%								288	1,440
Retirement plans		40	24	48	404	4	32	64		
Payroll admin		12		48	400	8	20	48		
Special projects		0	0	0	0	0	0	0		
MANUAL HOURS		308	48	736	7,187	72	380	1,392	1,237	11,360

	SVB	BLC	SSVB	NVB	NVDC	NVBC	BSC	ADMIN	ANNUAL HOURS
Staff support @ $24/hr	$4,224	$0	$8,640	$100,368	$576	$4,800	$17,280	$7,152	$143,040
Administration @ $30/hr	3,960	1,440	11,280	90,150	1,440	5,400	20,160	14,640	148,470
	$8,184	$1,440	$19,920	$190,518	$2,016	$10,200	$37,440	$21,792	$291,510
Staff support @ $25.50/hr	$4,488	$0	$9,180	$106,641	$612	$5,100	$18,360	$0	$144,381
Administration @ $32/hr	4,224	1,536	12,032	96,160	1,536	5,760	21,504	0	142,752
	$8,712	$1,536	$21,212	$202,801	$2,148	$10,860	$39,864	$0	$287,133
Monthly Personnel Support	$726	$128	$1,768	$16,900	$179	$905	$3,322	$0	$23,928 x12
Analysis/project Support	$0	$0	$0	$0	$0	$0	$0	0	0 x12
	$726	$128	$1,768	$16,900	$179	$905	$3,322	$0	$23,928

	1993 Budget	1993 Budget			
Version #1–Financial Services					
Direct Costs:					
Salaries & Benefits	$310,120.00	$310,120.00	Average working days		
Less:	0.00	0.00	In a month	21.00	
(with 20% benefits)	0.00	0.00	Working hours per day	8.00	
Total Direct Costs	310,120.00	310,120.00	Average hours in month	168.00	
Overhead	67,719.00	0.00	Number of employees	8.50	
Overhead rate		1.218			
Chargeable Costs	377,839.00	377,726.16	Total hours available	1,428.00	
Profit Margin	1.00	1.00	Number of months	11.735	
Costs	$377,839.00	$377,726.16	Chargeable Hours	16,757.58	
Per Unit Cost	$22.50	$22.50			
Version #2–Financial Services					
Direct Costs:	(staff)	(admin)			
Salaries & Benefits	$172,620.00	$137,500.00	Average working days		
Labor	0.00	0.00	In a month	21.00	21.00
(with 25% benefits)	0.00	0.00	Working hours per day	8.00	8.00
Total Direct Costs	172,620.00	137,500.00	Average hours in month	168.00	168.00
Overhead Rate	1.218	1.218	Number of employees	6.50	2.00
Chargeable Costs	210,251.16	167,475.00	Total hours available	1,092.00	336.00
Profit Margin	1.09	1.09	Number of months	11.758	11.669
Costs + Profit	$229,173.76	$182,547.75	Chargeable Hours	12,839.74	3,920.78
Per Unit Cost	$17.80	$46.60			

Bank B: Holding Company Management Fee Policy

The purpose of this policy is to define the framework within which Bankshares, Inc. determines the level of management fees charged to its subsidiaries and to describe the process Bank B will employ in administering the billing process in conjunction with services rendered to affiliate banks. Assessment of management fees is an important issue in banking and since Bank B and its affiliates have multiple regulatory considerations, this policy has been developed through a review of the various regulator rulings, with a primary focus on the process as supported by the Office of the Comptroller of the Currency via Supplement No. 1 to O.C.C. Circular No. 115.

We recognize that certain expenses incurred by Bank B while providing services to affiliate banks cannot be explicitly billed on an "actual cost and hours expended" identification. Under this policy, CFB will strive to utilize individualized billings which primarily incorporate identified services. Certain expenses as recognized in Supplement No. 1 to O.C.C. Circular No. 115, shall be billed on a pro rata basis to the extent they represent a legitimate and integral part of the overall services provided. Finally, this policy recognizes that certain expenses, which include debt service requirements of Bank B, expenses where there is no corresponding benefit to the bank, prepayment for services not yet rendered, and fees to subsidize unprofitable operations, do not represent areas in which the banks receive a benefit and accordingly shall not be assessed as management fees.

Classification of Holding Company Expenses

The following list of services provided and expense classification (i.e. the billing process type recognized as appropriate under Circular No. 115) has been extracted from Supplement No. 1 to O.C.C Circular No. 115 and expanded, as appropriate, to more accurately address services provided by CFB to affiliate banks.

Service

1.	Accounting	I.S.B.
2.	Corporate Audit	I.S.B.
3.	Corporate Tax Planning	Pro Rata
4.	Credit Examination	I.S.B.
5.	Financial Analysis, Planning & Reporting	I.S.B.
6.	General Legal Services	Pro Rata
7.	Holding Company Executive Management	Pro Rata
8.	Holding Company Occupancy Costs	Pro Rata
9.	Holding Company Staff Support	Pro Rata
10.	Investment & Money Desk Operations	I.S.B.
11.	Loan Review	I.S.B.
12.	Marketing Research	I.S.B.
13.	Marketing & Advertising - General	Pro Rata
14.	Marketing & Advertising - Specific	I.S.B.
15.	Operations & Services (Banks)	I.S.B.

16.	Personnel - Benefits & Salary Administration	Pro Rata
17.	Personnel Evaluation & Compensation, Staffing	I.S.B.
18.	Regulatory Relations & Planning	Pro Rata
19.	Security Measures & Procedures	I.S.B.
20.	Tax Preparation	I.S.B.
21.	Training	I.S.B.
22.	Other	I.S.B.

Individualized Subsidiary Billings

As identified, Bank B will utilize individualized subsidiary billings computed based on actual specific services rendered and charged at a rate which equates relative cost. Services rendered will be logged utilizing the format attached as Exhibit A. Relative cost shall be determined by incorporating all personnel related costs of providing the specified services.

Pro Rata Allocations

It is recognized that certain expenses cannot be allocated on an "actual cost and hours expended" basis and that those legitimate expenses will be assessed based on an affiliate pro rata level.

Market Value Allocations

Management of Bank B has reviewed the alternatives of billing services at cost, plus a reasonable profit and market, and has concluded that billings at cost will present the least amount of burden on affiliates. Further, a review of "market" rate fees reveals that market rate is not clearly defined, but ranges can be developed through a review of alternative providers of the service of like services. Our review has determined that the services of accounting firms provide excellent market value alternatives. Exhibit C presents the summary of market value rates at the present time.

Client Codes

BENS	COOP	HOTS
LFLS	DICK	HURN
MARS	LIDG	LEMN
PAYN	WAHP	PLAT
WHET		REDF
WIND		VERM
MN BANKS	CFB	
SD BANKS	CFSC	
ND BANKS	CFND	
ALL BANKS		

Allocation Codes

1. Per Bank (/17)
2. Per Bank Per State (MN/6, ND/4, SD/6)
3. Individual Hours
4. Pro Rata CFB*
5. Per Bank Per Region (SD Reg/5, ND Reg/6, MN Reg/5)
6. Regional Pro Rata*

*Pro Rata Allocation Index

1. FTE's (Full Time Equivalent Employees)
2. Total Loans
3. Total Deposits
4. Funds Management Portfolio
5. Total Assets

*Where the allocation of time is on a pro rata method (type 4 or 6), you must utilize the Pro Rata Allocation Index to appropriately identify the basis for allocation of time. The employee when using a pro rata allocation should strive to not use total assets as the allocation index. When allocating time on a pro rata basis, you must choose allocation code 4 or 6 (CFB or by region) and follow that with an allocation index. For example, credit work performed for all banks would be designated as 4–2.

Service	Billing Process
1. Accounting	I.S.B.
2. Corporate Audit	I.S.B.
3. Corporate Tax Planning	Pro Rata
4. Credit Examination	I.S.B.
5. Financial Analysis, Planning & Reporting	I.S.B.
6. General Legal Services	I.S.B.
7. General Credit Administration	Pro Rata
8. Holding Company Executive Management	Pro Rata
9. Holding Company Staff Support	Pro Rata
10. Investment & Money Desk Operations	I.S.B.
11. Loan Review	I.S.B.
12. Marketing Research	I.S.B.
13. Marketing & Advertising - General	Pro Rata
14. Marketing & Advertising - Specific	I.S.B.
15. Operations & Services (Banks)	I.S.B.
16. Personnel - Benefits & Salary Administration	Pro Rata

17.	Personnel Evaluation, Employment & Staffing	I.S.B.
18.	Regulatory Relations & Planning	Pro Rata/I.S.B.
19.	Security Measures & Procedures	I.S.B.
20.	Tax Preparation	I.S.B.
21.	Training	I.S.B.
22.	Other	I.S.B.
23.	Open Loan Pool	
24.	Open	

APPENDIX SIX

Communicating Corporate Culture: An Example

CHANGE... IT'S WHAT MAKES THE WORLD GO ROUND.

Deregulation, new regulation, new competition and changes in the marketplace have brought many changes to the banking industry. Today, it's no longer simply a question of planning for growth; it's a matter of survival.

The strange thing is, in spite of these rapid changes that are taking place, there are still basic common sense banking practices that are just as important today as they were over 100 years ago.

We could go 'round and 'round, dreaming up new and different ways to assure our future success. Yet nothing we do can ever replace our continuing focus on giving excellent service to every Sovereign Bank customer.

Our mission is to serve the loan and deposit needs of homeowners and mature savers. Sovereign's challenge is to continually improve that service in every way we can. To keep on the right track to ensure future success. And that's what this book is all about.

SURVIVAL OF THE FITTEST IS THE NAME OF THE GAME.

With deregulation, rapid changes in the marketplace and the economy, the players in the banking business have changed considerably. Many financial institutions across the country have fallen by the wayside. Others are teetering on the brink. But those most adept at serving a specific market niche will remain among the survivors.

Sovereign Bank intends to be a survivor.

For over 100 years, our efforts have been sharply focused on the homeowner's market. Our many mortgage products, including popular home equity lines of credit, offer a wide range of options. These, coupled with our quality team members, have made a big splash with today's homebuyers.

At Sovereign Bank, *our vision is that when homeowners think of a bank, they choose Sovereign.* It's up to every team member to make that vision a reality each and every day. If homeowner's do not choose Sovereign, either they are misinformed or we haven't done our job.

QUALITY SERVICE THROUGH QUALITY PEOPLE.

When quality, selection and price are comparable, the one thing that sets winners apart from the losers is always excellent customer service.

The same holds true in banking.

Only the best – those who give their customers the personal attention and consideration they deserve in a prompt manner – will survive in a competitive market. Which is why *putting our customers first and consistently exceeding their expectations is valued so highly at Sovereign Bank.*

The best team member is the one who sees a customer in every individual. And an individual in every customer. The one thought we should always keep in mind is that excellence in customer service starts with each of us.

Our differentiation must be based upon excellence in service through people.

SUPPORTING EACH OTHER... THE KEY TO SUCCESS.

By working together, our team members provide the momentum necessary to keep Sovereign Bank moving forward on the track of success.

Every team member plays a vital supporting role in accomplishing our organizational objectives. Each of us must demand excellence from ourselves, regardless of where we fit into the organization. Our success depends on how well we connect our individual talents together. And how effectively we build on one another's contributions.

Sovereign expects nothing but the best from each team member and in return shows extreme respect for each individual.

At Sovereign Bank, we can build a strong foundation by working together. Success can only come from teamwork. Which, in the end, helps all of us to come out on top.

FACING THE UPS AND DOWNS OF BUSINESS CHANGE.

Volatility and rapid changes throughout the financial world have put the banking industry on a veritable roller coaster ride.

White-knuckle drops in the stock market, breathtaking turns in investment opportunities and uncertain stops and starts in the housing market have combined to make banking customers nervous.

Change is inevitable. And sometimes the going gets tough. As team members, all of us must recognize these changes and develop the *flexibility* to meet them head-on. Our willingness to adjust to the conditions and influences that guide the banking business is imperative to ongoing success.

Staying flexible also means working smarter. That's why suggestions and ideas from team members on ways to improve the productivity and profitability of our company are more than welcome, they're a necessary part of our continued growth. Because we know there's always room for improvement.

STAYING AHEAD OF THE COMPETITION REQUIRES ALL OF OUR DRIVING SKILLS.

We cannot create the best bank for homeowners if we fail to keep pace with the marketplace. Maintaining our competitive drive is the name of the game.

We must constantly think of better and more creative ways to get the job done and to steer clear of obstacles in our path.

To drive Sovereign Bank safely and successfully toward our goals in the coming years, we must keep our eyes on the road. All of us must remain alert, look ahead and constantly move forward focusing our efforts on continued growth through sales, service and team members – both professionally and personally.

We must keep both feet on the pedals, ready to apply the brakes or step on the gas, as current conditions dictate. And through the entire journey, *we must maintain a low-cost operation while providing outstanding value.* It's the only way to be the leader, whether you are a bank or a manufacturing company.

WHEN THE CURRENT IS STRONG, WE CAN'T GO UNDER WATER.

While Sovereign Bank offers many types of real estate secured lending to thousands of homeowners each year, we are very conservative about the loans we approve.

We don't want business for business' sake. *We want good quality, low interest rate risk loans.* After all, if we put customers in a home they can't afford, we both lose.

As with every other business, we know we're going to take on some water now and then. But our objective is to prevent losses and do our best to keep the bank on an even keel.

After all, that's what our shareholders and team members expect. Because our team members don't just work for the company, they own part of it. And it's the reason why *we will continually seek to outperform our competitors in terms of quality of earnings, growth in earnings and return on money our shareholders have invested in Sovereign.*

OUR KEY TO SUCCESS: THE IMAGE WE BUILD TOGETHER AS A TEAM.

At Sovereign Bank, we firmly believe that our company image – the way we are perceived by our customers and the communities we serve – is a reflection of all our team members.

With the right attitude and teamwork, ours can be an exciting ride that will lift Sovereign Bank to new heights.

As a socially responsible corporate citizen, we remain committed to supporting the communities we serve. So it's easy to see why we encourage team members to continue their participation in a wide variety of activities and organizations that benefit others.

Our image as the homeowners bank is one of our most important assets. By dealing fairly and honestly with every one of our customers and team members and following through on our commitments, our reputation will continue to grow.

> # OUR SUCCESS DEPENDS UPON UNITING IN SPIRIT TO BE THE VERY BEST THERE IS!

As we enter a new era, let's remember the top priority we have established to guide Sovereign Bank into the future: *an unshakable commitment to teamwork and to excellence in customer service.*

Achieving this will not require rules and regulations to follow. It will call, instead, for a renewed spirit of dedication and performance from every team member. A spirit that will unite Sovereign into a cohesive, single-minded entity poised to meet the challenges of the future.

That's the kind of spirit that has made our country the best in the world. The same kind of spirit that will help our customers see banking with Sovereign in a whole new light.

Thanks to all the individual contributors, who endlessly provide the steam to keep Sovereign Bank on the right track and high above the competition.

INDEX